HOMES WITH CHARACTER

THIRD EDITION ———————— Hazel Thompson Craig

HOMES WITH CHARACTER

D.C. HEATH AND COMPANY
Lexington, Massachusetts

preface

The third edition of *Homes with Character* has been completely rewritten
in order to include contemporary housing concepts and expanding information on the social, psychological, economic, and managerial aspects of
housing. According to consumer spending figures, housing (that is, rent or
mortgage payments, home furnishings, and maintenance) now represents the
largest item in the family budget for the majority of families.

A home is more than shelter. In order to be satisfying, a home must meet
man's *physical* need for comfort, safety, and health; his *psychological* need
for privacy and security; and his *social* need for interpersonal relationships,
self-expression, and relaxation. The complexities of modern living—increasing
mobility, rising income, expanding suburbs, ever-present slums, easy credit,
technological progress, inflation, and persuasive advertising—have brought
housing into major focus here and abroad.

Housing needs vary with culture, climate, income, family composition and
ages, traditions and values, health and safety standards, available building
materials, and building technology. The rapid social and economic changes
over the past decade or so have been advantageous for some families and
disadvantageous for other families. It is the author's hope that the information in this text will be useful and enjoyable for all families in our diversified
society.

Homes with Character is organized in five units. The arrangement seems
logical in approaching the study of housing. However, a teacher may change
the sequence and the emphasis according to the background, interests, and
needs of her students.

Unit One, "Influences upon Housing," deals with our shelter heritage,
European influences upon American architectural styles, and the gradual
emergence of contemporary housing with all its satisfactions and increasing
problems. It is assumed that a knowledge of man's changing concepts of a
home will give a greater appreciation of the housing opportunities available
today, and a better understanding of our present housing needs, especially
in cities.

Unit Two, "Selecting a Home," focuses on the practical aspects of home
buying and renting. It includes the role of social and personal values, space
needs for livability, family income in relation to housing costs, factors to be
considered in financing a home, guidelines to follow in buying or building
a house, functional kitchen and laundry arrangements, storage provisions, and
the mechanical core of the home—heating and cooling systems, wiring, and
plumbing. Although geographical location, individual circumstances, and

local conditions influence the choice of a home, the basic information here should be helpful to anyone making the decision.

Unit Three, "Decorating a Home," emphasizes aesthetic values in housing —the application of art principles to wall and floor composition, the choice and arrangement of furnishings and accessories, the decoration of windows, and the effective use of color. A brief review of period and contemporary furniture styles is given, along with suggestions for combining different styles. The use of flowers and lighting in the decorative scheme is also discussed.

Unit Four, "Consumer Buying," includes suggested guidelines for selecting laborsaving equipment, rugs and carpets, bedding and household linens, dinnerware—dishes, glassware, and flatware—and furniture. If the consumer is to make wise decisions in the choice of home furnishings, she or he must become informed about grades, quality of materials, differences among brands, guaranties, life expectancy under normal use, and types of merchandise outlets. The consumer should also learn how to stretch the buying power of the dollar by properly caring for household equipment and furnishings.

Unit Five, "Maintaining and Improving a Home," concentrates on periodic and regular home maintenance, on making simple household repairs, and on home improvements—painting, wallpapering, laying floor tile, and making slipcovers and draperies. Methodical maintenance is necessary from the standpoint of economy and efficiency as well as for personal enjoyment; mastering the basic skills needed for home repairs and renovations can be satisfying as well as money-saving.

Each unit is followed by a list of books, booklets, pamphlets, and audiovisual aids, chosen to supplement and enrich classroom discussion. At the close of each chapter, activities are suggested to help students choose school and home problems or projects upon which they would like to work. The illustrations, which include photographs, drawings, and charts, have been selected to clarify and elaborate the text as much as possible.

The author expresses appreciation for the help given by architects, contractors, decorators, and librarians, especially Catherine Hay, head of the Art Division at the Carnegie Library in Pittsburgh. Without the enthusiastic cooperation of the editors and the art and photographic staffs of D.C. Heath and Company, the present edition of *Homes with Character* would not have been possible. A sincere thank-you is especially extended to Nancy Earnest and Eunice Maples, who typed the manuscript.

Hazel Thompson Craig

January 1970

Pittsburgh, Pennsylvania

contents

unit one

Influences
upon Housing

chapter one

OUR SHELTER HERITAGE

Most of us have become so accustomed to living in a modern world that we forget our indebtedness to past civilizations whose discoveries, inventions, and vision made our present way of life possible.

Man, the architect, has been ingenious in finding and using natural resources to improve his environment and provide greater comfort and convenience. Along with food and clothing, shelter has been one of man's most urgent needs. He has had to either find or devise some means of protecting himself from the weather and from intruders. In doing so he has had to avail himself of whatever natural hiding places or natural resources he could find.

With the discovery of fire and the invention of flint tools, man made his first step toward civilization. Fire kept him warm, provided light, served as a signal, changed clay into pottery, and helped in shaping tools and boats. The invention of flint tools helped him to kill and cut up wild animals for food, clothing, and shelter. By the time primitive man had begun to emerge from the Old Stone Age (Paleolithic Age), which is the first known period of prehistoric culture, into the New Stone Age (Neolithic Age) he had learned how to: (1) make bows and arrows to kill game, (2) design boats of reed covered with skins for navigating streams, (3) cut up animal hides with flint knives and make fitted garments to keep himself warm, (4) provide simple shelters of tree branches and animal skins for his nomadic existence.

Eventually, with the invention of the plow, the loom, and the wheel, or what sociologists refer to as the *tripod of civilization,* man ceased to be a nomad. The plow made cultivation of the land possible for an assured supply of food; the loom produced woven cloth for more versatile clothing. The wheeled cart made transportation faster. With a knowledge of cultivation, weaving, and transportation, family life began to develop in small villages, and the concept of home began to develop around the hearth.

Early in man's existence a spiritual need as well as a physical and a social need became important to his existence. This spiritual awakening led to the building of many edifices to the gods, and as civilization progressed, religious structures had a strong influence upon the homes of royalty and aristocracy and eventually upon domestic architecture.

GUIDELINES FOR STUDY

GENERAL IDEAS
TO CONSIDER

1. Shelter from the weather and from intruders has been one of man's most urgent needs from primitive times until the present.
2. The kinds of shelters man has devised have depended upon climate, terrain, natural resources, man's imagination, means of communication, and modes of transportation.
3. Human needs are physical, psychological, social, and spiritual. Man's striving for spiritual expression led to the building of religious edifices, which in many civilizations set a style for the homes of royalty and aristocracy.
4. The homes of people of the laboring class remained almost unchanged from ancient times until the Renaissance, after which a rising merchant class set new standards for domestic architecture.
5. After acquiring empire status, England led other countries in domestic architecture and gave a rich housing heritage to the American colonies.

WORDS, NAMES, AND PLACES
TO KNOW

Acropolis
atrium
Byzantine
Carlsbad Caverns
Charlemagne
flying buttress
Gothic
grotto
hogan
igloo
Jones, Inigo
kiln
lake dwelling
Macedonia
Mammoth Cave
Mayan civilization
Mecca
Medina

Mesopotamia
Minoan civilization
Minotaur
Mohammed
Mongolia
Neolithic
Paleolithic
Pantheon
Parthenon
pre-Columbian civilization
pueblo
Qumran
Renaissance
Sumer
Tower of Babel
windbreak
Wren, Sir Christopher
ziggurat

PRIMITIVE SHELTERS—PAST AND PRESENT

When we think of primitive shelters, we think of caves, tents, tree houses and houses on stilts, snowhouses, mud or clay huts, pueblos, and windbreaks. It may seem strange to us that primitive shelters mean home to many people in the world today.

Caves

Caves and caverns have always been favorite hiding places from bad weather and ferocious animals. Excavations of ancient caves indicate that man craved not only protection from natural elements but adornment for his body and his home. Archaeologists have found necklaces, earrings, and bracelets made of animal teeth, bones, and stones, and drawings on the walls of caves attest to primitive man's need for artistic expression. Caves have provided refuge since man first trod the earth. Throughout history people have fled to caves after floods, forest fires, economic crises, or wars have evicted them from their homes. In the heart of Germany caves have been occupied continuously since the Thirty Years' War (1618–1648).

Families of gypsies live in caves all over southern Spain. Much of the rock in this area is so porous that it is not difficult to enlarge caverns for cave dwellings. A cave dwelling may have several rooms with a front door opening onto a cobblestone street; and inside, it may have electric lights and running water from natural springs. The walls and dome-shaped ceilings are often whitewashed and decorated with gay designs and shiny copper utensils. Cave dwellers like to live in caves because they are cool in summer and warm in winter, and housing costs are low. Every now and then there is a church,

cinema, or shop in a cave among a row of dwellings. If you ever tour southern Spain, you will probably visit one of these gypsy caves where young men and women will entertain you with dancing and singing.

Many gypsy cave dwellers are skilled craftsmen, making ceramics, metalwork, and leather. These crafts date from the period when Spain was under Moorish rule, or from the seventh century until 1492, when the last Moorish stronghold in Granada was captured by the forces of Isabella and Ferdinand.

The water from a spring in the cave at Lourdes, France, is famous for its radioactive or seemingly superhuman healing powers. The rock shelters of the Holy Land are rich in ancient and Biblical history. A grotto, hollowed in the hillside and used as a stable at Bethlehem, was the birthplace of Jesus. The caves at Qumran, on the northwest shores of the Dead Sea, held secret until the mid-twentieth century many Old Testament writings dating from the time of Isaiah, the first great Hebrew prophet, who lived about the eighth century B.C. A cave protected the Prophet Mohammed (570–632 A.D.) from his pursuers during his flight from Mecca to Medina. Seeing the entrance covered with a spider web and a dove resting peacefully on the nest nearby, the angry mob ignored the cave.

In case of an atomic attack today some of the safest hiding places in America would be caves, such as the Carlsbad Caverns in New Mexico, the Mammoth Cave in Kentucky, and the Luray Caverns and other caves of Virginia.

Caves offer not only protection but mystery and adventure. In an attempt to fulfill his spiritual needs, primitive man performed sacred rites in caves. Men and children have lost their lives seeking lost treasures or adventure in caves.

Tents

Tents have taken many forms, and a variety of substances have been used for coverings. The simplest type of tent is the pole tent, typical of the wigwams and tepees of many North American Indian tribes. The Indians of the Great Plains covered their cone-shaped framework of tree branches with buffalo skins. Other tribes used tree bark as a covering. In the absence of the skins of large animals, the seed gatherers of California and the Great Basin covered their beehive-shaped framework with grasses. In winter they spread mud over the grass to shut out the wind.

Today the nomads of Mongolia live the primitive life of their ancestors. Because of the rugged weather their tents are more intricately constructed and more weatherproof than those of some other primitive groups. Their bee-hive structures, or yurts, are a mesh of latticework covered with large sections of heavy hair felt, which can be unlaced and folded for transportation. To the Western tourist landing by plane on the Mongolian desert, these simple homes, sparsely located on barren plains, are a dramatic contrast to the towering sky-scrapers, motor traffic, and deafening noises in the cities he left behind a few hours previously.

In refined versions, the tent is a favorite shelter for the camper today who wants to get away from the turmoil of city life. The cone-shaped pole tent is less popular, however, than the army pup tent or the wall tent with sides and gabled roof.

Tree Houses and Houses on Stilts

Primitive man found that high places as well as caves provided safety. Therefore, oblong tree houses, made of tree branches and grasses with ladders that could be pulled up from the ground, gave these men a feeling of security in areas of the world where caves do not exist. Today there are tree dwellers in many parts of Africa and in the islands of the Pacific.

The house on stilts has been common to inhabitants of lake and river regions where it would be impractical to build in swamps. We are perhaps more familiar with the Swiss lake dwellings because these were the first such dwellings to be discovered by archaeologists during the mid-nineteenth century. In pre-historic times lake dwellings were also common to areas in Ireland and Scot-land. These homes on stilts are to be seen today in parts of New Zealand and Venezuela.

Igloos, or Snowhouses

In parts of the frozen Arctic, particu-larly Baffin Land, where building materi-als are almost nonexistent most of the year, Eskimos build snowhouses, which they call igloos, from blocks of ice. They leave an opening at the top for light and for emitting smoke from the fire. In these ice-block houses intricate dome construction is used, and the houses are quite comfortable in below-zero weather. In lower Arctic regions where driftwood is plentiful, the Eskimos build log houses above a dugout in the earth, and in more southern regions they cover wall-tent structures with skins.

Mud or Clay Huts

Mud and clay can be found almost everywhere. Mud spread over a frame-work of branches has provided homes for primitive tribes where other natural building materials have been scarce. In our desert states today, adobe or earth houses are common. Very early in man's existence he found that he could mold small rectangular or square shapes from clay, dry these in the sun, and use them to build houses. We owe the discovery of brick making to primitive man.

Pueblos

The multistoried honeycombed structures of the Pueblo Indians are a fascination to the tourist. These are intricate structures, several stories high, with a maze of rooms for living as well as for religious, political, and social purposes. The crowded intimacy of this kind of communal society would be psychologically difficult for many people accustomed to space and privacy. However, Frank Lloyd Wright, the most famous of American architects, advocated communal living for architects and their families while they stayed at his two training centers.

Windbreaks

At the tip of South America, until recent times, lived the Ona and Alikuluf Indian tribes, who were guanaco herders. These nomads survived for centuries with only the skin of the guanaco, an animal similar to the llama, for protection. As the winds shifted they adjusted their skin garments over their naked bodies, covered only with animal grease, and at night used skins held in place by a few poles driven into the ice to break the wind. These people had adapted so well to their harsh climate that attempts by nineteenth-century scientists and missionaries to make their lives more comfortable had disastrous effects. The tribes that managed to exist with only the minimal shelter of windbreaks have almost disappeared today. Windbreaks are used nowadays mainly by farmers, to protect crops.

The American Indians and Eskimos, with a limited knowledge of technology, were very creative in their use of native materials appropriate to terrain and climate. Forest dwellers used tree bark and branches to build shelters; fishing tribes constructed theirs of driftwood. Huntsmen of the plains covered pole tents with skins of large animals, while seed gatherers used the skins of small animals sewn together or bunches of grass.

ANCIENT STRUCTURES

Mesopotamia

The first civilization in Mesopotamia or in the Middle East dates from about 3000 B.C. and is known as the Sumerian, named for the land of Sumer. This fertile land, so familiar to Biblical scholars, was fought over and occupied by one tribe after another for hundreds of years. As each new tribe captured this territory, the area conquered was named for the conquerors. The Babylonians, Chaldeans, Assyrians, and others ruled from time to time. During the occupation of these early tribes, the concept of religion expanded, and it was this concept that inspired the building of temples to the deities—a concept of architecture which reached its highest development with the cathedrals of the French Gothic and Renaissance periods of Europe.

Continuously awed by the mysteries of life—birth and death, famine and plenty, light and dark, fire and flood—which he could not explain, primitive and ancient man believed in spirits and invented many gods. Ziggurats (pyramids of rectangular forms, diminishing in size from bottom to top) rose to great heights, so that the priest could be closer to the gods. The Tower of

This model of Ur, an early city in Mesopotamia, shows laboring-class housing 4,000 years ago. Note ziggurat in background.

Babel (*Genesis 2*) was probably this type of structure.

The emphasis on warfare for the possession of fertile lands and upon religion for an explanation of the mysteries of life created two elite or upper classes—warriors and priests. Homes of these upper-class people were almost as elaborate as the temples of the gods with their courtyards and terraced gardens. (King Solomon's palace is described in *I Kings,* verse 7.) Homes of people of the poor laboring class were cone shaped or block shaped, often built in rows and covered with clay. For many thousands of years house forms remained unchanged for the poor classes. With a scarcity of rock and timber in Mesopotamia, mud, reed, and clay or brick houses were common. Eventually glazed bricks were used. From these glazed bricks evolved the beautiful mosaic work of Byzantium in the fifth and sixth centuries.

Egypt

In Egypt the abundance of stone influenced the building of pyramids to provide an eternal resting place for the rulers, or god-kings. During the Old Kingdom (roughly 2700–2200 B.C.) these tremendous and indestructible edifices were built and completely furnished, so that the god-kings would want for nothing in the afterlife. Homes for the laborers were crude rectangular structures, made of sun-dried bricks, with earthen floors.

In contrast to Mesopotamia, life in Egypt was orderly. The sun rose and set at about the same time each day; the Nile basin was inundated at approximately the same time each year, as the snows in the mountains melted. Mountains and rivers formed natural barriers to invading tribes. Stone (limestone, sandstone, alabaster, and granite) was plentiful and provided a building material with a high degree of permanence. However, the orderly life of the Old Kingdom began to disappear, as anarchy, civil war, and emphasis on materialism replaced a life of tranquility.

During the Middle Kingdom (roughly 2050-1800 B.C.) old ways changed. Temple tombs replaced pyramids as final resting places for royalty. Thereafter rulers patterned their great palaces after the royal temples. Entertainment, feasting, and dress became extravagant as emphasis on materialism continued. In the meantime the rulers had failed to provide for military protection, and the Egyptians could not withstand the first foreign invasions. The Hyksos, with horses and iron chariots, came from the Middle East, and the Middle Kingdom succumbed about 1800 B.C. The New Kingdom followed from around 1570 B.C. until around 1090 B.C.

During the New Kingdom and subsequent periods, holy priests, pharaohs, wealthy landlords, and other members of the elite lived in large villas with courtyards. These villas had colonnades, baths, and gardens covered with adjustable awnings. Many of our expensive houses today use these features.

Crete, or the Minoan Civilization

Until the present century little was known about this ancient civilization, which existed on the island of Crete between 2000 and 1200 B.C. In recent years scientists have begun to accept the theory that a terrific volcanic explosion on Santorin, a small island nearby, caused the sudden and complete destruction of Crete. Only the Minoans who were off to distant ports escaped annihilation.

During the mid-1890's Sir Arthur Evans, intrigued with the myth of the Minotaur, a sea creature that was supposed to have lived in the ancient labyrinth on Crete, became convinced that an exceptional civilization lay buried on the island. Evans set out to make excavations on this island where, according to legend, each year seven beautiful maidens and seven strapping youths were sacrificed to a sea monster called the Minotaur. When the Palace of Knossos was finally uncovered, it revealed a maze of rooms—throne room, courtrooms, a treasury suite, weaving quarters, bedrooms, kitchens, and bathrooms with flush toilets and two sets of drains. The women of Crete wore clothing far more intricately cut than any form of dress that was worn elsewhere until the fifteenth century A.D. Had this civilization continued, technology would probably have been far more advanced than it is today. Many secrets were buried with the lost civilization.

The island of Crete was strategically located for active trade with cities along the coasts of Asia, Egypt, and the Iberian Peninsula. The Palace of Knossos, and several other palaces uncovered more recently, have revealed a great deal about this ancient and advanced civilization. Colorful frescoes on the walls indicate that the Minoans enjoyed banquets where young women danced

The Palace of Knossos.

and played various musical instruments, and outdoor games where men and women, in short trunks, grappled with bulls. In the museum in the town of Heraklion, the tourist can see bathtubs, decorated urns, coins, statues, figurines, musical instruments, and many other items that were in use nearly four thousand years ago. It is possible that even the laboring classes on Crete lived far better than any laborers have lived until the present century.

Greece and Rome

During the Age of Greece (roughly 600–300 B.C.), worship of the gods motivated the building of the great temples, which have yet to be surpassed in architectural beauty. Greece was blessed with one of the most durable of building materials—marble, an inspiration to architects and sculptors. The Parthenon, with its friezes and awesome columns, stands in the Acropolis as a challenge to the architects and artists of all times. This beautifully proportioned structure, built to honor the goddess Athena Parthenos, was almost demolished when the Turks used it to store ammunition during a war with the Venetians in 1687 A.D. Great palaces, with courtyards and formal gardens, and public buildings were patterned after the temples of the gods.

The Romans (Roman Empire roughly 27 B.C.–476 A.D.) accepted the Greek gods and copied Greek architecture, but they added other engineering concepts, such as the dome, the aqueduct, and the bridge. The Romans did not limit their building materials to marble but used terra-cotta, limestone, brick, and cement, all of which offered greater building flexibility.

The Pantheon, originally built in 27 B.C. to honor all Roman gods, is the most perfectly preserved of all ancient Roman buildings. This ancient temple with its great curved dome (rotunda added in 123 A.D.) and magnificent colonnaded portico has inspired the designs for many public buildings in Europe and America.

Home architecture, at least among the wealthy classes, improved greatly during the Greek and Roman empires. Many aristocrats had town houses as well as villas in the country. Their houses had a central court, called an *atrium,* around which rooms were grouped. Other houses were built in rows very much like town houses today. Shops occupied the fronts of many buildings. Homes of the socially elite had baths with running water, sewer systems, and circulating hot-air heat through tiles in the walls. Oil lamps provided light. The Romans were the first civilization to use window glass instead of oiled paper in windows. Many of these living concepts were not paralleled in Europe or America until the nineteenth century. While the aristocracy enjoyed the good life, Roman laborers lived in mud or brick huts similar to those in Mesopotamia and Egypt or in apartment houses, some of which were as high as six stories, with a stairway in a central court.

Model of the Parthenon in Athens. (Courtesy of The Metropolitan Museum of Art, Purchase, 1890, Levi Hale Willard Bequest)

Byzantine Empire

During the early Christian centuries, the Roman Empire gradually declined because of incompetent rulers and corrupt government. One of the more able rulers, Constantine, after being converted to Christianity, founded New Rome, or Byzantium, later named Constantinople and, in 1929, given the name Istanbul by the Turks. This ancient city, the only city in the world built on two continents, straddles the Bosporus, which separates Europe from Asia. Constantine established the city in 330 A.D. and later built the world-renowned church St. Sophia. The original church was destroyed by fire and later rebuilt during Justinian's rule (527–565 A.D.). Byzantine architecture combined the classical elements of ancient Greece and Rome with the ornateness of Oriental architecture. The villas of the wealthy had mosaic tile floors, tapestries, and mosaic decorations on the walls. They also had beautifully landscaped courtyards, far excelling anything in Europe at the time.

MEDIEVAL CASTLES, GOTHIC AND RENAISSANCE CATHEDRALS

The Gothic period in architecture was an outgrowth of the Middle Ages, and the architecture of the Renaissance was a revival of the classic architecture of Greece and Rome.

Middle Ages—Feudal and Gothic Periods

As Constantine's empire flourished in the Middle East, Charlemagne, in the early ninth century, attempted to unite many of the expanding city-states of Europe into an empire as a protection against invaders. However, empire status was short-lived because wealthy, greedy independent landlords began to seize power over large tracts of land and to establish a manorial society

Bodiam Castle, Sussex, England. Vandal invasions after the fall of Rome caused powerful lords to build such fortresses.

Chartres Cathedral is an outstanding example of Gothic architecture.

composed of lords and serfs. Soon a feudal system emerged in Europe.

The homes of the landlords were quite unlike the ancient villas and town houses of previous civilizations. In the manorial plan a castle was built on the highest point of a large tract of land, and it was surrounded by a moat with a drawbridge. Below the castle the serfs and servants lived in houses similar to those allotted to the servant classes for several thousand years. These homes, with one or two rooms, were made of timber, brick, adobe, or stone, and had thatched roofs.

In spite of the beautiful wall tapestries, massive carved furniture, and huge ornamental fireplaces, the imposing castles were dreary, cold, and foul smelling from smoke and refuse. If ever you have the opportunity to take a trip up the Rhine River in Germany, you will see medieval castles high among the cliffs at every bend in the river. Many of these old castles all over Europe have been modernized inside and offer accommodations for tourists.

Our familiar church structures did not exist in the early Middle Ages. There were monasteries, where monks kept education and religion alive. Eventually many monasteries were built in the style of architecture known as Romanesque— less elaborate than later Renaissance styles.

During the twelfth century, the manorial system began to collapse as a new merchant class came into power and cities began to develop. Each community had a town square with market halls, guild headquarters, and a city hall. With greater social and economic freedom, the common people began to turn towards some form of spiritual expression. Inspired by the Crusades and by emphasis upon Christianity, the people began to build great religious structures or cathedrals with towering spires, with windows that had pointed arches, and with flying buttresses—known as Gothic architecture. Although the Gothic style originated in France, it obtained its name from the Goths, an early Germanic tribe who came to central Europe from Scandinavia. This new religious architecture had its counterpart in chateaus on large French estates, especially in Normandy. Homes on large tracts of land in America today show the influence of the Gothic period in a style called *Norman French*. Early New England homes with their high-pitched roofs showed Gothic influence,

The home of Johann Wolfgang von Goethe (1749-1832) at Frankfurt, Germany. Notice the gain in floor space with each story.

and in the nineteenth century many Victorian homes were called *Carpenter Gothic*.

Renaissance and a Revival of the Classic

The early Renaissance began in Florence and later moved to Rome. Because of their geographic location, the cities of Italy benefited from trade with the more advanced Middle and Far East and also from their rich heritage from Greece and Rome. Trade brought wealth, and with this wealth, architects attempted to adapt the classic elements of Greek and Roman architecture to current needs. In Rome the classic revival found its greatest expression in St. Peter's, begun in 1506 and finally dedicated in 1626. One of the leading architects of the Italian Renaissance was Andrea Palladio (1518-1580), whose books with plans based upon accurate measurements of classic architecture found their way to America as early as 1667. Jefferson's home, Monticello, in Charlottesville, Virginia, shows Palladian influence. In France the spirit of the Renaissance is exemplified in the Baroque architecture of the period of Louis XIV (1643-1715), especially in the palace of Versailles. This palace helped to establish the prestige of the French court, and every monarch in Europe tried to copy it.

The Renaissance found expression in England especially in St. Paul's Cathedral and in the large manor houses on country estates. From the reign of Queen Elizabeth, England began to progress rapidly due to increasing trade and to the influence of two leading architects, Inigo Jones (1573-1652) and Sir Christopher Wren (1632-1723). The Golden Age of furniture design in England occurred in the eighteenth century with such cabinetmakers as Chippendale,

The Half-timbered houses of medieval and early Renaissance England foreshadowed a popular style in America.

Sheraton, Hepplewhite, and the Adam brothers. The four Adam brothers were not only furniture designers; they were architects and community developers as well. They designed a pretentious suburban development along the Thames just outside London for wealthy sea traders, merchants, and other businessmen. Unfortunately there is little left of the planned community, named *Adelphi.*

During the eighteenth century English ties with America were strong, and the colonial city of Williamsburg, Virginia, is representative of English eighteenth-century architecture. With the late eighteenth century we bring this chapter to a close. From here on we shall trace home architecture as it developed in America.

SUMMARY

Next to food, shelter was one of man's earliest needs. Primitive man was ingenious in finding or creating a wide variety of dwellings—caves, houses suspended over water, snowhouses, tents, and huts. The materials used for these structures depended upon those available until means of transportation made it possible to transport materials from one place to another.

With the introduction of farming and herding during the Neolithic Age, community life became possible and with it a desire for spiritual expression. Every ancient civilization dedicated some type of structure to its gods. The people of Mesopotamia built ziggurats; the Egyptians, pyramids and temples; the Greeks and Romans, the most beautiful temples of all time. During the existence of these ancient empires, there was always an aristocracy made up of either the priestly class or warriors, and their homes or villas often reflected temple architecture. During the feudal period in Europe, the only religious structures were monasteries in isolated areas, and these structures had little influence upon domestic architecture. At this time a different kind of structure developed—the castle with a moat and drawbridge.

In the late Middle Ages a merchant class arose, and with it small towns or boroughs developed, causing the feudal or manorial system to collapse. A revival of Christianity during the Crusades coincided with the social and economic rise of the common people. Once again architecture found expression in the spiritual needs of the people. The Gothic period, which had its beginnings in northern France during the twelfth century, was the time during which many famous European cathedrals were built. The full flowering of the Renaissance in Europe followed the Gothic period, reaching England during the reign of Queen Elizabeth I. Domestic architecture in England was also a modification of church architecture. Because of wealth acquired during her period of empire, England led other European countries in the development of home architecture. No other European country bequeathed as great a home and housing heritage to America as did England.

THINGS TO THINK ABOUT AND TO DO

1. Discuss the importance of the tripod of civilization—or the loom, the plow, and the wheel—in relation to the development of present-day improvements in home living.

2. Display on the bulletin board illustrations of primitive structures, and indicate how climatic conditions and native materials influenced them.

3. Give a written or an oral report on primitive dwellings in some area of the world today and on family life in these dwellings. Choose one area of the world or one type of dwelling.

4. On a large map of the Middle East and Europe, trace trade routes of early civilizations—those of Mesopotamia, Egypt, Greece, and Rome. Display on the bulletin board illustrations of structures that developed in each civilization at its height.

5. Give some reasons why architecture differed so very greatly between contemporary civilizations—Mesopotamian and Egyptian.

6. Give a pictorial report on excavations on the island of Crete.

7. Show pictures of the Acropolis in Athens and tell something about its history.

8. Display on the bulletin board photos of public buildings in the United States today that reflect Greek influence.

9. Show slides of the ancient Roman ruins in Italy or in the Middle East. Include the Pantheon.

10. Give a report on the economic and social life of Constantinople between the period of the founding of Constantinople and its fall to the Turks in 1453.

11. Show slides of medieval buildings and how people lived in the Middle Ages. Discuss.

12. Show slides of towns in Europe (including Chester, England) during the late Middle Ages and the Renaissance, and comment on houses and living conditions.

13. Display on the bulletin board some of the great cathedrals, palaces, and villas of Europe (identify each), and indicate features that have been retained in our own churches and cathedrals, public buildings, and domestic architecture.

14. Write a summary of our shelter heritage, using as a basis the generalizations in the Guidelines for Study.

chapter two

EUROPEAN INFLUENCES UPON AMERICAN STYLES

Although a Viking, Leif Ericson, is credited with having been the first European to set foot on the American continent (about 1000 A.D.), early settlement and later colonization was done mainly by the Spanish, French, and English. Christopher Columbus, an Italian under Spanish sponsorship, discovered America in 1492, and in 1565 the Spanish made the first permanent settlement at St. Augustine, Florida. (The photograph opposite shows a house in St. Augustine which is thought by some authorities to be the oldest house in the United States.) The French explorer Jacques Cartier entered the New World by way of the St. Lawrence River in 1535; Quebec was founded in 1608; and by 1718 France had established trading posts and villages along water routes as far south as New Orleans. John Cabot from England landed on the coast of Labrador in 1497, but it was not until 1607 that an Englishman, Captain John Smith, made the first permanent English settlement at Jamestown, Virginia, and not until 1734 that Georgia, the last of the original English colonies, was settled.

After defeating Spain's so-called Invincible Armada in 1588, England became a new sea power in the world, more interested in trade with the East than in the colonization of America. Although France had substantial holdings in the New World, her prestige diminished after the long and extravagant reign of Louis XIV (1643–1715) and the ensuing French Revolution in 1789.

As a result of the French and Indian War (1754–1763) between England and France, England acquired all the French territory east of the Mississippi and all of Canada. After the War of Independence, the newly formed United States of America purchased the remaining Louisiana Territory from Napoleon in 1803, the proceeds of which he used to finance his campaigns in Europe, and in 1809 Florida was purchased from Spain by the United States.

Other European countries than those mentioned also left an impression upon American domestic architecture. During the early seventeenth century the Dutch were among the leading merchants of the sea, and they established fur-trading posts and villages on Manhattan Island and along the Hudson River. Among later comers to the New World were the Swedes, who

15

colonized New Jersey and the Delaware River valley, the Quaker
followers of William Penn, and the Germans, both of whom settled in
Pennsylvania.

Unfortunately time and the bulldozer have taken a heavy toll of early
American architecture. But we are indebted to many organizations for
preserving early landmarks all over the country—at Jamestown and Williamsburg in Virginia; at Plymouth and Salem in Massachusetts; at Natchez,
Mississippi; at Cape May, New Jersey; at Greenfield Village, Dearborn,
Michigan; and elsewhere. Through the Historic Sites Act of 1935, over six
hundred sites and buildings have been selected and studied, including
Sturbridge Village in Sturbridge, Massachusetts; Farmers' Museum at Coopers-
town, New York; and Mystic Seaport at Mystic, Connecticut. There may be
lovely historic buildings in your own community that you can help to
preserve as landmarks for future generations.

The authentic photographs of American architecture prior to the present
century should help you to appreciate your housing heritage and to recognize variations in styles of the past in today's homes. It is doubtful how
many, if any, modern house designs will survive as long as those of the
past did—some for three centuries or more.

GUIDELINES FOR STUDY

GENERAL IDEAS
TO CONSIDER

1. Early home styles in America differed greatly due to the variety of ethnic
groups, the socioeconomic background of the early settlers, the climate, and
the available building materials.
2. Most of the surviving early homes are of English origin because the majority
of settlers were English and because the French and Spanish lost control of their
colonial possessions.
3. A combination of French, Spanish, and English styles prevails along the Gulf
Coast, and Spanish adobe styles are prevalent in the Southwest.
4. The nineteenth century marked a period of growth in America and the revival
of many past styles as the newly rich competed for prestige.

WORDS, NAMES, AND PLACES
TO KNOW

adobe house
The Biltmore
Bok, Edward
The Breakers
bungalow
Cape Cod cottage
Carpenter Gothic

Cotswold
dormer window
Downing, Andrew J.
Dutch Colonial
Eastlake, Charles L.
English Half-Timbered house
Federal house

gable roof
gambrel roof
Garrison Colonial house
Georgian house
Greek Revival
House of the Seven Gables

Monterey house
Northern Colonial house
Saltbox house
Tiffany, Louis Comfort
Veblen, Thorstein
Victorian house

THE SEVENTEENTH CENTURY— PERIOD OF COLONIZATION

The reconstructed villages of the early settlers at Jamestown, Plymouth, and Salem give us a very good idea of how our forefathers lived during the period of colonization. The homes pictured in the restoration of Plimoth Plantation were far more comfortable than the original crude structures of our first settlers. Before they could erect these simple homes the Pilgrims lived either in dugouts or in bark-covered wigwams.

The early New England settlers used the house form they were familiar with in the old country, dating from medieval or Gothic times—a rectangular shape with a high-pitched or gable roof. Wood was as plentiful as it was in England, and it became the favorite building material. After the first sawmill was erected in 1648, many houses with walls made of split logs and caulking were covered with clapboard, and thatched roofs were replaced with shingles. The windows in New England homes were small to keep out the cold, and many were covered with oiled paper until glass became more plentiful. In fact, early colonists were reminded to bring oiled paper with them. Most New England homes had a vestibule to shut out the draft.

The following styles were typical in New England and New York during the seventeenth century—Northern Colonial, Saltbox, Garrison Colonial, Cape Cod, Multi-Gable, and Dutch Colonial.

Brewster House of Plimoth Plantation. (Courtesy of Plimoth Plantation).

Northern Colonial

The New England, or Northern Colonial, was one of the earliest homes built in America, and this style is popular today. It is characterized by its rectangular form, gable roof, plain clapboard exterior, and small windows. Present-day versions of the two- or two-and-a-half story home provide for maximum floor space and good room arrangement, with either a center hall or side-front entrance. The windows are larger than in colonial times and frequently have shutters. The door may have a plain pediment or a scroll-and-urn pediment, both decorative types of door

Northern Colonial—Amasa Gray House, Little Compton, R.I.

Saltbox—The Deming House, Wethersfield, Conn.
(Courtesy of The New-York Historical Society, New York City).

Garrison Colonial—Paul Revere's House, Boston, Mass.

framing. This type of home may be built on a relatively small lot in either flat or rolling country.

Saltbox

The Saltbox, named for its resemblance to early saltboxes, evolved from the early Northern Colonial. It was simply a means of providing more space on the first floor by adding a lean-to and by extending the gable roof at the back. The entrance and walls, with clapboard or shingle sides, are severely plain. Although the Saltbox is similar to the Northern Colonial, it is less popular in modern reproductions.

Garrison Colonial

One of the surviving Garrison-type homes is Paul Revere's home, the oldest wooden house in Boston. It was built about 1676, and Paul Revere lived in the house between 1770 and 1800. This style also dates from the late Middle Ages in England, when the upper floor projected beyond a lower floor in order to gain more floor space. The same type of construction is found in the blockhouses in restorations of forts. When the gable roof extends to the first floor, the second floor will have dormer windows. Originally the chimneys were rather loosely attached to one or both ends of the house, so that they could be knocked off in case they caught fire. In restorations there is usually one chimney. The main entrance may be centered or at one side, giving a choice of floor plans. Like other New England Colonial styles, the house is well suited to either level or rolling ground.

Cape Cod

This one-story or story-and-a-half house with a broad gable roof and sides covered with shingles, which are allowed to weather, originated on Cape Cod toward the end of the seventeenth century. There is a center chimney, which often separates living and sleeping quarters. Even when there is a second floor, the first floor usually has one or two bedrooms. Modern versions of the Cape Cod may be built with wood shingles, either painted or allowed to weather, or with aluminum shingles.

Cape Cod—Captain Gray House, Orleans, Mass.

Multi-Gable

This is not exactly a style but an early version of the extendable house. Just as the lean-to is characteristic of the Saltbox, the addition of wings with gabled roofs characterizes a New England house resembling the Cotswold, a stone farmhouse with several gables that derived its name from the Cotswold Hills in England. Often families would build a simple Northern Colonial house, and as the size of the family increased or as the family became more prosperous, they would build additions. The House of the Seven Gables, built in 1668 and made famous by Nathaniel Hawthorne, is an example of the many-gabled house of early New England.

Multi-Gable—House of the Seven Gables, Salem, Mass.

Dutch Colonial

In 1609 Henry Hudson sailed into what is now the harbor of New York and up the river which was later named for him. Even though Dutch colonization was brief in the New World, the Dutch left a rich heritage to American domestic architecture. The Dutch were an industrious, versatile, and home-loving people, who stressed friendliness, cleanliness, and comfort. They emphasized kitchen planning and provided cupboard space for food and utensils. The first Dutch homes did not have the familiar gambrel roof. Instead they had a steep gable roof with a

Dutch Colonial—The Schenck-Crooke House, Brooklyn, N.Y.

slight concave curve. When they built their homes in rows, as they did in cities, the top of the house at the front was built stepped-gable, fashioned to the ridge of the roof. We are told that this construction, typical of medieval Germany, helped the chimney sweeps to mount the roof with safety, but it may have been for beauty rather than function.

The climate in New York was less severe than in New England; so the Dutch were able to extend the roof to cover a stoop or small porch where people could sit on straight-back benches and chat. Another interesting feature of Dutch homes was the double door. The lower half could be kept closed to keep farmyard animals out of the house, while the upper half could be opened for ventilation. At first the Dutch used wood, but as soon as they could begin to make bricks, they preferred brick. Many homes along the Hudson River are built of fieldstone. The Dutch were often versatile in combining brick or stone with clapboard for the exterior and in using either a center or side entrance to change the floor plan. The gambrel, or broken gable, roof was a later development, possibly to save money by spreading out the roof and using dormer windows to provide light for the good floor space on the second floor. The use of brick or stone with clapboard or shingles also came later. This style, in many adaptations, is popular today, and it lends itself well to level or rolling country in moderate to cold climates.

THE EIGHTEENTH CENTURY—
PERIOD OF CONFLICT
AND EXPANSION

During the eighteenth century, domestic architecture in America followed contemporary Georgian styles in England. This was the period when England produced her greatest cabinetmakers and many important architects. The beautiful furniture of Chippendale, Hepplewhite, and Sheraton and the furniture and interiors of the Adam brothers, as well as imports of Oriental rugs and china, gave English homes an image of elegance.

On the American side of the Atlantic more comfortable and elegant homes were also being built. An aristocracy was beginning to develop in the North among shipbuilders and merchants; and in the South, among tobacco and rice plantation owners. There was also a growing professional class and an increasing emphasis upon culture— education, the theater, concerts, the arts, and libraries. More and more handbooks on building were available, showing elaborate paneling, stately entrances, ornamented ceilings, and beautifully landscaped gardens. The new homes were far more spacious than those in New England, and the windows were larger. Another feature was the provision for outdoor living in the form of balconies and verandas, or porches, especially in the South. The Georgian style was the basis for homes built from Pennsylvania to Florida, including the Greek Revival homes of the next century.

The Georgian

The visitor to Williamsburg will find many restored Georgian homes as a result of an extensive restoration project sponsored by John D. Rockefeller, Jr. in the 1920's. Williamsburg was chosen because not only was it the capital of the British colony in Virginia between 1699 and 1779, but the town was representative of eighteenth-century living. The Wythe House at Williamsburg is the purest example of Georgian architecture in America. Brick was the preferred building material for all buildings. Many of you may have visited the Governor's Palace, Capitol, Raleigh Tavern, and other restored buildings.

The Georgian house is a large rectangle with a hip roof and a symmetrical plan—that is, a center hall upstairs and downstairs, and chimneys at each end of the house. It conveys the impression of spaciousness, dignity, and elegance whether it is as plain as the Wythe House or a more elaborate adaptation with shutters and a paneled door set between Doric or Ionic columns. The rear is sometimes L-shaped or T-shaped, flanked by long porches. In many adaptations, the third floor may have dormer windows. An interesting feature of Georgian homes along the coast is the captain's walk, a relic of earlier New England homes. This rail, or fence, on the roof is sometimes called the *widow's walk* because it is where the captain's wife, when he was away, could watch for incoming fishing vessels.

Variations of this rather expensive and impressive home are to be seen all over the country. The style requires a large, fairly level lot.

Georgian—The Wythe House at Williamsburg.

Southern Colonial

In various interpretations, the Southern Colonial became popular in Virginia, Maryland, the Carolinas, and Georgia among wealthy plantation owners. Built of wood rather than brick, the floor plan was essentially Georgian. The verandas, or porches, with square columns reflected Mediterranean styles in Europe, and were later to be reflected along the Gulf Coast where the climate was mild. Many Southern Colonial homes borrowed the captain's walk from New England coastal Georgian

Southern Colonial—Mount Vernon.

homes. Original Southern Colonial homes had many separate buildings to the rear of the house for the kitchen, household help, and storage of food and supplies. Mount Vernon, George Washington's home near Washington, D.C., is a typical Virginia plantation home.

The Southern Colonial style took a little different form in the Carolinas because many of the Englishmen who settled there came by way of Bermuda and the West Indies where the climate was quite warm. They introduced some of the features of housing in the islands, such as porches on the first and second floors and stucco exterior walls.

Federal

The Federal bridged the eighteenth and nineteenth centuries—a transition from the pure classic English Georgian styles and the revival of Greek temple architecture. It was more Roman than Greek. Following the Revolution there was a general dissatisfaction with anything British, and many people rebelled against the Georgian. Thomas Jefferson was the chief exponent of the Federal style, and his home, Monticello, and the Rotunda at the University of Virginia in Charlottesville, Virginia, are excellent examples of the Federal period. Duncan Phyfe was the popular furniture designer of the period.

Federal architecture, like Georgian, makes use of brick and is based upon perfect symmetry. Jefferson used the plan book of the Italian Renaissance architect Andrea Palladio (1518–1580), who took exact measurements from many early Roman buildings for his handbook. Many public buildings today which date from the first half of the nineteenth century show a strong Federal influence. For home architecture, this style is suitable for large houses set in an expanse of rolling countryside.

Federal—Monticello, Jefferson's home, near Charlottesville, Virginia.

Creole

This style is a blend of Georgian, French, and Spanish architecture peculiar to the area around New Orleans. The French settled New Orleans in 1719 and made it the capital of New France. In 1722 a section of the city along the riverfront was fortified and named Vieux Carré. This is the French Quarter of New Orleans today, one of the most romantic areas in the United States. Before New Orleans became a part of the United States, it had been in Spanish hands through secret negotiations between France and Spain to keep out the English.

Creole architecture combined the most charming features of French, Spanish, and Georgian styles—the hipped roof and symmetry of the Georgian, and the balconies and verandas, with their lacy grillwork, and the romantic courtyards of the French and Spanish. Floor-length windows and louvered shutters, designed for ventilation and privacy, were French features. Fires in 1788 and 1794 destroyed many of these lovely structures. The Monterey styles in California resemble to a large degree the early Creole homes.

La Branche, a Creole house in New Orleans.

Monterey

This style developed during the late eighteenth and early nineteenth centuries. It is named for the Pacific coast city Monterey, which at that time (1769–1821) was under Spanish rule. Whaling ships from New England reached Monterey in 1796. Later the Gold Rush sent many people to California seeking fortunes, and as communities began to grow in southern California, the Monterey became popular. A replica of the original Monterey house is two stories high with a grillwork balcony around the second floor.

This "Monterey Saltbox" is an old whaling station. Built in Monterey in 1855, it has since been restored.

It has a low-pitched gable roof. In order to have more floor space many New England settlers in Monterey extended the roof at the back to produce a "Monterey Saltbox." The house is usually stuccoed and decorated with louvered shutters.

Spanish Mission

The Spanish Mission or Spanish Adobe house is a blend of the Pueblo Indian adobe or clay house and the Spanish architecture of the Moorish period. This particular style of adobe house originated with the Spanish missions of the late eighteenth century.

In 1789 Franciscan friars established twenty-nine Spanish missions, a day's journey apart, along a 600-mile road called El Camino Real in California. The Indians helped the padres build their missions of stone or sun-dried brick and clay, using heavy projecting log beams at the roof. The houses had very thick walls, which were effective in keeping out the heat. The typically Spanish red-tile roof, minus the beams, and an inner courtyard around a patio give this type of house a special charm. The Spanish Mission house is popular in the desert states, such as New Mexico, Arizona, and southern California.

The Carmel Mission in California.

THE NINETEENTH CENTURY—
PERIOD OF INDUSTRIAL
AND ECONOMIC GROWTH

The nineteenth century was a period of tremendous social and economic change. By the end of the century two extreme social classes had evolved in urban America, as well as a somewhat small middle class. The expansion of the factory system had produced a large class of low-paid, poorly fed, and inadequately housed families in our large cities. At the other extreme were the enormously wealthy families who had accumulated vast fortunes in railroad expansion, steel production, the fur and textile industries, banking, real estate, and merchandising. These were the families whose behavior Thorstein Veblen analyzed in his *Theory of the Leisure Class*. These people lived in mansions, owned summer homes and yachts, traveled extensively, entertained lavishly, and employed many servants.

Competition was keen in striving for social status. The moderately wealthy attempted to emulate the very wealthy in what Veblen describes as "conspicuous consumption." A home with servants, elegant dress, and expensive entertaining were visible symbols of the ability to spend. In home architecture many people went to extremes during the latter part of the nineteenth century in combining many European styles and adding all kinds of ornamentation to basic forms.

Early in the century the homes of the rising aristocracy on the southern plantations took on a different character from those to the north and east. As cotton cultivation became more profitable than rice, sugar, or tobacco, many plantation owners moved from Georgia and the Carolinas to the fertile Mississippi River delta states—Mississippi, Alabama, and Louisiana. An aristocracy had developed in this planter society, which wanted homes that would express affluence. The main floor of the house was often a floor above ground, reached by outside stairs, because the delta regions were often inundated when the Mississippi rose. Spanish and French verandas and balconies with grillwork were combined with eighteenth-century English-Georgian and nineteenth-century Greek Revival architecture. Many of these lovely homes are still to be seen in Natchez and other Gulf Coast and Mississippi valley cities.

The war between the North and South put an end to the planter society and the southern aristocracy, but due to their industrial and economic growth, the aristocracy of the North survived. These wealthy families became the socially elite or, in Veblen's language, "the leisure class." They began to build mansions inspired by English manor houses, Mediterranean villas, German castles, and Moorish and Oriental palaces. The Vanderbilt winter home at Asheville, North Carolina (The Biltmore), and the family's summer home at Newport, Rhode Island (The Breakers), are among the beautiful showplaces of the late nineteenth century.

The typical well-to-do home of the Victorian period had Brussels carpetings and carved black-walnut furniture upholstered in tufted velvet or horsehair, elaborately draped windows, and a lavish display of china and bric-a-brac. A trend toward replacing these furnishings with imported Oriental rugs, lacquered furniture, and Oriental screens began in the years after 1853 when Commodore Perry opened the ports of Japan to Western trade. For the two hundred years previously, Japan had been completely isolated from the West, during the militaristic rule of the Tokugawas.

During the latter half of the nineteenth century, less affluent families were becoming more conscious of their environment through the publication of a number of magazines that contained articles on architecture and decorating—*Godey's Lady's Book, The Ladies' Home Journal,* and *Harper's Bazar* (original spelling)—and through advances in technology. For example:

1844   The first machine for printing wallpaper arrived from England.

1848   Erastus B. Bigelow invented a loom for making Brussels and tapestry carpeting.

1848- The production of factory-made
1860   furniture quadrupled.

1850's Gaslights began to replace coal-oil lamps.

Sewer systems were installed by many cities.

1874 The electric light was patented by Edison.

1876 Iceboxes, with upper compartments for ice storage and lower compartments for food storage, were introduced.

Many laborsaving devices, although in the experimental stages, had their origins in the nineteenth century—the washing machine (1805), a furnace for central heating (1815), the flush toilet (1833), the vacuum cleaner (1859), the dishwasher (1865)—but it was not until the twentieth century that these labor-saving devices came into practical use. In fact, the only major invention in the area of home living developed entirely in this century has been air conditioning.

On the other hand, social and economic progress carried with it hardships and penalties for the poor urban laborer. Industry attracted families to cities faster than money and technology could provide adequate living and working conditions for them. Factories and tenement houses, with little light, ventilation, or sanitation, became "sweat shops." At the end of the century the contrast between the slum dwellers in large cities and the millionaires with town mansions and country villas was dramatic. However, we shall leave this period of social history, which continued into the following century, for the next chapter, and turn our attention to the types of architecture that developed before the twentieth century.

During the nineteenth century there were many revivals of previous periods, beginning with the classic revival of the Federal (more Roman than Greek), which spanned two centuries and lasted until 1820. After that the Greek Revival

came along, followed by the Victorian period—a term used to encompass a number of European revivals from the Middle East to Spain, but mainly the English Gothic.

The Greek Revival

The Greek Revival was an expression of the new public taste that was sweeping Europe and America between 1820 and 1840. The Greek temple with plain or fluted columns and Doric, Ionic, or Corinthian capitals formed the basis for large and small homes, state houses, and other public buildings in the United States. The roofs became almost flat, and all chimneys were suppressed. Cornices were carved with Greek motifs—the fret, anthemion, honeysuckle, and laurel wreath. Many old Georgian homes were updated with Greek columns and porticos.

Greek Revival—the courthouse in Stonington, Connecticut.

Victorian

The Victorian period is named for Queen Victoria of England, who became queen at eighteen and ruled from 1837 until 1901. This period in architecture as well as dress is often referred to as "the gingerbread age," a period of poor taste and an age of architectural horrors. Ghost stories invariably have their setting in deserted old Victorian homes or medieval castles. In spite of repeated criticism, there is something charming and nostalgic about nineteenth-century homes, especially those referred to as "Carpenter Gothic." If later, modern architects— Henry Hobson Richardson, Louis Sullivan, Frank Lloyd Wright, and others —had had their way, fewer of these homes would be left today. However, citizens in many areas of the country have been farsighted enough to save some of these Victorian homes for future generations to see. Not long ago the old homes at Cape May, an Atlantic seacoast resort, included so many "hopelessly Victorian" structures that the resort lost business, and the homes began to deteriorate. Today, these restored old homes give Cape May an air of distinction.

The Victorian period marks the end of traditional building methods and the beginning of the industrial age. Even before the Civil War more people were becoming conscious of domestic architecture and interior decoration through magazines. Many handbooks with building plans were available, and technological advances were spurring industry. The period between 1840 and 1900, except for the Civil War years, was one of the most significant in the social and economic advancement of our country. During these years, the first transcontinental railroad and the automobile speeded transportation;

A "wedding cake house" of Carpenter Gothic at Cape May.

modern farm machinery improved agriculture; the telephone, telegraph, photography, and the rotary printing press increased communication; modern factory machines, including the power sewing machine, automated industry; gas and electric lighting and better sanitation methods improved living conditions.

Among persons credited with influencing the taste of America during the nineteenth century were Andrew Jackson Downing and Charles Lock Eastlake. This was an age of experimentation and competition in housing, which produced a hodgepodge of architectural styles, but not all styles were equally bad. English Gothic domestic architecture was the basis for the majority of styles, but scarcely a period in history or a country in the world was overlooked by architects designing homes for clients who sought the ornate, the exotic, or the extreme in order to express individuality or to impress their social peers.

The Carpenter Gothic (see the illustration on this page) prevailed during the early Victorian period, followed by a number of European and Eastern

Above—Shadows-on-the-Teche, in New Iberia, Louisiana. Completed in 1834, this adaptation of a Southern Colonial home shows a blend of Greek Revival in the columns, Northern Colonial in the gabled roof, and Spanish in the second-floor veranda. Below—Boscobel, in Garrison-on-Hudson, New York. This house is an interesting Federal adaptation showing strong Adam influence and exquisite proportions.

These eclectic Victorian homes show the ingenuity of architects who tried to provide newly affluent families with homes symbolic of status.

Above—The Carson Mansion, built in the 1880's in Eureka, California, shows strong Gothic influence. Below—The Chaney House in Redlands, California, is a composite of gable and mansard roofs, Oriental tower and Chinese fret railing.

revivals. Later Victorian style, sometimes referred to as *Queen Anne Gothic,* was more elaborate and made of wood, stucco, or brick. It had little connection with Queen Anne's reign between 1702 and 1714, except perhaps that it included some features of English country homes. The *Gothic Revival* house of the early Victorian period, or period before the Civil War, competed with the Greek Revival for popularity and gradually replaced it. The landscape architect Andrew Jackson Downing, whose house plans appeared in *Godey's Lady's Book,* was the greatest advocate of the new architecture, which appealed to the newly affluent families of the nineteenth century. The interest in medieval chivalry and romance was increased by the popular literary works of the day—Alfred Lord Tennyson's *Idylls of the King* (legends of King Arthur) and Washington Irving's *Tales of the Alhambra.*

Actually the Gothic Revival was a revival of country homes of medieval England, one of which was the multigabled Cotswold, originating in the Cotswold Hills. However, not only gabled roofs, but turrets, towers, spires, long narrow arched windows, and porticos became incorporated in the plans. Gothic styles were copied in wood, on a smaller scale, by less affluent families. With the introduction of the scroll saw, a liberal amount of filigree and lacy trim was added to imitate Spanish grillwork. *Carpenter Gothic* was the name given the new architecture, in which the wood was often painted white. The popularity of the Carpenter Gothic spread north, south, and west as far as California. Former President Harry Truman's home in Missouri is an interesting example of Gothic architecture.

The term *eclectic* is used to include the great mixture of Gothic, Italianate or Tuscan, French Provincial, and Moorish styles that evolved from the drawing boards of architects in order to provide the newly wealthy with homes symbolic of prestige or sophisticated taste. Charles Lock Eastlake, an English journalist and architect, became critical of the emerging styles as well as of Carpenter Gothic.

A moralist as well as a journalist and architect, Eastlake preached against the insincere and deliberate imitating of foreign architecture for its symbolic significance. The home architecture he called insincere included the pseudo Italian or Tuscan villas, the elaborate French Provincial villas with mansard roofs (created during the reign of Louis XIV by the architect François Mansard), and the Oriental imitations with Moorish minarets or Japanese pagodas.

Eastlake introduced a style that is closely associated with Queen Anne houses (see pictures opposite). His homes were Gothic in form and designed to be sincere and functional.

With the American publication of Eastlake's *Hints on Household Taste* in 1872, his ideas had a definite influence upon general public taste, but the rising aristocracy continued to imitate the homes of the wealthy from all over Europe. The summer and winter homes of the Vanderbilt family are examples.

As the nineteenth century came to a close, the conflict between Victorian prudery and ornateness and modern boldness and severity was to continue. Edward Bok, famous editor of the *Ladies' Home Journal* at the turn of the century, was to influence public taste toward functionalism, and the jeweler Louis Comfort Tiffany was to appeal to the aesthetic senses in decoration, introducing stained-glass windows and lampshades.

Biltmore, the Vanderbilt winter home near Asheville, North Carolina, is a blend of Gothic and Renaissance architecture, imitating palaces in Europe.

A Charles Eastlake house.

A Queen Anne Gothic house.

The Victorians had no monopoly in borrowing from other styles. Atwood House, at Chatham, Massachusetts, is a Cape Cod adaptation with a gambrel roof.

European influence was also felt in the homes of the humble; the log cabin, built without nails, is of Swedish origin. This particular one was in the settlement where Abraham Lincoln was born (now located at Fort Harrod in Harrodsburg, Kentucky).

SUMMARY

From the first years of the seventeenth century until the end of the nineteenth century, America rose from a country sparsely populated with Indians and a few white people at Jamestown to a potential world power. The richness of her housing heritage, the variety of the settlers who came to her shores, and her favorable climate and varied topography have had a great deal to do with housing progress.

During the seventeenth and eighteenth centuries, domestic architecture was somewhat provincial—that is, certain styles prevailed in certain areas of the country. The early homes of New England with their compact floor plans and gabled roofs, the Georgian homes of the Mid-Atlantic coast with their spaciousness and symmetry, the Gulf Coast homes with their Spanish and French grillwork balconies and courtyards, and later the Greek temple homes of the Atlantic seaboard and the Spanish Mission structures of the Southwest and California gave a variety to American architecture found no place else in the world.

During the latter part of the nineteenth century wealthy merchants, businessmen, and industrialists set the pace in housing. Taste changed rapidly as new styles were introduced and technology increased. The century was a period of revivals, extremes, and extravagances. Toward the close of the century a middle class was becoming more prominent, and the trend toward smaller and more functional homes began.

THINGS TO THINK ABOUT AND TO DO

1. Locate on a map of the United States the areas where our early (seventeenth-century) homes developed.

2. Display on the bulletin board illustrations of seventeenth-, eighteenth-, and nineteenth-century homes in America, according to geographic location. A library file of clippings will be helpful. Discuss the differences in the types of homes, giving reasons for variations.

3. Display modern versions of early domestic architecture, and take a class vote on preferences. Compare the traditional homes with modern domestic architecture.

4. Form groups to tour various areas of your community, and take pictures of interesting older homes or buildings, even though they may look shabby. Identify the distinguishing architectural features.

5. Discuss the various building materials available in your area in relation to their popularity, cost, and appearance.

6. Using a slide or overhead projector, show pictures of some of the missions along El Camino Real, the 600-mile mission highway in California.

7. Show slides of homes and buildings in Williamsburg, Virginia, Greenfield Village at Dearborn, Michigan, Sturbridge Village in Sturbridge, Massachusetts, or any other living museum. Discuss the architecture and the home life that prevailed.

8. Conduct a class discussion on the many ways families accumulated wealth during the nineteenth century, and mention some of the wealthy families and their twentieth-century philanthropies.

9. Give brief reports on the evolution of our laborsaving equipment, such as washers, dryers, dishwashers, electric irons, and so on.

10. List each of the home styles discussed in the chapter, and give three characteristics of each.

chapter three

THE TWENTIETH CENTURY—END OF REGIONALISM

Changes are more gradual in housing than in any other area of living because the home is the biggest investment of a lifetime and homes last a long time. In many areas of cities today, handsome old homes stand near ultramodern apartments or deteriorating row houses. Many of our single-family dwellings dating from the early part of the century, as well as new homes, reflect architectural features from the past. It is interesting to follow the development of twentieth-century domestic architecture and note the factors that have brought about changes in housing concepts. Three factors have been largely responsible for the types of dwellings we have today—a tremendous growth in population, an accelerated technology, and a rising income.

At the turn of the century, our nation had forty-five states with a total population of seventy-six million people. Now there are fifty states with a total population of over two hundred million people. An increasing population has forced many families to move beyond the city limits and has made the price of land skyrocket. This shift in population has caused almost insurmountable urban problems.

A great deal of twentieth-century technology had its origin in the nineteenth century—the telephone, central heating, laborsaving equipment, the automobile, airplane, and movies, but these innovations did not become common until the first quarter of the twentieth century. It was not until the late twenties that electric refrigerators, washers, and radios came into popular use. It was not until the late forties that television became popular, and the late fifties that dryers, dishwashers, and air conditioners became common. These items, available only to the wealthy not many years ago, are in fairly general use today.

Family income has been rising gradually since the beginning of the century, and it is now at its highest in history in spite of payroll deductions. In the early 1900's, the average laborer earned $12 a week; the average stenographer, $10 a week; women clerks, $5 to $7 a week; housemaids, $3.50

a week; and the average garment worker in sweatshops, a meager $2.50 a week. Prices were low, too, but not compared with today's wages in relation to today's prices. The two-income family was rare early in the century because a woman was expected to give up her job when she married. It was a man's world.

Communication and travel were limited during the first two decades of the century, so that the average family did not question their position in life or the condition of their home. Advertising was in its infancy, so that people felt less need for many possessions. Regionalism in housing still prevailed. The West was considered a frontier, and much of Florida was a swampland. Gradually conditions changed, and people became more aware of what other people had and what they themselves might have. Magazines with pages on home architecture and decorating were the earliest media to influence the tastes of the middle class.

GUIDELINES FOR STUDY

GENERAL IDEAS
TO CONSIDER

1. Rapid social and economic changes, such as population density, building costs, and recreation trends, influence the style and type of dwelling.
2. Population shifts from rural to urban and from urban to suburban areas create housing problems, especially in cities.
3. Open-space development and cluster zoning provide for greater living enjoyment.
4. A scarcity of land and rising labor costs make provision of multi-family housing necessary.
5. Housing choices are increasing at most socioeconomic levels.
6. Improvements in housing for lower-income families and general civic improvement require the combined efforts of national and local government and other agencies and of private business and industry.

WORDS, NAMES, AND PLACES
TO KNOW

can-opener rehabilitation
cluster zoning
condominium
duplex
Falling Water
garden apartment
high-rise apartment
Hoovervilles
HUD

Mission furniture
mobile home
multi-family dwelling
new cities
open-space development
prefabricated house
row house
tenement
town house

THE FIRST TWO DECADES— APPEARANCE OF THE BUNGALOW

Between 1900 and the mid-1920's America changed from a rural society concerned mainly with producing enough food and other essentials for living to an urban society geared to consuming factory-produced goods. No longer was it necessary to preserve food and make clothes in the home. Electricity made it possible to discard the carpet sweeper, washboard, and flatiron. With the mass production of the Model-T Ford in 1915, more people were able to travel at their convenience and see how people lived in other parts of the country. Advertising, which gained impetus during the prosperous twenties, began to influence taste, and soon to many people psychological wants became almost as important as physical needs.

Early in the century three persons were to have a marked influence upon family taste and its expression in the home—Edward Bok, early editor of the *Ladies' Home Journal,* with his pages devoted to small homes; Henry L. Wilson, who called himself The Bungalow Man because of his promotion of the bungalow; and Elsie de Wolfe, actress-turned-decorator, who wrote one of the first books on popular decorating. She made her reputation by decorating the fashionable Colony Club in New York City, where she introduced gay flowered chintz for draperies and slipcovers, louvered screens in the dining room, and vanity tables with fancy chintz skirts in the ladies' lounge. Published in 1913, Mrs. de Wolfe's *The House of Good Taste* became the decorator's bible for many years.

The bungalow was the first functional home designed for families of modest income, although the term *functionalism* did not become widespread until after World War II, when the influence of Frank Lloyd Wright began to be felt. The introduction of the bungalow helped to increase the popularity of Mission-style furniture, a severely plain rectangular oak style that resulted from William Morris' handcraft movement of the previous century.

The bungalow is an almost square one-story or sometimes story-and-a-half structure with beamed ceilings and an overhung roof. It is a combination of Cape Cod cottage, Spanish mission-type home, and Swiss chalet. However, the name comes from the name of a low thatched-roof house in India. The house is informal, inexpensive compared with many types of homes, cozy, and adaptable to various terrains. The bungalow remained popular until the prosperity of the 1920's. Modern versions of the bungalow reappeared before World War II in the form of the California ranch house, but the ranch-house concept did not become popular until after the war.

A porch is a common feature of the bungalow.

Falling Water

THE ROARING TWENTIES—
MODERNISM VERSUS REVIVALS

After World War I, the country experienced greater prosperity than at any previous time. Women gained more freedom with the passage of the Nineteenth Amendment in 1919 than they had had before, and factories were booming, trying to meet the demand for new commodities. During the war, women left domestic service in droves to work in factories, and very few returned to domestic service afterward. Wealthy families with limited household help soon began to entertain in high-class restaurants instead of giving dinner parties at home. Observing this trend of the early twenties, a popular newspaper reporter coined the term *café society.*

With a scarcity of domestic help, laborsaving equipment was in greater demand than ever. Competition, plus increased advertising, induced manufacturers to improve their products.

Since many home chores were lightened and women were legally as free as men to work outside the home, the lure of two incomes encouraged more married women to enter the labor force. At the same time the movies and widespread car ownership were also causing values, wants, and needs to change.

During the twenties there was a trend toward modernism expressed by the *modernistic,* or a jazz-age interpretation of the prevailing modern movement. The modern trend had its beginning in 1913 with the International Exhibition of Modern Art at the Armory in New York City. This famous exhibit featured paintings by the modern artists Cézanne, Toulouse-Lautrec, Gauguin, and Picasso. Among the architects in sympathy with the new trend was Frank Lloyd Wright, whose architectural concepts of integrating the house with the land were to revolutionize domestic architecture of the future. Falling Water is one of the best examples of Wright's attempt to integrate the home with its surroundings.

This stone house was built over a waterfall at Bear Run, near Pittsburgh, Pennsylvania, for the Edgar S. Kaufmann family in the mid-1930's in the middle of the Great Depression.

In contrast to the modern trend in art, home furnishings, and architecture, there was an increasing emphasis upon antiques and older homes. The prosperity of the twenties made it possible for many well-to-do families to build large homes, and they turned their attention to styles of the past, as the newly rich had done in the nineteenth century. From England they borrowed the Half-Timbered Cotswold and Regency styles, from France the Norman-French and French Provincial styles, and from America many of the late Colonial styles. During this age of prosperity the bungalow, except in enlarged versions with basements, lost out because it was not pretentious enough for a more prosperous society. The modern ranch-style home, popular in California, had not yet made much

of an impression in other areas of the country. Bankers who controlled mortgage money considered these houses without attics and basements too great a monetary risk. Many of the large homes built during the twenties are popular today with people who like to renovate spacious older houses.

THE DEPRESSION YEARS—HOUSE CONVERSION AND LOW-INCOME HOUSING

The Wall Street stock-market crash of 1929 put an end to prosperity and curtailed the building boom of the twenties. Many families with large homes began to convert them into duplexes or apartment units. Second and third floors were often made accessible through outside stairways or fire escapes in order to save as much inside space as possible and still meet fire regulations. With living space at a premium, kitchens became kitchenettes; and dining rooms became dinettes. The

A Depression house converted into a duplex.

efficiency (one-room) apartment became popular, and with it the Murphy
bed that could be folded back into the
wall during the day.

However, many people could not
even afford to live in small improvised
apartments. When they lost their homes,
they sought shelter in warehouses, abandoned buildings, and shacks made from
material salvaged from trash heaps—
wood crates, sheets of metal, and canvas.
Groups of such dwellings became
known as *Hoovervilles,* a name coined
from that of President Herbert Hoover.

During the early years of the Great
Depression, while Hoover was still
President, he called a press conference
on home building and home ownership. This led to the Housing Act of
1934 under President Roosevelt's administration, which gave the Federal
Housing Administration (FHA) authority
to guarantee the payment of home loans.
The act also created the Federal Savings
and Loan Insurance Foundation to
protect savings in home-financing institutions. As a result of the Housing

Act, two years later the government
built a planned community for low-
income families at Greenbelt, Maryland,
just outside Washington, D.C. This was
to serve as a model for other areas of
the country.

THE POST-WORLD WAR II PERIOD—
TRACT DEVELOPMENTS
AND SLUM PROBLEMS

With materials and manpower released for peacetime use after World
War II, houses gradually became more
plentiful. FHA loans, which were first
made available through the Federal
Housing Administration in 1934, and
VA loans, which were made available
through the Veterans Administration
following World War II, made home
ownership possible for an increasing
number of families.

Tract Developments and
Prefabricated Houses

Many of these early postwar homes
were erected on tract developments by

Greenbelt, Maryland

The first Levittown, on Long Island, sprang up in only four years from bare pastures.

assembly-line methods. The houses were often small and poorly constructed, but they met an immediate need for a place to live shortly after servicemen began returning home. The early prefabricated house made from factory-produced walls, floors, and ceilings began to have a bad image. Only within recent years has the concept of prefabrication been acceptable in higher-price markets.

The man responsible for promoting assembly-line building was William Levitt, who is often referred to as *the Henry Ford of the housing industry*. In 1945 Levitt leveled 5000 acres of farmland on Long Island, New York, and erected Levittown, composed of 17,447 houses with identical floor plans and similar exteriors. He later built Levittown, Pennsylvania, and Levittown, New Jersey. By 1948 he was putting up 150 houses a week. Levitt's prices for houses were several thousand dollars less than those built by competitors. In the mid-sixties Levitt and Sons began to build houses in Europe to meet an expanding market.

Many factories are now equipped to

assemble the whole mechanical core of the house—plumbing for the kitchen and bathroom, and heating units and wiring for the whole house, as well as for any of the components just mentioned. However, in many communities union regulations and building codes prohibit builders from taking advantage of these advances in technology and cost cutting. But in spite of restrictions, factory-engineered homes represented twenty-five percent of all one- and two-family homes in 1968, or five times as many as in 1950. The greatest gains have been made in the range of $20,000 (minus lot) and over and in garden apartments.

Slum Problems and the Federal Housing Act

After World War II there was a greater exodus from the city to the suburbs than during the prosperous twenties. Cities began to deteriorate from the population shift. Tenement houses, built in the nineteenth century to accommodate the great influx of families seeking employment in factories,

The can-opener method: A preassembled core unit is raised from the street to the top of a seventy-year-old tenement house—

—and lowered through a hole in the roof.

became deplorable. Many were torn down but not replaced. Some, as in New York City, have been rehabilitated by the so-called *can-opener* method under the Rent and Rehabilitation Administration, with help from the Federal Housing Administration. In this approach to remodeling, an eight-by-eight foot shaft is cut through the center of the building. All debris is removed through the shaft, and then a core containing plumbing, heating, kitchen, and bathroom is dropped into place. The apartment units are then plastered and painted. The biggest advantage in this approach to rehabilitation is that families can be given better housing without moving from the neighborhood. However, the economy of remodeling —rather than building anew—has been questioned since several such buildings have been remodeled.

Cities continued to stagnate as slums expanded, smoke and smog polluted the air, traffic became snarled, and parking facilities became inadequate. The heart of the city began to die. Downtown theaters, shops, and department stores closed, and many businesses moved to the suburbs.

As the population shifted to the suburbs, giant shopping centers developed, further destroying the inner city. Formerly pleasant residential areas became blighted. With the exodus of large numbers of the middle class to the suburbs and continuing business failures, city income from downtown taxes was drastically reduced. By the late 1940's business and political leaders realized that conditions had to improve if cities were to survive.

After World War II, Pittsburgh was doomed to become a dead city buried in its own soot, smoke, and smog. Fortunately many of its leading business-men refused to accept defeat, even though many new businesses and industries passed up Pittsburgh for better locations and even though established businesses left or collapsed. The success story of Pittsburgh in ridding itself of smoke and smog and attracting new businesses and industries gained international recognition, even before the Federal Housing Act of 1949 triggered national urban renewal.

This Federal Housing Act authorized the Federal government to pay cities for at least two thirds of the difference between the cost of acquiring and clearing a blighted area and the price a private developer would have to pay for the land. Although slum clearance was the original goal, it was soon realized that cities had many other problems that were strangling them. The act was expanded to help cities get at the core of their troubles and to begin to remedy them in the erection of parking facilities, in the development of public parks, and in the restoration of older neighborhoods by remodeling rundown homes that were structurally sound. Over eight hundred cities have participated in the program.

Many people criticize the government's handling of urban renewal problems on the grounds that the cost of the programs exceeded the results obtained, that people had been evacuated from their homes before provisions were made for new housing, and that the new housing provided was too expensive for rehabilitated families. Nevertheless, government concern has helped to speed urban renewal, and to improve housing for the underprivileged. Businesses, industries, and insurance companies are helping to induce higher-income families to come back to the city by erecting skyscraper office buildings and apartments. A national agency active in rehabilitating neighborhoods

is ACTION Housing. This is a private, nonprofit civic organization organized in 1957.

THE SOARING SIXTIES— CHANGING HOUSING CONCEPTS

Housing concepts for apartments, town houses, single-family dwellings, and mobile homes have changed considerably within the last decade. The population explosion has increased the building of high-rise apartments; and new concepts, such as *open-space development* and *cluster zoning*, have influenced new suburban developments and new cities.

Open-Space Development and Cluster Zoning

Open-space development is a total approach to planning land use. In this approach a new land development is treated as a whole and broken up into areas for housing, recreation, and business. Cluster zoning is a tool used by planners that differs somewhat from conventional zoning, where minimum lot sizes are determined. Cluster zoning does not limit lot sizes but sets forth the maximum population density. Single houses, double houses, town houses, and apartments are built in clusters along winding roads, a lake, a small park, or a golf course. Buildings and lot sizes vary, but the total plan must provide for enjoyable living—safe automobile and pedestrian traffic, attractive housing and lawns, off-street parking, and adequate recreational facilities. Traditionally this is a return to small-town living, in the hope of bringing with it family stability and emphasis upon personal values more characteristic of communities before the midcentury. In some instances this approach has been successful, but in other instances the goals are more idealistic than realistic.

The same open-space-development concept is applied to new cities. Realtors consider 6000 acres as the dividing line between a successful *housing development,* with recreational facilities, nearby shopping center, and schools, and a *new city,* which is self-contained, with shopping areas, work opportunities, and recreational and cultural facilities.

New Cities

During World War II the government built three new cities near atomic energy plants—Los Alamos in New Mexico, Oak Ridge in Tennessee, and Richland in Washington. Among the new privately developed cities of the sixties are El Dorado Hills in California, built in

1961, and Reston in Virginia and Clear Lake City in Texas, built in 1962. So far the concept of new cities has not lived up to expectations because there are not enough jobs in the cities to attract people and the cities are too far away from existing jobs. However, these cities will be ideal places in which to live if the employment problems that are perplexing them can be solved.

Apartments

In the early 1950's apartment units accounted for about nine percent of all dwelling units; by the late 1960's, for forty-three percent. The trend toward multi-family structures continues because land is decreasing as a commodity and the population is increasing. It is predicted that in the future the average

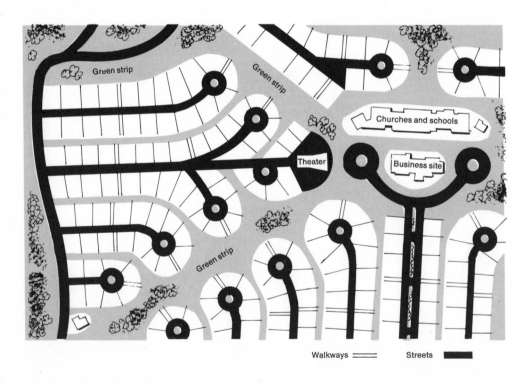

A plan for an open-space housing development, with cluster zoning, green strips, and a small community center.

person will spend about two thirds of his life in an apartment of some kind. The largest demand for apartments is from heads of families, couples, or single persons who are under twenty-nine and over fifty-five years of age.

Advances in technology have made the *high-rise apartment* possible. During the nineteenth century, the skyscraper began to appear among public buildings when steel, made by the Bessemer process, came into general use as a building material and hydraulic power became available to lift elevators. Electricity for elevator power and lighting and reinforced concrete (poured concrete over steel) hastened the erection of high-rise apartments in our large cities. Poured concrete became an important building material after its successful use in building the Panama Canal during the second decade of the present century.

There is no limit to the number of stories in a high-rise apartment building so long as adequate garage or parking space can be provided and so long as plans can meet local building codes. When an apartment building goes over three floors, the need for an elevator makes it more feasible to build at least six floors. High-rise buildings are going up in suburban areas as well as in large cities. (New York's newest high-rise building, the hundred-and-ten story World Trade Center, will top the world's highest building, the Empire State Building.) The new skyscrapers are called *microcities*. They are equivalent to a suburban living-shopping center with offices, apartment units, a department store, food and specialty shops, swimming pools, restaurants, and observation decks.

Many people prefer a *garden apartment* to a high-rise apartment because they feel less shut in. *Garden apartment*

Charles River Park, a high-rise apartment complex in Boston.

A garden apartment in Pittsburgh.

is a fairly general term used to describe any apartment building of three floors or less and up to twelve units with landscaped space around it. It may or may not have an elevator. Garden apartments are sometimes built in clusters in suburban areas with recreational facilities in common. They may be condominium (occupant owned) or rental units. Often large old homes on large lots in cities are redesigned and landscaped to make very attractive garden-type apartments with three or more units.

Town Houses

The town house is a compromise between an apartment unit and a single-family dwelling. It is the modern interpretation of the early row house, a dwelling form that dates from Roman times, where two houses in a row have a common wall. Its advantages are low cost where land values are high and a feeling of living in a home with a private entrance and patio or porch. Town houses in the suburbs appeal to young families who cannot afford to buy a home yet object to the confinement of an apartment. Town houses in the city appeal to older couples on a high income who like to be near business and cultural facilities. These town houses may have three floors with a small elevator. The garage, utility room, a recreation room, and half bath may occupy the first floor; living room, dining room, kitchen, and powder room, the second floor; and sleeping quarters with one or two baths, the third floor.

In some cities farsighted real-estate people have begun to reappraise many old row houses in once fashionable areas close to the city, and instead of demolishing them, they are rehabilitating them. On Old Society Hill in downtown Philadelphia a number of row houses

escaped the bulldozer by being purchased for $6000 each. After speculators restored them, they sold for $30,000, and the demand for these handsomely restored homes far exceeded the supply. In the Pacific Heights area of San Francisco, privately restored houses selling for $15,000 in the early 1950's were commanding prices up to $75,000 fifteen years later.

Single-Family Homes

The type of single-family home keeps changing to make a greater appeal to the potential buyer, usually the family with growing children. Single-family homes are not always built in cities or in isolated suburban areas. In the new open-space developments they are becoming a part of the overall plan where there are high-rise and garden apartments and town houses. The idea of mixing dwelling types and sizes is to encourage families to settle down in a large home until their children are grown and then move to a town house or apartment when the children leave home, or to encourage newlyweds to live in an apartment in the community until their children arrive and then to move into a town house or a small or a large home. Theoretically the idea is good, but with our present mobility rate it may not be practical. Nevertheless, homes in a well-planned community will always rent or sell.

Ranch styles have become popular as single-family homes in the moderately mild northern climates. Originally ranch-type homes were rather streamlined and modern in appearance, but models are now available in many traditional and provincial styles. Ranch-type homes require more land and may be more difficult to heat than two-story homes.

From the real-estate point of view, a family with children in grade school is

Town houses are a well-established tradition on Beacon Hill in Boston.

the best prospect for a large home, and builders try to cater to the wants and needs of such families at several price levels by offering: (1) a developer-built medium-priced home with limited changes allowed in the original plan, (2) a more expensive developer-built home with greater possibilities for variations, (3) a custom-built home with little or no limit on price. (Many low-cost to medium-priced homes are built by developers and are rented or sold through Federal financing.)

The Savings and Loan Fact Book for 1966 reported that the average home buyer in the midsixties paid $16,500 for a home in addition to the cost of the lot, driveways, and landscaping. The average new home had 1415 square feet of space, including hallways and closets. The average cost per square foot was $13.20 to $14.50. About three fourths of all financed houses had at least three bedrooms and more than one bathroom. These facts are significant, since savings and loan associations have the heaviest commitment of home loans of any lending institution.

In 1968 the Federal Housing Administration published a study indicating that homes bought with FHA-insured mortgages in the late sixties had more square

Mobile homes offer an attractive alternative in housing for families and individuals who want a flexible way of living at a modest cost.

feet of floor space (1284 versus 1258); one more bedroom, or four in place of three; more had two or more baths, and many more had air conditioning. However, between 1965 and 1968 building costs increased 20 percent, and in 1969 mortgage interest increased to a new high of 7 percent and over.

Mobile Homes

We used to think of mobile homes as eight-by-thirty-foot trailers attached to the rear of a car. They were places where families could live cheaply while on a vacation, or where migrant workers might be housed as they moved from one work area to another. The new mobile homes are twelve by sixty feet, and two may be attached side by side with doors between, or stacked one above the other with a stairway to the second floor. A mobile home is factory produced and hauled to a mobile-home park or other site where it becomes a permanent home. Parks may have lighted streets, sewer systems, and attractive landscaping. This kind of living appeals to young married couples, to retired couples, and to people who want a second or vacation home.

Mobile homes are said to account for over three fourths of all new homes selling for $12,500 or less in the midsixties. In 1968 there were nearly three times as many mobile homes sold as in 1961 (265,000 versus 90,200). Some mobile homes sell for as little as $5000. Most mobile homes come completely furnished with carpeting, furniture, equipment, draperies, and accessories. There are many additional costs, such as land rental, utility hookup, title search, and closing costs. It is not usually possible to secure financing by an ordinary mortgage, and mobile homes are not likely to appreciate in value.

THE ORIGIN AND FUNCTION OF HUD

In 1965 the Department of Housing and Urban Development (HUD) was created. The following government agencies became part of this new department in the President's Cabinet: Urban Renewal Administration, Federal Housing Administration, and Public Housing Administration. The new director of HUD urged all these agencies to become more concerned with: (1) improving the housing of low-income groups of all races, (2) resettling uprooted slum dwellers more quickly, (3) preventing urban blight, (4) encouraging racial integration, and (5) extending FHA mortgages to low-income families. In the past FHA mortgages have included mainly middle-income groups and houses outside the inner city.

The most important legislation for the underprivileged was the Housing and Urban Development Act of 1968. This law makes it possible for about 500,000 families to buy new homes through Federal subsidy of mortgages wherein one percent interest is paid by families making from $3000 to $7080 a year; and for about 700,000 additional families to rent units at low to moderate costs by paying no more than twenty-five percent of their incomes. This legislation is considered a *horn of plenty* for cities because it will aid slum fighters, government agencies, and lending institutions in an attempt to curtail city blight. Other provisions of the act apply to assisting new cities to get established, corporations to form partnerships for renewal programs, and individuals to secure more lenient mortgages under the Federal National Mortgage Association (nicknamed Fannie May).

SUMMARY

New building materials and methods, rising income, an expanding population, and shifts in population density have all influenced housing concepts and home construction during the twentieth century.

During the first quarter of the century, the urban population gradually surpassed the rural population, and income rose considerably. A new type of home, gaining in popularity, was the one-story bungalow with a wide overhung roof, which soon became popular in every area of the United States.

The general prosperity of the 1920's was accompanied by increasing automobile ownership, increased factory production of consumer goods, and accelerated advertising. Another population shift took place at this time, as people began to move to the outskirts of the cities and to build larger homes. The Great Depression of the thirties and World War II during the forties curtailed housing progress. The immediate demand for housing after World War II increased government interest in building homes and in home loans, especially for returning veterans.

The move to the suburbs during the fifties and sixties caused another shift in population density. About the middle of the sixties the suburban population exceeded the urban population. Many cities were threatened with stagnation in the postwar years, and in some instances cities were partially saved through private enterprise. Many more cities were helped after the passage of the Federal Housing Act in 1949, guaranteeing government subsidies to organizations willing to attack urban decay and slum clearance. As the urban problem became more acute in the sixties, the newly created Department of Housing and Urban Development granted additional help to cities with the passage of the Housing and Urban Development Act of 1968.

In recent years the trend has been away from single-family dwellings, except for families with moderate to high incomes. Multi-family dwellings in the form of town houses and garden and high-rise apartments are more economical to build. Mobile homes have become increasingly popular, despite some drawbacks. The concepts of open-space development and cluster zoning offer hope of combining traditional values of stability and sense of community with contemporary values of convenience and variety. As a solution to our population explosion and urban population shift, new cities are being built all over the country.

THINGS TO THINK ABOUT AND TO DO

1. Discuss how such factors as depressions, prosperity, population density, building costs, and building codes affect the housing market.

2. Give a brief report on Edward Bok and Elsie de Wolfe. Consult *The Tastemakers* by Russell Lynes.

3. Display illustrations of bungalows built during the early part of the century. Perhaps you can take some pictures of bungalows in your community.

4. Discuss some of the housing problems following World War II and the attempts made to solve them.

5. Assemble illustrations of prefabricated homes from builders' and homemaking magazines.

6. Discuss new community developments near you in relation to nearness to shopping areas, provision of recreational facilities, and general layout.

7. Display illustrations of older row houses and modern town houses, and make comparisons of living arrangements.

8. Read the advertisements in your local newspaper, and discuss the types of homes available in your area.

9. Collect illustrations of homes you like for a scrapbook.

10. What is being done in your locality to improve blighted areas? Who is providing the money for improvements? Can you offer suggestions for improving any part of your community? Can you help in any way with the task?

11. Read articles on urban renewal in current magazines, and discuss some of the problems facing cities.

12. Give brief reports on the Federal Housing Administration (FHA), Housing and Urban Development (HUD), and ACTION Housing.

13. Find out what new cities are being planned in the country and some of the problems being encountered. Consult such magazines as *Nation's Business, Fortune, House and Home,* and current news magazines.

14. Discuss factors leading to an increase in the development of multi-family dwellings. Visit one or two of these dwellings in your community.

Urban renewal is helping to revitalize the downtown areas of cities. Constitution Plaza in Hartford, Connecticut, which replaced a deteriorating commercial neighborhood, is considered a model of restoration.

REFERENCES FOR UNIT ONE

BOOKS

ACTION Series on Housing, *Housing Choices and Housing Constraints* (edited by Nelson N. Foote). New York: McGraw-Hill Book Company, 1960.

Allen, Frederick Lewis, *The Big Change*. New York: Harper and Row, 1952.

Beyer, Glenn H., *Housing and Society*. New York: The Macmillan Company, 1965.

Drexler, Arthur, and Daniel, Greta, *Twentieth Century Design*. New York: Museum of Modern Art, 1959.

Easton, Stewart C., *The Heritage of the Past*. New York: Holt, Rinehart and Winston, Inc., 1964.

Encyclopaedia of the Social Sciences, "Housing," Volumes 7 and 8 (pp. 496–499). New York: The Macmillan Company, 1948.

Gottlieb, L. D., *Environment and Design in Housing*. New York: The Macmillan Company, 1965.

Haas, Irvin, *Historic Houses and Restorations*. New York: Hawthorne Books, Inc., 1966.

Hoag, Edwin, *American Houses*. Philadelphia: J. B. Lippincott Company, 1964.

Hoebel, Adamson, *Man in the Primitive World*. New York: McGraw-Hill Book Company, 1958.

Life's Epic of Man. New York: Time, Inc., 1961.

Life's Picture History of Western Man. New York: Time, Inc., 1951.

Lynes, Russell, *The Tastemakers*. New York: Grosset and Dunlap, Inc. (paperback), 1954.

Maass, John, *The Gingerbread Age*. New York: Holt, Rinehart and Winston, Inc., 1957.

Nicholson, Arnold, *American Houses in History*. New York: Viking Press, Inc., 1965.

Pickering, Ernest, *The Homes of America*. New York: Thomas Y. Crowell Company, 1955.

Pratt, Richard, *Houses, History and People*. Philadelphia: J. B. Lippincott Company, 1965.

Quennell, Marjorie, and Charles, H. B., *Everyday Things in Ancient Greece*. New York: G. P. Putnam's Sons, 1960.

Quennell, Marjorie, and Charles, H. B., *Everyday Things in Roman and Anglo-Saxon Times*. New York: G. P. Putnam's Sons, 1959.

Shapiro, Harry L., *Homes Around the World*. New York: American Museum of Natural History, Natural History Press, 1945.

Shapiro, Harry L., *Man, Culture and Society*. New York: Oxford University Press, Inc., 1956.

Titiev, Mischa, *Cultural Anthropology*. New York: Holt, Rinehart and Winston, Inc., 1959.

United States Conference of Mayors, Special Committee on Historic Preservation (Albert Rains, Chairman), *With Heritage So Great*. New York: Random House, Inc., 1966.

U. S. Department of Housing and Urban Development, *Preserving Historic America*. Washington, D.C.: Superintendent of Documents, Government Printing Office, 1966.

Veblen, Thorstein, *The Theory of the Leisure Class*. New York: New American Library, 1954.

Welty, Paul Thomas, *Man's Cultural Heritage*. Philadelphia: J. B. Lippincott Company, 1965.

Williams, Henry L., and Williams, Ottalie K., *A Guide to Old American Homes*. A. S. Barnes and Company, Inc., 1962.

MAGAZINE ARTICLES

Fortune:
"The Coming Housing Boom," May, 1967 (pp. 135–137 and 230–232).
House and Home:
"Housing's Market Revolution," January, 1968 (pp. 49–59).
"How to Explode the Myth about Multi-Family Zoning," April, 1968 (pp. 84–85).
"The New Urban Market," October, 1967 (pp. 62–77).
"Stackup Housing: What Are Its Chances?" April, 1968 (pp. 86–95).
"The Village Shopping Center," October, 1968 (pp. 68–75).

FILMS, FILMSTRIPS, AND SLIDES
(See page 469 for name and address of source.)

A Is for Architecture. Traces the development of architecture from Egyptian and Greek times through Rome, the Renaissance, and French- and English-dominated periods. Sponsored by National Film Board of Canada. (30 minutes, color, IFB)

Ancient Egypt. Ancient Mesopotamia. Ancient Greece. Ancient Rome. (11 minutes each, CF)

Debt to the Past. Shows how all technological accomplishments may be traced to prehistoric times and how difficult survival would be today for a man dependent entirely upon nature.

Early America No. 1—Williamsburg, Sturbridge, and Plymouth. Shows buildings and many objects typical of early American towns. (13½ minutes, color, AF)

Early America No. 2—Mystic Seaport, Greenfield Village, The Alamo. Shows these restored areas in Connecticut, Michigan, and Texas. (13½ minutes, color, AF)

English Influences in the United States. French Influences in North America. Spanish Influences in the United States. (11 minutes each, color, CF)

Garden Apartments—The Early Years to the Present. Sixty-one 35-millimeter color slides trace the development of the popular garden apartment. (15 minutes, color, NAHB)

Megalopolis: Cradle of the Future. Shows problems resulting when cities, especially along the northeastern seaboard, become heavily populated. (21 minutes, color, EBF)

My American City. A documentary on the transformation of 12 acres of commercial slum area in Hartford, Conn., into the much acclaimed Constitution Plaza. (28 minutes, color, FHM)

No Time for Ugliness. Shows what happens to communities when people are apathetic and when they become concerned. Produced by American Institute of Architects. (45 minutes, color, SEF)

Open Space Communities. Shows how planned housing developments provide a new concept in living. (30 minutes, color, NAHB)

Our Inheritance from the Past. Shows origins of many present-day modes of shelter, transportation, and family living. (11 minutes, CF)

Public Housing: A 25th Anniversary Story, 1937–1962. Illustrates what has been done since the passing of the U.S. Housing Act of 1937. (30 minutes, 35 mm. filmstrip, NAHB)

Recreational Facilities in Residential Development. Eighty slides show the types of recreational facilities being included in subdivisions. (20 minutes, color, NAHB)

Shelter. Shows various types of shelters in important areas of the world and the variety of materials and labor required to build them. (11 minutes, color, EBF)

The Town House: Its Background and New Popularity on the American Scene. Slides and taped narration tell the story of the modern concept of the old row house. (18 minutes, color, NAHB)

unit two

*Selecting
a Home*

chapter four

SOCIAL
AND PERSONAL
VALUES IN
HOUSING

To millions of people all over the world, especially some of those in
Far Eastern countries, neither physical nor social nor psychological needs
have much meaning. For example 600,000 people in Calcutta, India, have
no home at all. They sleep on the sidewalks, beg for food, use public
fountains or rivers for bathing, and utilize the gutters along the street
for human waste. In many depressed areas in our own country, city tenements and rural shacks barely meet minimum physical needs for shelter.
Even though the Federal government is taking steps to relieve poverty, progress
is slow in many areas. Nevertheless, the majority of Americans expect
a home to provide more than a place in which to sleep and eat.

Our housing expectations are influenced by family traditions and values.
Some of the values that contribute toward satisfaction and enjoyment in
family living are comfort, convenience, economy, beauty, friendship, health,
safety, location, privacy, provision for personal interests, and, in some
instances, possessions indicative of status. These values vary according to
socioeconomic levels and the area of the country in which we live. Even
within similar socioeconomic levels some families may place a high value
upon expensive possessions—furnishings and works of art—whereas other
families may economize on possessions in order to have more money for
education, recreation, or travel.

During each stage in the family life cycle, personal and social needs
change, and therefore values change. Values also change with physical
and social mobility. When families move from one part of the city to
another or from one area of the country to another, they will evaluate
housing needs from new perspectives. There may be a strong need for
friendships within the immediate neighborhood when mothers are tied
down with young children. Moving is an emotional experience for young
families, and friendly neighbors can make moving less of a problem. On the
other hand, neighborliness may be relatively unimportant later in life.

GUIDELINES FOR STUDY

GENERAL IDEAS
TO CONSIDER

1. Personal values in relation to housing vary with environment, family social and economic position, and cultural background.
2. Values related to housing expectations change many times during the family life cycle and according to socioeconomic level.
3. Research in the apartment market indicates a segmented market, in which renters can be identified by their age, occupation, marital status, and value emphasis.
4. Potential home buyers represent three periods in the family life cycle, the beginning family and the expanding family being far better market prospects than newlyweds.
5. In suburban developments, friendships are often determined by wheel-traffic patterns and geographic boundaries.
6. As income rises the home and its location become more important as a status symbol.

WORDS AND TERMS
TO KNOW

community oriented
family traditions
home oriented
job centered
personal values
physical mobility
segmented market
social mobility
social traffic
socioeconomic level
status symbol
urban oriented
value emphasis

MEANING OF PERSONAL VALUES

Values are a combination of an individual's ideals, attitudes, goals, and tastes. They are controlled by tradition, cultural background, education, experience, and habit. Values govern our social behavior and individual judgments to a large degree.

We frequently judge the behavior of others by our own standards or system of values. When we live in one stratum of society, it is sometimes difficult to understand the values of families who live in a lower or higher stratum. Some of us, accustomed to a modest standard of living, may drive by spacious and beautifully landscaped suburban homes and question how some families can afford such extravagances. Some of us, accustomed to a high standard of living, may pass by run-down row houses in a blighted area and wonder how families can live in such dilapidated shelters. At the same time these shabby structures may look good to families accustomed to living in crowded, poorly kept tenements.

One of the greatest obstacles to slum clearance has been overcoming habit patterns based upon personal values. Many families, especially older ones, resent change because habits and expectations exist in regard to public assistance, such as free clinics, hospital and visiting-nurse care, food coupons, and rent subsidies. Despite apparent privation, many of these families have adjusted to existing social and economic conditions. To uproot them from one neighborhood and transplant them to another means a terrific emotional adjustment. A program of education is necessary to orient families to a new way of living. In some cities it has worked out better to improve structurally sound buildings, one at a time, and permit families to remain in a neighborhood to which they have become adjusted.

VALUES AND THE FAMILY LIFE CYCLE

No two households, even in the same neighborhood and living on similar incomes, will emphasize the same values. However, if we observe the housing behavior of the majority of families throughout the family life cycle, we will notice some common denominators.

In the original edition of this text we referred to one of the first studies made on personal values related to home living. This was a study in which Dr. Virginia Cutler listed the following ten values and asked a number of husbands and wives at three income levels (upper, middle, and lower) to rate them in order of importance.

comfort	health
convenience	safety
economy	location
beauty	personal interests
friendship	privacy

At the upper income level both husbands and wives stressed *comfort* and *friendship;* at the middle income level, *comfort* and *health;* and at the lower income level, *health, safety,* and *economy.* Since these values are also related to stages in the family life cycle, let us examine these stages.

Newlyweds

The cost of furnishing the first home is usually high, and therefore a young couple will place *economy* near the top of the list. Even when the wife works, there are many places to spend the extra money before a couple can begin to save for starting a family or a new home. The old custom of moving in with parents has almost disappeared in our country, but fortunately for many young couples, parents help to subsidize the cost of rent or contribute toward the cost of completing an education, acquiring furniture, or paying for a car. The first home is usually in an older apartment complex or in an older home converted into apartments. A minority of newlyweds may live in a single-family home or spacious apartment.

Beginning Family

Soon after the first child comes, the original home usually becomes crowded, making a move to a larger home necessary. The new home may be a two-bedroom apartment in a building similar to the first home or a better apartment building, or perhaps an apartment in the suburbs. By this time some couples have enough savings for a down payment on a small home in an area where other couples have similar incomes.

Even when the wife has mastered the routine of cleaning, marketing, and meal preparation, the arrival of the first child means a major adjustment for the new parents. There are not enough hours in the day for all the chores and some form of recreation. *Health* perhaps replaces economy on the scale of values because health is important to the father as provider and to the mother as homemaker. *Safety* and *comfort* are also high on the list. This is a period when *friendships* and *personal interests* should not be overlooked, although there may be very little time left over for these values.

Expanding Family

With the arrival of the second child, the father's income is likely to be larger, but expenses are mounting also.

At this time a move to the suburbs is typical if the second move was not of this type. If the family savings will not provide for a down payment on a home, a garden apartment or a small town house in a suburban area is often a compromise. *Health* of the children becomes important, so that fresh air and play space are essential. *Safety* takes on new meaning as young parents take precautions with outside steps and sidewalks, windows, wiring, and other home hazards. *Friendship* within the community assumes importance because the mother is usually without a car all day.

This is typically the next-to-longest period in the family life cycle. Emphasis is usually upon upgrading or improving family social status, so that at this time many families move to larger homes in better locations. Such values as *beauty* and *privacy* in the home become important for parents and children. As the children reach adolescence many parents want to give their children all the advantages they can. If the wife is not already working, she will often seek work to help pay off a mortgage or to send the children to college. Home ownership in a good suburban neighborhood or in a well-preserved urban neighborhood is considered a symbol of success. *Location* becomes a more important value.

Launching Family

During this period children are becoming independent and anticipating the breaking of family ties, yet they spend a great deal of time at home. The launching family requires the maximum of living space for *privacy, personal interests,* and *friendships*. To some families in this stage, *beauty* and *location* loom high as values. During the launching period, few people move to larger homes, although some families may make improvements on an existing home. Even though children leave home for further education, a job out of town, marriage, or the armed services, there are frequent periods of home-coming when space is needed. Even though income is high, excessive expenses associated with launching children may prevent parents from enjoying *personal interests* to which they have looked forward. This is a period when new interests and friendships become increasingly important to parents.

As they see new young families move into the neighborhood and their friends leave for smaller quarters or warmer climates, many parents begin to think ahead to the time when they will be alone. These families experience conflicting desires—to stay where they are and ignore change or to move into smaller quarters and start to make a new life. Most families take the road of least resistance and postpone making a change until some emergency arises or they are offered a good price for their home.

Later Years

With our increasing life expectancy this period is by far the longest in the family life cycle. A couple is usually reluctant to accept a new way of life unless poor health, financial difficulties, or the death of a spouse makes change necessary. With retirement, income is usually lower than in the peak years. *Economy* and *comfort* are next to *health* in the scale of values. For the couple with good health and no financial worries, these years can be really golden years free from responsibility. *Friendship* and *personal interests* can have greater meaning than ever before.

FAMILY LIFE CYCLE

Newlyweds	Childless
Beginning family	First child
Expanding family	Child bearing and rearing
Launching family	Children leave gradually
Later years	Childless — often only one spouse left

THE SEGMENTED APARTMENT MARKET AND VALUE EMPHASIS

VALUES	Distinctive Design	Economy	Common Recreational Facilities	Privacy	Location Close To City	Room Size	Interior Variety	Strong Management
Swingers		●	●		●			
Young Sophisticates	●			●			●	●
Newlyweds				●				●
Job Centered		●			●			●
Home Oriented					●	●	●	
Urban Oriented	●				●			●
Young Families		●	●			●		

RESEARCH IN THE AREA
OF HOUSING VALUES

Most conclusions on the behavioral aspects of the individual in regard to housing are based upon observation. Many of these observations are helpful, but they are insufficient in communicating psychological and social needs between people who live in homes (or apartments) and people who provide housing. A few studies have been made on personal needs in housing in recent years to provide architects and builders with pertinent information and to help real estate agents to do a better job of marketing.

Housing Patterns
and the Friendship Circle

Research in relation to housing behavior has revealed some interesting findings in large suburban developments regarding sociability. Whereas the city apartment dweller seldom knows his neighbor on either side or across the hall, friendship patterns in suburban planned communities are highly predictable. In the terms of William H. Whyte, Jr., author of The Organization Man, traffic, or the web of friendship, extends more easily in some directions than in others.

Planned suburban communities with low to medium rents are usually inhabited by young families, and the wife is not usually employed outside the home. (A childless employed couple in such a community can be a misfit.) Children are often responsible for friendship patterns. In a study reported in Whyte's book social traffic is often determined by wheel traffic—buggies, strollers, tricycles, skates. The families most centrally located have the greatest chance to meet people. Friendships will develop more frequently along the same side of the street and directly opposite rather than around corners or on parallel streets to the rear. These geographical boundaries are usually set for small parties and kaffeeklatsches.

Another interesting finding has been that each social area eventually develops a specific pattern of behavior. Incoming families frequently acquire the social habits of the area of which they become a part whether the community is bridge-party or sports minded, church or civic oriented. When vacancies occur, families in one area of a development often move to the area most likely to meet their friendship needs. It is not many years before each location develops a character, such as the complaining group, the partying group, the civic-minded group, the conservative group, and so on.

Apartment Rentals
and Personal Values

Young single or married persons, very young families, and older single or married persons make up the major part of the apartment market. Families whose heads are in the age range between twenty-five and forty-four are the prime home buyers. In the future the apartment way of life with shopping and recreational facilities nearby may become more familiar than now to families with growing children. As the suburbs move farther and farther away from businesses, landscaped apartments surrounded by parks but within cities may become more attractive to many people.

Apartment investors are aware of the type of potential renters and the rents they can expect when they draw up the blueprints for a building. In some areas apartments are designed mainly for retired persons; in others, for young business persons; in others, for small families; and in still others, for high-income renters. Builders in Dallas, for instance, have found that they can divide apartment renters into seven segments, according to their position in the life cycle and their value emphasis. Apartments in all large cities may not be so very definitely segmented, but distinct patterns tend to establish themselves over a period of time.

Dallas builders identify renter groups as follows (see chart, page 62):

□ The *young swingers,* or the young unmarried men and young unmarried women, who love parties and all kinds of fun, look for economical but attractive units in areas close to the city. They place high emphasis upon recreational facilities and fairly lenient management control. Dallas is typical of large cities where there are many young people in business and industry and where there is a large group of airline hostesses. In a similar area in California, in a new apartment building with extensive recreational facilities and planned weekend trips, the builder has limited all units to young unmarried persons. Although his control is rigid, he has a waiting list.

□ The *young sophisticates,* or the more mature, more reserved, more highly educated, and better-paid individuals, demand distinctive design, greater comfort and convenience, and strong management control. This group may snub apartments popular with young swingers.

□ The *newly marrieds* consider an apartment simply a stepping-stone in the family life cycle, something to be accepted until they can save enough money for a down payment on a home. They are not interested in a place to meet people and have a good time, even though these may have been high values during their unmarried days. Many wives still work, and they are reluctant to throw away their money on entertainment.

□ The *job centered* choose apartment living in order to be near a job and save commuting time. Making up this group are the single adults who are neither swingers nor sophisticates. Many are widowed or divorced.

□ The *home oriented* are mainly older persons who have given up their homes and want to retain some of the aspects of suburban life. They want attractive landscaping, attractive interiors, large rooms, and strong management control. These are people mainly in high-income brackets.

□ The *urban oriented* have never been particularly interested in suburban life or home ownership. They like the pace of the city, an apartment with character, independence from their neighbors, and strong apartment management.

□ Some *families with young children* prefer to continue apartment living for reasons of economy. They need large rooms and play space.

Values and Home Ownership

An extensive study costing $175,000 was made in 1966–1967 by *Project Home Committee,* an organization of twenty-eight major corporations, all but two of which manufacture building products. The study, "The Motivations Toward Homes and Housing," covered 2515 nonfarm families.

Findings confirmed observations that three basic home-buying markets exist, each representing a distinct period in the family life cycle. The study also brought out many new angles on sales approach, which may or may not be desirable from the home buyer's point of view, especially if he is not conditioned to subtle sales approaches.

The three major markets and the buyer approach in each follow:

☐ The *newlyweds* market is largely dominated by rental units, but there is still a sizable market for the first home. About thirty percent of newlyweds are home buyers. The newly married couple seeks privacy and independence from parents. Husband and wife try to agree upon the same values, but if they were to be frank with each other, their views would vary. The husband is more likely to view a home as a *private retreat;* the wife is more likely to view it in terms of her *future role as homemaker.*

With these findings at hand, home builders and sellers are advised to: (1) stress the importance of independence, freedom, and privacy; (2) casually mention the provisions made for future needs; (3) assure the financially insecure couple that a future resale will not be difficult should the need arise; (4) point up the ease of maintenance, especially if the wife is employed; (5) convey the idea that a house is a place in which to have fun as well as to eat and sleep.

☐ The *beginning-family* market is quite large, representing the biggest single swing toward home ownership. This market will expand well into the 1970's due to the large birthrate following World War II and the constantly increasing formation of new households. During this house-hunting period, both parents focus attention on the needs of children, and the husband begins to accept his role as that of *second fiddle.* The idea of home ownership is sometimes more idealistic than realistic because many couples do not realize the responsibilities that go with it.

At this period in the family life cycle the seller is advised to: (1) stress factors that relate to the welfare of the children, such as good schools, playgrounds, traffic safety, and adequate recreational facilities; (2) stress privacy and quiet

CHANGES IN VALUE EMPHASIS OF HOME OWNERSHIP DURING THE FAMILY LIFE CYCLE

NEWLYWEDS

BEGINNING FAMILY

EXPANDING FAMILY

for parents, due to a carefully worked out floor plan and soundproofing; (3) de-emphasize adult activities in the neighborhood because there is little time for such things; (4) emphasize the home as a *family nest,* as putting down roots, and as providing status; (5) explain the equity that can be built up and the advantages in being able to deduct interest and taxes from income tax as contrasted with paying rent; (6) point out the convenience features that a new home has over older homes that may need improvements or remodeling. □ The *expanding family* with children in school may have a head of the family between thirty-five and forty-four years old. In the late 1960's and early 1970's, this market is much smaller than the beginning-family market because the heads of these families were born during the depression when the birthrate was low. This market will be larger when the large group of younger heads of households reach this age range.

At this stage in the family life cycle husband and wife are more likely to differ in their value emphasis than at any other period. There is less uniformity in their emphasis upon needs of the children. The husband begins to think of a home in terms of peace and quiet, but the wife has become accustomed to noise and activity. The wife wants a more attractive place in which to entertain because this does two things—provides prestige and makes her feel that she is still very important to her husband. Two-story homes with distinctive exteriors imply status and are therefore popular with home buyers at this stage in the family life cycle. Two stories are also popular with these families because they provide greater room separation and less noise.

Sales approach at this market level is to: (1) emphasize the importance of

newness and additional conveniences to the wife and greater space for teen-age children; (2) point out the provision for quiet areas for parents; (3) mention the desirability of the neighborhood and stress the nearness to sports and outdoor recreation, community affairs, and cultural opportunities for parents; (4) indicate the importance of an attractive home as a status symbol; (5) mention the home as a good investment for a resale.

How soon potential buyers will become immune to these new sales pitches is anybody's guess. Former emphasis upon space, convenience, quality, easy maintenance, and the like is less effective as more and more homes offer these values. However, there is still room for improvement in individual rooms, as the same study indicated. More husbands than wives were pleased with entrances and kitchens in model homes; both expressed satisfaction with living rooms and bedrooms; neither liked· the dining room (not enough space for storage or entertaining), the storage areas (inadequate), and the backyards (not appealing without landscaping).

Values and Advertising Appeal

A study made by the National Association of Home Builders in 1966 to determine what motivates families to look at new homes is entitled "Concept-Motivation Study on New Housing." Copies of this study are available from NAHB in Washington, D.C., for $25. Many public libraries have copies. In this extensive study nearly 8000 persons in forty-five market areas were contacted, most of whom expected to move within two years. One purpose of the study was to find out how to advertise in order to give new homes good sales exposure.

Subjects were asked to rate a number of phrases used to attract buyers to new suburban developments. Traditional advertising slogans, such as *maintenance free, quality guaranteed, modern conveniences,* rated low in advertising appeal because home buyers now take these things for granted. Rated highest in sales appeal was *culture in suburbia,* followed by *luxury homes* and *prestige community.* A suburban community offering cultural opportunities, such as music centers, playhouses, libraries, drama groups, and good schools, had the best chances of attracting prospective buyers.

MOBILITY AND VALUE EMPHASIS

When we speak of mobility, we are referring to *physical mobility,* or moving from one place to another, as well as *social mobility,* or striving to improve social status. Physical mobility frequently accompanies social mobility.

Physical Mobility

Unless the family head is a doctor, a dentist, a lawyer, a person with his own business, or is otherwise self-employed, a family can expect to move about once every five years. Many

Research in concept motivation shows that advertising slogans play a large part in attracting buyers to new housing developments.

young families will move more often. Families with a frequent moving pattern are low-income families, families in the armed services, families whose head is a young business or industrial executive, and those who are perpetual renters. This situation did not prevail during the early part of the century. The expansion of business and the rise of junior executives, the turnover in the teaching field, and the increase in government and armed-services personnel have increased physical mobility. Promotions within local businesses and industries sometimes cause families to look for new residences in the same community.

Increased mobility has influenced social values. When families remained in the same community for a lifetime, the community set up certain unwritten codes of behavior and enforced them effectively. Far more responsibility now lies within the home. Families must learn to compensate for the lack of community controls by setting up and adhering to their own standards of behavior. With every move, roots are torn up and values are challenged. Sociologists tell us that we can maintain a greater feeling of personal security in times of change by upholding time-tested family traditions and values. Closely knit family relationships become important as children enter school. Adjustments to adolescence are far easier also if the family is able to share and enjoy working and playing together.

Social Mobility

Location of a home is an important value to many families seeking upward social mobility. In every community there are neighborhoods and streets that have a higher rating or prestige value than other neighborhoods and streets, and as income rises, many families like to improve their social position as well. Terrain and elevation of land tend to relate to prestige value. In ancient times the cliff dwellers were the elite. In our present society family social status frequently rises as the ground rises. Homes partway up a hilly terrain usually have more prestige appeal than homes at the foot of the hill, and the homes on top command not only a better view but also a higher price tag. If the terrain is level, prime locations are often near rivers, lakes, or golf courses.

SUMMARY

Values are deep-rooted in an individual's concepts of housing. Many families uprooted by urban renewal may resent change, even if they can move to a better housing development. At every level of society it is difficult to understand and appreciate family housing values at other levels.

Some research has been done regarding values and housing concepts and expectations, and observations indicate a relationship between personal values and housing expectations. In some parts of the country apartment managers can predict fairly accurately the type of renters an apartment will attract. Older families are more averse to change than younger families until they are faced with an emergency that makes a move necessary. The move they make will depend upon their economic limitations and social needs.

Even though values are slow to change, it is evident that value emphasis does change during the family life cycle and also with physical and social mobility. Some families place emphasis upon prestige symbols as they move up the social ladder. Young suburban families place a great deal of emphasis upon friendship. Some studies indicate that friendships are predictable according to where the family lives within a suburban housing development.

THINGS TO THINK ABOUT AND TO DO

1. Discuss how personal values influence your reactions to new situations and to homes of different types.

2. Examine the real estate section of your Sunday newspaper and notice the type of advertising slogans most often used. Bring in clippings and explain to the class why (or why not) the slogans would be effective.

3. From magazines cut out illustrations of homes or apartments with floor plans which might be desirable at each stage during the family life cycle for a family of four—father, mother, son, and daughter. Indicate why.

4. Comment on housing patterns and the friendship circle. Can the friendship pattern be applied to your community? Consult Chapter 25, "The Web of Friendship," in *The Organization Man* by William H. Whyte, Jr.

5. Visit a new housing development nearby, and report on the types and sizes of houses and sizes of lots. Note recreational facilities.

6. Why do you think it is difficult for most older persons in areas undergoing urban renewal to adjust to improved housing?

7. List on the chalkboard the housing values discussed in this chapter. Discuss and tell how you would rate them. Also tell how you might rate them if you were within the age range of your parents or your grandparents.

8. Discuss the meaning of physical and social mobility and any relationship between the two.

9. Take a poll of the class to find out how many moves each student's family has made over the student's lifetime.

10. Discuss what is being done in your community to improve housing conditions by private enterprise and by government leadership.

11. Discuss the segmented rental market in Dallas in relation to potential or actual apartment renters in your own community.

12. Discuss the study made by Project Home Committee and your impressions of the sales approach for each home market.

chapter five

SPACE NEEDS
FOR LIVABILITY

Adequate space for living is important to one's general welfare. Behavioral scientists have observed that people tend to follow the same pattern as rats do when they are overcrowded. Rats react by becoming apathetic or rebellious. Their sense of responsibility, general health, and entire social order begin to break down under the pressure of overcrowding.

Overcrowding in our large cities has forced many families into the suburbs in search of more space for indoor and outdoor living. Conversely, as commuting distances to and from work have increased, a movement back to the cities has begun. City planners are beginning to set aside more space for indoor and outdoor living; home and apartment builders are making scientific studies of space needs in the home and attempting to turn these findings into better planned homes and apartment units.

At present there are many agencies—both government and private— concerned with better housing, the best known of which is perhaps the Federal Housing Administration (FHA). Among other organizations interested in space standards are the American Public Health Association, the United States Savings and Loan League, the National Association of Home Builders, and life insurance companies offering home mortgages.

Although recommendations vary somewhat with different organizations, it is possible to establish certain standards for judging living space in a floor plan. For example, an individual needs about 400 square feet of floor space for general comfort, but as the number of persons sharing a home increases, a little less living space per person is required because such areas as kitchens and halls serve as common space. Standards for obtaining an FHA loan may serve as a guide for judging minimum living space, but more generous-size rooms are desirable if one can afford to pay for the extra space. Aside from cost, a number of factors influence the criteria for judging space in a home: the period in the family life cycle, the number of persons in the home and their ages, the amount of time spent in the home, and the types of interests and hobbies.

GUIDELINES FOR STUDY

GENERAL IDEAS
TO CONSIDER

1. Space and how it is used affect the physical, psychological, and social reactions of individuals and in turn the general welfare of society.
2. Federal and private lending agencies concerned with loans and family living conditions have set space standards for individual rooms in a house.
3. Space requirements change frequently during the life cycle, especially when an individual's status changes from that of a single person to that of sharing a two-person household and later to family status.
4. By understanding space requirements a potential home renter or buyer has a better understanding of housing needs.
5. Adequate storage space and efficient traffic patterns in a home contribute toward personal satisfaction and enjoyment by the occupants.

PHRASES TO KNOW

clearance
conversation circle
cross traffic
house zoning
traffic pattern

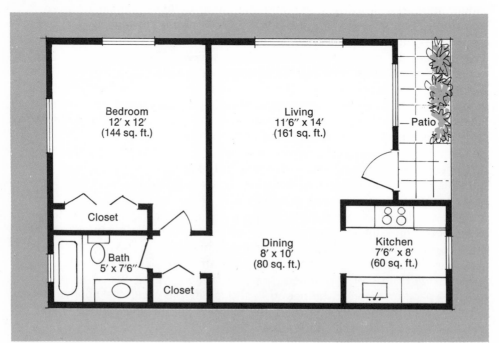

This one-bedroom unit meets FHA room size standards.

FHA RECOMMENDED ROOM SIZES

Living Unit	Living Room	Dining Room	Kitchen
1 bedroom	160 sq. ft.	80 sq. ft.	60 sq. ft.
2 bedrooms	160 sq. ft.	80 sq. ft.	60 sq. ft.
3 bedrooms	170 sq. ft.	95 sq. ft.	70 sq. ft.
4 bedrooms	180 sq. ft.	110 sq. ft.	80 sq. ft.

SPACE REQUIREMENTS

Since space is very important to our welfare, we shall examine some of the space criteria used by various agencies. These include FHA (see table above), American Public Health Association, U. S. Savings and Loan League, and National Association of Home Builders.

Federal Housing Administration Standards

The FHA has established minimum room standards which a house must have before it can qualify for an FHA loan. These standards are based upon the number of bedrooms: the more bedrooms, the larger other rooms must be. The master bedroom must provide a minimum of 120 square feet; and all other bedrooms, a minimum of 80 square feet. The minimum width for the living room must be 11 feet; for the dining area and bedroom, 8 feet. (It is preferable for a bedroom to be 9½ feet.) Passage space between kitchen counters or counter and wall cannot be under 3 feet 4 inches. (A 4-foot clearance is preferable.) You will note in the table above that as the number of bedrooms increases beyond two, the size of other rooms must also increase in order to provide extra living space.

Space requirements for FHA loans are low compared with those that are preferred by other agencies. Most life insurance companies require larger rooms for home loans. To qualify for a Metropolitan Life Insurance Company loan, a house must have a living room 196 square feet; the master bedroom, 171 square feet; other bedrooms, 110 square feet; and the kitchen, 112 square feet.

American Public Health Association Housing Recommendations

In order to provide for health and safety the American Public Health Association, through its Committee on the Hygiene of Housing, has made the following recommendations in square feet of floor space:

1 person	400 square feet
2 persons	800 square feet
3 persons	1000 square feet
4 persons	1200 square feet
5 persons	1450 square feet
6 persons	1550 square feet

After the first two persons, the average number of square feet per person decreases because there are many areas in common use, such as the kitchen, the living room, and the bathroom. With the addition of the third bedroom, another bath or powder room may be desirable.

U. S. Savings and Loan League Recommendations

The U. S. Savings and Loan League, in 1966, published a *Construction Lending Guide,* a five-volume detailed study for its 5100-member savings and loan associations. The study placed emphasis upon proper zoning—for example, separation of sleeping, living, and working areas within the home—for comfort and efficiency. A number of recommendations are summarized:

☐ Provision for a family entrance other than the front door, so that family members can pass back and forth between kitchen and bedrooms without going through the living room.

☐ Allowance for at least one conversation circle 10 feet in diameter in the living room without traffic interference. This requires a living room at least 12 feet by 16 feet (longer if part of the room is used as a passway). A 14-foot by 18- or 20-foot living room is a better size.

☐ Location of bedrooms away from street and inside noises, such as kitchen motors and living-room TV and hi-fi. It is preferable to locate bedrooms for young children near the parents' bedroom, but teenagers' bedrooms should be more remote from the parents' bedroom. Of course this is not always possible unless families move or remodel their homes. When the master bedroom has its own bath, the separation is less important.

☐ Provision for the kitchen to connect with the dining and service areas, and placement of work centers in the kitchen, so that cross traffic will not interfere with work.

☐ A width of 3 to 4 feet for halls, and provision for handrails on stairways.

☐ Doors at least 2½ feet wide.

☐ Windows located no higher than 3 feet from the floor for easy exit in case of fire. Windows should be at least 24 by 30 inches in overall size. In case of fire, high awning-type or sliding windows do not provide proper exit.

☐ Provision for a 2-foot clearance between wall and doors in clothes closets, and an 18-inch clearance in linen closets.

National Association of Home Builders' Report on House Sales

When six hundred members of the Builders' Economic Council of the National Association of Home Builders (NAHB—headquarters in Washington, D.C.) were interviewed concerning 1965 home sales, the following facts came to light. Of all the new homes built in 1965, slightly over six out of ten had two or more baths; over eight out of ten had either garages or carports; seven out of ten had family rooms with the highest percentage in the West (81%) and lowest in the Northeast (57%); eight out of every ten kitchens provided built-in ovens or ranges, dishwashers, and garbage disposers.

SPACE RECOMMENDATIONS TRANSLATED INTO FLOOR PLANS

It is one thing to read about space requirements, but quite another thing to translate these figures into floor plans. Even when we are aware of space needs, the cost of a home providing these needs may seem excessively high or be more expensive than a family can afford.

Factors Affecting Living Space

The high cost of land, building materials, and labor influences the amount of living space a builder can provide and a family can afford. The size of the family and the ages and sizes of the children also influence space requirements and affect the amount of money a family has available for housing.

Using the recommendations of the various agencies concerned with housing betterment, we shall attempt to translate space needs into some sample floor plans for individuals and families.

Desirable Space Provisions for Small Apartments

SINGLE PERSON. The efficiency apartment illustrated here, which is confined within an area of about 22½ feet by 17½ feet (including partitions), provides just under 400 square feet of space, or the amount recommended by the American Public Health Association for one

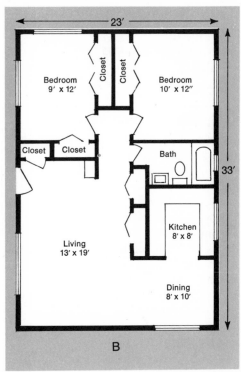

B

This two-bedroom plan has 759 square feet plus partition space. It meets the APHA recommendation of 800 square feet for two persons. However, three persons might live in the apartment very comfortably.

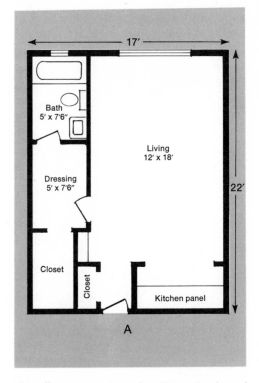

A

This efficiency apartment has 374 square feet of usable floor space. Partitions make up the other 26 square feet needed to meet APHA standards.

person. Careful arrangement in the floor plan shown provides ample space for dressing, storage, cooking, and living. Note the thicker walls between the bathroom and the living room to provide minimum sound transmission. Many single persons can afford much more space, but it is possible for one person to live comfortably within the space provisions shown.

TWO OR THREE PERSONS. The two-bedroom apartment shown provides between 700 and 800 square feet of space (including closets and partitions). Adequate wall space is provided for furniture arrangement. The square feet of living-room and bedroom space more than meets FHA requirements.

Recommended Minimum Floor Space for Individual Rooms

LIVING ROOM. Although living rooms are often 11 feet wide, 12 feet is considered a good minimum width. The smallest living room for comfort and livability by Metropolitan Life Insurance Company standards for home loans is 12 feet by 17 feet. When there is more than one door, a 12-foot by 19-foot living room is preferable to accommodate extra traffic between doors. A comfortable living room for good furniture arrangement is 14 feet by 18 to 20 feet. When the dining area and living area are not separated, there can be an illusion of more space in a 14-foot by 20-foot room than in two small rooms.

DINING AREA (OR ROOM). It is desirable to have a dining room or an area large enough to seat eight persons. The smallest table accommodating eight persons is 40 inches by 72 inches. This size table will seat three persons at each side and one at each end. A linear space of 21 to 24 inches should be allowed for each adult. The smallest room capable of accommodating a 40-inch by 72-inch table, eight chairs, and a serving table is about 9½ feet by 12 feet. If the dining area forms an L with the living area, the dining area need not be as long as 12 feet. Many dining areas in apartments are 9 feet by 9 feet and 9 feet by 10 feet, but this size crowds the person who may be serving and removing food.

BEDROOMS. The Small Homes Council of the University of Illinois considers 9½ feet by 18 feet (171 square feet) the smallest master bedroom that will comfortably accommodate twin beds. To qualify for a loan, the Metropolitan Life Insurance Company also

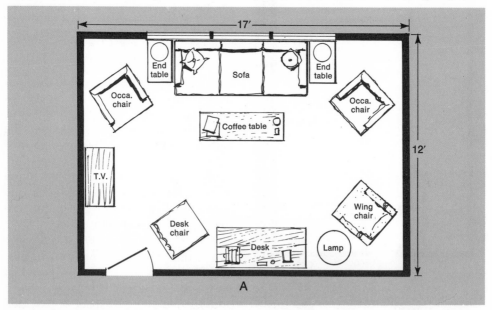

This plan shows the smallest living room for comfortable furniture arrangement by Metropolitan Life Insurance Company standards. A distance of 15" is needed between coffee table and sofa. The room will seem more spacious if the coffee table is eliminated and a long, low, narrow chest placed between the wing chair and occasional chair.

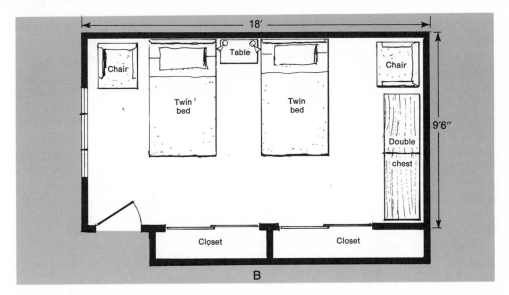

This is the smallest-size master bedroom that allows for twin beds and good traffic flow. A space of 2' 6" is needed between beds, 3' between bed and chest of drawers, and 3' 6" between end of bed and wall.

requires that the first bedroom have 171 square feet. The FHA requires only 120 square feet for the first bedroom in order to qualify for a loan. FHA requirements would provide a bedroom 10 feet by 12 feet or 9½ feet by 13 feet—perhaps a little crowded for twin beds or a king-size bed. A second bedroom, according to Metropolitan Life Insurance Company standards, must have 110 square feet; according to FHA standards, 80 square feet.

The space between the end of the bed and a dresser on the wall opposite should be 3 feet in order for drawers to open with ease. Space between beds should be 2½ feet.

KITCHEN. An 8-foot by 8-foot two-wall kitchen is the most compact for maximum storage and efficiency for a family of three or four. Eight feet will accommodate cabinets, range, refrigerator, dishwasher, and sink—all of which are about two feet deep—on opposite walls with adequate space in between for work. A U-shaped kitchen may also

be provided in an 8- by 8-foot space. The U shape will provide a little more counter work space but some less-easy-to-reach storage space than the two-wall kitchen. A 7- by 9-foot or 7- by 10-foot kitchen lends itself better to an L-shaped arrangement. The corner cabinets will require lazy-susan shelves for maximum storage. The one-wall kitchen is used when less space is required, or in case a long one-wall kitchen 6 to 7 feet in length may parallel a living room and permit more usable space in the living room. (These types of kitchens are explained in Chapter Nine.)

The smallest kitchen that will provide adequate cabinet and work space and also space for a table to seat three or four persons is 9½ by 12 feet. This kitchen has about 114 square feet. The minimum kitchen space requirement for a Metropolitan Life Insurance Company loan on a home is 112 square feet. This kitchen will accommodate a wall oven as a second oven in addition to a regular range and also a dishwasher.

The floor space may be slightly reduced and satisfy standards if the dishwasher and wall oven are omitted and a range substituted for the burners. This is because these additions require approximately 8 square feet more of floor space and use up 16 feet of storage space.

BATHROOM. The minimum-size bathroom containing a small shower stall and a door that opens into the room is 4 feet by 5 feet. If a standard 5-foot tub is used, the minimum size is 5 feet by 7 feet 2 inches or preferably 5 feet by 7 feet 6 inches. A small counter-top vanity can be used in either size. In expensive homes and high-rental apartments, a bathroom should be large enough for a linen closet and a longer vanity counter. Compartmented bathrooms are becoming more common in high-priced homes, especially in the first bathroom. The value of a compartmented bathroom is questionable when bedroom space must be sacrificed to provide the extra bathroom space.

LAUNDRY. The minimum space for a laundry center must provide for the use of a washer, a dryer, and a worktable or cabinet for supplies. By stacking the two units one above the other less space is needed. Two separate units can be accommodated in a 5-foot by 5-foot space on one wall or in a 3-foot 8-inch by 7-foot space provided the two pieces are on opposite walls. An ironing area requires a space 4½ feet by 6 feet whether it is a separate space for permanent use or space in a kitchen or bedroom for occasional use.

Chapter Nine discusses further the kitchen, laundry, and closets.

PLANNING FOR MAXIMUM
LIVABILITY

The amount of floor space is not as important as how it is planned for use.

Proper zoning, or the separation of areas used for quiet and relaxation and work and activity, will make home living more enjoyable.

During the 1950's the keynote in family living was *togetherness,* and architects introduced the open-plan concept in housing in which traffic flowed easily from one area of the house to another. The kitchen and family room were often in the center of the house. The open plan provided for little quiet or privacy for anyone, and parents began to feel a need for better zoning. The two-story house increased in popularity because living and quiet areas could be more easily defined. However, any well-designed house should provide adequately for quiet and activity zones.

Livability of Older Homes

One reason for the current popularity of older two-story homes in well-established areas is their provision for adequate space for social and personal needs. During the expanding family stage many families—families who can afford extensive remodeling if necessary—like the kind of space older homes provide. Older homes often have a family sitting room that can become a *family room,* a large company parlor that makes a gracious *living room,* a large *dining room* which many families prefer to a dining area, a pantry and often a butler's pantry, either of which can be converted into a *powder room.* The upstairs usually has three or more bedrooms and often storage rooms. Even though there may be only one existing bathroom, it is frequently not difficult to find space for a *second bathroom.* The attic provides additional storage space, and the basement has adequate space for a *laundry* and *recreation room.* Remodeling possibilities are often interesting but costly to carry out.

For families who can afford it, a separate dining room may be desirable. To be able to serve the family dinner in an attractive, relaxed atmosphere is important during the expanding and launching stages in the family life cycle. The social experiences children have in learning good table manners, in participating in conversation, and in serving company or special-occasion meals are invaluable, and these experiences will be among their most cherished family memories in the future.

In our complex age it is not easy to have family meals together every evening because many husbands are late coming home from work and children have basketball, baseball, dancing lessons, and club and school meetings that compete for time. Nevertheless, psychologists emphasize the importance of the family dinner in creating good family relationships and in developing poise and a feeling of security in children. The evening meal should not be sandwiched in between other activities but be the highlight of the day.

Making Living and Recreation Areas More Satisfactory

Aside from mealtime sociability, a home should provide for the development of personal interests. Often this means providing additional room space for indoor hobbies or collections and other personal interests, as well as storage space for equipment used in outdoor activities.

OUTDOOR ACTIVITIES. Families who enjoy outdoor sports will need extra storage space for equipment. Here is a list of outdoor activities that may require special storage space for equipment:

badminton	gardening
baseball	golf
basketball	hockey
bicycling	hunting
boating	ice skating
bowling	roller skating
camping	skiing
croquet	swimming
fencing	tennis

INDOOR HOBBIES AND COLLECTIONS. Family members may have special hobbies or collections that require storage space for display as well as a place in which to pursue these activities. Collections and hobbies include:

Hobbies	Collections
basketry	antique furniture
block printing	antique glass
bookbinding	autographs
ceramics	bottles
embroidery	butterflies
knitting	buttons
leather tooling	coins
metalcraft	dolls
model building	jewelry
painting	miniature furniture
pets	rare books
photo developing	rare prints
sewing	records
short-wave radio	shells
weaving	stamps
woodshop	

A collection of campaign buttons displayed on burlap boards.

PERSONAL INTERESTS. Aside from providing space for storing equipment and supplies necessary for active sports, hobbies, and collections, there are space requirements for special interests. When there are small children, space for play and for storing toys is important. Some families enjoy entertaining, and these families may want a large living room, a larger than average kitchen, maybe a recreation room, and a patio. Musically talented families need floor space for an organ or a piano and storage space for smaller musical instruments and sheet music. The family that emphasizes reading and study may need more bookshelf space and study areas or perhaps a separate library or study.

Providing for Quiet and Sleeping Zones

Any house, either two-story, split-level, or ranch type, can have well-defined quiet and activity areas through good planning. When bedroom and living room walls are adjacent, a closet or storage wall between can serve to reduce noise. It is also important to locate bedrooms so that they are not in the line of traffic between the living room and the bathroom or the living room and entrances or kitchen. When you examine house plans, you will want to keep these suggestions in mind.

FLOOR PLANS AND TRAFFIC PATTERNS

A home which provides for efficient, convenient, and safe traffic will be more livable than one which does not. Factories are far ahead of the home in providing for safe traffic. In factories cross traffic through work areas is not permitted, but in many homes children dart back and forth through the kitchen, dining room, and living room, causing

falls, breakage of china, damage to furniture, and jangled nerves. Falls account for half of all home accidental deaths. The largest number of falls occur in kitchens, in bedrooms, in bathrooms, and on stairways. Many of these accidents could be avoided with better traffic lanes. Poor traffic lanes not only cause accidents but they interfere with conversation, study, listening to music, or watching television in the living room. Poor traffic patterns can sometimes be corrected.

It is seldom possible to satisfy all space and traffic requirements in a home. Frequently adjustments can be made to an existing floor plan, or space can be added to a floor plan before a home is built. By the addition of a foot or two to the planned width or length of the house the home may become far more livable. *The additional cost per square foot is usually under the quoted average cost per square foot.* This means that if the builder estimates the total cost of the house at $18 a square foot (including flooring, walls, heating, plumbing, and so forth), an additional foot along one side will cost somewhat less than $18 a square foot.

Let's study the following floor plans in relation to traffic patterns:

Living-Dining-Food Preparation Zone (Floor Plans A–B)

The two plans of the living area of a home shown opposite indicate how preliminary planning by adding a few extra feet can provide for greater livability. Let us criticize Plan A and compare it with corrected Plan B.

CRITICISM. The traffic pattern in Plan A crisscrosses through the main living area. Entering through the sliding doors that separate the dining area and the terrace, a person with an armload

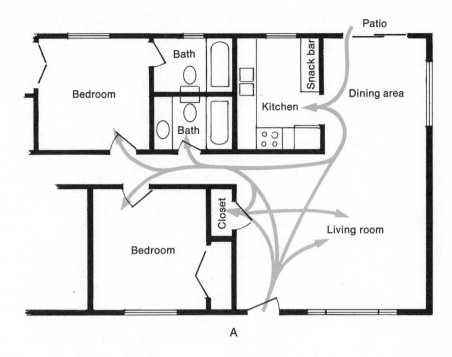

A

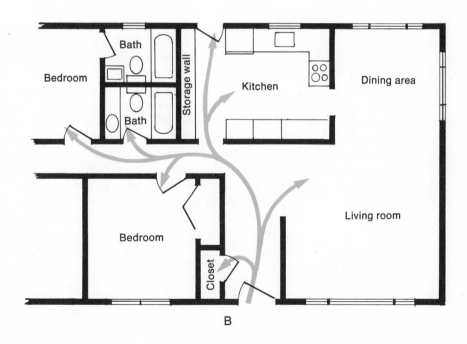

B

Floor Plan A: Poor traffic lanes through living areas.
Floor Plan B: Improved traffic lanes (with 3 additional feet).

of groceries must avoid bumping into the dining table and chairs. The absence of a kitchen door makes more cleaning necessary in the dining area and wears out the carpet quickly along the line of traffic. The kitchen provides no space for cleaning equipment—vacuum cleaner, broom, mop, and scrub bucket. Family members have no privacy in entering the home and reaching the bedrooms or bathrooms because the living room is open to all traffic.

No major work center is located under the kitchen window, a desirable feature, since a view reduces fatigue and prevents a closed-in feeling. Although there is a snack bar for eating in the kitchen, it is like eating in a hurry at a short-order counter, with little or no provision for sociability.

On the credit side of the floor plan, kitchen and bathroom plumbing is concentrated on one wall to reduce the cost of more expensive two-wall plumbing. Bathrooms provide a sound barrier between bedrooms and kitchen.

CORRECTION. The addition of three feet to the width of the house will correct most objections. The additional three feet provides space for a hallway at the entrance, for a kitchen door, for a storage closet for food and cleaning equipment, and for privacy for any family member to enter the house and go to either the bedroom or the kitchen without going through the living room. Note that the three additional feet in the kitchen place the kitchen door off center with the front entrance, so that guests cannot look directly into the kitchen. The coat closet has been conveniently placed near the front door. The double closet along the hall provides an excellent sound barrier for the bedroom. There is also more wall space for arranging furniture in the living room. Conversation circles need not be used as passways.

Sleeping and Quiet Zone (Floor Plans C–D)

Upon casual observation Plan C seems to be spacious, to provide ample storage space, and to produce good traffic lanes, but upon close study there are many points to criticize.

CRITICISM. The bathroom at the end of the hall is visible to the living area. The door into the 11½- by 14-foot bedroom is not only far from the bathroom but in a bad location in relation to bed placement. Occupants of the master bedroom are exposed to hall traffic should the door be left open while they are moving back and forth to the bathroom and closet. There is no wall space for a chest of drawers and dresser if twin beds are used. Bathrooms that are so widely separated increase plumbing costs. The closet in the master bedroom is not arranged for maximum use. All closets are a little small.

CORRECTION. Placing the two bathrooms adjacent to each other will reduce plumbing costs. The 5- by 8-foot bathroom instead of a 5- by 7-foot one (*minimum size which will allow a door to open*) permits a vanity basin and cabinet in the master bathroom and a small linen closet in the family bathroom. Greater privacy is afforded occupants of the master bedroom as well as those of other bedrooms in using the bathrooms. The large closets serve as sound barriers between rooms.

In Plan D children can occupy the bedrooms at the left, giving the parents privacy and quiet. The den-study in Plan D at the right provides another retreat for parents for hobbies or watching television. It is possible to arrange double or single beds and twin chests of drawers or dressers in all bedrooms. The time to check for good traffic lanes is during the paper planning stage.

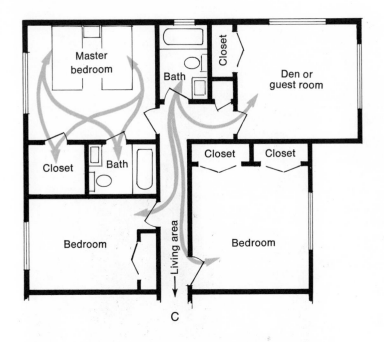

C

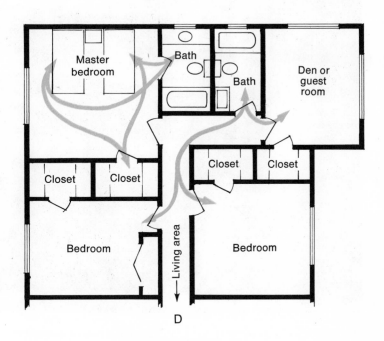

D

Floor Plan C: Poor traffic lanes in sleeping area.
Floor Plan D: Improved traffic lanes in sleeping area.

This basement area in an older home has been converted to a family recreation room that can double as an extra guest room. The linoleum floor with area rug is reasonably priced but handsome, as are the furniture pieces (modular units that can be added to for an expanding family).

SUMMARY

Many groups have been concerned with housing space which provides for health, safety, efficiency, and living enjoyment ever since the Industrial Revolution. However, only lately has a scientific approach to housing space been undertaken. A lending agency, whether it be FHA or a life insurance company, sets up minimum space requirements before granting loans. Space needs change during the life cycle, ranging from a recommended 400 square feet for a single person to 1500 or more for a family with two to four children.

If living space is to be satisfactory, it must provide for livability, including adequate storage space for food, clothing, cleaning supplies, and cultural or recreational needs. Floor plans should provide for sleeping areas to be separated from the noise of recreational and food preparation areas. Traffic should not interfere with conversation circles in the living room or work in the kitchen.

THINGS TO THINK ABOUT AND TO DO

1. List and identify all the agencies you can that are concerned with house livability.

2. Find floor plans with living room, bedroom, and kitchen that meet FHA and Metropolitan Life Insurance Company space standards. Make comparisons.

3. Bring to class floor plans of apartments or houses meeting the total space requirements set down by the American Public Health Association, and mount the best example of each on the bulletin board. Use suitable captions. (Use information on page 73.)

4. Select a floor plan that appeals to you, and check it against the recommendations of the U.S. Savings and Loan League for arrangement (page 74) and for space recommendations for individual rooms under FHA and Metropolitan Life Insurance Company requirements (page 73).

5. Discuss factors that influence the amount of living space (or size of home) a family can afford. If space is inadequate, suggest means of making available space more usable.

6. Make a list of your family's activities, hobbies, and personal interests, and suggest how to obtain space for individual needs.

7. Select any floor plan for a two- or three-bedroom home, and criticize the traffic pattern. Using tracing paper, suggest how you might improve the traffic pattern.

chapter six

FAMILY INCOME RELATED TO HOUSING COSTS

Before an individual or a family can know how much can be spent safely for housing, they must know what costs are involved, understand all sources of income, and be able to estimate expenditures. When this information is known, it is not difficult to approach budgeting, or the distribution of income, on a sound basis. The housing dollar must provide for rent or for payments on a mortgage, which usually include prorated taxes, interest, and insurance. Maintenance and repairs, utilities, and home furnishings are also part of the housing dollar.

Once you have an idea of how much you can spend for rent or for monthly mortgage payments, a real estate agent will be able to help you find a home you can afford. You may want to weigh the advantages and disadvantages of renting and buying. Whether you decide to rent, buy, or build a home you will need certain guidelines. It is usually wise for a young couple to rent for a while, not only because it is an economic necessity for most young couples, but also because the experience gained in renting provides a valuable background for judging a home you may want to buy or have built in the future.

Families expect more for their housing dollar than they did a generation ago. This is evidenced by the fact that the 1967 *City Worker's Family Budget* (a periodic survey made by the Bureau of Labor Statistics of the U. S. Department of Labor) refers to the newer budget as one planned for *moderate living*. The 1947 term *adequate living* is no longer used. Over a period of twenty years the budget necessary for a city worker with a wife and two children to live moderately has more than doubled.

Today's family is extremely mobile, so that moving costs are also important in planning the distribution of income. Even though many large businesses and industrial firms may pay part or all of moving expenses, most families have many additional expenses when they move. It may be necessary to make some home improvements or buy new draperies or carpeting or additional furniture.

GUIDELINES FOR STUDY

GENERAL IDEAS
TO CONSIDER

1. Housing represents the highest cost in most family budgets and therefore involves careful decision making.
2. Salary and wages account for the main source of income, but there are also other sources.
3. Good home management increases spendable income.
4. Certain housing expenses do not change greatly from year to year, whereas other expenses may vary.
5. The *City Worker's Family Budget* offers a guide to families in the middle-income bracket for the allocation of income.
6. The decision whether to rent or to buy a home depends upon many factors, including available money, attitudes toward owning property, and mobility of the chief provider.
7. Salary, amount of savings, and other financial commitments determine the price a family can safely pay for a home.

WORDS AND PHRASES
TO KNOW

bonus
dividends
equity
fixed expenses
flexible expenses
home management income
income tax
inflation
interest
landlord
lease
rental deposit
seasonal income
self-employed person
spendable income
vacancy clause

SOURCES OF INCOME

Income generally includes salary or wages received over a period of time—weekly, monthly, quarterly, semiannually, or annually. In addition to regular salary or wage income, families may receive income from interest or dividends on investments, from rent, from royalties, from bonuses, from commissions, and so on. Once in a while a family may receive unexpected income from an inheritance, a gift, or part-time work. The majority of families plan their yearly income around a salary or wage income on either a weekly or a monthly basis.

The husband or father is considered to be the chief provider, but it is becoming more and more common for both husband and wife to be employed. In some families older children may earn regular income, part or all of which may go toward the support of the family.

Workers who are paid by the job or on a daily or hourly basis find it difficult to distribute income evenly over a year, especially if the total yearly income is low. Migrant workers in such fields as lumbering, crop picking, or fishing earn seasonal income, and these workers sometimes have difficulty budgeting income. Self-employed persons may have less difficulty budgeting income and expenses if they have average or above average total annual income. In this category are artists, writers, photographers, small shop owners, farmers, cattle raisers, doctors, and lawyers. When income varies greatly from month to month or from year to year, it is recommended that the total income be averaged on a three- to five-month or three- to five-year basis.

Another source of income, although not always thought of as such, is home management income, or income saved by family members who help with household management and maintenance. A great deal of money can be saved when all family members make an effort to curtail spending by taking better care of clothing and home furnishings or by cleaning the home rather than paying to have it cleaned. Two families with the same number of children and approximately the same income may not spend money in the same way, so that one family is continually borrowing and the other family is continually saving.

Before making any kind of spending plan, or budget, a family should list money income from all sources and deduct such items as income tax, social security, and health insurance payments. What is left is considered *spendable income.* At no other time in history have so many families had so much spendable income as at present.

ITEMS OF EXPENDITURE

Some expenditures vary little from month to month or from year to year, whereas others may vary a great deal. Expenditures that vary little are referred to as *fixed expenses* and those that vary greatly are referred to as *flexible expenses.*

Fixed Expenses

Fixed expenses include the cost of housing, such as rent or home-mortgage payments, taxes, and insurance. Payments on a car, interest on borrowed money, public-utility bills (water, light, heat, and telephone), transportation related to employment, and church and club contributions are also more or less fixed expenses. Of course fixed expenses change during the family life cycle. It is difficult to reduce fixed expenses during any period without being willing to lower one's standard of living. At any period in the family life cycle it is not difficult to estimate fixed expenses if you keep receipted bills or canceled checks.

Flexible Expenses

Flexible expenses include food, clothing, new furnishings, health expenses, education, car expenses, recreation, charitable gifts, and personal expenses. Of all flexible expenses food will vary the least, for food is a big item in the family budget and there is an inflexible amount below which an adequate diet cannot be provided.

The money spent on clothing and home furnishings will depend somewhat upon how family members take care of these items and how much they can save by making clothing and home repairs. If a family will look for so-called leaks in spending, such as buying at expensive stores at peak prices, paying excessive charges for credit buying, indulging in impulse buying, and so on, waste can be eliminated without causing any sacrifice. Becoming expert at careful planning and comparative shopping can work wonders.

There is no foolproof spending plan to fit all families because too many variables enter into budgeting—the number of family members and their ages, the geographical location of the home, the family's outstanding debts, and the willingness of family members to think in terms of long-term goals, such as a trip, a new home, or an education, instead of in terms of short-term wants. However, some budget guidelines will be helpful as a starting point. After a year of record keeping it will be easier for a family to determine where some costs can be reduced in order to have enough money for special needs.

The City Worker's Family Budget as a Guide

For a number of years the Bureau of Labor Statistics in the U.S. Department of Labor has conducted studies in twenty major cities in the United States to estimate what income a family must have for adequate living. One of the most comprehensive studies was made in 1946–1947 and was followed by an interim study in 1960–1961. The most recent study was made in 1966 and published in 1967.

The hypothetical family, used in all studies, consists of a husband in his late thirties, a wife a little younger, a boy thirteen, and a girl eight years old. The mother is not employed outside the home, and there are no dependents outside the immediate family. In the original study the term *adequate living* was used as a standard, and it was assumed that the average city family rented a home. Since the study made in 1946–1947 and the interim study made in 1960–1961, technological advances in all areas of living and rising income have changed living concepts, so that in the recent study the term *moderate living* has replaced *adequate living*. The new study also includes nonmetropolitan areas, or communities of from 2500 to 50,000 persons. And since about three fourths of all urban families either own homes or are paying off a mortgage, estimates have been established for home buyers in addition to home renters.

Adequate living was originally defined as including the following: a five-room home or apartment, a used car, central hot and cold running water, a gas or electric range, and a washing machine. The new term *moderate living* not only includes the provisions for comfortable living but adds more space, better home furnishings, and perhaps a clothes dryer, as well as a more liberal allowance for clothing, transportation, and meals out. A number of costs rose greatly between 1946–1947 and 1966–1967. For instance, personal income tax, which represented about 12 percent of all budget items in 1966–1967, was more than double the earlier percentage. However, spendable income is greater now than ever in spite of rising income tax, more costly health insurance, and inflation. For a number of years inflation has caused the dollar to lose from 3 to over 5 percent a year in buying power. Yet many families have discretionary income, or income left after providing the essentials, to spend exactly as they please.

In the cities studied, the total cost of an adequate standard of living for a family of four averaged about $4200 in the late 1940's. At the time of the interim study in 1960–1961, the figure had risen to $6100, representing a 45 percent increase. In the 1966–1967 report an average income of $9191 was needed for moderate living in urban areas of the United States. The cost of a moderate budget varied from $9376 in metropolitan areas to $8366 in smaller cities, where a much smaller sampling was used. It was estimated that homeowners in a metropolitan area needed $800 more a year than renters. From these estimates we might conclude that on the same income a renter family could save $800. However, the homeowner is constantly building up equity or savings in a home each time he makes a mortgage payment. The homeowner has another advantage in that he may deduct interest on the mortgage and taxes from his income tax. Of course the figures used in the study are based upon prevailing costs in all areas and not on how actual families spend their money.

CITY WORKER'S FAMILY BUDGET (1966–1967)

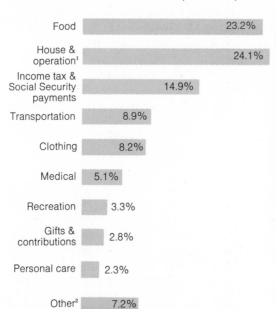

Food — 23.2%

House & operation[1] — 24.1%

Income tax & Social Security payments — 14.9%

Transportation — 8.9%

Clothing — 8.2%

Medical — 5.1%

Recreation — 3.3%

Gifts & contributions — 2.8%

Personal care — 2.3%

Other[2] — 7.2%

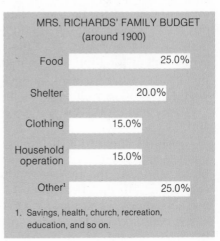

MRS. RICHARDS' FAMILY BUDGET
(around 1900)

Food — 25.0%

Shelter — 20.0%

Clothing — 15.0%

Household operation — 15.0%

Other[1] — 25.0%

1. Savings, health, church, recreation, education, and so on.

1. Includes rent or mortgage payments, utilities, and maintenance.
2. Reading and education, 1.3%; occupational expenses, 0.9%; life insurance, 1.8%; miscellaneous, 3.2%.

The table opposite shows the amount of money considered necessary for budget items and the approximate percentages of each item in the *City Worker's Family Budget*. Housing costs for the first time have exceeded food costs. Housing costs are highest in the Northeast and lowest in the South. In New England and along the Middle Atlantic coast, land is scarce and costly near large cities, and the cost of labor in building houses is higher than in other areas of the country. The cold climate also affects housing costs. Homes can be built less expensively in the South because basements are not needed and labor costs less. As a rule fuel costs are less in the South unless homes are air-conditioned throughout.

The *City Worker's Family Budget* is fairly generous in comparison with what low-income families can afford. Low-income families may have to spend as much as twenty-five or twenty-six percent of their income for food and up to thirty percent for housing. Naturally this limits the amount left for all other items. As income rises, a smaller percent is spent for food and shelter, although more money may be spent. A higher percent, as well as more money, may be spent for clothing, recreation, and transportation.

It may be interesting to compare a budget suggested by Mrs. Ellen H. Richards, one of the pioneers in home economics, at the beginning of the present century with today's *City Worker's Family Budget*. The chart on page 91 gives details. At that time there were no life or health group insurance plans, no social security, and few pension plans. Saving for future security was an individual matter. There were no laborsaving devices as we know them because electricity was just becoming common for home lighting only.

The cost of living was about a fourth of what it is today, but salaries and wages barely covered essentials. There was no discretionary income for psychological needs and almost no advertising to create such needs.

RENTING VERSUS HOME OWNERSHIP

Whether you rent or own a home will depend upon many factors. Newlyweds seldom have enough money for a down payment on a home. Young families in which the head is a young executive may move too often to want to worry about buying and selling a home. Some people do not want the responsibility of all the repairs and improvements necessary in a home. Here are some considerations for potential renters or home buyers.

Advantages of Renting

Some people are better off renting, at least during part of the family life cycle. For instance: (1) A young married couple seldom have the money or the experience necessary to buy a home. (2) The junior executive, who is likely to be transferred frequently, may have to sell a home at a sacrifice each time he moves in order to have a down payment for a new one. (When his position appears to be more permanent, home ownership may be desirable.) (3) People who have little interest in keeping a home in good repair, in landscaping, and in lawn care are likely to neglect a home and cause it to depreciate in value. (4) The suburban homeowner who dislikes commuting long distances and paying extra transportation and parking costs may prefer to rent near the city, especially after the children leave home.

Budgeted items of the CITY WORKER'S FAMILY BUDGET, 1966–1967	Average family expenditures[1]			% of nat'l au. income spent for each item
	In large cities	In small communities	National average	
Flexible items				
Housing[2]	$2286	$1894	$2214	24.1%
Food	2173	2005	2143	23.2
At home ...... $1824　　Meals out $319				
Transportation[3]	815	813	815	8.9
Clothing and upkeep[4]	767	709	756	8.2
Medical care (including insurance)	481	411	468	5.1
Recreation	310	291	306	3.3
Gifts and contributions	259	231	253	2.8
Personal care	218	194	214	2.3
Life insurance	160	160	160	1.8
Reading and education	130	76	120	1.3
Occupational expenses	80	80	80	0.9
Miscellaneous	294	287	293	3.2
TOTAL SPENDABLE INCOME	$7973	$7151	$7822	85.1%
Fixed items				
Personal income tax	$1112	$ 935	$1080	11.8%
Social Security and disability payments	291	280	289	3.1
TOTAL INCOME	$9376	$8366	$9191	100.0%

1. The total incomes given for these columns are an estimated average for a family of four with a moderate standard of living. The figures are based upon the assumption that three fourths of the families are homeowners and one fourth are renters.
2. Housing includes rent or mortgage payments, utilities, equipment, furnishings, insurance on household items, and property taxes (for homeowners).
3. Transportation includes automobiles and public conveyances.
4. Clothing costs break down as follows: wife, $187; husband, $174; boy, $168; girl, $154; upkeep, $72.

Advantages of Home Ownership

Home ownership has many obvious advantages over renting, provided the owner does not anticipate frequent moves and the location of the home is in a neighborhood that is more likely to appreciate than to depreciate in value. Some advantages are: (1) An equity or savings is gradually built up, even though a large portion of a mortgage payment goes into interest. (2) Interest payments and those for real estate taxes may be deducted from income tax. (3) Home ownership provides many psychological values that are difficult to measure, such as personal satisfaction, independence, and security. (4) Investment in a home is often a hedge against inflation as the dollar buys less and less each year.

GUIDELINES FOR RENTING

A renter is concerned about the neighborhood in which he lives, the general appearance of the property, the size and location of rooms, the nearness to shopping centers, and if there are children, the nearness to schools and churches.

In addition to these considerations, there should be an understanding between a tenant and an apartment landlord regarding services to be provided, restrictions to be imposed, convenience and safety factors, and obligations concerning the lease. The house renter has more responsibilities for services than the apartment renter; so not all of the following guidelines apply to house renters.

Provision for Services

TRASH REMOVAL. Find out who is responsible for removing trash and where trash is to be deposited.

MAIL AND LAUNDRY. Find out if there are individual mail boxes and if coin-operated washers and dryers are available. If no provision is made for home laundry, find out where the nearest commercial laundry or coin-operated laundry is located.

PARKING. In some areas of cities overnight parking is forbidden, and this may necessitate renting a garage some distance away if no garage or parking space is provided.

DECORATING AND REPLACEMENT SCHEDULE. In most new apartment buildings there is a schedule for painting walls, replacing laborsaving equipment, and so forth, but in older buildings the tenant may be expected to take care of decorating and to provide or replace a refrigerator, range, garbage disposer, and so on.

JANITORIAL SERVICES. You should have an understanding as to who is responsible for cleaning halls, stairways, sidewalks, and windows. These responsibilities should be the owner's in a large apartment building. Windows are usually cleaned outside twice a year. Also installing and removing screens should be the owner's responsibility in a large, new apartment building.

Restrictions

Most apartment owners have restrictions concerning pets especially if the floors are carpeted. Others have restrictions about installing air conditioners unless the tenant pays for the current. In some instances families with young children are not permitted.

Convenience and Safety Features

Noises are increasing inside dwellings, on the street, and in the air. An apartment building near an airport, factory, or railroad may be noisy. An apartment unit near an elevator or a laundry room may be objectionable. There are safety factors to be considered also, such as railings on stairs; lights in stairways, in halls, and at entrances; sufficient fire exits; and adequate wiring. Many older buildings remodeled into apartments do not have adequate wiring. Ask questions about wiring and circuit breakers. Note where outlets are placed in the living room for lamps, in the kitchen for appliances, and in the bathroom for an electric razor.

Landlord and Tenant Obligations

TERMS OF LEASE. Before signing a lease make sure you understand the terms. If you sign a lease for a year and decide to move at the end of eight months, you may be responsible for paying the full year's rent before you can move. If the place is subsequently rented, you will usually receive a refund for each month's rent collected from another tenant. Most leases carry a penalty clause requiring the renter to pay an additional fee if the rent is not received before a certain date. Some leases have a sixty-day vacancy or transfer clause—that is, the tenant or the landlord reserves the right to break the contract with a sixty-day notice. This clause protects both parties.

RENTAL DEPOSIT. In order to protect equipment, carpeting, walls, and so forth, many landlords require a deposit of a hundred dollars or more to keep in escrow. When the tenant moves, the cost of repairing any damage is deducted from the deposit, and the remainder of the money is returned to the tenant.

PAYMENT OF UTILITIES. In some cases the owner pays only water and sewer charges, while in other instances the owner may pay for heat and/or electricity.

GUIDELINES FOR DETERMINING THE COST OF A HOME

The potential home buyer will want to know how much he can safely spend for a home. Many factors will affect this spending, such as family size and composition, ages of family members, number of family members employed full- or part-time, future salary potential of the head of the family, savings on hand, the amount of the down payment, and what family members are willing to sacrifice in order to own a home. Here are some guidelines for determining how much a family can afford to pay for a home.

□ Pay no more than two to two and a half times annual family income after deductions. To be on the safe side this should be based only upon a husband's income because a wife's income is not always dependable during child-bearing years. Until recently the Federal Housing Administration ignored the wife's income in all instances when granting FHA-insured mortgages.

□ Invest no more in a home than a hundred times one week's take-home salary or wages. For example, if one week's earnings are $180, a house should cost about $18,000.

□ Pay no more on a monthly mortgage (including payment toward principal, interest, taxes, and insurance) than 20 to 25 percent of monthly take-home pay.

□ Plan to spend 1 percent of the cost of the house on yearly upkeep if it is a new home or at least 2 percent if it is an older home.

The following description of the average FHA house in 1968, along with a cost analysis, may help a potential home buyer. However, it must be remembered that yearly inflation at the rate of 3 to 5 percent will cause these figures to rise.

The typical house in 1968 was a one-story slab-foundation building with frame construction and an attached two-car garage. The average lot contained 7842 square feet and cost $3690. The average house had six rooms (three bedrooms) and two bathrooms. At an average cost of $12.75 a square foot, the cost of the house was $18,808. The down payment was $1120; the mortgage, $17,695; closing costs, $430; and monthly mortgage payments, $141. The average buyer earned $10,580 a year, or approximately $732 per month after deductions.

One-story homes accounted for 84.3 percent of all homes built with an FHA mortgage; two-story, for 10.4 percent; and split-level, for 5.3 percent. A slab foundation was typical of 52.1 percent of homes; crawl space, of 28 percent; and a full or half basement, of the remainder. Slightly over 77.4 percent were of frame construction; slightly over 22 percent, masonry; and between 6 and 7 percent were fabricated. Other features included ranges in 68 percent, ventilating fans in 54.2 percent, garbage disposers in 40.5 percent, dishwashers in 30.5 percent, central air conditioning in 24.3 percent, and refrigerators in 20.8 percent. In a few instances automatic washers and dryers were part of the package, but in most instances families supplied these on their own. Over 65.6 percent of the homes had one and a half bathrooms.

Mortgage companies financed 65.9 percent; state banks, 12.8 percent; national banks, 8.6 percent; savings and loan associations, 6 percent; insurance companies, 2.2 percent; and savings banks, 1.5 percent. These figures are for FHA mortgages only. Turn to the next chapter to find out how mortgage debt in general is distributed. Note especially the chart on page 103.

COSTS AND CONSIDERATIONS IN MOVING

If you follow the pattern of many of today's families, you will probably move about every five years.

Moving in any instance is expensive and frustrating. If your first home is a small apartment, your first real moving experience may be to a larger apartment or perhaps to a home. If you have only a minimum amount of furniture, you may enlist the help of your friends and move everything in a station wagon, or you may consider renting a self-help truck. Before you try a do-it-yourself means, make sure your decision is wise. There is always the possibility of personal injury and damage to furniture, and if you use nonprofessional help, you may not be able to collect any kind of insurance in case of accident. Young people offering their services to friends on moving day have sometimes suffered severe injuries.

It is advisable to secure moving estimates from two or three reliable moving firms. If you are planning a move from one large city to another, find out whether it is more economical to move by rail or by motor freight. Remember that careful planning ahead of time can lessen many problems.

Preparing to Move
□ Make plans to terminate your lease or sell your house as soon as a move is certain. It is usually wiser to place the sale of a house in professional hands than to try to make a personal sale. Real estate agents are aware of local housing values, and they are skilled in dealing with prospective buyers.
□ Contact several reliable movers in advance, and obtain comparative costs. When satisfied with an offer, confirm the contract and moving date.

□ Several weeks in advance arrange with utility companies to have water, gas, electricity, and telephone service terminated. Investigate the need for having major laborsaving equipment removed and installed in the new home.

□ Notify the following about your change of address: local businesses; insurance companies holding any kind of home, automobile, life, or hospital insurance policies; subscription departments of magazines; friends and relatives. You may request special change-of-address forms from moving firms.

□ Cancel all delivery services, such as newspaper, laundry, and milk.

□ Write letters of resignation to local organizations unless certain memberships can be transferred. Notify your church of your change of address, but retain your membership until you have made new contacts.

□ Assemble valuable papers, such as legal documents; insurance papers; canceled checks for at least five years (these are good receipts if a question should arise about unpaid bills); mortgage-payment receipts; and any other papers relative to the purchase of a house, or valuable furs and jewelry, birth certificates, health records, and children's school records. Although some families take these items with them in a car, it is wise to send them by registered mail.

□ For future convenience take along a copy of the local telephone directory.

Dealing with Movers

Surveys indicate that the most common complaints against moving companies are: (1) failure to arrive on the promised day for either pickup or delivery; (2) underestimating costs for packing and shipping; (3) loss of or damage to possessions; (4) difficulty in collecting money for damaged goods.

Take these precautions if you move:

□ Make sure to have in writing the charges agreed upon, including optional services and liability coverage in case of damage, as well as dates of pickup and delivery. It may be hard to obtain firm dates on small loads, especially if you are moving to a small community, because small loads are stored until there is enough for a truckload going in the same direction. Charges for local moving are made by the hour. Intercity and interstate charges are based upon distance and weight. Large items, such as pianos, carry extra charges.

□ Find out how you can cut costs by doing some or all of the packing yourself. Books and clothing are easy to pack. However, china and crystal are not so easy to pack, and if you pack these items and breakage occurs, you will not be reimbursed.

□ Take a complete inventory of all possessions. Label all boxes, barrels, and drawers. Count and number all.

□ Tag all items according to where they are to be placed.

□ Arrive at your destination before the moving van arrives. Have a money order, a traveler's check, a cashier's check, or cash ready for the driver. Personal checks are not acceptable as a rule, and it may be difficult to obtain cash or a cashier's check in a strange city.

□ Direct the placement of furniture as it is delivered. Placement is included in the cost estimate.

□ Note damage to furniture or furnishings. Secure estimates for replacement or repairs. Within several days write a letter to the central office of the moving company and state the damage done and possible costs for replacement or repairs. Keep a carbon copy of your letter. If your letter is not answered within thirty days, have the secretary of the Better Business Bureau or your lawyer write to the moving company.

CONSUMER PRICE INDEX (1957-59 = 100)

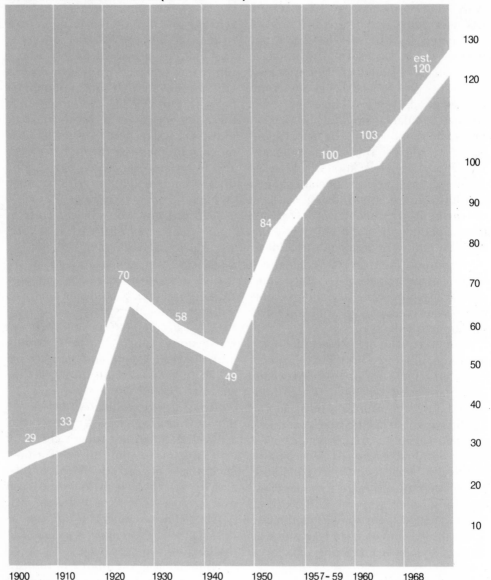

INFLATION IN THE UNITED STATES—1900-1968

Between 1900 and 1968, consumer prices rose more than 400 percent. With the 1957-59 dollar as a basis, it would have taken about $120 to purchase in 1968 what could have been bought for $29 in 1900. However, during the early part of the century almost all income went toward paying for physical needs. The rising standard of living has increased people's social and psychological needs.

SUMMARY

A home is a business on a small scale. Family members who earn or help to spend income should know how to manage money so that special needs as well as essentials may be provided for. Housing, including home furnishings, home maintenance and repair, and utilities, is the largest item in the budget at most income levels. It may be second to food at low-income levels. Some families prefer to spend the housing dollar for rent and others for home ownership. In some instances it may be wiser to rent, but there are satisfactions in ownership.

The renter needs many guidelines, so that his rental dollar will give satisfaction. He should investigate the services, restrictions, and conveniences provided by the landlord. He should understand the terms of the lease, the disposition of the rental deposit, and the obligations for the cost of certain utilities and services.

In an age of increasing mobility it is important to plan ahead of time for moving, so that not too many things will be left to chance. It is also advisable to compare moving costs and to know how to deal with movers. Careful preliminaries can lessen the frustrations of moving.

THINGS TO THINK ABOUT AND TO DO

1. Discuss with your family the amount of monthly income that can be used safely for housing.

2. List on the chalkboard ways you can save money (management income) if you want to allow more income for housing.

3. Using the table on page 93, work out monthly and weekly costs for all items listed in the *City Worker's Family Budget*.

4. Suppose that a family's take-home pay is $5000. Reverse the percentages for food and housing in the *City Worker's Family Budget*, and based on these and other percentages work out the cost distribution of a yearly and monthly budget for a $5000 income.

5. Using the guidelines on page 95, determine the price range for a home that families in the following income levels (after taxes) can afford: $5000, $6500, $8500, $10,000. Assuming that mortgage payments should not exceed 20 percent of income, determine yearly and monthly mortgage payments.

6. On the bulletin board arrange a display of homes in the price ranges above. A

multi-list real estate firm may provide such photographs.

7. Debate the proposition: "It is more economical to rent than to buy."

8. Discuss experiences your family and older friends have had in: (1) renting, (2) buying older property, (3) buying new property.

9. List questions you would ask a landlord: (1) if you were renting the third floor of his home, (2) if you were renting an apartment in a large, moderately priced apartment building.

10. List some inconveniences and hazards often prevalent in an older home converted into apartments.

11. Discuss experiences you and other class members have had with moving.

12. List precautions you would consider most important in making arrangements with a moving company if you should move.

13. Compare the moving rates of the following agencies concerned with moving: (1) large van companies, (2) freight by truck or rail, (3) rent-a-truck service companies. Consider convenience as well.

chapter seven

HOME
FINANCING

Six out of every ten families in the United States are homeowners, but most homes carry a mortgage. Few families buy a home outright, and many take as long as thirty-five years to pay for a home. Government subsidies are making home ownership possible for more families of modest means. Recently the Federal Housing Administration has agreed to secure home loans on condominium town houses and apartments, a step which is also increasing home ownership. Unfortunately some families have no business owning homes because they cannot afford them or will not take care of them. When they cannot make their mortgage payments, foreclosure steps are necessary, and by this time many homes are in a very rundown condition.

Home ownership involves more than meeting monthly mortgage payments. When you are renting a home, the landlord is responsible for general maintenance and repair, but when you own a home, your housing budget must allow for all upkeep and improvement. Adequate insurance must be carried, and the amount of insurance should be checked from time to time as improvements are made and as rising labor costs increase the cost of replacing a home in case of total loss by fire. A homeowner's insurance policy gives comprehensive coverage for fire damage as well as for damage from other causes, and in addition, it provides personal liability insurance at a lower cost than can be provided by a number of separate policies.

Since home ownership represents the largest single investment of a lifetime for most families, it is important for the prospective home buyer to understand what agencies offer home financing, to be able to evaluate the types of mortgages available, to judge mortgage-contract provisions, and to understand the legal procedures in the purchase of a home. In some instances sales agreements have to be canceled because buyers have been financially unprepared to meet closing costs. Sometimes families are not prepared to pay the extra cost of assessments for public utilities, such as sewer provisions. Also, few home buyers realize the importance of checking liens against the property, or easement rights for utility companies.

GUIDELINES FOR STUDY

GENERAL IDEAS
TO CONSIDER

1. A knowledge of where to apply for a home loan, of mortgage terms, of interest rates, of legal documents, and of closing costs is essential to the potential home-owner.
2. Mortgage contracts vary in terms of mortgage type, interest rates, and provision for paying off the loan in advance.
3. The services of a lawyer may prevent misunderstandings at the time of settlement and future legal problems.
4. Adequate insurance protects the homeowner against fire, theft, and other damage as well as injury or accidental death to anyone on the property.

WORDS AND TERMS
TO KNOW

abstract
amortized mortgage
appraisal
assessment
closing costs
deed
down payment
easement
escrow
Federal Housing Administration
Federal Reserve System
foreclosure
forgery
hand money
heir
hidden hazards
homeowner's insurance
interest
joint tenancy
liability insurance

lien
loan
mortgage
multi-listing
mutual savings banks
notary
open-end mortgage
package mortgage
prorated
real estate broker
repayment (of loan)
sales agreement
saving and loan associations
solicitor
survey
title
title insurance
Veterans Administration
zoning ordinance

LENDING AGENCIES

The most important financing agencies, or sources of mortgage credit, from the standpoint of volume are savings and loan associations, commercial banks (and trust companies), mutual savings banks, and life insurance companies. Other sources are mortgage companies, real estate and construction companies, and individuals. Aside from these private lending institutions, there are government agencies under which loans are insured but not actually made. Savings and loan associations have accounted for the largest volume of home loans since the passage of the Housing Act of 1934, giving the Federal Housing Administration authority to insure home loans.

Life insurance companies have built their business on long-term investments, and home financing has been an important source of income. The Federal government through the FHA will insure a home loan by a private lending institution if the lending institution finds the property meets certain standards and the buyer's income and

debt obligations meet its yardstick. War veterans have an advantage in securing loans through the FHA at lower rates than nonveterans, and they may also secure a guaranteed loan through the Veterans Administration (VA) and a private lending agency. With the recent building boom, real estate companies and building contractors have begun to grant loans on approved property if the buyer can qualify financially. All lending agencies are strict about property appraisals and the credit rating of potential buyers.

PROPERTY APPRAISAL

Sometime before a sales agreement is entered into, financial arrangements must be made for obtaining a mortgage. The financing agency will have the property appraised to determine its realistic value, or what price it might bring on a quick sale if the buyer should default in his payments. The amount of the mortgage depends upon this appraisal, along with the size of the down payment.

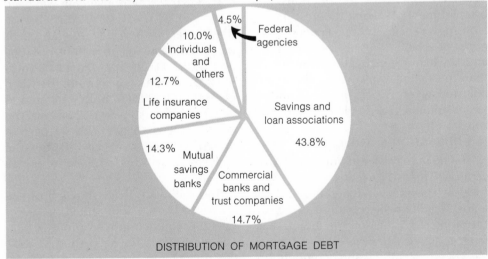

DISTRIBUTION OF MORTGAGE DEBT

This chart shows the approximate percentages of outstanding mortgage debts held by various lending agencies on nonfarm one- to four-family homes in 1967.
(Source: Housing and Home Finance Agency, Washington, D.C., *Housing Statistics—Annual Data,* 1967.)

An *appraisal* and an *assessment* are not synonymous. An assessment is the price placed on property by tax assessors for state and local taxes. The appraisal is frequently higher than the assessment, and the buying price is sometimes higher than the appraisal—especially in expensive residential neighborhoods.

TYPES OF MORTGAGES

In general there are three types of mortgages—conventional, Federal Housing Administration (FHA), and Veterans Administration (VA).

Interest rates on mortgages and the term or duration of the mortgage vary with the lending institution, the section of the country, and the nation's economy. The amount required for the down payment also varies according to lender and locality. Individual savings and loan associations may establish their own interest rates, according to conditions in the locality and current reserves. The Federal Reserve System, which was established by an Act of Congress in 1914, has as one of its functions the establishment of bank interest rates. Housing agencies of the Federal government establish interest rates on FHA and VA loans, which may seem lower than prevailing rates, but which are adjusted when a percentage is added to the quoted rate for loan insurance.

Conventional Mortgages

The down payment required on conventional loans is usually higher than the down payment on federally financed loans. Traditionally about a third of the appraisal value of the house has been required. However, when money has been plentiful and competition keen, the down payment on a conventional loan has been as low as 20 percent. Savings and loan associations and commercial banks usually prefer conventional loans. As has already been mentioned, the price one pays for a house may be either *higher* or *lower* than the appraisal value. In case the buying price is *higher than the appraisal value,* the buyer must provide the difference in the down payment. Suppose a buyer wants very much to live in a particular neighborhood, and the appraisal value of the house is $25,000, but the owner hold out for $26,500. In addition to the down payment on $25,000, the buyer would have to include in his down payment the difference between $25,000 and $26,500 or an additional $1500.

Federal Housing Administration (FHA) Mortgages

FHA-insured mortgages are available to both nonveterans and veterans, but veterans have an advantage over nonveterans in needing a smaller down payment. Suppose a single-family home costs $25,000. The nonveteran will need 3 percent of the first $15,000 cost on the house, whereas the veteran needs no down payment on a house costing up to $15,000. On the next $5000 (over $15,000) or on any amount between $15,000 and $20,000, both veteran and nonveteran must pay 10 percent. The veteran needs to pay only 15 percent of any amount over $20,000, but the nonveteran will be required to pay 20 percent.

The following chart shows how the down payments will differ. In every case the figures must be rounded out. Therefore, on a house costing $25,000, the nonveteran must have $2000* for a down payment, but the veteran needs only $1000*.

	Nonveterans	Veterans
First $15,000	$ 450 (at 3%)	—
Next $5000	500 (at 10%)	$500 (at 10%)
Over $20,000	1000 (at 20%)	450 (at 15%)
	*$1950 or $2000	*$950 or $1000

The FHA sets up standards for home mortgages with regard to room sizes, plumbing, heating, construction, and so on (see Chapter Five). Lately the FHA has permitted the cost of wall-to-wall carpeting to come under the mortgage. Formerly floors had to be finished wood, resilient tile, or roll goods. Buyers had to pay for carpeting exclusive of the mortgage. With the trend toward laying carpet over plywood panels or concrete, the use of carpets that are less expensive and more durable and the demand for carpeted floors, the FHA permits the use of carpet. A more durable quality is required for heavy-traffic areas than for areas receiving ordinary traffic. However, there is no definite scale for measuring quality. Although FHA loans accounted for only 20 percent of merchant-built homes in 1967, FHA standards are widely used by builders and lending agencies.

Veterans Administration (VA) Mortgages

Following World War II, war veterans, including those of the Korean conflict, were granted VA mortgages requiring no down payment. The date for applying for these loans has been extended from July 25, 1967, until July 25, 1970. Although no down payment may sound attractive to the person with little cash, the large amount of interest paid over the mortgage period places a high total cost on the house.

INTEREST RATES AND REPAYMENT PERIODS

The interest rates and the length of the repayment period will influence the total cost of a house. When mortgage money is plentiful, as it was in the early 1960's, interest rates are low, and when mortgage money is scarce, as it was in the middle and late 1960's, interest rates are high.

Interest rates on FHA and VA loans are fixed by law, and they are usually lower than interest rates on conventional loans. Origination costs, or *initial service charges,* may be charged by the mortgage holder of either government-insured or conventional loans. These charges on FHA and VA loans are fixed by law. They sometimes make the total charge on a government-insured loan higher than it would be on a conventional loan where such charges are not fixed.

You can save money on the total cost of a home by (1) making a large down payment, (2) shopping for the lowest interest rate available, or (3) paying off the mortgage in a short period of time. Note in the following tables the savings that can be realized at *different interest rates* and at *different repayment periods* on each one thousand dollars of a loan.

TABLE 1

Monthly Payments[1] and Total Interest Charges for Each $1000 Borrowed Over a 20-Year Period at Different Interest Rates[2]

Interest rate	Monthly payment	Total interest (over 20 years)
6½%	$7.46	$789.38
7	7.75	860.72
7½	8.06	933.42

1. Monthly payment figures shown include only principal and interest. Actual payments may include prorated taxes and insurance, thus removing the risk of having the buyer fail to pay his taxes and insurance. Most lending agencies prefer to include all possible financial obligations of the buyer in the monthly mortgage payments. As taxes, insurance, and other costs go up, the monthly payments are increased proportionately.
2. New mortgage interest rates as of 1969 averaged 7.45 percent, whereas existing mortgages are generally 6 percent or below.

TABLE 2

Monthly Payments for Each $1000 Borrowed at 7 Percent Over Different Repayment Periods[1]

Repayment period	Monthly payment	Total interest
10 years	$11.61	$ 393.30
15 years	8.99	619.69
20 years	7.75	860.72
25 years	7.07	1120.34
30 years	6.65	1395.09

1. Monthly payment figures shown include only payment toward the principal and interest. Actual payments may include prorated taxes and insurance.

TYPES OF MORTGAGE CONTRACTS

Mortgages may be arranged in a number of different ways. The most common types of contracts are described briefly below.

Packaged Contract

The packaged contract permits the borrower to include equipment for the laundry and kitchen, carpeting, and other items under one contract. These items will have worn out before the mortgage is liquidated or paid off. A lender might question including such items because their life expectancy is short in comparison with the life expectancy of the structure and of the plumbing, heating, and cooling systems.

Open-End Contract

The open-end mortgage is advantageous to the borrower who anticipates future property improvement. As he pays off part of the principal, he is permitted to extend the mortgage balance at the same rate of interest so long as the new loan does not exceed the original amount. Thus the borrower saves the cost of refinancing.

Amortized Mortgage

The amortized mortgage pays itself off over a certain period, which may be as long as thirty or even thirty-five years on an FHA loan. Each month a certain sum is paid, which usually includes payment toward the principal, interest, state and local taxes, and insurance. Some lending institutions will permit the buyer to pay for taxes and insurance when due rather than hold prorated payments in escrow (safekeeping). It is usually advisable to limit the duration of the mortgage to twenty or twenty-five years because continuous

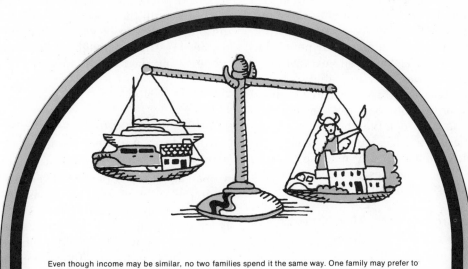

Even though income may be similar, no two families spend it the same way. One family may prefer to live in a small home, drive a large car and take many trips whereas another family may enjoy a large home and cultural activities and be satisfied with a small car.

A large down payment and a small loan or mortgage will give more equity in a home than a small down payment and a large loan or mortgage. The larger equity makes it easier to borrow when need arises.

interest charges increase the total cost of the house. Even on a typical twenty-year amortized mortgage, about half of each month's mortgage payments during the first eight to ten years will represent interest. It is advisable to obtain a mortgage that can be paid off ahead of time without paying a penalty, thus saving considerable interest. Conventional mortgages usually carry this clause, but a penalty may be charged on FHA mortgages for paying off the mortgage ahead of schedule.

Straight-Term Mortgage

The straight-term mortgage was common until after the first quarter of this century. In this type of mortgage interest must be paid regularly, and the principal must be paid after a set number of years. It is used now mainly in short-term construction loans.

FORECLOSURES

When mortgage payments cannot be met, the lending agency may foreclose on the property or take it over for a resale. The foreclosure rate on mortgages is low during good times. For instance, during the early 1960's there were only slightly over four foreclosures for every thousand mortgages. The rate was highest for FHA- or VA-insured mortgages because as a rule these borrowers are less financially secure than others. A number of factors may cause a foreclosure: death or severe illness of the homeowner, work layoff, and marital difficulties leading to separation or divorce or indifference. Many homeowners are not ready for the responsibilities of home ownership. Not only do they default in their payments, but they often allow their homes to deteriorate for want of repair. The foreclosure loss from FHA-insured loans has been

criticized. Many homeowners keep up payments until they move, but they let the property go to pieces. In many instances FHA has rehabilitated rundown property and paid for the loss.

LEGAL DOCUMENTS

Sales Agreement and Hand Money

If, after seeing a number of homes with an agent, a prospective buyer finds a home that he wishes to purchase, he may make an offer. The real estate agent will write up a tentative sales agreement (sometimes called a *binder,* an *offer,* or a *contract*) with the amount of the offer written into the agreement. The offer is usually below the listed price, but the seller seldom expects to receive the price listed. If the offer is unsatisfactory to the seller, he may make a counter offer, and bargaining may ensue until the seller and the buyer agree. When an agreement is reached concerning price, a final contract or sales agreement is in order, indicating the selling price agreed upon by the seller and the buyer, the date of transfer of the property, and other incidentals relative to the sale.

As part of the sales agreement the real estate agent will require *hand money* or *earnest money,* which may range from a few hundred dollars to a few thousand dollars, depending upon the price of the house. This sum is usually held in escrow by the real estate company or person transacting the deal. This transaction protects the seller. If the buyer should break the contract, he must be willing to forfeit the money to the seller, since he may have prevented a sale to another party. If the contract is not broken, the hand money is credited to the buyer's costs at the closing.

Abstract, or Title

An abstract is a description of the property with a history of former ownership. A lawyer will investigate this document to make sure that the new owner will have a clear title to the property.

Survey

The abstract and the deed are usually sufficient in determining land boundaries, but a survey is the best protection in any future disputes regarding paths or driveways. Although many buyers do not consider a survey necessary, a lawyer will be the best judge in helping the buyer make a decision.

Deed

The buyer's lawyer or the real estate lawyer (solicitor) will prepare the deed before the closing date. The deed is the written instrument transferring ownership. It must be signed by the buyer and the seller and their signatures witnessed and sealed by a notary public. The mortgage company usually holds the deed until the mortgage is paid, but the buyer may request a copy of the deed.

Title Insurance

Title insurance protects the buyer, and it is worth the additional cost if any of the following problems should arise: the possibility of forgeries, erroneous land descriptions, false heirs, an incompetent person making a will, or a supposedly dead person suddenly making claims. The American Land Title Association (Washington, D.C.) refers to these pitfalls as *hidden hazards* in purchasing property.

ROLE OF REAL ESTATE BROKER AND LAWYER

In some instances the owner may sell a house and save the real estate agent's commission (six percent or more). However, this may not always be wise, especially in instances where property is not selling fast. An experienced real estate agent can give the house greater exposure to prospective buyers and handle appointments, sales agreements, and other services more expeditiously than the owner. Often he can give the homeowner a larger profit than the owner can make himself. If a house is *multi-listed,* all real estate dealers in the area will be able to show it to potential buyers. Sometimes an owner will give an exclusive listing to a certain real estate firm for a short time before having the property placed on multi-list.

The real estate broker, or agent, is the middle man, or bargaining agent, in a sales transaction. The person interested in buying a home may contact one or more real estate agencies selling homes in the area of the city where the buyer may want to live. The agent will show the buyer pictures of homes with a full description of location, number and size of rooms, assessment value for tax purposes, and local and state taxes. It saves time for the buyer and the agent if the buyer can give the agent an idea of his price range, a description of his needs, and a list of preferred localities.

Liens and Easements

Many real estate deals are consummated without a personal lawyer. Lending agencies have their own solicitor or lawyer. However, the lawyer's fee may be well worth the cost to an inexperienced buyer or seller. The lawyer will be able to present precautions to take before entering into a sales agreement and see that the buyer has all the necessary legal protection, such as a clear property title as well as a properly drawn and executed abstract.

The lawyer may examine the title to make sure that it is clear. He may recommend title insurance and examine the abstract to make sure that the history of the property is correct, that there are no liens (personal charges or claims) against the property, and that there are no easement or encumberment rights which permit a third party—perhaps a utility company—to run wiring or sewers through the property. No one wants ugly power lines crossing the front of a house or holes in a lawn.

Zoning Ordinances

Either the buyer or his lawyer should look into zoning ordinances to make sure that the property will be protected from the erection of any undesirable structure in the future—a filling station or hamburger stand, for example. In areas where the size of lots, amount of setback of the house from the street, type of structure, and height of buildings are established by zoning codes, the neighborhood will be more stable. Homes located near zones termed *commercial* and *industrial* will be less desirable as residences, although such property may become valuable as a business site. If additions or improvements are anticipated in the future, it is especially important for the buyer or lawyer to look into zoning laws. Sometimes a variance (permission to break certain codes) can be obtained in the future, but one must be certain of local building codes ahead of time. In one instance a man bought an older home, obtained a building permit for remodeling, and did the job himself. When the building was inspected, the inspectors found that he had provided a dwelling for four families in an area zoned for one- and two-family dwellings. The owner had to convert the house back into a two-family dwelling, thus greatly increasing his costs.

HOME INSURANCE

Before taking possession of property, the buyer should obtain the following insurance: (1) *comprehensive personal liability insurance* to protect any member of the household in case of accident or to insure payment of bills for injuries received by any guest, stranger, or delivery person while on the property; (2) *fire, theft, and extended coverage insurance* to insure recovering some of the loss in case of fire, theft, vandalism, damage from landslides, or other falling objects, or structural collapse of any part of the building. A *homeowners's policy* for homeowners or a *tenant's package* for renters will include all types of insurance, and it is generally cheaper than separate policies. Insurance policies should be considered before the final settlement, so that the new owner will be fully protected immediately.

About 90 percent of all homes are insured against fire, but most of these homes could not be replaced for the sum collected in case of a serious fire. For example, it may cost $24,000 to replace a home originally costing $18,000 because of rising labor costs and inflation, which devaluate the dollar over 4 percent a year. In estimating income tax, your home (on paper at least) depreciates in value each year, unless you build an addition or modernize a bathroom, a kitchen, or the exterior. When improvements are made, the insurance should be increased.

Here are a few other things to think about regarding home insurance:

☐ Consider the cost of extra living expenses should the damage be extensive enough to necessitate living elsewhere during repairs.

☐ Take an inventory of all possessions, including the date when each was bought and the original cost. For an additional record, you may want to photograph areas of the house.

☐ Consider a $50- or $100-deductible clause because this will reduce your payments.

☐ Never arrange for insurance on the telephone. If you are in doubt about the reliability of an agent who comes to your home, telephone the Better Business Bureau in your community in his presence.

☐ Delay signing any papers after a fire, theft, or other casualty until you are satisfied that the adjustment is fair.

☐ Contact your insurance agent at once after a fire, theft, or other calamity.

THE CLOSING, OR SETTLEMENT

The real estate agent will arrange a date when the buyer and the seller can meet to close a sale. The buyer should be notified ahead of time concerning the amount of the closing costs. Sometimes a buyer cannot raise the several hundred or so dollars needed for all final costs, and it may be necessary to cancel the contract.

Buyer

Typical closing costs to the buyer are the following:

Title examination

Appraisal fee

Credit report (investigation of ability to pay)

Deed transfer tax (often 1 percent of the sale price to the city or borough and another 1 percent to the state; sometimes 1 percent paid by both buyer and seller)

Recording mortgage

Recording deed

Notary public fee

Prorated taxes (buyer's share of annual tax)

Prorated insurance

Preparation of necessary papers

Settlement fee

Application for liens

FHA title insurance or other title insurance

Seller

Typical closing costs to the seller are the following:

Preparation of deed

Realtor's fee (frequently 6 percent of the selling price)

Deed transfer tax

U. S. documentary stamps

Prorated taxes and insurance (Amounts are deducted from the costs if taxes and insurance were paid for the entire year.)

HUSBAND-WIFE OWNERSHIP

In generations past when women had few legal rights, *joint tenancy,* or *husband-wife ownership* of property with rights of survival, was not common. Many states did not recognize joint tenancy. Now joint ownership of property of any kind with survivorship rights is fairly common.

The *advantages* of joint tenancy probably outweigh the disadvantages for the following reasons: (1) the survivor automatically becomes full owner of the assets without waiting a long period for a legal settlement; (2) the value of property and other assets is kept private; (3) joint owners have a greater personal interest in investments; (4) legal costs and executor's fees are kept at a minimum.

The *disadvantages* are (1) a survivor may remarry, and the entire estate can pass on to the new spouse, depriving the children of the earlier marriage of their inheritance; (2) an unstable marriage with divorce a possibility may create problems.

A lawyer who is familiar with state laws concerning the disposition of property is the best judge when in doubt about joint ownership.

SUMMARY

It is advisable for the inexperienced buyer to shop around for a house and compare costs, lot size, house construction, and adequacy of space. It is also important to investigate various financing agencies for the best type of financing. It is not always best to settle with the lending institution requiring the lowest down payment because a larger down payment saves interest.

Veterans may qualify for both FHA- and VA-insured loans with low financing and a long period over which to repay the loan. However, many lenders prefer conventional loans. As a rule a penalty is charged if an FHA loan is paid off in advance, but this is not true of conventional loans.

The potential home buyer should understand the terms involved in a real estate deal, including closing costs. This is so that he can have the money on hand needed to close the transaction.

THINGS TO THINK ABOUT AND TO DO

1. Make a list of the various types of lending agencies in your area. Appoint several persons in your class to find out the terms regarding home loans at local banks, savings and loan associations, and other lending institutions.

2. From a local realtor secure several sheets illustrating and describing homes in a moderate-price range in your vicinity, and mount these sheets on the bulletin board.

3. Have two class members volunteer to make an appointment with someone in the mortgage department of a local lending institution to find out (1) the required down payment on a new $20,000 home, (2) the monthly payments on a 20-year and a 30-year mortgage at prevailing interest rates, (3) the total cost of interest on a 20- and a 30-year mortgage.

4. Discuss the advantages and disadvantages of FHA and conventional mortgages.

5. Give some reasons for foreclosures. Find out about foreclosures in your community and what happens to the property afterwards.

6. When is a sales agreement in order, and what does it include?

7. Why is a survey recommended even though the deed and abstract describe the property? Find out survey costs in your community.

8. What is title insurance, and why is it advisable to take out such insurance?

9. List all kinds of insurance policies available on a home, and discuss each. You may want to invite an insurance salesman to discuss problems of home insurance with the class.

10. Using the closing costs listed in the text, ask a real estate agent or a lawyer to indicate approximate amounts under each item for both a buyer and a seller.

Newspaper cartoons like this one have, in recent years, provided a satirical commentary on trends in the housing market. Such graphic devices can alert people to the need for making a careful, intelligent decision on buying a home.

chapter eight

BUYING
OR BUILDING
A HOME

A home is man's refuge and his castle. It can be a place of solitude and loneliness or a place of friendships and happiness. A house may have a prestige address and the most beautiful furnishings money can buy, but it is not a home if its occupants are unhappy or dissatisfied.

A home, whether it is a city apartment or a suburban ranch house, must satisfy social and personal needs. The money spent for a home must bear some relationship to income if the family is to be free of excessive financial worries. Some families are better off spending the housing dollar for rent, whereas others are happier owning a home. To a certain degree guidelines are similar either for renting or for buying an apartment or a home. However, if ownership is the goal, the location and character of the neighborhood are even more important than for renting. Renters can move when the lease expires, but homeowners have too much invested to move frequently.

The location, size, and topography of the lot, the exposure of the house, the exterior and interior finishes, and the floor plan are important considerations in looking for a home. The scarcity of land has limited the size of lots and increased the price, especially in desirable urban areas and in suburban areas near large cities. It has become so expensive to build a single-family dwelling that many families are forced to buy a unit in a multi-family building. More and more families in the expanding stage of the family life cycle are considering apartment ownership. The newer apartment buildings provide many family recreational facilities and many are built in parklike areas. Two types of apartments that may be purchased are the cooperative, dating from the 1920's, and the condominium, originating in the 1960's. In this chapter we shall discuss the location of the house, how to judge an existing house, how to judge a builder-built house in a tract development, and some of the considerations in planning and building a home, as well as owning an apartment.

GUIDELINES FOR STUDY

GENERAL IDEAS
TO CONSIDER

1. The type of lot (location, size, shape, land contour, exposure, subsoil) will influence the style, size, and cost of a house.
2. The cost of an existing house must include the buying price, closing costs, and anticipated repairs, improvements, and additions.
3. Major improvements, such as plumbing, wiring, a new kitchen, or room additions, should be in keeping with the resale value of the house and the cost of other homes in the neighborhood.
4. An understanding of architectural terms (blueprints, detail drawings, side elevations, and so forth); of construction methods; of ways of finishing walls, floors, and ceilings, and of controlling sound and humidity is essential for a home builder.
5. Advances in technology influence housing forms, function, and living patterns, but existing building codes curtail progress.

WORDS AND PHRASES
TO KNOW

balloon framework
blueprint
building code
built-up roof
casement window
ceramic tile
condominium apartment
cooperative apartment
crawl space
decibel
detail drawing
double-hung window
downspout
duofold door
elevation (drawing)
exposure
flashing
flush door
footer
gutter
gypsum board
insulation

mechanical core
millwork
mobile home
paneled door
parquet floor
perspective drawing
plywood
post and beam
scale
sheathing
shingles
slab foundation
subfloor
subsoil
symbol
tack strip
tongue and groove
topography
two-by-fours
vapor barrier
vertical section
zoning ordinance

GUIDELINES FOR LOT SELECTION

The location, size and shape, contour, and type of soil are important in lot selection. The lot also determines the exposure of the house. Zoning ordinances control the type of structure that can be built. If there are no gas, electricity, or sewer connections, these will be additional costs.

Location

Many families with children look for a location near public transportation, schools, and a local grocery store or market, so that it will not be necessary to own two cars. After children leave grade school, it is less important to be within walking distance of a school because there is usually bus service to and from large high schools. It is also less important to be within walking distance of large shopping centers and church because most family members may be able to drive or to go by public transportation to suburban shopping centers and church.

Other factors to consider in choosing a location are local provisions for trash removal; for fire and police protection; for water, sewer, electricity, and gas connections; and for recreation. Future assessments for these improvements in partly developed areas may be expensive.

NEW DEVELOPMENT. Homes in subdivisions are frequently attractive, especially if the developers have left some natural landscaping. As a rule, however, the bulldozer rips out all trees in an area where popular-priced homes are to be built. You can reduce some of the risk in investing in a home in a subdivision if you do the following: (1) Judge the housing division by its lower-priced homes, not its higher-priced ones, because these establish the real value of the division. (2) Buy in a subdivision near an older well-established neighborhood or in the direction in which the community is expanding. (3) Buy one of the medium- or lower-priced homes. (4) Avoid buying where the down payment is very low or where there is no down payment because homes in these areas may change hands frequently as families fail to keep up payments and the property becomes run down. (5) Avoid buying a home near a fire station, a filling station, or too near a public playground.

ESTABLISHED NEIGHBORHOOD. If you are buying a home in an established neighborhood, you will want to take a close look at other existing homes. Your investment in an established neighborhood will probably be safe if lawns and backyards are well kept, if exterior finishes are in good condition, and if the majority of the homes are owner occupied. If a number of homes in the area are for sale, you should find out the reason.

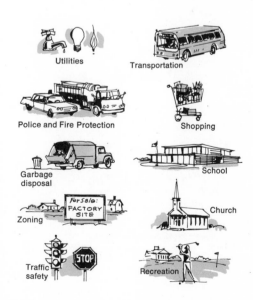

Utilities　　　　Transportation

Police and Fire Protection　　　　Shopping

Garbage disposal　　　　School

Zoning　　For Sale: FACTORY SITE　　　Church

Traffic safety　　STOP　　　Recreation

TWO-STORY HOUSE
Lot coverage: 725 sq.ft.
Living area: 1200 sq. ft.

RANCH-TYPE HOUSE
Lot coverage: 1344 sq. ft.
Living area: 1200 sq. ft.

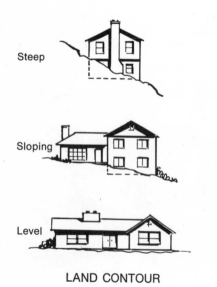

Steep

Sloping

Level

LAND CONTOUR

Size and Shape of Lot

The size and shape of a lot will determine the type of house that can be built on it. A rectangular lot should be a *minimum of 50 feet wide.* Each foot over 50 feet in width and over 100 feet in depth increases the value of the lot in a good neighborhood. Desirable lot sizes are as follows: 50 feet by 100 feet, *fair;* 60 feet by 125 feet, *good;* and 75 feet by 150 feet, *excellent.* However, attractive homes are being built on much smaller lots. In areas where land is scarce and high in price, architects can plan two-story rather than ranch-type houses (see the illustration on this page) on 60-foot by 100-foot lots.

Odd-shaped lots are less desirable than rectangular lots unless the area of the house can be related to the area of the lot. Corner lots have advantages and disadvantages. There is greater freedom in locating a house for good exposure on a corner lot, but assessments for street improvements, such as sewer installation and sidewalks, may be doubled. There also may be more snow to shovel off sidewalks in winter.

Topography

The topography is important for two reasons. First, both surface and underground water, if there is any from springs, should be free to drain away from the homesite. A damp basement can be a nuisance as well as an expense. Second, the topography of the land will influence the design of the house. A one-story house is best adapted to level land; a split-level house, to sloping land. If the land is steep, a half story may be on the lower level with a full story on the upper level.

Soil and Subsoil

The soil and subsoil should be ascertained before buying a lot on which to

SUN CONTROLS

Awnings   Trees   Overhangs

CONSIDERATIONS IN SOLAR ORIENTATION

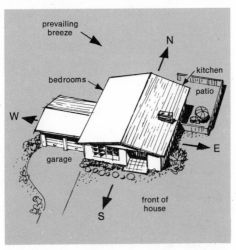

build. If there is limestone below the surface, the expense of excavating for a basement may be great. If the lot is marshy or underlaid with quicksand, it may be difficult to lay a foundation. If the area is over an abandoned coal mine, there may be danger of erosion.

Exposure

The exposure will influence the design of the house. If a terrace or a patio is to be enjoyed, it should not be located on the west where it will receive the hot afternoon sun. A living room exposed to strong north winds may be uncomfortable in winter. The term *solar orientation* means placing a house in relation to the sun. A southern exposure for the major areas of the house is the most desirable because with this exposure in the living areas of the house the sun gives warmth and light in winter and shade can be controlled in summer. See the illustration on this page.

Zoning Ordinances

Zoning ordinances determine the types of structures that can be built in certain areas. The most expensive locations call for single-family dwellings with adequate side yards. On locations termed *boulevards,* apartment buildings and shops may be erected. Areas zoned *industrial* or *commercial* are not desirable for home locations. Sometimes such property is bought on speculation for future resale at a high price to a business or industrial firm.

GUIDELINES FOR JUDGING AN EXISTING HOUSE

Sales of existing houses are about double the sales of new houses. In the mid-sixties, the average price paid for an existing house was $17,300, whereas $22,000 was the average price paid for a new house.

The best way to judge an existing house is to have a contractor or an architect go over it and give you an opinion. He will tell you where the bearing walls, or walls that support the house load, are located so that you may avoid expensive changes in these areas should major changes be necessary or desirable. He will also be able to explain where you can put in a powder room or a new bathroom or kitchen without adding too much new plumbing installation. He should also be able to evaluate the heating system and the adequacy of the wiring.

It is important to inquire about state and local taxes, insurance costs, and heating or heating-and-cooling bills.

Here are some special features to check on the exterior of an existing house:

1. *Roof:* Check for loose shingles, loose tile, or worn spots in a built-up roof (one made of several layers of paper, tar, and fine gravel).

2. *Chimney:* Note the condition of the chimney. Bricks and mortar should be in good repair. If the flashing (metal used for waterproofing) around the chimney is loose, water may leak into the house.

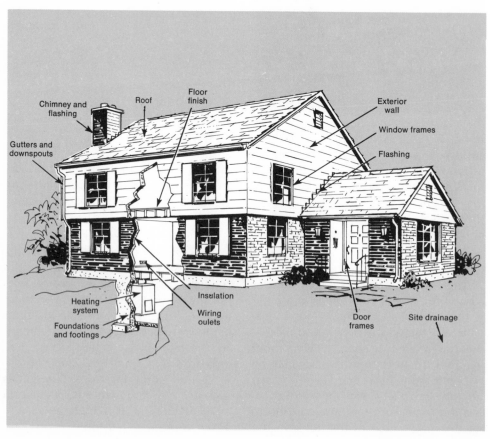

3. *Foundations and footers:* If there are severe cracks at the corners of the building, and if floors creak or appear to be uneven inside the house, the foundation may be weakening and the cost of improvements may be prohibitive.

4. *Gutters and downspouts:* Gutters and downspouts must be in good shape and be free of leaves, or they will clog up and overflow, or they may even crack open in winter.

5. *Doors and windows:* Doors and windows should have a good surface finish and fit tightly.

6. *Exterior finish:* If the exterior is brick, check the caulking around the bricks to make sure that little pointing (or new caulking) will be necessary. If the exterior is painted, make sure that the finish is not peeling or blistering.

7. *Insulation:* Make sure that the walls are insulated to prevent moisture condensation, that floors above unheated garages and porches are insulated, and that the roof has insulation as well as good ventilation.

Check these features in the interior of an existing house:

1. *Basement:* There are two things to look for in the basement—dampness and termites. Notice the floor and corner walls to make sure that they are dry, and notice wood joists to make sure there is no evidence of termites.

2. *Inside walls and ceilings:* Note not only the condition of the ceilings and walls but also the wall space available for furniture arrangement.

3. *Windows:* Look for well-fitted easy-to-operate windows. Weather stripping will save heating and cooling bills. Inquire whether screens, shutters, storm windows, shades, and the like are included in the sale price.

4. *Convenience outlets and switches:* Check the walls for switches at doors and for convenience outlets at least 3 to 4 feet apart or at special places where you will need them.

5. *Floors:* Note condition of wood floors where used, of resilient tile floors in the kitchen or bathroom, and also of concrete floors in the basement.

6. *Kitchen:* In older homes, kitchens often have to be remodeled. This may mean new plumbing and wiring as well as new cabinets and equipment. It is wise to get some cost estimates if remodeling is anticipated.

7. *Stairways:* Inside stairways should have 7- to 8-inch risers and 10-inch treads. All stairways should have handrails and a light switch at the top and bottom of the stairs.

8. *Storage:* Make sure there are sufficiently large storage closets near entrances and bathrooms and in bedrooms. A storage wall or pantry in or near the kitchen, in addition to cabinets, facilitates housekeeping.

In a house today, unlike one fifty years ago, a third of the purchase investment is tied up in mechanical equipment—central heating; plumbing for the bathroom, kitchen, and laundry; and wiring for lighting and electrical appliances. These items have become necessities, whereas many of them were above the expectations of the average family during the first quarter of this century.

Check these features in the mechanical core when judging a house:

1. *Wiring:* Note the electric lines leading into the house. (Consult Chapter Ten.) Inquire about wiring for special equipment, such as a washer, dryer, dishwasher, or large air conditioner.

2. *Heating:* Find out the age and condition of the heating unit as well as its kind of operation. If you are considering central air conditioning, find out the cost. Ask the owner about annual heating bills.

3. *Plumbing:* Copper piping is preferable, although some newer homes have plastic pipes. Iron pipes will erode. Turn on all faucets, and note any stopper leaks and the speed at which the water disappears down the drain. Flush toilets and immediately turn on the water to note any change in pressure. Look for accessible shut-off valves under sinks and other fixtures.

GUIDELINES FOR REMODELING

Your family may buy a house with the thought of remodeling it, or you may already own a house which you would like to remodel. The most frequent remodeling jobs include the addition of a bedroom, a bathroom or powder room, a recreation or family room, or a new kitchen. A new heating system is expensive. Central air conditioning is usually prohibitive in older houses because it is too expensive to insulate adequately walls, ceilings, floors, and windows. Through-the-wall room air conditioners are more satisfactory and more attractive than window units, but they are more expensive to install.

Remodeling may be advisable under the following conditions: (1) The house is structurally sound. (2) It is not in need of an entirely new heating system and all new plumbing (unless the quality of the structure and the character of the neighborhood justify the costs). (3) The cost of remodeling does not exceed more than half of the purchase price (unless the family can afford to invest more than is wise, simply for family enjoyment and regardless of resale value). (4) The cost of purchase and remodeling will not place the house in a price range far above other homes in the neighborhood.

Some people who are experienced in carpenter work, in painting, and in laying parquet floors or tile can save a great deal of expense by doing these jobs. Such work as wiring, heating, and plumbing calls for professionals. The person who wishes to remodel a home should have an architect draw up plans if changes are elaborate. Either the owner, the architect, or the contractor will have to obtain a building permit before remodeling is attempted, and plans must conform to local codes.

GUIDELINES FOR BUILDING

The home builder who expects to work intelligently with an architect in planning a home should understand basic styles, building plans and terminology, foundation construction, exterior and interior wall and ceiling finishes, and flooring, roofing, and millwork terms. This section will be helpful in building a new house or in judging a new developer-built house.

Basic Models

There are four basic models: two-story, split-level, split-entry, and ranch. (See illustrations, pages 124–125.) These models may be had in many sizes, a variety of floor plans, and a choice of exterior design—contemporary, Colonial, French Provincial, Spanish Colonial, and so on.

Building Plans

The following is a list of terms that are necessary in understanding plans:
☐ *Blueprints, or working drawings:* A set of scale drawings that show actual measurements of floor plans, elevations, and necessary details
☐ *Perspective drawing:* A pen-and-ink drawing that depicts the home with proposed walks, drives, and landscaping
☐ *Scale:* A unit of measurement to show the plans in exact proportion

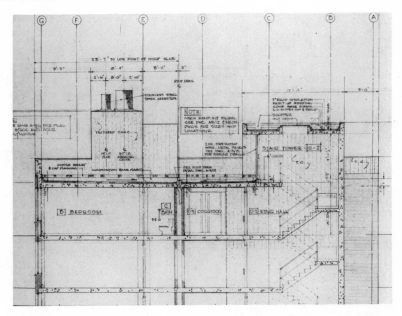

An elevation of an apartment house.

□ *Floor plans:* A layout of each story, indicating room arrangements and room sizes, fireplaces (if any), closets, halls, windows, and entrances

□ *Elevations:* Line drawings that show front, side, and rear views of a house with windows, doors, porches, and chimneys included

□ *Vertical section:* A drawing that shows any part of the house as it would look if you could see through it

□ *Detail drawing:* A drawing that shows an enlarged view of construction details, such as fireplaces, stairways, bookcases, or special features

□ *Landscaped drawing:* A drawing (usually in color) that shows the location of the house on the land with suggested walks, driveways, shrubbery, and other plantings

□ *Symbols:* Abbreviated pictures that represent outlets for gas, electricity, telephone, and television; placement of doors and windows and of plumbing, heating, and cooling fixtures; and type of materials to be used

Foundations

Houses are built on *slab foundations,* over *crawl space,* and over *basements.* Reinforced concrete *footers* must be used under all foundations to support bearing walls, or the walls that carry the house load.

SLAB FOUNDATION. The concrete-slab foundation is used for one-story houses where the ground is level and where underground water may create a water problem in a basement. If a slab foundation is used, it is important to provide for adequate storage facilities, heating ducts, water lines, and plumbing fixtures within one story. Adjustments in these areas will be costly after the concrete foundation is laid. Formerly a concrete floor limited the choice of floor coverings, but new materials and new methods of laying traditional materials have expanded choices. Many but not all resilient floor coverings can be laid on grade level (a floor of ground level). The tack-strip method of laying carpeting makes it possible to lay carpet

SPLIT-LEVEL HOUSE
Living area: 1472 sq. ft.

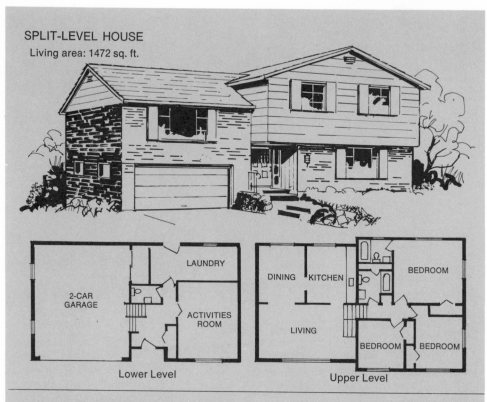

LAUNDRY

2-CAR
GARAGE

ACTIVITIES
ROOM

Lower Level

DINING   KITCHEN

BEDROOM

LIVING

BEDROOM   BEDROOM

Upper Level

SPLIT-ENTRY HOUSE
Living area: 1140 sq. ft.

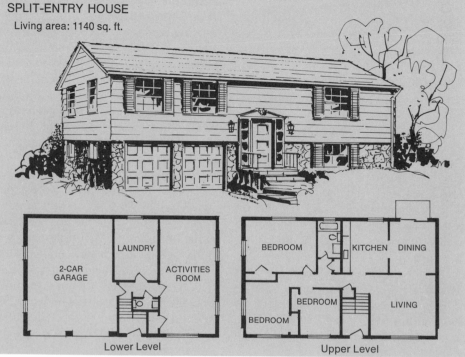

LAUNDRY

2-CAR
GARAGE

ACTIVITIES
ROOM

Lower Level

BEDROOM   KITCHEN   DINING

BEDROOM

LIVING

BEDROOM

Upper Level

TWO-STORY HOUSE

Living area: 1010 sq. ft.

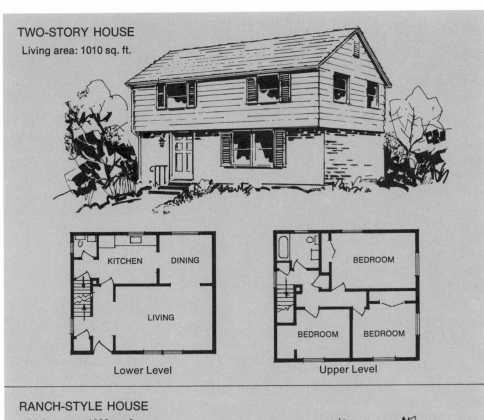

KITCHEN   DINING

LIVING

Lower Level

BEDROOM

BEDROOM   BEDROOM

Upper Level

RANCH-STYLE HOUSE

Living area: 1200 sq. ft.

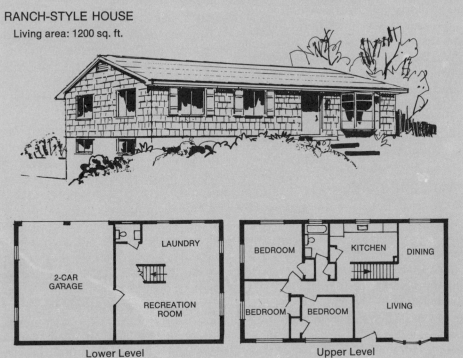

2-CAR GARAGE

LAUNDRY

RECREATION ROOM

Lower Level

BEDROOM   KITCHEN   DINING

BEDROOM   BEDROOM   LIVING

Upper Level

on a concrete floor. A tack strip is a strip of wood about the width of a yardstick with short needles to grip the edges of the carpet and hold it in place. Steel runners, anchored to concrete, make it possible to lay oak flooring so that it looks as though it is laid over a wood subfloor. Wood blocks, resembling parquet floors, may also be laid over concrete.

CRAWL SPACE. A house built over crawl space is raised several feet off the ground—high enough for a person to crawl under the floor to repair heating and plumbing installations. Insulation is not always used above the crawl space in temperate climates, but it is recommended in cold climates. Wood flooring or subflooring is generally used for houses with crawl space.

BASEMENT FOUNDATION. A basement is desirable, especially if a lot slopes from a flat area at the front to a depth of six or eight feet at the rear. A basement may provide space for storage, for recreation, and for laundry equipment. On sloping land the basement walls may be higher on one side than the other. It is preferable to face above-ground-level side elevations with brick or siding materials to match the exterior walls. The provision for flooring over a basement foundation is the same as for crawl space.

Walls and Framework

Walls that hold up the house are constructed by three methods: (1) conventional or balloon frames, (2) post-and-beam construction, and (3) concrete-block construction.

In the conventional method 2-inch by 4-inch boards are nailed to joists at the floor and ceiling at 16-inch intervals. When window walls became popular, the conventional method was unsatisfactory because the span was too wide

for adequate support of these large windows. Post-and-beam construction provides for wide spaces between upright supports or studs. Concrete-block construction is increasing in popularity in warm and temperate climates and where central air conditioning is to be used. Concrete-block walls have advantages over wood because they are more soundproof and fireproof. However, conventional wall construction is more popular in colder climates because there is less moisture condensation inside the home.

In large buildings steel and reinforced concrete or concrete poured over iron or steel is used in the construction.

Wall and Ceiling Finishes

OUTSIDE WALLS. Exterior walls may be covered with a number of materials— wood, plastic, steel, or aluminum siding; stone or brick veneer; wood or asbestos shingles; or vertical tongue-and-groove boards. (See the illustration on page 131.) As already indicated, exterior walls may be constructed of concrete block or poured concrete, and glass is popular. As a rule for appearance' sake no more than two materials should be combined on outside walls.

Wood siding costs less than plastic, steel, or aluminum siding, and wood is less noisy during a rain. However, the limited length of wood boards means piecing, whereas plastic and metal siding may be cut any length. Wood must be painted at regular intervals, or it will decay. Masonry materials, such as stone, brick, and slate, require little maintenance, but the initial cost is high. Painted concrete or cinder-block exterior walls are popular in southern climates. However, they are less popular in northern climates because changing temperatures sometimes create moisture condensation that causes paint to peel.

Glass walls are popular in homes where there is a view. In order to reduce heating bills, insulated glass (two pieces of glass laminated with a film between) should be used, and in order to be safe, the glass should be shatterproof. When glass walls are used, the room must be protected from the sun by extending the roof (see page 119). Electronic glass, whereby the sun's rays can be controlled, is being used in expensive homes, but it is too costly as yet for general application.

INSIDE WALLS. Inside walls may be finished with plaster, wallboard, sheetrock (plain or wood-grain finish), ceramic tile, or wall paneling. Inside concrete-block walls may be plastered or left plain and painted. Plaster is also applied over a ⅜-inch gypsum lathboard, and it gives an excellent finish. However, plaster is messy, and it cannot be painted until it is thoroughly dry, which may take a very long time unless the temperature is warm and the humidity is low. Some people prefer to tint plaster rather than wait for plaster to dry and then be painted. When the tinted walls become soiled, they may be painted at the occupant's convenience. Plaster sometimes cracks as the house settles and may need patching. This is another good reason for postponing painting. Plasterboard (referred to as *dry wall*) is a less expensive substitute for plaster and requires no drying time. Plasterboards are butted together and nailed to the upright studs. Nail holes are filled in, and the seams are covered with tape before painting. Smooth plaster or plasterboard walls may be papered or painted.

BASEMENT WALLS. Basement walls below ground level require special treatment before the earth is filled in to prevent dampness in the finished basement. During construction the masonry should be made as watertight as possible on the outside and the inside. If the basement walls are made of cement or concrete

THREE TYPES OF WALL CONSTRUCTION

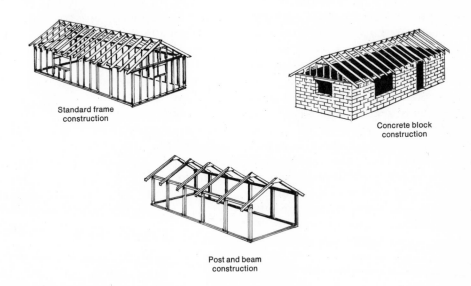

Standard frame
construction

Concrete block
construction

Post and beam
construction

block, they may be finished inside with a special concrete paint. If wood paneling, plasterboard, or sheetrock is desired, the walls must be furred in first—that is, strips of wood must be nailed along the floor and ceiling to which upright 2-inch by 4-inch boards are nailed at 16-inch intervals. There are special nails for nailing concrete. A *vapor barrier* or insulation material should be placed between the wall and the wallboard finish in order to absorb moisture.

CEILINGS. Ceilings may be treated with any of the materials used for inside walls, except ceramic tile. In hallways and recreation rooms it is advisable to use acoustic tile for the ceiling. Acoustic tile comes in a number of sizes and patterns, and it may be used in any room of the house. It is recommended especially for family rooms and recreation rooms.

Millwork

Windows of all kinds, framed and ready to set in the framework of the house, and interior and exterior doors come under the term *millwork.* Interior baseboards, closet fixtures, kitchen cabinets, and stairways are also millwork items. All of these items are pretreated and ready for paint or varnish.

WINDOWS. Windows are available with wood, aluminum, or steel frames. Because it is a nonconductor of heat and cold, wood adapts itself well to cold climates. Where there is a great deal of moisture or the possibility of termites, wood is less desirable. Aluminum and steel have won acceptance in temperate and warm climates. Marble windowsills are popular in all climates, but the initial expense is high. In order to save fuel, windows need to be weather-stripped in temperate climates, and in colder climates, storm windows

need to be used—at least on the windy side of the house.

Windows come in many styles. *Double-hung* windows are the most commonly used. *Awning-type* and *ranch* windows in single or multiple design are used more frequently in contemporary homes. *Casement* windows are used in all types of houses. These are shown in the illustration on page 244.

DOORS. As a rule paneled doors are used in traditional homes; and flush doors, in contemporary homes. The Dutch door, or double door, is used in some Early American designs. Louvered doors are frequently used for closets and as swinging doors between the kitchen and pantry, hall, or dining room. Louvered closet doors ventilate the closet, but they also let in dirt. Duofold closet doors, when opened, make the entire closet available for use, but they project into the floor area. Sliding doors expose only one section at a time, but they do not project into the room.

Roofing

Before the roof finish is applied, the studs, or supports, are covered with wood sheathing and with an underlay of roll roofing made of asphalt or saturated felt. The sheathing lends rigidity, and the underlay acts as a wind and moisture barrier.

Roofing materials include asphalt shingles, cedar shingles and shakes, asbestos tile, slate shingles, and aluminum shingles. On a flat or low slope, a built-up roof with chips or gravel is used. Wood, asbestos, and asphalt shingles are used to cover sloping roofs. On heavy sloping roofs, tile or slate is often used.

A built-up roof is not used if the roof has more than a slight pitch because the gravel used in building up the roof will wash off. A built-up roof consists of layers of roofing felt (three to five layers) covered with fine gravel, which is adhered with a tar compound. Even though a drain and downspout take off rain and melted snow from a flat built-up roof, a great deal of moisture may remain on the roof if rains continue and if the roof is not slightly slanted toward the drain.

Insulation

Insulation is important in keeping out drafts and reducing heating bills in cold climates and cooling bills in warm climates. If electric heating and cooling are used, the house should be completely insulated. In cold climates specifications call for 3-inch insulation in inside walls and in floors over a crawl space and for 6-inch insulation in the ceiling. In temperate climates ceiling insulation should be 3 inches; side-wall insulation, 2 inches; and slab foundation, 1¼ inches. With a slab foundation a 2-inch rigid insulation strip is required around the perimeter of the floor set in from outside walls a distance of 1½ to 2 feet. In conventional construction insulation is used as a vapor barrier between the inside and the outside walls in order to absorb moisture and thus to prevent outside paint from peeling.

Insulation comes in roll, batt, board, and bulk forms. Some sheathing materials for roofs have an insulation backing. Bulk insulation may be blown or poured between ceiling rafters or wall studs; roll and batt insulation is laid in place or attached with a staple gun.

Insulating materials between inside walls in the home provide an excellent sound barrier—especially when a bathroom wall is adjacent to the living room, or a kitchen wall is adjacent to a bedroom. Sheet cork makes a good insulator

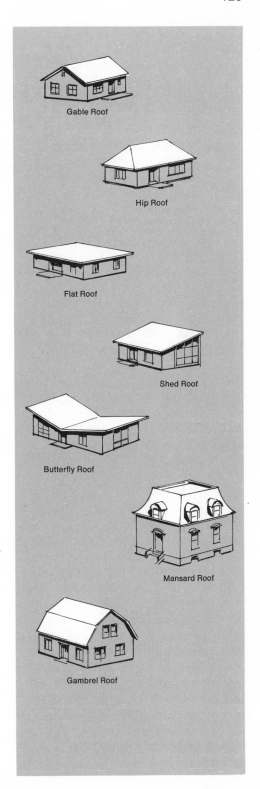

Gable Roof

Hip Roof

Flat Roof

Shed Roof

Butterfly Roof

Mansard Roof

Gambrel Roof

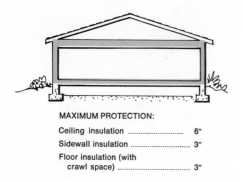

MAXIMUM PROTECTION:

Ceiling insulation .... 6″

Sidewall insulation .... 3″

Floor insulation (with
   crawl space) .... 3″

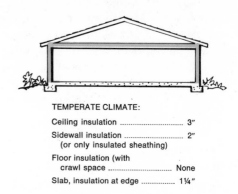

TEMPERATE CLIMATE:

Ceiling insulation .... 3″

Sidewall insulation .... 2″
   (or only insulated sheathing)

Floor insulation (with
   crawl space .... None

Slab, insulation at edge .... 1¼″

when installed underneath flooring or behind gypsum wallboard. It comes in rolls 4 feet wide and 100 feet long. It can be stapled or laminated into place. If a house has an attic, the space over the ceiling should be insulated; if the roof is flat, the roof should be insulated; and if the house has no basement, the floors should be insulated. The accompanying illustrations show where and how to insulate.

Noise Control

Noise has become such a problem that some housing codes now include specifications for sound control. Advances in technology have increased noises inside and outside the home. Television, hi-fi, dishwashers, food disposers, vacuum cleaners, and other laborsaving equipment have made the home as noisy as a factory. Airplanes, buses, trains, automobiles, motorcycles, power lawn mowers, and in some instances motorboats create a constant hum outdoors. The noise and vibrations of the sonic boom (noise created when planes travel faster than sound) are forcing offices and schools to be constructed underground in some areas.

The principal of an eighteen-room underground school in Lake Worth, Texas, stated that he would not change his underground school for anything. The sonic boom has been a greater nuisance near large airfields than elsewhere.

Noise is measured in terms of decibels. A decibel is the smallest degree of sound difference detected by the human ear. Accordingly the rustle of leaves registers about 10 decibels; a whisper, about 20; average office noises, about 50; ordinary conversation, about 60; noises in crowded restaurants, at large receptions, and at benefit parties, 80 or more decibels. The exhaust of a big jet at a distance of fifty feet makes a noise of 135 or more decibels. If a person is constantly exposed to noises of 120 decibels, damage may be caused to the inner ear or that person may suffer physical or emotional disorder. It is becoming customary for owners of large apartment buildings to advertise that noises never exceed 45 decibels, a fairly tolerable amount of noise. The Federal Housing Administration plans to include noise control in its building codes.

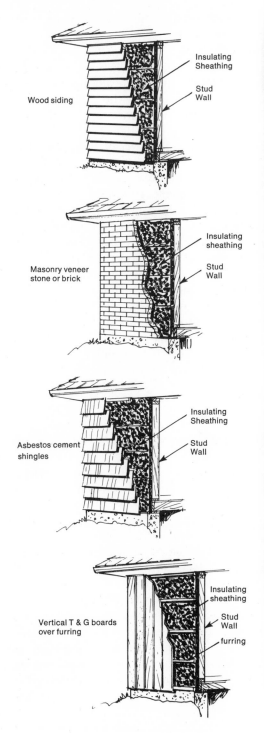

Wood siding

Insulating
Sheathing

Stud
Wall

Masonry veneer
stone or brick

Insulating
sheathing

Stud
Wall

Asbestos cement
shingles

Insulating
Sheathing

Stud
Wall

Vertical T & G boards
over furring

Insulating
sheathing

Stud
Wall

furring

Installing insulation.

It is possible to reduce unpleasant noises by observing the following recommendations: (1) Stagger the studs in walls, so that insulation materials can be laced between studs before applying lath and plaster. (This means making the walls six inches thick instead of the usual four inches.) (2) If conventional four-inch walls are used, place batts of insulation between the studs. (3) If bathrooms are back to back, use insulation and stagger the fixtures, especially the toilets because toilet noises are sometimes amplified from room to room. (4) Select toilets with a silent flush mechanism. (5) If a hot-water heating system is used, install separate return ducts, and if hot air is used, look for a quiet blower. (6) Install acoustic tile or acoustic plaster in the ceilings. (7) Use wall-to-wall carpeting and lined draw draperies. (8) Look for air conditioners, disposers, dishwashers, lawn mowers, and other motorized equipment with quiet motors.

Cutting Costs in Building

The following suggestions will cut building costs considerably:

☐ Build a rectangular two-story house. As a rule this type of structure costs less than a ranch or a split-level house.

☐ Limit the amount of grading, filling, and excavating as well as the length of driveways and walks and the number of steps.

☐ Use local building materials and local labor. If materials and workmen are imported for any distance, costs mount rapidly.

☐ Use prefabricated components, such as windows, doors, wall siding, flooring, roof trusses, and baseboard.

☐ Use standard plumbing and wiring installations.

☐ Avoid using many special windows, such as dormers, and special paneled doors because they require more labor to produce.

☐ Consider initial costs as well as maintenance. It may be less expensive in the long run to use aluminum siding, which is expensive but which needs very little maintenance, rather than wood siding.

☐ Consider the area of the country in relation to the framework of the house and the type of windows. For example, a concrete-block house with metal window frames may not be desirable in climates where winters are very cold and summers are very hot. Conventional framework and wood window frames will produce less moisture condensation in the walls and on the windows.

☐ Use a slab floor or a crawl space if the substratum is stone and expensive to excavate or if the land is moisture ridden, requiring expensive wall construction for a basement.

Technological Advances in Building Materials

Every few years the National Association of Home Builders (NAHB) constructs a research house to test new building techniques. Research House No. 6 was completed in Montgomery County, Maryland, in 1966. The object of the research is to test new materials and to discover means of reducing building costs and methods of providing a stronger structural system. Reports on the feasibility of using various materials and methods are made over a period of three years. Builders take advantage of the findings when they undertake new construction. However, building codes are slow to change and many tested innovations are generally prohibited. Consumer resistance to new ideas, as well as building codes, has sometimes deterred building progress.

It is impossible for the average consumer to appraise new building materials and construction processes. But at the same time it is important for a consumer who wishes to build or remodel to discuss new ideas with architects and contractors.

The concept of prefabrication, or off-site construction, has prevailed in many areas of housing. Among newer applications of off-site construction is the installation of plumbing and wiring systems prefabricated into the walls.

Plastics in many forms have found wide use in the building trades. Plastics are used for plumbing pipes and joints, for siding for outside walls, for gutters and downspouts, and for coating wood paneling and wood window frames on the outside.

Steel, popular as a building material in large structures for nearly a century, is used in the foundation and framework construction of homes, for outside clapboard, and for framing doors and windows, but steel is expensive for the average home builder. Steel foundation girders may be used over a far greater foundation span than wood.

Aluminum, durable and easy to maintain, has many home construction uses. It is used for insulation, for screen-storm doors and windows, for gutters and downspouts, for awnings, for railings and shutters, and as a vapor barrier.

Many of the newer building materials cost more than traditional materials, but gradual acceptance is increasing the supply and helping to reduce costs.

APARTMENT OWNERSHIP

The Cooperative Apartment

During the 1920's America imported a European apartment concept—the cooperative apartment. In cooperative apartments, tenants own shares in the business venture, and a board, elected by the shareholders, makes the rules governing management. The first cooperative apartment in the United States was erected by members of the Amalgamated Clothing Workers' Union in 1926. Thereafter a number of similar projects met with failure, and it was not until after World War II that the cooperative-apartment concept spread.

The cooperative apartment has some advantages over renting: (1) the landlord's profit is eliminated; (2) taxes and interest are deductible in income tax; (3) an equity or savings is built up; (4) a permanent home is guaranteed; (5) owners may make decisions about maintenance and services.

On the other hand, the cooperative apartment has disadvantages: (1) the down payment may be high; (2) property value may depreciate if the neighborhood changes; (3) a management board may not always be as easy to deal with as a single manager; (4) there is less independence in selling an apartment unit than in selling a home because the management board must approve all transactions; (5) expenses can increase if the management board votes to increase improvements and services.

The Condominium Unit

The Housing Act of 1968 (mentioned in Chapter Three) provided for another type of apartment ownership—the *condominium*, an apartment unit in a multi-family building. These apartments, the purchase of which may be financed through the Federal Housing Administration (FHA), are unlike a home on a lot and are sometimes referred to as *parcels of space*. The cost of a condominium under the Housing Act of 1968 was limited to $25,000, and the maximum loan maturity was set at

thirty years. Under condominium ownership the owner pays taxes, insurance,
and utilities and in addition a monthly
fee to the management office for maintenance of the outside of the building
and grounds.

The FHA points out some differences
between cooperative and condominium
apartments:

☐ In the *cooperative* apartment the
tenants own shares of stock with the
right to occupy a specified unit. In the
condominium the tenant has the title
to the unit, and in addition to his own
unit he may own up to three other
units.

☐ In the *cooperative* apartment the
occupants of each unit have only one
vote regardless of the size of the unit.
In the *condominium* owners vote on a
proportionate basis.

☐ Under *cooperative* ownership taxes
are included in the monthly carrying
charges. *Condominium* owners pay taxes
in the same way as they would in buying
a home, usually with the mortgage
payments until the mortgage is paid
and afterwards when tax bills are due.

☐ In the *cooperative* apartment the
entire project must remain solvent or
the individual owner may be responsible
for cooperative debts. In the *condominium* the tenant is responsible only
for his own mortgage payment and
taxes, and his share of management
debts.

SUMMARY

No one can expect to find satisfaction in selecting a home without having
some kind of guides to follow. Renter and buyer have some guidelines in common, but the buyer has a far greater responsibility because a home usually represents the largest investment of a lifetime, and it is not easy to move when things
go wrong. The stability of the neighborhood is a prime consideration in buying
a home. Ordinances, zoning codes, and provision for utilities should be investi-
gated before making a purchase. A home in a neighborhood where home ownership is general or in a new development situated in the direction in which the
city is expanding is likely to appreciate in value.

The size of the lot and the location of the home on the lot will affect the
desirability and the comfort of the house. The contour of the land will influence
the style of the home; it will affect the drainage of both surface and underground
water. The character of the subsoil will influence the kind of foundation. If a
location is desirable and the lot has an existing home, the buyer should have a
contractor or an architect check the foundation, exterior and interior walls of
the house, wiring, heating (and cooling), and plumbing.

The potential home builder will gain valuable experience by observing homes
under construction.

In addition to buying an existing home or building a home, there is a choice
of buying a cooperative or a condominium apartment.

THINGS TO THINK ABOUT AND TO DO

1. Find out the size of some of the lots in your neighborhood. This information will be included in the abstract to the property or in the county tax assessor's office. Or secure a number of multi-list sheets of houses for sale in your area, and compare the lot sizes with recommendations given in the text.

2. On the chalkboard list in order of importance the factors under lot selection mentioned on pages 117–119 in the text. Can you add other factors?

3. Weigh the advantages and disadvantages of buying a new home located in a suburban development and buying an existing home in a well-established suburban neighborhood.

4. What are some important considerations in judging an existing house?

5. In groups of three or four, visit homes advertised for sale, and check the location and the exterior appearance. You may want to develop a scorecard in class for judging these houses. Discuss your findings in class.

6. Check the interior of your own apartment or house with your parents and list possible improvements.

7. Report to class on a remodeling job you know about in terms of satisfaction and cost.

8. Find out how to interpret the symbols on a blueprint of a house, and discuss these with the class.

9. Discuss the uses and the advantages and disadvantages of the three types of foundations mentioned—slab, crawl space, and basement.

10. In teams of two or three study a block of homes in any convenient location. Note the kind of exterior, type of windows and doors, and the presence or absence of storm windows or screens, porches, railings, and the like. Discuss in class.

11. Visit a millwork showroom, and observe the items that can be purchased ready to install.

12. Find out what types of roofing materials are most popular in your area and why.

13. Discuss the kinds of insulation and their uses. Display various types.

14. Indicate ways you can reduce noise in a new home and in your present home.

15. Make a list of new materials used in home building, and tell where each may be used.

16. Explain the differences between *co-operative* and *condominium* apartments.

17. Show as many of the films listed on page 183 as time permits. Discuss.

chapter nine

KITCHEN AND LAUNDRY ARRANGEMENTS, STORAGE SPACE

Few people remember the old-fashioned rural kitchen so very typical of American homes during the early part of this century. Sounds and smells, as well as furnishings, combined to give the kitchen a character all its own.

The water from a single faucet in the sink dripped rhythmically into a washbasin below; the fire in the big iron stove crackled merrily; the floor boards groaned under the vibration of the rocker; and the clock on the wall ticked away the passing hours. All kinds of tantalizing odors emerged from homemade treats stored in crocks and jars behind cupboard doors. Occasionally the water basin under the wooden icebox overflowed and trickled silently over the linoleum. The small light bulb dangling from a single cord in the ceiling was not always dependable as a source of light.

Nevertheless, the kitchen was the pulse of the home. Family members washed at the kitchen sink before meals and bathed, with some degree of privacy, in a round tub placed near the stove every Saturday afternoon. On winter evenings members of the family congregated in the kitchen to prepare food, eat supper, study, mend, crack nuts, and play games until it was time to scurry off to chilly bedrooms.

Some time during the latter part of the first quarter of this century, social and economic progress began to change this familiar and comfortable scene. Gradually we became a society of city dwellers living in more compact homes, centrally heated and provided with indoor plumbing. Kitchens became small and less personal. There was no place for the rocking chair and family gatherings. Electricity or gas made the coal stove and wooden icebox obsolete. Packaged food in airtight containers sealed in all tempting odors. During the 1930's the kitchen became a subject for scientific research. Kitchens with stark white metal cabinets, ranges, and refrigerators became so stereotyped that in the 1930's and 1940's they

137

resembled hospital clinics. However, as research continued, kitchen planners became aware of the need not only for efficiency and convenience but for beauty as well.

Even though the kitchen has changed, it is still the center from which many activities must be controlled, especially during the early stages in the family life cycle. Its location and arrangement are important to good management and pleasant family relations.

Laundries have undergone change also. Washtubs, washboards, hand wringers, clothes boilers, and clotheslines are becoming collector's items. Automation and fabric engineering to reduce the need for ironing have changed former concepts of laundering equipment and procedure. A washer and dryer can be stacked in a small closet to take care of the laundry needs of many families.

As basements and attics have been eliminated, more thought must be given to storage needs in modern homes. With an attic, a basement, and perhaps a spare bedroom, there was always some place to put items not in daily use. Few homes had built-in closets, so that two storage pieces of furniture were considered essential for the bedroom—a long, low chest with a lid for bedding and a tall, narrow wardrobe for clothing. People had fewer clothes and less need for them, since activities outside the home were limited. There was less need for closet storage both for clothing and for other items than there is now.

Working wives and mothers today would find it even more difficult to fill two roles if progress in home planning did not keep pace with progress in general .

Regardless of whether she fills two roles, today's homemaker wants a kitchen that is as attractive, efficient, and convenient as possible and storage areas and a laundry that will best serve a family's needs. This chapter will examine general kitchen requirements, suggested layouts, and space standards, as well as laundry recommendations and storage needs.

GUIDELINES FOR STUDY

GENERAL IDEAS
TO CONSIDER

1. The kitchen is the control center in the home while children are young, thus making its location important in relation to play areas, the laundry, other rooms in the house, and entries where daily deliveries are made.
2. Easily maintained surfaces in the kitchen and bathroom reduce the home-maker's fatigue.
3. A multipurpose kitchen will help the homemaker dovetail hobbies, recreation, and other duties with her meal-preparation work.

4. The decision to have a home laundry and where to place it will depend upon the stage in the family life cycle, the layout of the house, and attitudes toward doing laundry at home.

5. The trend toward eliminating basements and attics makes it more important to plan efficient work and storage areas.

6. Storage facilities must be adequate, economical, and flexible to facilitate housekeeping and to provide for an orderly environment.

WORDS AND TERMS TO KNOW

air duct
base cabinet
ceramic tile
corridor kitchen
double-bowl sink
exterior-grade plywood
island kitchen

melamine (for counter tops)
multipurpose kitchen
panel kitchen
peninsula kitchen
polyester (for counter tops)
work flow
work triangle

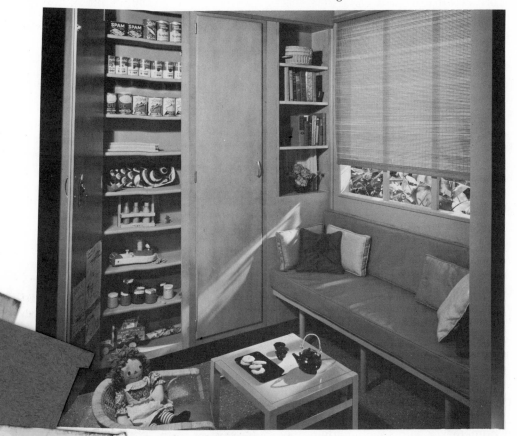

...cludes play space for small children plus a mending and menu-planning center. ...or cookbooks and sewing basket, and the narrow shelving which makes all ...accessible.

GENERAL KITCHEN CONSIDERATIONS

If you are building a house, you will have some freedom about the size and location of the kitchen. If you are remodeling a home, you may be able to change an existing kitchen. But if you are renting a house or an apartment, there are few changes that you can make in the size or arrangement. In order to facilitate work, you will have to plan storage carefully, so that food and supplies will be stored as near as possible to where they are used.

Location and Use

Since the average homemaker spends more time working in the kitchen than anywhere else in the house, the kitchen should be located conveniently, cheerful in appearance, well lighted, sanitary, well ventilated, and easy to keep clean. For work efficiency and safety, the work area should be as free as possible from traffic hazards.

The kitchen should have a direct connection with the service entrance (preferably not through a garage), the dining area, and the front entrance. It should be possible for the homemaker to pass from the kitchen to the master bedroom without going through the living area. If there are young children, it should be possible to supervise an indoor and an outdoor play area from the kitchen. It is also desirable to have enough space in the kitchen for occasional family meals.

Some workers like a multipurpose kitchen, so that they may dovetail food preparation with other activities, such as ironing, sewing, or a special interest. A homemaker with small children may want to fence off a play area in the kitchen for a few years, and use the space later for a breakfast nook or an activity center. Every kitchen should have a planning area with a place to sit down and with a drawer or shelf for cookbooks and other planning needs.

Cabinet Surfaces

Kitchen cabinets should be verminproof, and surfaces should be easy to maintain. The finish should be resistant to water, alcohol, abrasion, and fire.

Cabinets come in a choice of materials: metal, solid wood or plywood with a choice of flush or paneled doors and drawers, and sheet plastic laminated to plywood. Solid-wood and plywood cabinets come in natural grain ranging from light birch to dark walnut. Solid-wood cabinets may also be had with a durable enameled surface resembling wood grain. Laminated-plywood cabinets are available in numerous finishes, including wood grains.

Metal cabinets meet the requirements for kitchen cabinets, but metal is noisy and will chip and rust. If metal cabinets have to be refinished, the doors, drawers, knobs, and handles must be removed. The paint should be sprayed rather than brushed on to avoid brush marks because metal does not absorb paint the way wood does. Wood and laminated-plastic cabinets are quieter than metal. Laminated plastic is more abrasion resistant than natural wood, but if doors and drawers have to be replaced, it is difficult to match the original finish. Wood can be sanded, stained, and finished more satisfactorily than other materials.

Cabinet Types and Sizes

Base cabinets are available with all drawers or with a drawer at the top and shelves below. Standard-size base cabinets are 24 inches deep and 36 inches in height. Wall cabinets are available with shelves only. They are 12 inches deep and 30 inches in height, unless they are to be hung above a sink or refrigerator. Both base and wall cabinets are from 12 to 42 inches in length. Cabinets for a wall oven or utility storage are 24 inches deep and 84 inches in height. Oven cabinets are 24, 27, and 33 inches wide, and utility cabinets are 12, 18, and 24 inches wide. If it is desirable to have a counter space longer than a combination of standard-size cabinets, filler strips may be used between cabinets to accommodate the counter top. There should be a distance of 15 inches between base and wall cabinets to allow space for using portable appliances.

Cabinets come with numerous accessory units, such as a bread box, cutlery drawer, towel rack, sugar and flour containers, ventilated vegetable drawer, and so on. If cabinets within the work area do not provide enough storage space and if the kitchen is large enough, a pantry wall cabinet can be added.

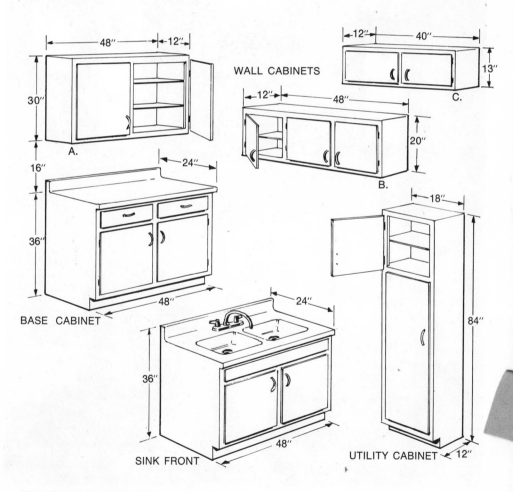

The dimensions shown here are typical; cabinet widths can vary widely. Wall cabinet A above is a standard size; B can be used over a refrigerator; C, over surface burners.

Kitchen carpeting is durable and restful, as well as attractive. The appearance of this U-shaped kitchen is enhanced by including both an old-fashioned and a modern stove.

Counter Surfaces

Plastics laminated to plywood are heat resistant up to 275 degrees or over, and these finishes are the most popular choice for counter surfaces. There are two kinds of thermoset laminated plastics sold under various trade names—*melamine* (high pressure) and *polyester* (low pressure). Both are available in a wide choice of colors and patterns. Both are tough, stain resistant, flame resistant, and abrasion resistant, and both are easy to maintain. Low-pressure, or polyester, laminates are not quite as resistant to heat or abrasion as high-pressure ones. A cigarette will burn polyester laminates, but it will not burn melamine laminates. Vinyl plastic is durable, but it is less resistant to stains and abrasion than the above-mentioned surfaces. Burning cigarettes and a very hot iron will melt vinyl plastic.

Other counter surface materials are inlaid linoleum, marble, stainless steel, ceramic tile, and wood. Linoleum absorbs water and stains; it will buckle if water seeps under it; it is damaged by heat and abrasion. Marble is seldom used because it is expensive, difficult to keep clean, and noisy. Stainless steel is used frequently in large commercial kitchens where there is a lot of steam and in humid climates. It is not as colorful, as stain resistant, or as quiet as plastic surfaces. Most stains on stainless steel can be removed with rubbing alcohol or a special cleanser for metals. Ceramic tile is durable, waterproof, and stain resistant, but the grout used to fill the joints is susceptible to grease and stain. Unless wood is well seasoned and treated for resistance to water, grease, and stains, it is less desirable as a surface finish except in areas where dough is rolled out or cutting is done. Of course cuts will show on wood, but on the other hand, wood will not dull knives.

Floor Coverings

All kitchen flooring materials should be laid over smooth, moistureproof subflooring. If the subflooring is made of narrow boards closely joined, it may be possible to nail loose boards in place and sand the surface before laying resilient tile, sheet vinyl, or linoleum. Otherwise exterior-grade (moisture-resistant) plywood must be nailed firmly on top of the subfloor and the joints must be filled in with grout before laying any resilient flooring material, if a smooth-looking surface is to be obtained.

Kitchen carpeting can be laid over ordinary wood floors, provided they are fairly smooth, or over exterior-grade plywood subflooring. Linoleum, vinyl-asbestos tile, and pure vinyl are easily maintained flooring materials for the kitchen. Asphalt, rubber, and cork tile are not recommended because they absorb grease.

Tests by the National Bureau of Standards show that there is no more *give* with wood, asphalt- or rubber-tile, or inlaid-linoleum flooring than there is with concrete, insofar as human fatigue is concerned. Vinyl cushioned tile and heavy inlaid linoleum are slightly more restful. However, rubber heels do more than anything else to absorb shock and reduce fatigue on hard-surface floors. Carpeting made especially for the kitchen absorbs more shock than any of the above-mentioned flooring materials. Regardless of this selling feature, families with small children usually prefer resilient floor coverings to carpeting. For a more detailed discussion of floor coverings consult Chapter Thirteen, pages 230 to 235.

This one-wall kitchen with an undercounter refrigerator is suitable for an efficiency apartment, especially in a basement. The hood over the stove conceals both the ventilation unit and artificial lighting. The pegboard helps to maximize storage space.

Lighting

Artificial lighting for the kitchen is discussed in Chapter Eighteen. However, a rule of thumb for natural lighting is that the window area should account for 10 percent and preferably 15 percent of the floor area. Of course windows facing another building receive very little natural light. In many large apartment buildings, kitchens and bathrooms have no natural light or ventilation. They must depend upon artificial light and air ducts. For economy reasons halls, elevators, bathrooms, and kitchens in large apartment buildings are placed on inside walls to save as many windows as possible for living and sleeping areas.

For best light reflection, walls should be a light color and ceilings should be white. Next to white, which may be glaring, cream, yellow, and soft pink are the best light reflectors. Semigloss paint, vinyl-coated wallpaper, or rubber-coated fabric wall cover is recommended for kitchen walls. Light-colored cabinet, counter, and floor surfaces will also reflect more light than dark surfaces —the lighter the value, the greater the reflection.

KITCHEN ARRANGEMENTS

Kitchens are usually planned around three major pieces of equipment—range, sink, and refrigerator. These three basic appliances form what kitchen engineers refer to as the *work triangle*. In this work triangle it is preferable to place the sink between the range and refrigerator. A double-bowl sink is recommended if

FOUR BASIC KITCHEN LAYOUTS

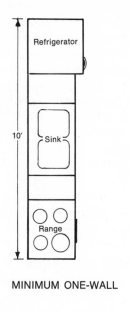

MINIMUM ONE-WALL

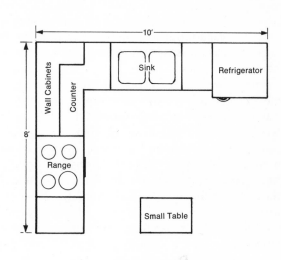

MINIMUM L-SHAPE

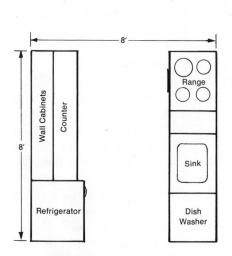

MINIMUM TWO-WALL

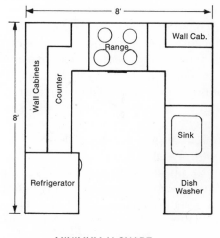

MINIMUM U-SHAPE

there is no dishwasher. If there is a dishwasher, it should adjoin the sink on the right or on the left, depending upon the space available and the work flow, or direction of work. A wall oven may be placed outside the work triangle because it is used less frequently than the burner surface.

Four basic arrangements, or layouts, may be used to accommodate the work triangle: one-wall or panel-type kitchen, two-wall or corridor-type kitchen, L-shaped or corner kitchen, and U-shaped or three-wall kitchen. Modifications of these basic layouts are the broken corridor, the broken L shape, and the broken U shape. The peninsula, island, and multipurpose kitchens are further variations.

One-Wall or Panel Kitchen

When space is limited, as in an efficiency or one-bedroom apartment, the one-wall kitchen may be a necessity. This type of kitchen is not recommended in a home or for a large family because there is too much lost motion between work centers. For maximum efficiency in a one-wall kitchen, the sink should be placed between the range and the refrigerator with enough space on either side for stacking clean and soiled dishes. Entrance doors should not open against the counters.

Compact packaged one-wall units with a cooking surface, undercounter refrigerator, sink, and wall cabinets are available in 39-inch lengths. Similar models with oven and base-cabinet space are available in lengths up to 72 inches.

Two-Wall or Corridor Kitchen

The smallest kitchen area that will accommodate a two-wall layout comfortably is 8 feet by 8 feet. This allows approximately 2 feet at each side for counters and major appliances and 4 feet in between for working. The corridor kitchen provides the greatest amount of undercounter storage space for its size. However, if the kitchen has an outside door at one end and a door to the dining room at the other, there will be a traffic problem. A corridor kitchen in an apartment usually has one dead end, making deliveries necessary through the main entrance. To reduce hazards and increase working efficiency in a corridor kitchen, the sink and range should be placed on the same wall because this will be the area of most activity.

L-Shaped or Corner Kitchen

The L-shaped kitchen is an efficient one in which to work because work areas are uninterrupted by traffic. Two walls are free for doors, a cleaning closet, and a table for eating. An L-shaped kitchen may include a peninsula and have a washer and a dryer on an adjacent wall. One objection to the L-shaped kitchen is the somewhat inaccessible corner storage. However, revolving shelves in a corner cabinet make the space more useful.

U-Shaped
or Two-Corner Kitchen

The U-shaped kitchen is popular because it is compact, step saving, and usually free of cross traffic. The sink should be placed at the inside or center of the U with the range near the dining room and the refrigerator near the rear entrance. In a large U kitchen there may be a counter for eating or a washer and a dryer along one side of the U. The principal objection to the U shape is having two corner cabinets, where storage space may be inaccessible.

Variations

PENINSULA KITCHEN. If the kitchen area is large, a peninsula may provide additional undercounter storage and a counter space for work or for eating. The peninsula may serve as a divider between the kitchen and the dining area or the kitchen and the laundry area. Wall cabinets may be suspended from the ceiling, making a pass-through between the base and the wall cabinets.

ISLAND KITCHEN. The island kitchen is often designed to provide more work space in a large kitchen, but it can be a nuisance if there is a great deal of traffic in the kitchen. The island may be placed inside a U-shaped or L-shaped kitchen. It may contain a sink or a range with work space or an eating area at one end. It must be well planned to be useful.

MULTIPURPOSE KITCHEN. If a kitchen is moderately large, it may contain anything from a sewing corner or a loom to a large play area for children. An L-shaped kitchen lends itself best to multipurpose use.

For information about buying kitchen equipment and appliances, see Chapter Twenty.

THE WORK TRIANGLE AND SPACE STANDARDS

The diagram on this page indicates the work triangle made by the range, sink, and refrigerator. The sum of all sides of this triangle should be less than 23 feet for maximum efficiency, although in very large kitchens it can be as large as 26 feet.

The following space recommendations are made in locating cabinets and providing for counter space:
☐ Place the sink 12 to 15 inches from each corner of an L or U turn.
☐ Provide 15 to 18 inches of counter space on the latch side of the refrigerator for loading and unloading.

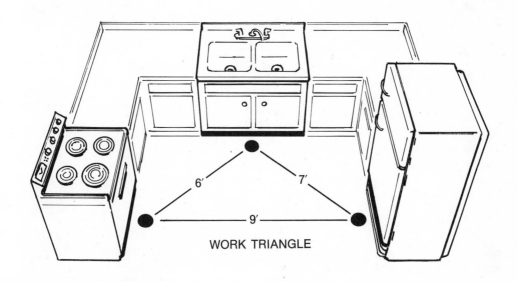

WORK TRIANGLE

The storage cabinet in this kitchen can be shut off with sliding doors when not in use. Notice the many conveniences—dividers for baking utensils, a graduated spice rack, a pegboard for measuring cups and spoons, and a pull-out chopping block.

□ Provide a counter space of 24 to 36 inches on one side of the sink (a dishwasher may be under this counter space) and a counter space of 18 to 30 inches on the other side of the sink. More space will be needed for stacking soiled dishes and pots and pans than for stacking clean dishes.

□ Provide 15 inches of counter space somewhere near the wall oven, if one is used, to set down hot containers.

□ Make sure that somewhere in the assembly there is an uninterrupted work area of 36 to 42 inches for mixing or other food preparation, preferably between the range and the sink.

For storage in a liberal-size kitchen provide a total of 10 linear feet of base cabinet frontage; a medium-size kitchen, 8 linear feet; and a minimum-size kitchen, 6 linear feet. Corner space is not counted as usable storage space, although it does serve to hold a mixer, canister set, or mixing supplies.

KITCHEN STORAGE

Work in the kitchen revolves around three main areas: the sink and mixing area, where most food preparation and dishwashing take place; the range and cooking area, and the serving area, from which food is placed in dishes and carried to the table. It will facilitate work in all these areas if the items used in each area are stored where they can be easily reached. Reaching and bending for supplies interferes with efficiency. Although each kitchen will contain different types of equipment and utensils, the following suggestions should be helpful.

Sink and Food Preparation Center

It will pay dividends in time and energy saved if you work at proper storage until you are satisfied that every item is stored for convenience and efficiency. Can you add others to this list?

Mixer and blender

Clean towels and dishcloths

Knives, forks, large spoons, kitchen shears

Garbage pail and garbage bags

Measuring cups and spoons, biscuit and cookie cutters

Strainers, colander, and lemon squeezer

Mixing bowls, molds, egg beater

Paper towels, wax paper, metal foil, transparent plastic wrap

Fruits and vegetables not needing refrigeration

Seasonings, spices, flavorings, sugar, flour, shortening, coffee, tea, and similar items

Range and Cooking Center

Many homemakers prefer to store frequently used pots and pans in deep drawers rather than on shelves. Flat utensils for stirring may be stored in compartmented drawers or in a wall rack. Items to be stored at this center include:

Saucepans, double boiler, lids

Cake pans, pie pans, muffin tins, and cookie sheets

Cake turner, ladle, spatula

Frying pans, roasters, coffeepot, and teapot

Serving Center

The serving center should be near the dining room. The following items should be stored in this area:

Trays of various sizes

Toaster, waffle iron, and similar appliances

Serving bowls, platters, and gravy bowl

Frequently used table linens

Bread box, cookie and cake containers

GENERAL LAUNDRY REQUIREMENTS

There are several recommendations for the placement of a laundry. Equipment for the laundry will vary according to individual family needs and to the space available.

Location

Many homemakers with small children prefer having the laundry in or near the kitchen, so that laundry work can be dovetailed with food preparation and the supervision of children. On the other hand, it seems inconsistent to some people to have dirty clothing and laundry odors in an area of the home where cleanliness is of prime importance. When the laundry is part of the kitchen, it is not only timesaving but economical because plumbing installations are often reduced.

The bathroom is another possible laundry location. Some advantages are: (1) soiled clothing accumulates in the bathroom; (2) plumbing is provided; (3) the floor and wall finishes are not harmed by moisture. Disadvantages are: (1) laundry odors, additional moisture, and noise may be objectionable in the sleeping area; (2) sorting, washing, and drying clothes may interfere with using the bathroom.

If space permits, a small utility room adjoining the bathroom may be desirable, especially if the homemaker does not have to supervise young children.

This laundry shows efficient use of space. It provides both good storage and a pleasant place to work.

With an upstairs laundry, ironing can be done in the same room or in a bedroom and the entire process can be done without moving the clothes from floor to floor.

The basement is desirable for a laundry, especially when an indoor or outdoor play area is adjacent and when there is a clothes chute. The basement should have a floor drain for overflow of water. Space in a basement will allow for using a basket on wheels to transport wet clothes, a drying rack for special items, a table for sorting and treating items for special stains and for folding clean articles, and a sewing center for mending clothes before they are washed. There may be a disadvantage in keeping an ironing board in the basement if it is used frequently between laundry periods.

Laundry Equipment

If space is sufficient, the following laundry equipment is recommended in addition to a washer and a dryer:

Clothes basket or wheel-mounted laundry cart

Laundry tub or large basin (necessary with semiautomatic washer) for special jobs

Counter or sorting table

Supply cabinet

Ironing board

Steam-dry iron

Clothes rack

Mending equipment

Laundry Procedure

Although this is not a book on the care of clothing and household textiles, it seems important to indicate certain laundry procedures that will produce satisfactory results.

WASHING. It is important to preserve the manual of directions and the guarantee that come with a washing machine.

□ Study the book of directions before attempting to use an automatic or a semiautomatic washer. This will explain how to wash various fabrics, the parts of the washing cycle, the time necessary, maximum and minimum loads, and so on.

□ Sort items according to washing requirements. This means that dark socks, slacks, and dresses should not be washed (or dried) with any item that will shed lint. This also means washing table linens separately from wearables. It means washing special garments, such as washable-woolen and permanent-press items, precisely according to recommendations. Delicate items may have to be placed in a mesh bag for washing. If any garment has seams that might ravel during tumbling or agitation, the seams should be overcast first.

□ Note special stains and follow directions for removing them. Avoid using chlorine bleaches on wool, silk, or resin-treated cottons. Use water and fabric softener according to directions.

DRYING. Note any special instructions for temperature and drying time if an automatic dryer is used. Many items need no ironing if they are taken off the clothesline or removed from the dryer and folded immediately. You should avoid overdrying in an automatic dryer because overdrying will take some of the life out of linen and make it difficult to remove wrinkles from garments made of man-made fibers. Separate items according to those that need no ironing, those that need only touch-up ironing, and those that need to be sprinkled and ironed.

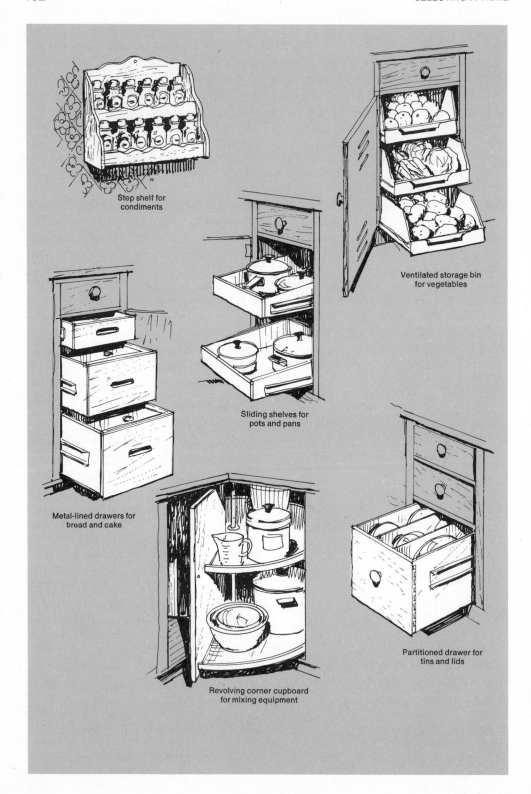

Step shelf for
condiments

Ventilated storage bin
for vegetables

Sliding shelves for
pots and pans

Metal-lined drawers for
bread and cake

Partitioned drawer for
tins and lids

Revolving corner cupboard
for mixing equipment

LAUNDRY PLANNING

KEY:
- 1. Preparing
- 2. Washing
- 3. Drying
- 4. Dampening and folding
- 5. Ironing
- 6. Folding and hanging
- 7. Storage

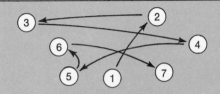

Haphazard Placement

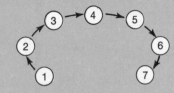

Planned Placement

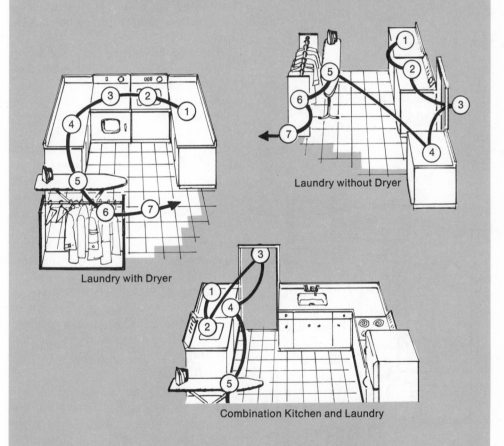

Laundry without Dryer

Laundry with Dryer

Combination Kitchen and Laundry

CLOSETS AND STORAGE WALLS

General Requirements

Minimum standards for storage in homes and apartments require a closet near the entrance, a linen closet near the bathing and sleeping areas, a closet in each bedroom, and a utility closet in or near the kitchen in addition to base and wall kitchen cabinets. Additional provision should be made for special equipment, such as books, records, and games, and awkward-size items, such as musical instruments, sports equipment, and some hobby supplies.

If storage space is to be satisfactory, it must be: (1) conveniently located, (2) easily accessible, (3) economical to build or buy, (4) flexible enough to meet the changing needs of the present family and future families who may occupy the house. If closets or shelves are too far away from where clothes are put on and taken off or where toys, games, and books are used, clothing will be tossed over chairs and other items will be left almost anywhere. If shelves are out of reach or if articles are completely concealed by other storage items, it will become a chore to find things. When a closet door or drawer is opened, one should be able to see everything with a minimum of effort.

Storage Needs in Areas of the House

The items to be stored in various areas of the house will determine the type and amount of storage space required, as the text below indicates. Closet doors made of louvered metal or wood are popular in modern homes because they permit air to circulate and keep clothes fresh. Their main disadvantage is that they collect dust and add to maintenance time.

Well-organized closets can save time and effort.

THE LIVING AREA. This area may include the living room, study, family room, or any other area in the house where family members spend a great deal of time. There should be an entrance closet large enough for coats and other storage and a closet in every room in the living area. The following items may require storage in the living area:

coats, jackets, sweaters, hats, scarfs

umbrellas, overshoes (unless provided for elsewhere)

card tables, folding chairs, games

phonograph records, music, musical instruments

camera, projector, projection screen, slides, and film

golf clubs, tennis rackets, and other sports equipment (unless provided for elsewhere)

books, magazines, writing supplies

THE DINING AREA. Dining needs vary greatly with the size and composition of the family, its socioeconomic level, the amount and type of entertaining done at home, and the area of the country in which the family lives. Some people like to entertain more formally indoors during the winter months, while other families enjoy informal entertaining outdoors during the summer season. Some families have no need for large embroidered tablecloths and table mats requiring special ironing, but prefer plastic mats and permanent-press or paper napkins. One homemaker may like to use a separate tarnishproof chest for silver, while another may prefer a shallow buffet drawer with compartments. In general the following items will require dining-area storage:

tablecloths, table mats, napkins

china and serving dishes used in the area

tableware and glassware used in the area

flower containers and candle holders

serving trays (if not stored in the kitchen serving area)

silver service and punch bowl and cups (if owned)

The dual-purpose buffet here not only stores dining equipment, but also serves as a divider between the library and the dining area (foreground).

THE SLEEPING AREA. The bedrooms should provide storage space in chests, dressers, and closets for all personal items, including clothing, and certain items of bedding, such as an extra cover or pillows.

Bedroom closets should open into full view; or if sliding doors are used, into half view. Although shelves are sometimes placed in the center of a closet, it is more economical to install them at the end to use otherwise lost space. Shelves need to be 12 to 14 inches deep. If there are growing children in the family, closet rods and shelves should be adjustable.

Provision must be made in the bedroom for storing the following items:

coats, jackets, dresses, trousers, skirts

hats, shoes, purses

flat items, such as blouses, sweaters, shirts

belts and ties

sleepwear used daily

clean sleepwear and underwear

books and study supplies, or toys and games in children's rooms

luggage; toilet and grooming items

In addition to providing adequate storage space, it is also important to

A man's closet with built-in dresser.   A woman's closet with convenient shoe rack.

This linen closet, with its pull-down shelf for sorting and its folding doors, could be built by a do-it-yourselfer.

select closet accessories that will aid in the proper care of clothing. These include see-through garment bags; plastic containers for shirts, blouses, and sweaters; special hangers for heavy garments, trousers, and skirts; racks for ties, belts, and shoes.

BATH AND BED LINEN STORAGE. Except for medicine cabinets, few bathrooms have storage facilities. In new homes the basin is often recessed in a counter, with a cabinet beneath. This provides storage space for extra soap, cleansers, toilet paper, and small towels.

Somewhere near the sleeping area shelves must be provided for bedding not in use. A hall linen closet may fill this need and also provide space for the following:

hamper for soiled clothes

extra soap and cleaning agents

toilet paper and cleansing tissues

bath towels, hand towels, washcloths

enema bag, heating pad, hot-water bottle, ice bag

sheets, pillowcases, blankets

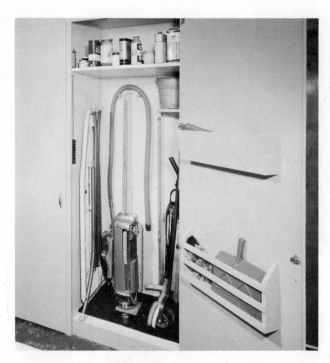

A storage bin on the door helps keep this utility closet orderly.

UTILITY AREAS. Somewhere near the back door there should be space for work clothes and children's play clothes and overshoes if dirt is to be kept out of the house. In or near the laundry, there should be a small cabinet or shelves for laundry supplies. In or near the kitchen, there should be a cleaning and general utility closet for the following items:

vacuum cleaner, hand vacuum (if used), carpet sweeper, dry mop

ironing board and iron (if not stored in a separate laundry area)

broom, whisk broom, dustpan and brush

scrub bucket, sponges, wet mop

paper bags and dustcloths

soaps, detergents, and other cleansing agents

tool panel for frequently used tools, such as hammer, screwdriver, and so on

Storage Walls

When storage space is scarce or when it might be desirable to divide a large room into two rooms or into a room and a hallway, a room divider storage wall is useful. This may be an island extending into the room or an entire wall. A storage wall in the kitchen is convenient for storing packaged food or dinnerware. A storage wall in the living room may contain a television, a phonograph, sections for record storage, shelves for books, a desk, a place for a projection screen, and other items.

A storage wall built into the rooms of growing children provides space for books and study needs or games and toys. Many companies make sectional units that can be purchased one piece at a time, until a permanent wall arrangement can be made. The storage walls pictured on pages 160 and 161 will give you some idea of their versatility.

SUMMARY

An intelligent and efficient homemaker will be keenly aware of good organization because good organization means the effective management of time and energy. Since the kitchen is the place where much work is done, it deserves special study. Scientific studies have provided architects, builders, manufacturers of kitchen cabinets and kitchen equipment, and homemakers with measurements desirable for cabinet surfaces, storage drawers, and shelves. Studies have also shown the best placement of cabinets and major appliances for a logical and efficient flow of work.

If a homemaker understands something about good kitchen arrangement, space standards, counter and floor coverings, cabinets and laborsaving equipment, she will be better able to judge a kitchen in an existing home or to plan a kitchen in a new home.

With the general acceptance of automatic or semiautomatic laundry equipment, most of the work is taken out of laundering. It is no longer necessary to have a lot of space for laundry tubs, a washer, clotheslines, and drying racks. However, even with fully automatic equipment it is necessary to know how to sort items to be washed and to use the proper setting on automatic appliances.

Although there are certain requirements for storage closets in newly built homes, few families ever have enough storage space. Often it becomes necessary to use the available space as efficiently as possible. When space is lacking, storage walls help to keep many homes more orderly.

THINGS TO THINK ABOUT AND TO DO

1. Show illustrations of pioneer kitchens, of kitchens during late nineteenth and early twentieth centuries, of kitchens during the 1930's, and of present-day kitchens. These may be found in public library files. Compare and discuss.

2. Bring to class floor plans for houses and discuss the location of the kitchen as a control center.

3. Mount on the bulletin board illustrations of all the kitchen layouts mentioned in the text, including island and peninsula types. Discuss what you like and do not like about each.

4. Obtain samples of various counter-surface materials (melamine, polyester, vinyl, and so on) from a kitchen-planning center. Study and discuss.

5. Collect bulletins or folders on cabinet types and sizes from nationally advertised manufacturers of kitchen cabinets.

6. On graph paper (¼ inch = 1 foot) plan some kitchen layouts, using the dimensions indicated in the folders just mentioned. Make a side elevation also. Sink sizes will be indicated in the folders. Use the following range sizes: small apartment size, 21 inches; regular size, 30 inches; larger size, 40 inches. Refrigerators are 28 inches; 30½ inches, and wider. Dishwashers are 24 inches wide. Use the space standards on pages 147–149 here. Determine whether you will use standards for a minimum-, medium-, or liberal-size kitchen. Check the work triangle as you plan.

7. Check the kitchen in your own home against some of these criteria, and discuss with your parents ways of improving your kitchen without major remodeling.

8. Visit kitchen-planning centers in your community and new model homes, and note kitchen layouts, materials used for counter surfaces, and storage facilities.

9. Indicate some advantages of having one wood surface—part of a counter or a pull-out board—in the kitchen.

10. Assemble various types of kitchen floor coverings. Examine them, and discuss the advantages and disadvantages of each. You may want to refer to Chapter Thirteen also.

11. Rearrange your own kitchen storage for greater efficiency.

12. Discuss some advantages and disadvantages of coin-operated laundries. Compare the service and the cost with those of a home laundry, including the initial cost of the latter.

13. Collect booklets on automatic washers and dryers, and discuss their use. You may want to refer to Chapter Twenty also.

14. Compare various possible laundry locations, and select the one you think you would prefer. Give your reasons.

15. Mount on the bulletin board illustrations of various kinds of closets. Discuss them as to size, arrangement, and appearance.

16. List the items to be stored in your home, room by room, and work out a plan for more efficient storage if it should be needed.

17. Assemble closet accessories from a department store, and discuss the usefulness of each in the proper care of clothing.

Storage for games and sports equipment.

This bedroom can provide privacy for both its occupants by means of folding doors. The versatile storage wall contains a desk unit as well as shelving.

chapter ten

HEATING, COOLING, WIRING, AND PLUMBING

Not many years ago fireplaces and stoves were the only means of heat, and houses were often cold and drafty. Central heating was developed and gradually accepted during the first quarter of the present century. The early furnaces burned coal, had to be fired by hand, and were completely devoid of automatic controls.

Central cooling, unlike central heating, is still a luxury in most areas of the country. Room air conditioners, however, are quite common.

The general acceptance of laborsaving equipment and of improvements in lighting over the last thirty years has made the wiring in over half of the homes in the country entirely inadequate for today's needs. Overloaded wires in the walls of homes, especially wires leading to the kitchen, have been the cause of many fires. When older homes are remodeled, one of the major costs is rewiring.

Out-of-date plumbing can be a detriment to the resale value of a home. New plumbing is costly, but in home remodeling it is foolish to install expensive bathroom, kitchen, and laundry equipment without having pipes, drains, and sewer connections checked first. Corroded pipes, leaky joints, and poor drains will be constant problems.

The average consumer is not expected to be an expert on heating, cooling, wiring, and plumbing, but a certain amount of basic information is helpful in building or remodeling a home and in judging a new or an older home. For instance, a couple evaluating an older home or a home in the blueprint stage should consider the adequacy of wiring for future use, the location of outlets and switches for convenience and efficiency, the heating or heating-cooling system in relation to efficiency and operating costs, and perhaps the need for an extra bathroom. The following information is for the layman and not the heating, electrical, or plumbing expert.

GUIDELINES FOR STUDY

GENERAL IDEAS
TO CONSIDER

1. Science and technology make it possible for man to control the temperature, humidity, light, air purity, and sound transmission in his home.
2. The type of wall construction, the size and placement of windows, the amount of insulation, and the solar orientation of a house influence the comfort of the occupants.
3. Air pollution, increasing noise from air and ground traffic, and need for labor-saving equipment are important considerations in home planning.
4. The type of heating system will depend upon the climate, the style of home, its thermal design, cost of local fuel, and family income.
5. Adequate wiring is necessary for comfort, safety, and efficiency.
6. For reasons of economy, provision for future plumbing needs should be included in the original plans for a house.
7. Plumbing-installation costs can be reduced by concentrating the plumbing in one or two areas. Maintenance costs can be reduced by installing quality materials and by using dependable labor.

WORDS AND TERMS
TO KNOW

adequate wiring
ampere
automatic controls
circuit breaker
fuse
heating cable
heat pump
kilowatt
low-voltage system
National Electrical Code
radiant heat
receptacle (electrical)
reverse trap
siphon jet
temperature zoning
thermal design

HEATING AND COOLING NEEDS

Factors that will determine the satisfaction and efficiency of the heating or heating-cooling system are suitability to the climate and to the prevailing exposure, style and size of the house, care exercised in the installation of the system, and judgment used in the selection of the controls. In hot and temperate zones it is advisable to plan for central cooling when the house is constructed, even though the system may not be installed until a later date. The installation will cost less at the time of building and will increase the resale value of the house. The heating or heating-cooling requirements for a remodeled older home will be quite different from those for a compact new home on a slab foundation.

During the planning stage, a heating-cooling engineer can estimate closely the size of the furnace and cooling unit which a new house will require. He can do this by measuring the cubic feet of air space; knowing the type of walls and the number and size of windows; and being aware of provisions made for such items as weatherstripping, storm doors, and storm windows. He will also need to take into consideration outdoor temperature range and prevailing house exposure. By estimating heating and/or cooling needs and knowing the cost of the fuel to be used, it is possible to determine yearly fuel bills fairly accurately.

Humidity and Air Purification

Unless they are very active, the majority of people are comfortable in a room with a temperature between 72 and 75 degrees Fahrenheit and with a relative humidity between 30 and 60 percent. Constant high humidity gives

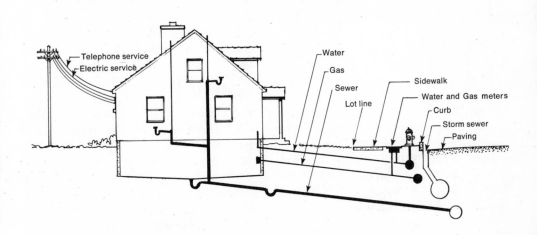

Every house depends upon certain public services, which include overhead or underground electric and telephone wires; water, gas, and sewer lines; and a storm sewer to dispose of surface water.

an oppressive feeling and causes condensation on windows in cold weather. When the heating system is designed to throw warm air toward the windows, condensation is reduced. If dampness in a home becomes a problem, a room or furnace dehumidifier can help to control the amount of moisture in the air.

Clean air is as important to health and comfort as temperature and humidity. People with allergies will be more comfortable if the air is free of dust, odors, and pollen. It is possible to install an air-purifying system (not always an air-cooling system) in older homes as well as in newer ones. A heating contractor will be able to recommend the most satisfactory system for any type of home.

Automatic controls provide comfort as well as convenience. Automatic controls include room thermostats, combustion controls, and safety devices. If these are properly installed, the home can be comfortably heated and cooled with a minimum of drafts and objectionable noises.

Sun Controls and Ventilation

Man in hot climates devised many ways to make a house comfortable long before the concept of mechanical air conditioning came into being. The Moors built row houses along very narrow streets to keep out the hot sun. If you visit Spain today, you can see in the older sections of many cities some of this construction reminiscent of Moorish occupation. In our Southern states people built homes with breezeways and porches to shield the house from the sun's rays. In many areas people have installed attic fans to suck the warm air out of the house and pull in the cool night air. Hillsides, trees, grape arbors, tall hedges, roof overhangs, and roof insulation have all been effective in combating the heat.

Heat in a house exposed to the sun all day can build up to 140 degrees under the roof, while the inside is 90 degrees. A light-colored roof is about 20 percent more effective in keeping out heat than a dark-colored roof. Practical ways of reducing the heat in the house are as follows:

SOLAR ORIENTATION. By exposing major walls and glass areas to the south, it is easier to protect them from the summer sun. Also additional warmth and sunlight enter the house in winter. A northern exposure produces opposite effects, and east and west exposures are difficult to protect because of the low angle of the sun in early morning and late afternoon. (See also page 119.)

WINDOW PROTECTION. In the south of Europe homes have heavy Venetian-type blinds on the outside of the house rather than on the inside, and during the time the sun strikes the windows, the blinds are closed tightly. Outside installation is nearly twice as effective as inside installation. Other methods of keeping out the hot sun are the use of heavy draw draperies with insulated linings; laminated window shades that let in very little light; and awnings of cloth, metal, or plastic.

OVERHANGS. In the past people built homes with porches, but overhangs and terraces have become popular, especially on one-story houses. An overhang is more effective on southern exposures than on eastern and western exposures because of the low angle of the summer sun. Overhangs must be planned in accordance with the latitude of the area and window height.

WALLS AND FENCES. Walls and louvered fences give fairly good protection on eastern and western exposures.

TREES. Tall deciduous trees, which give shade in summer and permit light in winter, are excellent sun protectors especially if they shade part of the roof.

VENTILATION. Many homes have roof ventilators which help to reduce heat by allowing cool night breezes to pass between the roof and the second-floor ceiling. Rooms that permit cross ventilation stay fairly comfortable.

FANS. Exhaust fans, attic fans, and ordinary floor fans remove hot air or keep air in circulation for greater comfort.

INSULATION. Insulation has been mentioned earlier. Insulation comes in many forms, and requirements differ in different types of home construction. (See pages 129–130.)

Types of Heating Systems

All heating systems should be designed to keep the temperature of a room relatively uniform in all areas. A thermometer on an inside wall may register 80, but if the outside walls or large glass areas are poorly insulated, or if the heat is poorly distributed, a person may feel uncomfortably cool near them. The cold air from the outside wall may cause a floor draft. Radiation may draw the heat from a person's warm body toward the cold wall.

Heating systems that are in most common use are *warm air* and *hot water*. With more compact and better insulated homes, steam heat is less popular than in former years. Combination heating-cooling systems, in addition to being popular in year-round relatively warm climates, are becoming more prevalent in expensive homes in temperate zones, especially in areas where summers are hot.

A central-heating system includes the furnace or boiler, ducts or pipes which distribute heat, room heating units, and controls.

A brief discussion of heating systems follows:

WARM-AIR SYSTEM. The warm-air system in some form is probably the most common type of home heating. In this system heated air is distributed throughout the house from heating units located in the floor, along the baseboard, or in the wall. It is important to concentrate warm-air supply lines near the base of large glass areas. It should be possible to adjust the louvers, so that the warm air is forced onto exterior walls and glass areas to counteract drafts. Individual-room returns or a large central return·in the hall (with enough air space under doors) carries off the cool air.

Warm-air systems are relatively low in initial cost; they provide almost instant heat and adjust rapidly to changing temperatures; the air can be filtered as it circulates; and there is no danger of having water pipes freeze in winter. On the other hand warm-air systems are a little noisier than hot-water systems; there are other air currents in the room, and the heat may fluctuate a little more.

A *gravity warm-air system* is adequate for a small compact house, but this system requires a basement, and large ducts occupy valuable basement space. A *forced warm-air system,* in which a blower is used, can be used in houses with a slab floor, a crawl space, or a basement. A blower in the furnace forces warm air through ducts and draws the cool air back to the furnace through return ducts. Forced warm air causes noise as the blower goes off and on.

A *warm-air perimeter-loop system* is used in many homes with a slab foundation. In this system ducts extend from a furnace in the utility room to a duct embedded in the perimeter of the concrete slab. This system minimizes cold drafts from floors and windows. It is also possible to use air conditioning with this type of installation.

HOT-WATER SYSTEM. A hot-water system provides the most uniform heat, especially when baseboard radiators or convectors are used around the outside walls. In this system water is heated in a boiler and circulated through pipes to radiators or to individual convectors or baseboard units. Some hot-water pipes have fins to produce greater radiation. With a hot-water system, hot water for home use can be had by installing coils in the heating unit. However, many people prefer a separate hot-water heater.

A gravity hot-water system is quiet and economical to install, but on the other hand, it responds slowly to temperature changes. It also requires a basement because the boiler must be lower than the individual heating units. A forced hot-water system may be installed in houses built on a concrete slab, over a crawl space, or over a basement. In some slab-foundation construction, the pipes are concealed in the floor, walls, or ceiling. Special insulation is required for this type of heating, and it responds more slowly to changing temperatures than when baseboard units or exposed radiators are used. This type of forced hot-water heat is comparable to electrical panel or radiant heating.

A forced hot-water system provides even, quiet heat, but until recently it has been fairly expensive. Costs have been cut in a number of ways without interfering with efficiency, so that the cost of this heating system compares favorably with warm-air systems. Two disadvantages of hot-water heat are the need to drain the radiators if the house is unoccupied in freezing weather and the need to release air from the pipes occasionally to avoid knocking.

STEAM HEAT. Steam heat is seldom used in new houses, unless they are large houses in cold climates. Steam heat is often noisy, and it cannot be adapted to air conditioning. A separate air-conditioning system must be used.

ELECTRICITY AS A SYSTEM AND FUEL. Electricity provides fuel for central-heating systems and also for other methods of heating. Several types of electrical heating are described briefly:

A heating cable, or electric-resistance wires, may be embedded in the ceiling or floor in the same way that hot-water pipes are concealed to provide panel or radiant heat. The temperature in each room is controlled with a thermostat.

A baseboard may contain an electric heating element similar to the element in an electric range, or a baseboard may contain an electric element and pipes for circulating hot water. The hot-water type is preferable. Contact with a heating element similar to that in a range will cause a burn, and curtains containing man-made fibers will scorch when they touch the element.

Wall panels may be placed in the wall, preferably under windows, to provide heat. Some installations require fans. A ceiling fixture, working on the same principle, is often used in a bathroom to provide additional heat on cold days. Wall panels that both heat and cool are also available. They are popular in motel rooms and in compact apartments or rooms in a large older house that need extra heat in winter and cooling in summer.

The heat pump is a most satisfactory means of providing year-round climate control. In the winter the pump extracts heat from the outside air, ground, or well water, and distributes heat through a duct system in the house. In the summer the operation is reversed for cooling. In very cold climates a heat pump may not provide enough heat from the elements, so that additional electric-resistance units may be required. Heat pumps may be placed outside near the garage, in a breezeway, or on the roof.

An electric furnace may be used in areas of the country where rates are low. This method of central heating also provides central air conditioning, humidity control, and electrostatic air filtering.

Since electric heating is still relatively expensive, a house must be well insulated in order to help keep costs down.

HEATING AND COOLING COMBINATIONS. Now that central cooling is becoming more common, the feasibility of combining the heating and cooling systems should be studied during the house-planning stage, because some heating systems are better adapted to air conditioning than others. The cost of combining a hot-air heating system and a cooling system in the average house may add no more than six to eight hundred dollars to the total cost. Provision for total air conditioning also includes moisture and pollution control—desirable features for persons who suffer breathing difficulties or who have allergies caused by pollen or dust. Even when central air control is not available, homes may be equipped with a central filtration system, and a dehumidifier may regulate the moisture in the air.

Central heating and cooling may be provided in some hot-water systems. It is possible to pump chilled water through hot-water pipes for cooling, but separate conveyors are preferable. It is expensive and difficult to provide central air conditioning in older homes because of the cost necessary for proper insulation. Ceilings in older homes are usually over eight feet high; insulation

HOT-WATER RADIATION HEATING SYSTEM
PLUS OVERHEAD AIR CONDITIONING

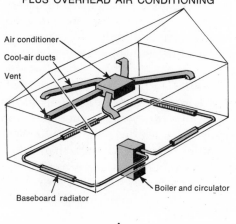

Air conditioner
Cool-air ducts
Vent
Baseboard radiator
Boiler and circulator

A

FORCED WARM AIR HEATING SYSTEM
WITH AIR CONDITIONING ADDED

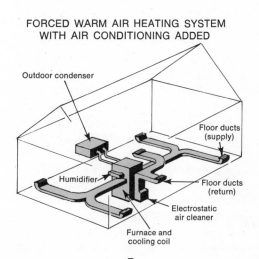

Outdoor condenser
Floor ducts (supply)
Humidifier
Floor ducts (return)
Electrostatic air cleaner
Furnace and cooling coil

B

A combination heating and cooling unit adds greatly to the comfort and convenience of life in variable climates.

is often inadequate. It would be necessary to lower the ceilings and provide adequate insulation in walls, ceilings, and windows to operate a central cooling system economically. Although valance heating-cooling has been in use for over a decade, it has only recently become popular. In this type of heating, water is circulated through tubes with fins concealed in a narrow metal valance around the perimeter of the ceiling. In summer water is cooled to 35 to 45 degrees Fahrenheit and in winter it is heated to produce the desired temperature. Air is circulated by convection and radiation.

Valance heating-cooling leaves the maximum of usable floor space, eliminates drafts, dehumidifies in summer, operates quietly, and can be used effectively in remodeling. It is also easy to install thermostats in each room or in any future additions for zone control. Of particular advantage is its use in kitchens where floor space is an important item.

Air conditioners installed through walls or in windows are fairly satisfactory for older homes. A heating engineer can determine the size of an air conditioner needed by measuring the cubic feet in the room, by considering the number of persons using the room, and by estimating the loss of air through windows, archways, stairways, and doors. An air conditioner with too large a capacity is not desirable because it will go off and on too frequently and will not keep the temperature as even as one of average capacity for the room.

Temperature Zoning

It is usually desirable to have bedroom temperatures cooler than living-area temperatures. With electric heating, individual thermostats control room temperatures. When only one thermostat controls the heat, the units—registers or radiators—may be turned down, but the temperature cannot be controlled accurately. With a hot-water system it is possible, although more expensive, to have separate thermostats in two or three areas of the house. Some people who live in larger homes find it cheaper to install two furnaces—one to control the temperature in sleeping areas and the other to control the temperature in living areas.

Evaluation of Heating Fuels

It is not possible to list fuels in the order of cost because there are too many variables. In some areas coal is plentiful and less costly than other fuels; in other areas gas is available at very low rates; in still other areas electricity rates for home heating are very reasonable. Competing fuel producers can quote figures indicating the advantage of any particular type of fuel. For example, the Electric Heating Association reports that between 1946 and

1963, according to Bureau of Labor figures, oil retail prices rose 36.9 percent, gas rates jumped 45.4 percent, and electric heating rates dropped 21.5 percent. On the other hand, producers of oil for heat can quote figures to imply that fuel oil would have to quadruple in price to equal the present cost of electric heat. Fuel dealers sometimes use numerous inducements to home builders and buyers, ranging from trading stamps to installation allowances for each piece of equipment installed.

Electric heat is ideal in many ways, but if it is to be economical, local rates must be low and the home must be adequately insulated. Heating engineers use the term *thermal design* to describe home insulation. Gas and oil dealers criticize the thermal design that meets electric-heat specifications, saying that the structure is too airtight to provide desirable humidity and to allow odors to dissipate. The proper installation of dehumidifying and air-filtering machinery can overcome these objections. Many factors compensate for the high installation and operation costs of electric heat, such as convenience, cleanliness, safety from explosion, and compactness of the unit. In areas of the country where electricity for heating is becoming more competitive with other fuels, many new homeowners prefer to pay a little more for heating and cooling in order to save the space required by hot-air ducts or to be relieved of the worry of having water pipes freeze in case the heating system should break down.

A local heating engineer, architect, or contractor can give you the best advice on what fuel is most economical and satisfactory for the design of your house and for your locality should you ever build or remodel a home.

WIRING AND ELECTRICAL NEEDS

Because faulty wiring and overloaded circuits cause high annual property losses as well as loss of lives, as a home dweller you should know something about adequate wiring. Many fires start in the walls when too many electrical appliances are in use, causing the insulation on the wires to burn out. When you connect a number of electric cords, octopus fashion, into one outlet, you signal danger. When you stand in a bathtub, a shower, or a wet laundry area and reach for a switch or screw in a bulb, you may risk your life.

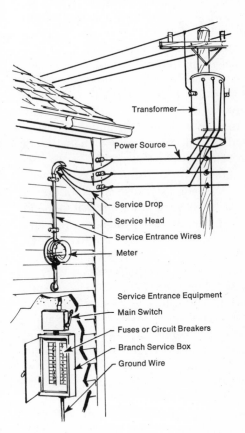

Transformer

Power Source

Service Drop

Service Head

Service Entrance Wires

Meter

Service Entrance Equipment

Main Switch

Fuses or Circuit Breakers

Branch Service Box

Ground Wire

Service Entrance Equipment

Safety Regulations and Warning Signals

CODES AND STANDARDS. A wiring system is safe if it conforms to the requirements of the National Electrical Code, local building codes, and the standards of the utility company providing the power. One safety requirement of the National Electrical Code is that all appliance outlets in damp areas be grounded to prevent shock or fire. All outlets, or receptacles, in new construction must be grounded. Bathroom switches and outlets must be out of reach of bathtubs and showers. All supplies used in wiring should bear the UL label of the Underwriters' Laboratories, Inc., a nonprofit organization under the sponsorship of the National Board of Fire Underwriters.

Safety is also guaranteed by insulated flexible cords wired according to use. For example, small appliances may need heavier wire than ordinary wire used on lamps. Ordinary extension cords should be no longer than 10 feet for safety. It is not a good idea to join a series of extension cords because power is lost. Extension cords for power tools and other equipment that demand excess current carry heavy wires and come in lengths from 15 to 35 feet. *Never use an ordinary extension cord with heavy-duty equipment.*

BUILT-IN SAFETY DEVICES. In addition to built-in safety factors in wiring and in appliances, there are other automatic protective devices or warning signals. When a circuit is overloaded, a fuse or circuit breaker will cut off the current. Every home (or apartment) should have one or more service equipment panels with fuses or circuit breakers to all branch circuits. *Fuses,* which usually screw in like light bulbs, may have a 15-, 20-, or 30-ampere capacity.

If you have occasion to replace a blown fuse, make sure that it has the proper ampere capacity. In new construction the National Electrical Code specifies that fuse receptacles be coordinated with fuses so that it will not be possible to insert the wrong fuse.

Circuit breakers (push-button or handle type) are more satisfactory and safer than fuses. When a circuit is temporarily overloaded, the circuit breaker will be released. To restore power the homemaker needs only to press a button or push a handle, whereas she might not know what ampere-capacity fuse to use. Circuit breakers, like fuses, are chosen according to the power needed and come in 15-, 20-, 30-, 40-, and 50-ampere capacities. If the same fuse or circuit breaker continues to interrupt current, it may be necessary to add another branch circuit.

You will have certain warning signals if there is too much strain on the power even before a fuse or circuit breaker shuts off the current. The lights will dim or the television picture will fluctuate when a major appliance, such as a toaster, mixer, or vacuum cleaner, is in use. Families keep adding more and more laborsaving appliances without realizing how much more power is needed. The warning signals just mentioned should alert you and your parents and cause you to consult your power company (your landlord if you are renting) about your increasing power needs.

Adequate Wiring

The diagram on page 173 shows the essential parts of a home wiring system. Three service wires, or power conductors, from the utility distribution system reach the house either overhead or underground. They come together at a weatherhead and are funneled through a hollow tube to the meter and service-equipment panel. A grounding conductor connects the wiring system with a grounding rod (this may be a cold-water pipe) that acts as a safety device in preventing fire or electrical shock.

In addition to understanding fuses and circuit breakers, you should also be familiar with the following terms and their application to adequate wiring.

AMPERE CAPACITY. An ampere is a unit used to measure the electrical rate of flow (comparable to gallons of water per minute). A 60-ampere service is the minimum acceptable by the National Electrical Code. This service is adequate for homes up to 1000 square feet of floor space for lighting, portable appliances, and an electric range or clothes dryer or water heater, but not all three. Additional major appliances will require separate service wires.

In most new construction the minimum is a 100-ampere service. This flow of power will be adequate for lighting, portable appliances, a range requiring 10,000 watts, and other equipment totaling up to 8000 watts (see wattage needs, page 176). A 150-ampere service will provide for a 13,500-watt range, a clothes dryer, and a room air conditioner up to 5000 watts, plus other appliances totaling not more than 8200 watts. If electric heating is used, a 200-ampere service is required. Large homes with complete heating and cooling systems require a higher ampere capacity.

CIRCUITS. A circuit consists of two or more wires carrying the flow of electricity from the supply source to the outlet and return. The circuit breaker or fuse is the safety device on a particular line of electrical flow.

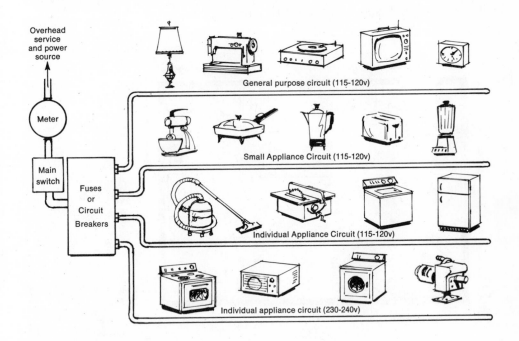

Overhead service and power source

Meter

Main switch

Fuses or Circuit Breakers

General purpose circuit (115-120v)

Small Appliance Circuit (115-120v)

Individual Appliance Circuit (115-120v)

Individual appliance circuit (230-240v)

This diagram shows adequate wiring voltage for general usage and appliances. (See pages 175–176 for an explanation of volts.)

There are three types of circuits:

Lighting and general-purpose circuits are for general lighting and small appliances not generally used in the kitchen. Each room should be served by more than one circuit, so that there will always be a source of light. A general rule is to provide one 20-ampere, 120-volt general-purpose circuit for every 500 square feet of floor space. A 15-ampere, 120-volt circuit may be used for a floor area up to 375 square feet.

Appliance circuits are special circuits to provide power for portable appliances used in the kitchen and in other work areas of the home. Two 20-ampere, 120-volt circuits for small appliances should serve the dining-kitchen area.

Special-purpose circuits are for individual appliances that are installed more or less permanently, such as a range, a dishwasher, a dryer, and power tools.

OUTLETS. These are points in the wiring system that supply power for lighting or for appliances. Convenience outlets are also referred to as *receptacles* and include the following types: duplex; clock outlet; combination switch and receptacle; weatherproof receptacle (necessary outdoors); TV outlet; and special outlets for dryer, range, and so on. In some instances a multi-receptacle for three or four plugs may be desirable. A multi-outlet panel is recommended for kitchens.

It is important to locate receptacles or outlets conveniently in every room of the house. Here are a few guidelines:

☐ Place outlets so that no lamp or appliance plug is more than six feet from a source of power.

☐ Never place outlets behind large pieces of furniture because they will be inaccessible without the use of an extension cord.

☐ Never let a cord extend across a doorway. Each narrow wall requires an outlet.

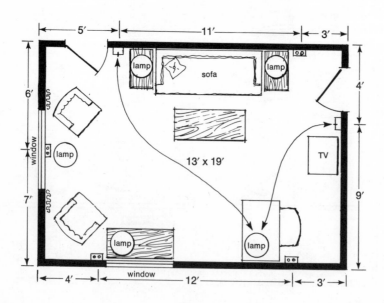

This floor plan shows correct placement of convenience outlets—all are accessible to points of use. The wall switches next to the doors turn on the desk lamp—a good safety feature, since few living rooms have overhead lighting controlled by a switch.

☐ Place outlets in living and sleeping areas about 18 inches from the floor; in the dining room, at table height as a rule, or about 36 inches from the floor; in the laundry, at washer height and near the source of water; in the kitchen, above counter height.

☐ Be sure to have an outlet in hallways for the vacuum cleaner and perhaps for a night light.

☐ Provide one or more outlets near the bathroom mirror for an electric razor. Medicine cabinets often come equipped with one or more outlets.

In addition to convenience outlets, it is necessary to consider other lighting needs before construction or remodeling begins. Ceiling lighting is recommended for all rooms except the living room, and many areas will need decorative lighting in the walls or ceiling.

SWITCHES. Every wiring system has a main switch which turns on and shuts off all the power. Any time that electrical work is being done, this switch should disconnect the flow of current into the house. There are many kinds of individual switches. Some recommendations for the choice and placement of individual switches follow:

☐ Place all switches on the latch side of the door for convenience.

☐ Place switches so that it is always possible to light the area ahead without walking through a room or a hall. Entrance switches should light the outside and inside entrances and turn on one light in the living room. It should be possible to turn off these lights without retracing steps.

☐ Place two-way switches at the top and bottom of steps, at each door in a bathroom if it serves two rooms, and also at the kitchen and garage doors.

☐ Use pull-chain switches in closets, in storerooms, and in other less frequently used areas.

☐ Use weatherproof switches outdoors.

☐ Use dimmer switches in areas of the house where you might want to control the lighting.

☐ Use an automatic switch device to turn on and turn off lights in certain areas of the house if you expect to be away from home frequently at night. This is one way to discourage burglars who might be tempted to enter dark homes.

One of the most convenient switching systems is low-voltage or remote control. In this system a panel of wall switches controls a special low-voltage circuit, which in turn is wired to a relay that operates the line-voltage switch. This is a relatively inexpensive system for remote control if it is included at the time of construction. From a panel in the bedroom, for instance, you can turn on the coffeepot, the TV, or any light in the house or in the garage. A low-voltage system is a good protection against burglars.

VOLTS. A volt is the unit used in measuring electrical pressure (comparable to pounds per square inch of water

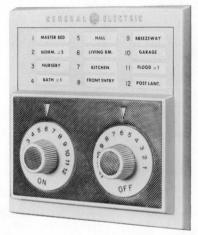

A panel like this in a central location makes it possible to control lighting throughout the house. By turning the dials, and pushing or releasing the knobs, one can operate lighting fixtures individually or in combination.

pressure). Homes, hotels, office buildings, and so forth are wired for either 120-volt or 240-volt current (sometimes referred to as 115- and 230-volts). You have probably noticed that electric razors and irons may be adjusted for either current by flipping a trigger. If you plug an appliance requiring a 120-volt current into a receptacle producing 240 volts, the appliance may be ruined. It is becoming customary to wire the receptacle so that it will take either 120 or 240 volts by having a built-in appliance adapter. When you are using any electrical appliance for the first time, make sure to check the voltage of the appliance with the voltage of the receptacle in the place where you might be using it.

WATTS. A watt is a unit of power (the product of amperes times volts) used by lights, appliances, or equipment. For example, a circuit with 15 amperes and 120 volts will provide 1800 watts, the average wattage for general-purpose circuits. Average power requirements for a number of appliances are given below. Each appliance you use will have watts indicated.

A kilowatt is equal to 1000 watts. Electrical bills are stated in terms of kilowatts.

Small appliances (average wattage)

baker (portable)	800–1000
blender	250
clock	2
coffee maker	440–1000
deep-fat fryer	1350
electric blanket	200
hair dryer	250
heating pad	60
iron	1000
knife sharpener	100
mixer	100
portable heater	1000
radio	100
roaster	1650
refrigerator	150
sewing machine	75
skillet	1100
television	300
toaster	1150
waffle iron	1100

Major appliances (average wattage)

automatic dryer	4500
automatic washer	700
built-in bathroom heater	1500–2500
dishwasher-waste disposer	1500
fuel-fired heating system	800
range	10,000–13,500
room air conditioner	1500
water heater	2500–5000
water pump	300–700

PLUMBING NEEDS

Plumbing should be carefully planned for present and future needs during the blueprint stage in construction, even though an extra bathroom, a dishwasher, or a laundry may not be installed until a future date. It is economical to concentrate plumbing, so that fixtures for bathrooms, kitchen, and laundry can be placed on adjacent walls in a one-story house or vertically in a one-and-a-half- or two-story house. The diagram on the next page shows an economical arrangement of pipes for minimum plumbing needs.

General Requirements

The minimum plumbing needs in a home are for a lavatory, a toilet, and a bathtub in the bathroom; a sink in the

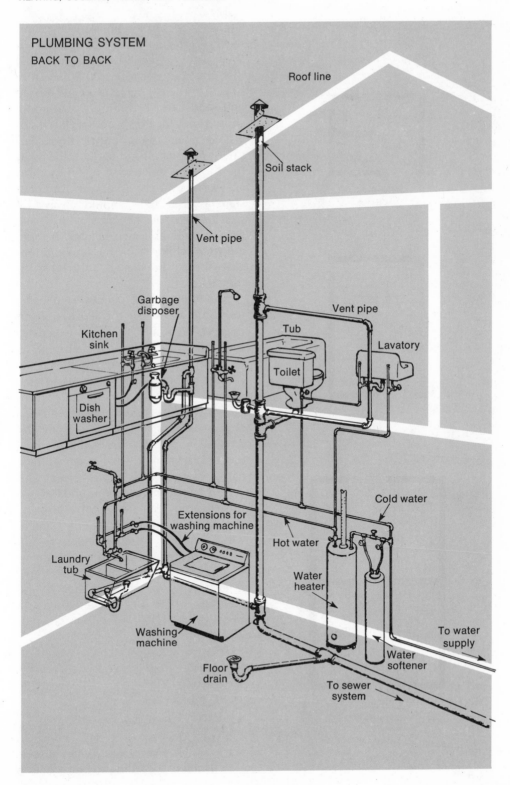

PLUMBING SYSTEM
BACK TO BACK

Roof line

Soil stack

Vent pipe

Garbage disposer

Vent pipe

Kitchen sink

Tub

Lavatory

Toilet

Dish washer

Cold water

Extensions for washing machine

Hot water

Laundry tub

Water heater

Washing machine

To water supply

Floor drain

Water softener

To sewer system

MINIMUM
4′ x 5′

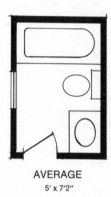

AVERAGE
5′ x 7′2″

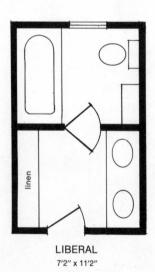

LIBERAL
7′2″ x 11′2″

kitchen; a tub in the laundry; and faucets for two hose connections in the yard. A second bathroom or a first-floor powder room (in a two-story house) provides greater convenience and adds resale value. A bathroom should be located so that it is not visible from the entrance door. For safety reasons also, it should not be at the top of a stairway. If a bathroom in an existing house is at the top of a stairway, the stairs should always be well lighted and, needless to say, have one or preferably two railings. If there are small children in the family, a firm gate should be placed at the top of the stairs.

Minimum space needs for a bathroom are shown in the illustration on this page. Usually, the more expensive the home, the larger the bathroom. A bathroom that is 6 feet 6 inches by 8 feet 8 inches not only permits a much more flexible arrangement but relieves the crowded feeling of the more common size bathroom that is 5 feet by 7 feet 2 inches. A larger bathroom may be compartmented—that is, a wall may partially isolate the water closet and another wall may accommodate two washbasins. Families with growing children like this arrangement. Families with teen-age daughters who tie up the bathroom for long periods shampooing and setting their hair often have a lavatory installed in an area of the bedroom where it can be enclosed as a closet or be concealed with a screen or wall divider.

The choice of water closets, lavatories, tubs, showers, and kitchen sinks is discussed briefly.

Water Closets

Water closets, or toilets, come in many styles and prices. Water closets are classified according to water action

—siphon jet, reverse trap, or washdown. The siphon jet is the most efficient; it has the largest trap, quick and fairly quiet flush action, and the volume of water in the bowl is extra large for maximum cleanliness. A deep water seal gives greater protection against sewer gases than either the reverse-trap or washdown types. The reverse-trap-bowl type has a smaller water surface, or volume, and a trap that requires less water for operation. Unlike the other two types, the washdown has a trap in front of the bowl. Its construction is simple, but it is noisy.

In addition to being classified according to water action, toilets are marketed according to design and shape of the bowl and seat. The conventional (elongated) bowl is three inches longer and more expensive than the cadet type. Cadet types are used in most apartment buildings and in moderate-priced homes because they save floor space and money. The most expensive water closets are made in one piece that hangs from the wall to facilitate cleaning the floor. Next in cost is the one-piece floor-supported type. The two-piece type with a tank on the wall and bowl on the floor is the least expensive.

Lavatories

The vitreous-china lavatory is generally preferred, although an acid-resistant porcelain enamel on cast iron is somewhat cheaper. Lavatories are available in several sizes. The most popular sizes are 21 inches deep by 24 inches long and 18 inches deep by 20 inches long, the larger size being preferable unless space is at a premium. A lavatory with a ledge, splash, or shelf at the back helps to keep water off the floor. Wall-hung lavatories are supported by brackets or legs. The lavatory may be 33 to 36 inches high.

A custom-made lavatory-cabinet combination costs at least twice as much as a regular 21- by 24-inch lavatory. Factory-built models cost somewhat less. A lavatory cabinet has a counter with storage space beneath and a splashboard at the back. In a large bathroom there may be counter space for two vanity bowls with storage space beneath. Lavatory cabinets come in heights of 31 inches and 34 inches, but the height may be increased by increasing the toe space underneath.

Tubs and Showers

If there is only one bathroom in the house, a tub with a shower fixture is preferable to a shower stall. The combination of tub and shower is more versatile, and the resale value of the house is increased. The 5-foot tub is the most popular choice. Some people prefer a 5-foot 6-inch tub if space permits. A receptor-type tub from 36 inches to 38 inches long, 39 inches to 42 inches wide, and 12 inches high is popular in homes where there are small children or semi-invalids who need help with bathing. The smaller type tub adapts itself well to shower equipment especially if it is enclosed on three sides.

An average-size bathroom.

A second bathroom may have a shower stall. A shower with a seat and a long handrail is safer for older persons, and certain precautions can help increase the safety of a tub—a handlebar or handle grip at shoulder height and another within reach of a person sitting in the tub. Slip-proof adhesive strips in the tub will help to prevent falls. Sliding glass doors that enclose a shower in a tub prevent an overflow of water on the floor, but they increase the problems of cleaning, and they are in the way when small children are being bathed.

Prefabricated tubs and showers now come in one-piece models that are part of a wall ready for installation. They cost less than traditional equipment.

Kitchen Sinks

The most commonly used sink is acid-resistant enamel over a cast-iron base with an integral drain set into a plastic-covered counter top. Stainless-steel sinks are more expensive but easier to maintain. A double-bowl sink is preferable to a single-bowl sink if there is no dishwasher. If there is a dishwasher, a single-bowl sink takes up less counter space and accommodates larger pots and pans than one side of a double-bowl sink.

SUMMARY

Comfort and convenience are important factors in the enjoyment of a home and also in its resale value. The provisions for heating the home in winter and keeping it comfortable in summer, for wiring the home for proper lighting and well-placed convenience outlets, and for meeting plumbing needs adequately are important to the home builder and buyer.

There are numerous ways to reduce the heat load in summer, among which are trees, solar orientation, good ventilation, awnings, overhangs, and insulation. The heating system and the source of heat will depend upon the geographical location of the home, its size and exposure, the cost of available fuels, and the cost of various heating systems. It is usually advisable to provide for future cooling needs, even though a cooling unit may not be installed at the time of building.

To be safe, a wiring system should conform to the requirements of the National Electrical Code. When wiring is inadequate, there are warning signals that should not be ignored, because inadequate wiring causes many fires. If fuses keep blowing out, if the television flickers, or if lights become dim when appliances are being used, wiring should be checked.

The areas in which plumbing provisions should be made are the kitchen, bathroom, laundry, and outside connections for hoses. If plumbing pipes can be concentrated on one wall in a two-story home or on adjacent walls in a one-story home, costs can be cut. Although the average-size bathroom is 5 feet by 7 feet 2 inches, it is desirable to have one a little larger when possible. If there is no dishwasher in the kitchen, a double-bowl sink is preferable to a single-bowl sink.

THINGS TO THINK ABOUT AND TO DO

1. List some of the factors related to home heating and cooling that you would want to discuss with an architect if you were building or buying a home. Use role playing to demonstrate a meeting with an architect.

2. Find out from a local heating engineer or a representative of the gas, oil, or electric industry how he would go about estimating the annual heating bill for a house heated by his type of fuel.

3. Place a thermometer and a barometer in your home or classroom, and check the temperature and humidity daily for a week.

4. Find out what firms in your area provide for home air purification. Determine the cost of installing equipment, where and how it can be installed, and what it can be expected to do.

5. Differentiate between a *gravity* and *forced* warm-air heating system, a *gravity* and *forced* hot-water heating system.

6. Give some reasons why steam heat is less popular now than in former years. Find out whether steam heat is used in your immediate neighborhood, and if so where.

7. Discuss some pros and cons of central cooling systems in a home or an apartment.

8. Mount on the bulletin board illustrations showing various methods of using electricity for heating. A local heating firm or power company will have brochures. Explain how radiant or panel heating may be provided by either hot water or electricity.

9. Discuss some advantages and disadvantages of panel or radiant heating.

10. Discuss popular heating fuels in your community as to cost and satisfaction.

11. Check your home wiring against some of the safety provisions and warning signals discussed in the text. Examine all the cords on lamps and appliances and replace frayed or worn cords.

12. Check the service panel in your home to find out how many circuits there are and whether fuses or circuit breakers are used. If they are not labeled, label where each leads and indicate the ampere capacity of each.

13. Find out where your electric meter is located and the average number of kilowatt hours of electricity you consume monthly. How many special-purpose circuits have you?

14. Find out whether your electric current is grounded.

15. On quarter-inch graph paper make a drawing of a two-bedroom home, and indicate where you would place convenience outlets and switches. Work in pairs.

16. Define a *low-voltage system* and give its advantages.

17. Make a list of all the lights in your home and also all appliances (other than those requiring special circuits), and indicate the total wattage. How many circuits should you have?

18. Assemble illustrations of various types of toilets, tubs, showers, and lavatories, and discuss their characteristics.

An attractive powder room, well located for guests.

REFERENCES FOR UNIT TWO

BOOKS

Abrams, Charles, *Man's Struggle for Shelter in an Urbanizing World*. Cambridge, Mass.: Massachusetts Institute of Technology Press, 1964.

Allen, Frederick Lewis, *The Big Change*. New York: Harper and Row, 1952.

Allport, Gordon, and others, *Study of Values*. Boston: Houghton Mifflin Company, 1957.

Churchill, Allen, *Remember When*. New York: Golden Press, Inc., 1967.

Galbraith, John K., *The Affluent Society*. Boston: Houghton Mifflin Company, 1958.

Gordon, Leland, and Stewart, M. Lee, *Economics for Consumers*. New York: American Book Company, 1967.

Harmon, A. J., *The Guide to Home Remodeling*. New York: Holt, Rinehart and Winston, Inc., 1966.

Lynes, Russell, *The Tastemakers*. New York: Harper and Row, 1954.

Maisel, S. J., *Financing Real Estate: Principles and Practices*. New York: McGraw-Hill Book Company, 1965.

Murray, R. W. *How to Buy the Right House at the Right Price*. New York: P. F. Collier, Inc., 1965.

Oppenheim, Irene, *The Family as Consumers*. New York: The Macmillan Company, 1965.

Perl, Lila, *The House You Want: How to Buy It*. New York: David McKay Company, Inc., 1965.

Rose, J. G., *The Legal Adviser on Home Ownership*. Garden City, N.Y.: Institute of Legal Knowledge, 1964.

Troepstrup, Arch W., *Consumer Problems and Personal Finance*. New York: McGraw-Hill Book Company, 1965.

U. S. Department of Labor, *How American Buying Habits Change*. Washington, D.C.: Superintendent of Documents, Government Printing Office, 1959.

Warner, W. Lloyd, and others, *Social Class in America*. New York: Harper and Row, 1949.

Whyte, William H., *The Organization Man*. New York: Simon and Schuster, Inc., 1956.

Williams, Robin, *American Sociology*. New York: Alfred A. Knopf, Inc., 1960.

MAGAZINE ARTICLES

Fortune:
"The High Rise Monotony of World Housing," July, 1968 (pp. 73–81).
House and Home:
"Housing's Market Revolution—and What It Means to Builders," "The Multifamily Boom in Suburbia," February, 1968 (p. 71).
"Segmented Demand: Is Today's Apartment Market Divided into These Seven Renter Types?" April, 1965 (pp. 94–99).
"Who Really Buys Your Houses and Why?" November, 1967 (pp. 82–85).

BOOKLETS AND PAMPHLETS

Superintendent of Documents, U. S. Government Printing Office, Washington, D.C. 20402:
   Bathrooms, Misc. Publication No. 988 (5¢)
   City Worker's Family Budget, Bulletin No. 1570-1 (75¢)
   Dining Areas, Misc. Publication No. 960 (5¢)
   Home Heating Systems, Fuel Control (30¢)
   Planning Bathrooms, Home and Garden Bulletin No. 99 (15¢)
   Planning Your Home Lighting, House and Garden Bulletin No. 138 USDA (20¢)
   Where Not to Build ($1.00)
University of Illinois, Small Homes Council, Urbana, Ill. 61801 (Pamphlets 15¢ each):

A1.3 *Financing the Home*	F4.6 *Flooring Materials*
A2.0 *Business Dealings with Architect and Contractor*	F6.0 *Insulation*
	F11.0 *Window Planning Principles*
C1.1 *Hazard-Free Houses for All*	G3.1 *Heating the Home*
C5.1 *Household Storage Units*	G3.5 *Fuel and Burners*
C5.32 *Kitchen Planning Standards*	G4.2 *Electrical Wiring*
C5.33 *Separate Ovens*	G5.0 *Plumbing*
C5.4 *Laundry Areas*	G6.0 *Summer Comfort*
C5.9 *Garages and Carports*	

   (Write to the following addresses for current lists of literature, with prices. Also use coupon services in magazines to send for material on bathrooms, kitchens, walls, floor coverings, and so forth.)
National Adequate Wiring Bureau, 155 E. 44th St., New York, N.Y. 10017
U. S. Gypsum Company, 101 S. Wacker Dr., Chicago, Ill.

FILMS, FILMSTRIPS, AND SLIDES
(See page 469 for name and address of source.)

   A Good Kitchen in Your Home. Gives help on kitchen planning. (47 slides, USDA)
   A House Is a Living Thing. Shows how good planning can restore an old house to meet modern needs. (13½ minutes, color, BBB)
   How to Fight a Fire in the Kitchen. Shows how to cope with small fires in the kitchen. (5 minutes, color, AF)
   Keys for the Homes of Tomorrow. Shows ways home economics courses prepare for successful living. (27 minutes, color, AF)
   Patterns of Time—The Hardwood Story. Shows how hardwood patterns are selected and matched and how hardwood plywood is made. (13½ minutes, color, MTP)
   What You Should Know Before You Buy a Home. Shows important factors to consider before buying a home, such as location, space, conveniences, age, and cost. (27 minutes, color, MTP)
   Wise Use of Credit and Personal Financial Planning. Two films showing how to budget and plan for the future, according to the National Consumer Finance Association. (22 minutes, color, AF)
   Your Money and You. Gives practical help in managing money. (35 minutes, 72 frames, HFC)

Decorating a Home

chapter eleven

THE APPLICATION
OF ART PRINCIPLES

Our physical and social environment is important to our well-being. To the person who has been at work all day, home is a haven of rest, a place in which to relax and renew one's energy and interests for another day, a place in which to enjoy one's family and entertain friends. If a home is to provide satisfaction and happiness, its furnishings and decoration should conform to the family's pattern of living and their likes and dislikes. A home must also meet certain standards of comfort, convenience, economy, and ease of maintenance. Being able to apply the principles of design to furnishing a home is not a panacea for all environmental difficulties, but it can help to provide beauty and order.

Good interior design can be achieved by learning the meaning of the *elements of design*—line, form, texture, and color—and by learning how to apply the *principles of design*—balance, proportion, rhythm, emphasis, and harmony. *Line* not only establishes direction but is symbolic of mood and important in conveying illusions of height or breadth. *Form* is the shape that objects take—rectangular, square, triangular, oval, round, and so on. The shapes of objects in any area should be relatively harmonious with each other and with the size and contour of the area in which they are used. All forms have *texture*—smooth or rough, shiny or dull, soft or hard. Some textures combine better than others. *Color* is such an important element of design that it is treated separately in the following chapter. In addition to having elements of design, objects may be purely functional or purely decorative or both functional and decorative. When decoration is applied it should be consistent with the design and use of the object.

When you become thoroughly familiar with the elements and principles of design, you will find that they apply to spacing the typing on a page, selecting the clothes you wear, arranging furniture or flowers, landscaping a home, setting a table, hanging pictures, placing rugs, or almost anything else you do.

GUIDELINES FOR STUDY

GENERAL IDEAS
TO CONSIDER

1. The elements of design—line, form, texture, and color—are the components an artist or a decorator uses to create something interesting or attractive.

2. The principles of design are the laws that govern the way an artist or a decorator uses design elements to create anything of interest or beauty.

3. Structural design is the fabricating of materials to produce an object that is either utilitarian or both utilitarian and interesting. Decorative design means that decoration has been applied to the structure.

4. All independent forms that contribute to the whole must be harmonious with each other and with the space confining them in order to create unity.

5. Interior decoration is successful when it conforms to the laws of design and when it serves the needs of the occupants of a room or a home.

WORDS AND TERMS
TO KNOW

abstract design
contemporary (furniture)
conventionalized design
decorative design
dominant lines
Early American (furniture)
environment
floor composition
French Provincial (furniture)
function
highboy
natural design
progression
structural design
subordinate lines
traditional (furniture)
Victorian (furniture)
wall composition

THE ELEMENTS OF DESIGN

It is difficult to separate the elements and principles of design because you cannot use the elements of design without employing design rules or principles. The elements are line, shape or form, texture, and color.

Line Establishes Direction

The artist working on a flat surface first establishes line direction or motion. Some lines are dominant, and others are subordinate. In some instances lines may be so conflicting that they create confusion. In other instances lines may be so repetitive that they convey an impression of monotony, or so vibrant that they create an atmosphere of excitement.

Lines take four general directions— vertical, horizontal, diagonal, and curved. By combining directional lines there is no limit to design possibilities. Designers have found that lines have certain psychological associations. For example:

Vertical lines point toward the sky and seem to convey an impression of dignity, discipline, and strength. In architecture vertical lines are exemplified in tall monuments and skyscrapers; in nature, by Lombardy poplar trees and tall grasses; in home furnishings, by a high secretary, highboy, vertical mirror, or vertical picture.

Horizontal lines are down to earth and suggest serenity, repose, and relaxation. In architecture horizontal lines are noticeable in contemporary or ranch-type homes; in nature the setting sun over the ocean or across a plain suggests horizontal lines; in the home a sofa, a low chest, or a long low bookcase emphasizes horizontal line movement.

The use of vertical, horizontal, and curved lines in decorating.

Diagonal lines are active and seem to disturb the dignity of vertical lines and the tranquility of horizontal lines. However, they break the monotony of vertical and horizontal lines. In architecture slanted and pointed roofs produce diagonal lines; in nature mountain peaks and rocks suggest diagonal direction; and in the home diagonal lines are expressed in stair rails and in some fabric designs.

Curved lines are graceful and suggest youth, gaiety, and subtle motion. Architects make use of curved lines in arches and domes; nature uses curved lines in clouds, leaves, and winding streams; and in home furnishings curved lines are prominent in furniture design and window decoration.

A knowledge of when and how to use and combine various lines will help you in decorating your home.

Form Relates to Shape

Lines help to give an object form or shape. Whereas the landscape artist works on flat surfaces to give an illusion of form, the sculptor and the furniture designer work with solid or plastic materials to create many forms and shapes. Chairs, sofas, tables, and lamps take many shapes in which either straight, diagonal, or curved lines predominate. Some shapes are more pleasing than others. Rectangular shapes are associated with masculine rooms and contemporary furnishings, whereas oval or curved shapes are associated with feminine rooms and Victorian furnishings. When you study furniture design, you will notice that during some periods rectangular forms dominate furniture styles, and in other periods curved forms dominate. A room is more interesting when different forms are combined. The form or shape of an object should have some relationship to its function, but its function need not always be utilitarian. For example, some shapes, such as large objects of art in a hotel or apartment house lobby or in a park or city square, may be functional only as objects of beauty.

This brings us to two design terms that we should understand—*structural* and *decorative* design. Most modern furniture depends solely upon structural lines and texture for beauty. Eighteenth-century furniture depends upon both structure and decoration because many pieces are carved or inlaid. You will notice as you study period furniture that the structural and decorative lines are interrelated.

A fabric may be structured to produce design; that is, the warp may be set up to produce a plaid, stripe, geometric, brocade, or damask design. A plain fabric may have an applied or a decorative design. This is usually printed on the surface, and it may be a *natural* design, a *conventionalized* design, or simply a *geometric* or *abstract* design, such as checks, dots, blocks, or stripes. The illustration on page 192 shows these types of design.

Decorative design must be in keeping with structure and function. For instance, embroidery on dishcloths or sequins on flyswatters are not consistent with the use of these items. The following criteria will help you to judge structural and decorative design:

1. Will the structure or form serve its function? For example, no matter how attractive bookends may be in form, they must also be heavy enough to function in supporting books.

2. Are all parts of a structural design in good proportion? A very heavy chair with short pipelike legs may sit squarely on the floor, but the legs are out of proportion to the chair.

3. Does the decoration improve the appearance of the structural form? If not, it should be omitted.

4. Are the decorative lines in harmony with the texture as well as the shape of the object? For example, Indian motifs would be out of place on a fine china plate but appropriate on pottery.

Texture Applies to All Forms

Texture may be rough or smooth, shiny or dull, porous or firm. The same form—a sofa, for example—will look quite different upholstered in homespun, mohair, or damask. A floor will change its character depending upon the texture used—tile, wood, or carpeting. Certain textures are compatible, whereas others clash.

The furniture used in a room will determine to a large extent the textures suitable for rugs, drapery fabrics, and wall finish. For example, traditional or eighteenth-century furniture is made

Above: This nineteenth-century chair, made of painted birch, depends upon decorative design for its beauty. (Courtesy, Museum of Fine Arts, Boston) *Below: The Barcelona chair, designed by Mies van der Rohe, uses chromium-plated steel and leather in a superb structural design.*

of fine mahogany or walnut, often carved or inlaid. Furniture of this period looks best with rather rich textures, such as brocade, damask, velvet, fine linen, and smooth firmly woven cotton; and with silver, brass, and alabaster accessories. French Provincial and Early American furniture is often made of light and more informal woods—maple, birch, or fruitwoods—which are compatible with chintz, gingham, and other informal fabrics; and with copper, pewter, and pottery accessories. Contemporary furniture may be made of light or dark wood, metal, or plastic, but it is streamlined. It combines nicely with rough textures and bold patterns and with wood and wrought iron accessories.

When period styles are combined, as they are quite often, the shape of the room and the predominating style will determine the best choice of textures. All the textures should harmonize. It might be possible for an experienced decorator to combine homespun and satin in the same room, but the amateur is more successful in combining homespun with cretonne and satin with brocade.

Color

Color is such an important element of design that an entire chapter has been devoted to it. You may refer to Chapter Twelve for an application of design elements to the use of color.

THE PRINCIPLES OF DESIGN

Design principles are time-tested laws that help us to achieve pleasing effects in home furnishings, landscaping, or selecting clothes. These principles are *balance, proportion, rhythm, emphasis,* and *harmony* or *unity*. They are all interrelated.

Balance Means Equilibrium

When furniture, pictures, or colors are balanced, a feeling of satisfaction and rest is projected. When objects are out of balance, the effect can be quite disturbing. For example, when all the upholstered pieces of furniture are at one end of the room or when a single bright-colored chair has nothing in the room to balance it, the effect is like a seesaw with all the weight on one end.

Balance may be secured by placing identical objects on each side of a center point, or by placing unequal objects at unequal distances from a center point. The former arrangement produces *even balance*—sometimes called symmetrical or formal balance. The latter produces *uneven balance*—sometimes called occult or informal balance. A room looks more interesting when both types are used.

A

Proportion Means Good Space Relationships

Pleasing space relationships are important in designing a dress, in hanging pictures, and in arranging furniture. As a rule, it is better to break up spaces unevenly; that is, a belt should not divide a dress equally; a door should not divide a wall equally; and a piece of furniture should not divide a space equally.

The ancient Greeks were masters in the application of the principles of design, as all their great temples and statues show. They developed a scale of space relationships that avoids monotony. According to the Greek laws of proportion, flat areas are divided in the following ratios: 2:3, 3:5, 5:8, 8:13, and so on. With a little practice the eye can distinguish between interesting and uninteresting space relationships.

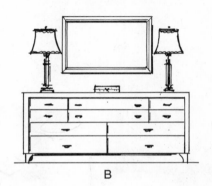

B

We cannot discuss proportion without mentioning scale because the terms are similar in that they deal with space relationships. Furniture must be chosen in scale to a room; lamps, tables, and accessories grouped about a sofa or a chair must be chosen in scale with the dominant object; a picture over a fireplace must have the right proportions and be in scale with the fireplace. The illustration on page 196 shows how the law of proportion and scale can be used effectively.

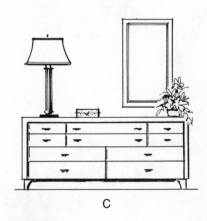

C

A shows lack of balance—the lamp is too tall to balance the jewelry box. B shows even balance, with smaller lamps in symmetry. C shows uneven balance, with one large lamp and a small, vertical mirror.

Rhythm by repetition provides a graceful window grouping. The curving lines of the window are repeated in the placement of furniture, in the shapes of individual pieces, and even in the drapery fabric.

Rhythm and Motion

The art principle called rhythm is used to create motion and to carry the eye from one area to another without abrupt interruptions. We can create rhythm in a number of ways: (1) by the *repetition* of lines, shapes, or color; (2) by *gradation* or a gradual progression of sizes in the arrangement of pictures on a wall or objects on a shelf or chest; (3) by using lines in *opposition* or at right angles in the treatment of windows —for instance, where tailored draperies are used with a straight-edge cornice; (4) by *transition* or by connecting straight lines with curved lines as in the use of curved cornices or swags of draperies at the top; and (5) by *radiation* when many lines radiate from a central point.

Emphasis Creates a Center of Interest

Usually an observer is attracted to one particular part of a room. It might be a painting around which a color scheme is planned, a beautiful rug, an interestingly arranged set of shelves, beautiful windows, or an attractive fireplace. The skilled decorator knows what to emphasize and how to avoid overemphasis. The amateur may have a pleasing, restful room, but may lack the skill or knowledge necessary to give a room character or to focus attention on an interesting structural feature or home furnishing item. Overemphasis, which gives an impression of clutter, is far less desirable than underemphasis, which often conveys a feeling of simplicity. As a rule, it is advisable to focus attention upon an area of a room that is seen as one enters the room. Study the illustrations throughout the text, and see how experienced decorators use emphasis.

Rhythm by RADIATION

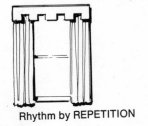

Rhythm by REPETITION

Rhythm by OPPOSITION

Rhythm by TRANSITION

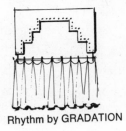

Rhythm by GRADATION

Five ways to create rhythm in window treatments.

Many elements in this room convey an impression of harmony, including the use of objects in scale with each other. The arrangement of furniture and pictures gives a rectangular "feel," softened by the graceful lines of the chairs and the window treatment. What basic idea do you think is expressed here?

Harmony or Unity

Where colors, lines, and shapes are related in a floral centerpiece, painting, dress or room arrangement, unity or harmony will prevail. In producing harmony or unity, the artist, dress designer, or interior decorator usually aims to express an idea in combining art elements—lines, form, texture, and color. For example, the decorator may aim to express masculinity or femininity, formality or informality, ruggedness or refinement, classic simplicity or contemporary boldness. If lines, shapes, textures, and colors are coordinated with the general idea and the art principles are observed, the decorations in a room will be harmonious. However, this does not mean that we cannot mix furniture styles or have some freedom in the choice of fabrics. Tasteful blending of unlikes can contribute to harmony.

While studying this chapter you will want to turn to Chapters Fourteen and Sixteen and note further application of the principles of design to window decoration and furniture arrangement.

FLOOR COMPOSITION. The following suggestions may be helpful in the arrangement of furniture so that it conforms to the principles of design and so that good traffic lanes are created:

☐ Study the room you are decorating from all angles. Try to visualize its strong points and its weak points.

☐ Buy furniture that will be in scale with the room. Measuring the room and the furniture will help.

☐ Draw a floor plan on graph paper (¼ inch equals 1 foot) and cut out to-scale furniture templates. Place the templates on the floor plan, showing the floor space each item of furniture will cover.

☐ Place large pieces first, such as sofa, bed, chests, and so forth. Chairs may be placed diagonally. However, large items are seldom placed diagonally.

☐ Balance large pieces on walls facing structural features, such as windows or a fireplace, or on a wall opposite other large pieces.

☐ Use area rugs in a large room or a dining area for a furniture grouping.

☐ Place a piano on an inside wall for protection, and place a baby grand piano so that the pianist can face the room.

☐ Use room dividers, such as shelves, cabinets, or planters, to separate areas in a large room.

☐ Arrange chairs and sofas for conversation groups, so that chairs must not always be moved.

☐ Mark on the floor plan traffic lanes that will need to be used in getting from room to room and area to area. Improve these if necessary.

☐ Avoid overcrowding.

WALL COMPOSITION. Good floor composition is the basis for good wall composition. A few additional suggestions are helpful:

☐ Balance vertical and horizontal shapes in a room.

☐ Avoid placing a tall bookcase between two tall windows. Place a tall piece of furniture on a wall opposite tall doors or windows.

☐ Show good transition in the placement of wall objects, lamps, and furniture groupings.

☐ Avoid using too much even balance in a room. Some even balance is necessary to give a room repose, but overdoing it creates monotony.

☐ Group wall accessories, such as pictures, shelves, wall brackets, and so on, over low cabinets so that all space relationships are pleasing.

☐ Avoid hanging pictures stairstep fashion except perhaps along a stairway.

☐ Consider the many types of wall accessories—pictures, mirrors, wall clocks, barometers, hanging shelves, lamps, wall brackets, and so on—and choose those best suited to your decorating plan.

☐ Consider the effect of different window treatments, since windows are such an important part of wall composition. Details will be given in Chapter Fourteen.

OTHER FACTORS
IN SUCCESSFUL DECORATING

While keeping in mind the aesthetic values in decorating, you must not overlook other values. For example:

☐ *Does the house look as if it is planned for the people who live in it?* If a family like outdoor life and simple living, they may not be happy in a home with a formal atmosphere or in a home that is cluttered with bric-a-brac, no matter how attractive it is.

☐ *Are the art principles observed without decreasing comfort and efficiency?* A home should look "lived in"—not like a showroom in a furniture store. However, this does not mean that it must look lived in to the point of always presenting an untidy or unkempt appearance.

☐ *Is the furniture functional in design and arrangement?* It is quite possible to become so enthusiastic about achieving an artistic effect that function is overlooked. If a living room has tables without drawers and no place for the storage of records, writing supplies, or other items it will not be very conducive to efficient living. Beautiful kitchen equipment and attractive walls and windows cannot compensate for inconvenient kitchen storage.

You may want to review the chapter on values in housing while studying this chapter. If so, see Chapter Four, pages 57 to 69.

Every feature of this arrangement is evenly balanced, including the design on the wall paneling, yet the total effect is neither contrived nor rigid. Why?

SUMMARY

Some people have a natural talent for selecting clothes, arranging flowers, and combining home furnishings, whereas others must learn and apply the rules. In learning these rules, one must develop certain concepts about line direction, shapes and sizes, texture, and color combinations. It is important to know how to discriminate between structural and decorative design, so that emphasis and unity can be achieved. Texture is also an important element of design. Certain textures for floors, walls, and furniture combine to produce harmony, others to produce discord.

Art principles govern the choice of lines, shapes, texture, and color. Balance may be even or uneven. Proportion relates to scale and requires that line and form have pleasing relationships. Rhythm relates to line movement that is pleasing to the eye. Emphasis creates a center of interest, thus avoiding monotony. Harmony is achieved when the requirements of other art principles have been met. The principles of design apply to both floor and wall composition. When arranging furniture, begin with the largest pieces and avoid having too much weight in one area. Begin the wall composition by emphasizing a focal point—windows, fireplace, or an object of art.

THINGS TO THINK ABOUT AND TO DO

1. Consider the importance of physical and social home environment to you. Write two or three paragraphs on this subject and then discuss your ideas with other class members.

2. Display a number of reproductions of paintings, and indicate the lines that predominate. How do you react to line direction? Contrast your emotional reaction to different line directions.

3. Study the clothing of class members and objects in the room in relation to line and form, and make comments on your findings.

4. Mount on the bulletin board illustrations of rooms that show the use of vertical, horizontal, diagonal, and curved lines, and discuss the effects produced.

5. Mount on the bulletin board pictures of furniture showing good and poor form or shape. Indicate those that convey a feeling of masculinity; those, of femininity.

6. Bring to class clippings showing structural and decorative design. Indicate how the decorative design is achieved and the form it takes; for instance, conventional,

natural, or abstract. Does the decorative design enhance or detract from the structural design?

7. Display a number of textures for floor, wall, and furniture coverings, and demonstrate how some combine better than others.

8. Mount on the bulletin board black-and-white illustrations of contemporary, traditional, and provincial rooms, and using the samples collected for item 7, select texture and color combinations for each room.

9. Bring to class clippings of rooms showing uneven and even balance, pleasing proportions in the choice and arrangement of wall composition, and the interesting use of rhythm and emphasis. Write a description for each clipping. Keep these in your decorating file or notebook.

10. Discuss the importance of such factors in decorating as considering the likes and dislikes of the people who live in the home and weighing beauty against comfort and function.

chapter twelve

THE MAGIC
OF COLOR

Perhaps nothing is as important as color in home decoration. Unless we are blind, we are constantly aware of color, and we consciously or unconsciously react to the colors around us. We become accustomed to associating certain colors with the way we feel. We use color to give an illusion of closeness or distance, colored lights to direct traffic, and colored filing cards in business codes. At present colored advertising far outsells black and white advertising. We see color built into everything we use—metals, wood paneling, concrete, mortar, window shades, kitchen appliances, automobiles, and clothing. We know that background colors may increase or decrease working efficiency and may cheer or depress children in hospitals.

Light is the source of color and is necessary to our full enjoyment of it. A knowledge of the physical, chemical, and psychological aspects of color is important to our understanding of color. For example, black absorbs light and white reflects light; these facts explain why black clothing and black roofs hold heat, whereas light clothing and light roofs reflect the rays of the sun. Studies reveal that individuals have strong likes and dislikes for certain colors. Furthermore, over the years each color has acquired a certain symbolism, illustrated by such phrases as "in the pink," "green with envy," "yellow"—meaning cowardly—and "true blue."

Certain colors are very stimulating in a decorative scheme, and others create a sense of rest. The colors used in a particular room should therefore be selected with the function of the room in mind. Other factors to be considered in choosing colors are whether we want a room to appear warm or cool, whether we want it to look larger or smaller, and whether or not the choice will blend with colors in adjacent rooms or hallways. The background colors can be enhanced by attractive accents.

If we are to be able to use color effectively, we must become familiar with terms describing its application, such as hue, value, and intensity, and we must know similar and contrasting color harmonies. Some of us may be fortunate enough to have a natural gift for using color, whereas others may have to develop a color sense through study.

GUIDELINES FOR STUDY

GENERAL IDEAS
TO CONSIDER

1. Color is of prime importance in the decorating scheme because it not only contributes to beauty but also affects the way we feel and behave.
2. Colors have been subject to fashion change since ancient times. Changing color emphasis in decorating affects many industries—paint, textile, carpet, tile, and industries related to all accessories.
3. A knowledge of terms related to color, such as hue, value, intensity, and standard color harmonies, is basic to using color effectively in the home.
4. Color plans will give satisfaction if the following factors are considered: family preferences, room exposure, room size and shape, and decorating theme.
5. Colors may change their appearance under warm sunlight, ordinary daylight, and either incandescent or fluorescent light.
6. Colors may appear different in different textures.
7. In addition to planning color schemes from standard color harmonies, one can use a figured carpet, wallpaper, a drapery fabric, a painting, or an heirloom to establish a color scheme.

WORDS, TERMS,
AND NAMES TO KNOW

Adam brothers
Antoinette, Marie
Baroque style
Chippendale, Thomas
color symbolism
color trend
de Wolfe, Elsie
du Barry, Madame
eclectic approach
fluorescent light
Gainsborough, Thomas
genre painting
heirloom
Hepplewhite, George

hue
incandescent light
intensity (of color)
Munsell System
Pompadour, Madame
Prang, Louis
primary color
Reynolds, Sir Joshua
Rococo style
Romney, George
secondary color
Sheraton, Thomas
tertiary color
value (of colors)

APPROACHES TO THE STUDY OF COLOR

We have a number of scientific approaches to the understanding of color. The *physiologist* studies the effect of color stimulation upon the eyes. Experiments have shown that so-called eye-rest colors—soft greens, blue-greens, and off-whites—should be used in offices, factories, hospitals, and classrooms where there is a great deal of concentration or routine activity. In your own study area you can avoid eye fatigue if you eliminate strong surface contrasts. For example, the contrast created by a dark-surface desk and white paper will cause more eye-strain than a light-surface desk and white paper. For this reason large, light-colored desk pads are used for work on dark-colored desks.

The *physicist* studies color in terms of light waves. Ordinary white light contains all colors, which our eyes, unaided, cannot detect. (A rainbow or a prism shows the entire spectrum.) When all rays of light are reflected, a surface appears white; when certain light rays are reflected and others are absorbed, various colors appear; when all the rays of light are absorbed, the surface appears black. Applying this principle to clothing and housing, we can understand why light-colored clothing and light-colored rooftops keep out heat by reflecting light waves and why dark-colored clothing and roof-tops hold in heat by absorbing light waves.

The *psychologist* studies the effect of color upon the emotions. Red is a stimulating color, and it is frequently used in carpeting or for walls in night-clubs and special dining rooms, but red in large areas is not recommended for school use or for dining rooms where

groups of children study or eat. It is too stimulating. Blues and greens are far more relaxing.

The *chemist* studies ways and means of producing beautiful dyes and paints. Until the mid-nineteenth century pigments for paints and dyes came from natural sources—iron oxide, iron sulfate, tree bark, plants and plant roots, berries, and insects. Now paints and dyes are largely synthetic. The chemist endeavors to perfect permanent dyes for all the new fibers and outdoor paints and produce colors that will endure exposure to atmospheric gases and temperature changes.

The *artist*—painter, interior decorator, dress designer, and textile designer—is constantly experimenting with colors to produce new color combinations for interiors, for clothing, and for woven and printed fabrics. Color is sensitive to fashion change. A color may be fashionable during some periods in history or during some seasons of the year.

COLOR SYMBOLISM

Color has many associations for which we often use the term *color symbolism,* such as "feeling blue," "in the red," and so on. The ancient Greeks associated *black* with life because out of the dark night day was born. We have associated black with death since Anne of Brittany wore black in the sixteenth century to mourn the death of her husband, Charles VIII. *Red,* because of its association with blood and fire, has always symbolized danger. One is in difficulty when his accounts are "in the red." Because the heart is red and love was believed to begin in the heart, red is also a symbol of love. Black and red are two of the most dramatic decorating colors (if we can stretch a point and call black a color).

Yellow has symbolized cowardice and jealousy and also wisdom and gaiety. It was sacred to the ancient Chinese, a symbol of power to pre-Christian rulers because it resembled gold, and thus a color disdained by early Christians. Yellow is associated with cheerfulness because it is the color of the sun. Nature uses *green* in the greatest abundance (except perhaps brown), and therefore green has become a symbol of life, fertility, and vitality. Pagans used green in their outdoor ceremonies, and for this reason early Christians banned its use. The Moslems associate green with sacredness; the Irish, with good luck; but to many people it means envy. Perhaps we can trace this association to Old Testament times when tribes fought over fertile valleys because land with water meant their livelihood. Yellow and green are two of the most popular colors in home decoration.

Except for the blue sky and blue water, *blue* is one of Nature's rarest colors. Blue symbolizes truth and honor, and from this symbolism the terms *blue blood* and *true blue* originated. *Purple,* although quite similar to blue, has had different associations. In ancient times purple pigments were rare and expensive, and only royalty could afford purple fabrics. Early Christians eliminated this color because of its cost and royal symbolism. Hebrew priests used purple curtains in the holy places in their temples. The fact that these holy places were reserved for high and learned priests is the reason why purple has been symbolic of wisdom and mystery. In the Middle Ages it became associated with penitence. Blue has been far more popular in decorating than purple, except for short periods during the nineteenth and twentieth centuries.

ORIGIN OF COLOR TRENDS

Colors, like fashions in furniture and dress, have gone through periods of popularity since ancient times. Many color trends in furnishing are short lived.

Early Civilizations

The Egyptians and Greeks used rather sharp, clear colors. The bright colors in evidence in Egyptian tombs and described in early Greek literature, plus those seen in the excavations of the buried cities of Pompeii in Italy and Knossos on the island of Crete, attest to the popularity of bright colors in many ancient civilizations. Time and weather have erased the bright colors that decorated the sculptured figures on the temples of the Greeks, such as the Parthenon. But when Pompeii was excavated in the eighteenth century, there was a revival of classic colors and designs.

The Romans established the dramatic black and white color scheme when Emperor Hadrian used black and white marble chips for mosaic floors in his villa. Marie de Médicis, second wife of Henry IV of France, used black and white floors in a number of châteaus that were built under her direction. The popular decorator Dorothy Draper and the well-known artist-designer Cecil Beaton have used black and white with a flair. The dramatic black and white Edwardian costumes used at the races in *My Fair Lady* were creations of the late Cecil Beaton. During the eighteenth century, the English artist Josiah Wedgwood created many beautiful teapots and urns of black Ethiopian marble overlaid with white.

Renaissance

Renaissance colors were rich but not bright or light, although gold and white were often used in wall and furniture decoration. Renaissance paintings are seldom used to establish a color scheme because they are usually dark and the subjects—often of a religious or allegorical nature—are not appropriate for many homes. The Dutch artists of the period have produced colorful genre paintings (subjects of everyday life) which often establish color schemes for Provincial rooms.

The Eighteenth Century

The pretentious Baroque styles and colors of the period of Louis XIV are most at home in palaces, such as Versailles and the many country palaces of Europe copied from this spectacular palace outside Paris. When Louis XIV's rule of seventy-two years ended and Louis XV came to the throne, court life had begun to change. The salons and boudoirs of this period, dominated by Madame du Barry and Madame Pompadour, called for light buoyant colors, and many of our present colors were named by these popular hostesses. Flowers and foliage provided the background for the paintings of the French artists Fragonard and Boucher, and the colors in nature inspired the light and gay color schemes of the day. This period is referred to as the French Rococo. Marie Antoinette, wife of Louis XVI, merely exaggerated the trends set by Madame du Barry and Madame Pompadour.

During this period in history (the eighteenth century), the practical English were taking a lead in home furnishings. The English, always enthusiastic about nature and the outdoors, came under the influence of the French social reformer Jean Jacques Rousseau (1712–1778), who stressed a return to the simplicities of nature in rebellion against prevailing court extravagances.

The eighteenth century was known as the Georgian period, or the Golden Age of Furniture, in England, when architecture and home furnishings developed to their highest degree. The period was dominated by the artists Romney, Reynolds, and Gainsborough; by the cabinetmakers and designers Chippendale, Hepplewhite, Sheraton, and the Adam brothers; and by the ceramic craftsmen Wedgwood and Spode. Wedgwood medallions, panels, and fine pottery were developed from jasper, an uncrystalline variety of quartz capable of taking stains of almost all colors. Trade between England and India and China brought brighter Oriental colors into vogue, but lovely soft colors prevailed in paintings, fabrics, rugs, and wallpaper. If you have ever visited historic Williamsburg, Virginia, you will have some conception of the colors used during the eighteenth century.

The Nineteenth Century

The nineteenth century, the latter part of which (insofar as design is concerned) is referred to as the Victorian period, was a period of industrialism when somber colors came into fashion —mauve, wine, old rose, sage green, and buff. The good Queen Victoria probably had less influence upon color choices than that exerted by the growth of industry. The vibrant colors typical of the court and country life of the eighteenth century could not hold up in the soot that was constantly being emitted from factory smokestacks and steam locomotives. Dusty colors were popular because they showed the dirt less than clear light colors. Thus the nineteenth century is remembered as a period in which muted colors were fashionable.

The Twentieth Century

Elsie de Wolfe, former actress and socialite, is often referred to as America's first interior decorator. As people tired of drab colors and heavy fabrics, she introduced during the early twentieth century light colors in the use of gay chintz. However, her dark green soon became her decorating trademark. In her own words it kept her "in tune with nature." In the late twenties, the decorator Syrie Maugham, wife of the famous English novelist Somerset Maugham, started a vogue for all-white rooms, a trend which is revived from time to time.

The Armory show of 1913, or the International Exhibition of Modern Art, in which paintings by Matisse, Gauguin, Cézanne, Van Gogh, and other modern artists were shown, started a trend toward vibrant colors which was interrupted by the Great Depression of the thirties and World War II of the forties. The sharp and often striking color combinations of these artists continue to influence contemporary decoration.

Interior decorators try to keep fashions in home furnishings on the move to stimulate business, just as couturiers do in the dress-fashion business. Color trends often start when a well-known decorator designs a room around a color that has been dormant for several seasons. Fortunately for the consumer, fashions in furnishings change at a less rapid pace than in clothing. New color combinations appearing in home furnishings magazines make some homemakers dissatisfied with their present furnishings. Some follow new trends and thus stimulate business in the paint, wallpaper, carpet, and fabric industries, whereas others wait until refurbishings are needed. A few years ago when it was suggested to a popular New York decorator that she had not used pink for a long time, she created a pink, red, and white room. This was a fresh change from traditional color schemes, and immediately pinks and reds became popular. A pink and brown and pink and orange trend followed. For a period, blue and avocado were popular. Actually *orange* and *pink* (a light value of red) and *blue* and *avocado* (a dull yellow-green) are sets of neighboring colors on the color wheel (see page 208).

Color psychologists began to enter the decorating field during the late 1940's by introducing eye-rest colors for hospitals, offices, and factories. Paint companies produced paints to meet the recommendations of the color psychologists. The light reflection of many standard colors was indicated on the paint-can label. For example, an off-white, called *color-conditioning white,* has the highest light reflection of all colors with a count of 86 percent. Ivory and sunlight yellow follow with a light reflection of 68 and 66 percent respectively. By contrast, deep green, deep blue, and deep rose drop to about 15 percent in light reflection and require much more artificial light for reading and working comfort.

There is no reason why you should slavishly follow popular color trends in home furnishings, unless the new colors are colors you like and can live with, and unless new decorating is necessary. You can admire the new colors in magazines and in the homes of friends who may have them. If the new colors are your favorite colors and you decide to use them, do so with discretion so that the color combinations will not date your decorating scheme.

The following discussion of color terms and color harmonies will help you to be discriminating in the use of color.

THE COLOR WHEEL
AND COLOR CLASSIFICATION

The color wheel on page 208 includes twelve colors, and these colors are classified as *primary, secondary,* and *tertiary.* This color arrangement is based upon the Prang System. The name originated with Louis Prang (1824–1909), who in 1882 formed the Prang Educational Company, nationally known distributors of art supplies. The *primary* colors are *red, yellow,* and *blue;* these are basic colors from which any other colors can be produced. The *secondary* colors are *orange* (a combination of red and yellow), *green* (a combination of yellow and blue), and *purple* (a combination of blue and red). *Tertiary* colors come in between the six primary and secondary colors to produce *red-orange, orange-yellow, yellow-green, green-blue, blue-purple,* and *purple-red.*

There are other color systems, one of which is the Munsell System. It starts with five principal colors and has five intermediate colors, with a total of ten colors in the color wheel instead of twelve as in the Prang System. Orange is eliminated as a principal color. Although the Munsell System has merit in that it produces less contrast in color combinations, we shall base our color study on the Prang System with its three basic, or primary, colors.

THE DIMENSIONS OF COLOR

For want of a better term we use *dimension* to refer to hue, value, and intensity, all of which are important in using color. We can take any of the pure *hues* (colors), change their *value*

(make them lighter or darker), and change their *intensity* (make them brighter or duller).

Hue is another term for the name of a color. We might say that red, yellow, blue, and so forth are generic names for colors—family names, so to speak. A red hue can mean red from pale pink to crimson as well as orange-reds or purple-reds in wide ranges. We may accept blue as a background hue for a room if it is light and has a touch of green to produce a turquoise, whereas we might reject blue as a background hue if it is a strong purple-blue. It is important to develop an eye for color, so as to be able to discriminate between color combinations that are almost right and those that are really effective.

Value refers to the lightness or darkness of a color. Light color tones are called *tints;* and dark color tones, *shades.* Sky blue, shell pink, and Nile green are tints, and royal blue, rose, and forest green are shades. When mixing paints, you can lighten colors by adding white, and darken colors by adding black. However, you should add black very slowly because it can change some colors very quickly.

Intensity refers to the brightness or dullness of a color. Kelly green, fire-engine red, and sunflower yellow have high intensities. Although experienced decorators may use intense colors for all or some of the walls in a room, the amateur is advised to use intense colors in very small amounts to accent a color scheme. If when painting a wall you find the color is too intense, you can subdue or neutralize it by adding a small amount of its complement, or the color opposite it on the color wheel. For example, red will tone down bright green, but too much red will make green almost gray.

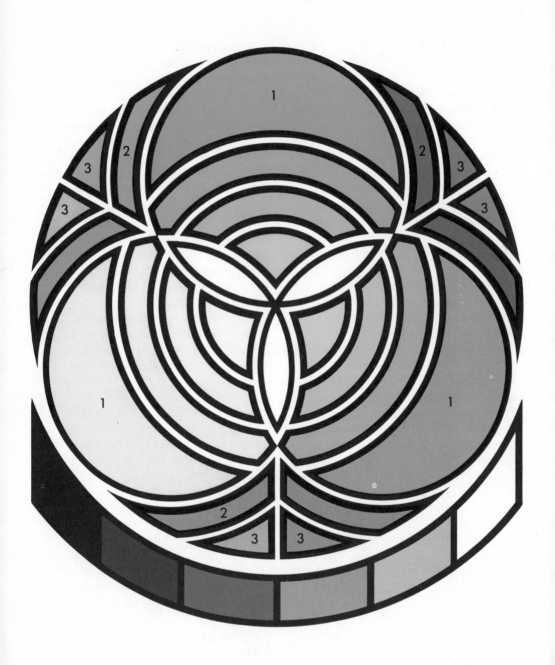

Key: (1) indicates the primary colors—red, blue, and yellow; (2) the secondary colors—purple, green, and orange; (3) the tertiary colors—purple-red, blue-purple, green-blue, yellow-green, orange-yellow, and red-orange. At bottom: the value scale of black.

When you understand the meaning of hue, value, and intensity and how to apply the principles of design, you can use color with confidence.

STANDARD COLOR HARMONIES

In connection with the color wheel and its twelve hues and the variations in intensities and values that hues can have, we shall discuss standard color harmonies that are scientifically planned to produce pleasing and often dramatic color schemes.

Color harmonies may be *similar* or *contrasting*. Similar harmonies are produced from colors close together on the color wheel; and contrasting harmonies, from separated colors.

Similar Color Harmonies

Similar color harmonies are *monochromatic*, or a harmony produced by use of one color in a number of values and intensities, and *analogous*, or a harmony produced by the use of colors that are close neighbors on the color wheel—for example, yellow, yellow-green, and green. (See pictures, pages 200 and 212.) Similar harmonies tend to unify a room and give an illusion of more space, but some contrast in value and intensity is needed to avoid monotony.

Contrasting Color Harmonies

Contrasting harmonies are *accented neutral, split complementary, complementary,* and *triad*. An *accented-neutral* harmony is the use of a noncolor, such as white, black, or gray (made by mixing opposite colors), or sometimes a grayed beige or tan, with a color accent, such as red, yellow, or blue. An accented-neutral color scheme can be very dramatic (see page 212).

To produce a *complementary* color harmony, two opposite colors on the color wheel are used—for example, red and green in varying intensities and values. When used together, opposite colors tend to emphasize each other. This means that a light-pink wall will look pinker when soft green or even blue-green draperies are used than when either light-blue or beige draperies are used. A *split-complementary* color harmony uses three instead of two colors. In place of the opposite color from red (green), for instance, the colors on each side of red's complement (green) are used—yellow-green and green-blue.

A *triad* color harmony is produced by using three colors that are an equal distance apart on the color wheel. This harmony requires a little more skill in handling to avoid too much color contrast and a somewhat disturbing effect.

THE POWER OF COLOR

Color has magical powers. No other element of design is as effective as color in creating a mood, changing the size or shape of a room, camouflaging awkward looking furniture, or focusing attention on prized possessions. Warm colors, such as yellow, orange, and red, tend to *advance,* and cool colors, such as greens and blues, tend to *recede* within the room.

The same living room might be decorated in cool colors—for instance, blues and greens with lots of white—and give a feeling of *restfulness;* or with vibrant splashes of warm and cool colors and give a feeling of *excitement;* or perhaps in soft pale yellows and greens and give a feeling of *gaiety.*

Any color has force, especially if its complement is used as a background color—for instance, a violet chair against

A storage area with a triad color harmony.

A colonial living room in complementary colors, with accents.

An analogous color harmony.

An accented-neutral color harmony.

a yellow wall will stand out much more than when violet is used against a background of an adjacent color, such as blue. A handsome piece of furniture in brown wood tones, such as mahogany or walnut, will have greater emphasis against blue and blue-green walls than against beige walls because brown (dark orange) and blue-green are complementary colors. On the other hand, color can be used to camouflage unattractive furniture by blending it into the background. A sofa with poor proportions can be slipcovered in a fabric with a slight surface pattern (or muted pattern effect) a little darker than the wall, and its lines will appear indistinct. Colorful cushions can be used for accent.

Warm, fairly intense colors used on the walls of a large room make it seem smaller and more intimate. However, warm colors in tints, such as pale yellows and pinks, can make a room appear larger, although not so successfully as a pale cool color. Because cool colors (especially light blues and greens) tend to recede, using them on walls can make a room appear larger.

FACTORS DETERMINING COLOR CHOICES

Factors which often determine color choices include family preferences, exposure of the room, physical characteristics of the room, colors used in adjoining rooms, decorating theme, and so on.

Family Preferences

Perhaps the most important factor in using color is to make sure that the colors will please the occupants of the room. No matter how attractive the colors may be in a room, in a magazine, or in the home of a friend, they must give the people who use the room a feeling of satisfaction. Some people have definite dislikes regarding color. There are people who have a strong dislike for green, for example, although it is a popular decorating color.

Exposure of the Room

The power of color to make a room feel warm and gay or cool and relaxing has already been discussed. A room with a south or even a southeast or southwest exposure will have a great deal of natural warm sunlight. Therefore, it is usually advisable to use *cool* colors for the major areas—walls and floor. On the other hand, a room with a northern exposure will have less natural warm light; hence it is advisable to use *warm* colors to compensate for the general coolness. A kitchen is one of the most lived-in rooms of the house; hence exposure will have a lot to do with the choice of colors for large areas —walls and floors. If rooms are not lived in much during the daylight hours, it becomes less important to consider exposure in the choice of color, and personal choices may take priority over exposure.

Physical Characteristics of the Room

We discussed the power of color in creating optical illusions—that is, in causing the walls to advance or recede. Dark, bright, and warm colors used on the walls of a small room will make the occupants of the room feel crowded and perhaps depressed. A light wall color with a matching color in the draperies and woodwork, a lighter value on the ceiling, and a slightly darker value in the carpeting will give a room a feeling of space.

If a room is cut up with offsets, chimneys, windows, and doors, greater unity can be achieved by using the same color on all surfaces or by using a printed wallpaper, by using a companion print in the drapery fabric, and by painting the woodwork the same color as the background of the print. This treatment may have too much pattern for some people. If so, either the printed wallpaper or the printed drapery fabric may be omitted and a solid color matching the background of the print used instead.

If a room has a normal eight-foot ceiling or a lower one, it is advisable to paint the ceiling off-white or a tint of the color used on the walls to give a feeling of height. On the other hand, a high ceiling, often found in older homes, may appear lower if it is painted a little darker than the walls. A dark ceiling will require more artificial light because it will have little light reflection.

A square room can be made to appear more oblong by the skillful use of color. For example, an off-white or creamy yellow paint may be used on three walls and a turquoise blue on the fourth wall to give an illusion of length. If you do this, be sure to mix a little of the off-white or creamy yellow with the blue to key it to the predominant color. A sharp cool blue, while giving an illusion of greater distance, may be too unrelated to the white or yellow.

A room that is too long and narrow can also be given an illusion of better shape through the application of color. If one of the end walls is painted a warm advancing color, or covered with a wallpaper or drapery fabric with warm colors in the design, the room will appear to have better proportions.

The use of color to create optical illusions can be supplemented by such ideas as lowering a ceiling by panels or arranging furniture skillfully.

Adjoining Rooms and Present Furnishings

It is not often that we can change the entire color scheme of a house or even its living area. We usually have to key a new color scheme to an existing rug, sofa, or draperies or to colors in adjoining rooms. It is a good practice not to use more than two or three colors in a single room or living area where rooms and halls are closely connected. After studying all present furnishings and determining how you might shift rugs or furniture to another part of the house, you will have to work colors that you cannot change into the new color scheme.

You cannot use one set of colors in a living room, another in the hall, and still another in the dining room if these areas are adjoining and if you expect to achieve unity. Colors should flow from one room to another. If a house is small, the best way to give a feeling of unity and space is to use wall-to-wall carpeting in the living room, hall, and dining room in a medium-light color. The hall wallpaper, if figured, may suggest color schemes for adjoining rooms. But for a feeling of maximum space, paint the living room, hall, and dining room walls the same color, preferably a light color. Window treatment and accessories can give each area individuality or character.

Decorating Theme or Room Character

Houses and rooms within houses, like people, develop a certain character. If you are trying to achieve spaciousness, study an Egyptian, a Greek, a Japanese, or a contemporary room where simplicity is the keynote. If you are aiming at dignity and formality, study rooms furnished in the Georgian period. If you like coziness and informality, study Provincial and Early American rooms.

A room takes on character according to the way it is used. A living room is more or less impersonal, and therefore colors should not be too stimulating. Bedrooms are for relaxing and sleeping; hence bedroom colors and design should be more or less restful. A family room or kitchen or dining room may be more colorful because these rooms are activity rooms and places where family members can be informal. You can be as original and bold as you please in choosing and combining colors in playrooms.

Other Factors

Other factors that may influence color choices are texture and artificial light. *Incandescent* light is a bit yellow and it tends to fuse yellow into existing colors, making yellows and greens more sharp, blue more green-blue, and purples almost brown. *Fluorescent* light drains color out of furnishings. This type of lighting is frequently used in bathrooms and kitchens, and sometimes colors are greatly distorted. It is possible to use fluorescent light bulbs that do not influence light reflection too greatly.

Texture influences the apparent color of textiles and other furnishings. Even though the same dyes are used for a linen or satin drapery fabric and a wool or synthetic carpet, the resulting colors will look different. In choosing colors it is always advisable to bring fabric or rug swatches to the room where these items will be used. You can judge better how they will fit in with present furnishings and how they will appear under daylight and artificial light.

The Oriental rug has influenced the choice of colors throughout this room.

STARTING POINTS
FOR COLOR SCHEMES

You may find a starting point already established if you move into a home or an apartment with painted walls and wall-to-wall carpeting that would be expensive to change. The question of changing the wall color may not present an insurmountable problem if you can afford the cost of a coat of paint and labor or if you do the painting yourself. If you should own an Oriental rug you will have to consider the predominating colors in it when establishing a color scheme. Existing wood-paneled walls also may have to be considered in a color scheme.

Here are some helpful suggestions for developing color schemes:

START WITH WHAT YOU CANNOT CHANGE. If a rug or an allover carpet is green or if an Oriental rug has a great deal of red and blue, you cannot ignore these existing colors. It will be helpful to start a clipping file of ideas for a suitable color scheme. There are bookstores in most cities that sell old magazines cheaply. In addition to this source, you can go through current decorating magazines; note advertisements for carpet, paint, draperies, and furniture; and write for special brochures. After you have chosen several possible color schemes for your existing colors, display the clippings on a wall in the room, and study them for a few days.

START WITH WALLPAPER OR A PRINTED FABRIC. This is a trick used at times by all decorators. The artist who created the print will have partially solved your color problems. The print will suggest not only colors to use but also the proportion in which to use them. (See page 218 for a discussion of proportion in the use of color.) Note the colors that dominate the print. If you are using figured wallpaper, you may want to wallpaper three walls of a room and paint one wall the color of the wallpaper background; then you can use a drapery print to match. Avoid selecting a color that is used in very small amounts to repeat in major room areas because it may be too insignificant to be effective. By holding fabric swatches and large paint cards against the print, you can soon find the two colors to use in the largest quantity. If you wish, you can pick up a third color for emphasis, which can be used in accessories. It is not always necessary to use a third color especially if you use two colors in more than one value. For example, if you have a drapery print with a white background and a design that uses several values of blue and yellow-green, you can use a medium-blue carpet, light-blue walls, an avocado sofa or chairs, and white lamps. In a large room the print can be repeated in a sofa or chair; in a smaller room, in sofa cushions. Additional upholstered furniture can be covered in a neutral fabric with a woven pattern.

START WITH A PICTURE OR AN HEIRLOOM. A painting, a prominent vase, a textile hanging, or an attractive quilt may provide an interesting color harmony. It is wise to assemble swatches of fabric, carpet, and paint samples, and study them in the room. Use the colors that dominate the painting or art work in decorating the largest areas of the room. This should insure the application of good proportion in the use of color.

START WITH A FAVORITE COLOR. If you have a favorite color and it happens to be orange, you may want to select a burnt-orange carpet. Your next consideration will be the walls. Off-white or light-yellow tones or even turquoise will go with orange. By adding a very small amount of the rug color to the wall paint, you can key together the carpet and the walls. Your next step may be to find a window fabric. If you like a feeling of space, match the window fabric to the walls and secure your pattern emphasis in the choice of a painting or a wall hanging for a prominent wall area. This hanging must have fairly large amounts of the two colors you have already selected. Other colors in the hanging will give you a key to the colors for accessories.

USE THE ECLECTIC APPROACH. The term *eclectic* is frequently used in decorating to describe a combination of furnishings in colors that defy general rules. Some people have the ability to ignore rules and to express independence and imagination, whereas others must be governed by certain rules.

USE A STANDARD COLOR HARMONY. Pleasing color harmonies can be developed according to the rules for standard harmonies. The above sources for developing color schemes may or may not combine colors ordinarily used in standard color schemes. However, they provide some measure of guidance for the beginner in attaining success. Illustrations in this chapter show color schemes derived from standard color harmonies as well as from printed fabrics and wallpaper, paintings, and heirlooms.

PRINCIPLES OF DESIGN APPLIED TO THE USE OF COLOR

The principles of design apply to the use of color as well as to the use of line, area, and shape. For example, *balance* must be observed in the distribution of color.

The delicate color scheme used here focuses attention on the heirloom bedspread.

Balance

If two colors predominate, they should not be used in equal amounts in furnishings. Neither would you place all items of one color on one side of a room and all of another color on the opposite side. Two chairs of the same color may balance each other on opposite sides of a fireplace or a table. On the opposite side of the room a color in a figured sofa may repeat the chair color, or cushions on the sofa may pick up the chair color for balance.

Proportion

Colors should be used in varying proportions. The wall area, including doors and windows, represents the largest mass. The room will appear in larger proportion if walls, doors, and window fabric are all one color. As a rule light and neutral colors may be used in larger proportions than bright colors, but high-fashion decorators may take the liberty of painting walls or ceiling a strong color or using a strong-colored carpet. Other decorators may use a large printed background with draperies or a bedspread of matching print. However, large areas of vivid color or figured wallpaper and matching textiles are disturbing to the average person who must live with them.

Rhythm

Color rhythm may be obtained by repeating the colors in a figured fabric or carpet, in a painting, or in an object of art. However, spotty repetition may create a staccato rhythm that can be disturbing. Color transition from one room to another is necessary in observing the principle of rhythm. In a small home wall-to-wall carpeting in the living room, hall, and dining room with related colors used in these areas will create rhythm. In a large home a figured wallpaper in the hall may suggest colors for adjoining rooms. Color gradation is evident in a monochromatic harmony where the wall, floor, draperies, and furnishings are variants of one color.

Emphasis

Color may be used to emphasize beautiful furniture by contrast or by repetition. A drapery fabric that uses a color which repeats the wood—cherry, walnut, maple—will emphasize the warm wood tones. A plain, light background will always emphasize any dark-wood furniture more than a medium-colored or figured background. If overstuffed furniture is awkward in shape, it may be de-emphasized by blending it into the background colorwise. As a rule, in any decorating scheme, one color predominates and provides emphasis.

SUMMARY

Color is so very important to our environment and emotions that it has been the concern of physiologists, physicists, psychologists, and chemists as well as of painters and designers of clothing and home furnishings. We are all aware of color symbolism when we use such expressions as "feeling blue" or "in the red." Colors come and go in popularity in the same way as furniture and dress fashions.

When we understand the color wheel and the relationships of colors in different intensities and values, we can develop greater confidence in combining colors.

In addition to knowing how to select and combine colors, we must consider other things, such as family preferences, room exposure, size and shape of the room, the effect of colors used in adjoining rooms, and how colors react under changing light.

Although a painting, a drapery fabric, or wallpaper may provide keys to good color schemes, we must also know how to apply art principles to the use of color if we are to be pleased with the results.

THINGS TO THINK ABOUT AND TO DO

1. Name and describe the scientific approaches to the use of color. Tell the story of how some manufacturer of household furnishings studies color.

2. How do the artist, dress designer, and interior decorator influence color trends? Use some of the references suggested, and report to the class the story of how some color or color scheme became popular.

3. List on the chalkboard the three primary and the three secondary colors on the color wheel, and conduct a class discussion regarding color symbolism.

4. Find illustrations from library files to show how color was used by such ancient civilizations as those of the Egyptians, Greeks, and Romans and during such historic periods as the Renaissance, the French eighteenth century, the Victorian era, and contemporary times.

5. Conduct a class demonstration (using tempera colors) to show how primary colors may be combined to produce all other colors, and how the value and intensity of colors may be changed.

6. Mount on the bulletin board illustrations to show the power of color—that is, how it can change apparent room dimensions and temperature. This will include examples of good color schemes for rooms of different exposures and different sizes.

7. Name all the factors to be considered in arriving at a color scheme and discuss the importance of each. Go on a field trip to observe examples of the application of these factors.

8. Mount on the bulletin board illustrations showing how the color of furniture, accessories, and textures may influence the character of a room.

9. Tell how you would use colors from the following sources in planning the floor and wall covering, drapery and upholstery fabrics, and accessories in a room: faint figured wallpaper, figured fabric, a large painting, and an heirloom, such as a quilt or wall hanging.

10. Using the above illustrations, explain how you would use the principles of design —balance, proportion, rhythm, and emphasis—in the color schemes.

11. Collect some clippings of good color schemes, and put them in a scrapbook or portfolio.

chapter thirteen

BACKGROUNDS
FOR FURNISHINGS

Walls and floors are the principal backgrounds which provide a setting for room furnishings. The ceiling treatment must also be a part of the decorating plan. It should never compete for interest, but blend into the general decorating theme. During the Renaissance period and the eighteenth century, ceilings were quite decorative, and in early American homes beamed ceilings were common. In recent years acoustic tile ceilings have been used for their functional as well as their decorative effect.

Walls may be finished in many ways depending upon the condition of the walls, the cost, and the size, shape, and character of the room. Paint, wallpaper, and paneling have been the most common wall finishes, but emphasis upon integrating indoor and outdoor living has popularized the use of glass, brick, and shingles for indoor walls. Formerly hardwood floors in the north and hardwood or terrazzo floors in warm climates were considered to be the best floor finishes. On these floors either scatter, area, or room-size rugs were used, ranging from expensive Orientals to inexpensive cotton shag rugs. Wall-to-wall carpet, once a prestige symbol, has become more common in recent years all over the country. The introduction of inexpensive rug fibers and a tackless method for laying carpet, plus easy-to-lay tiles of wood or resilient substances, give the homeowner a choice of floor covering over a concrete or plywood base.

In earlier chapters many of the factors that influence a decorating plan have been discussed. These include physical features of the room, present furnishings, family preferences, size and shape of the room, exposure, and the character of adjoining rooms. You may want to review some of these factors as you study this chapter.

We are concerned here mainly with choices of wall finishes and floor coverings. The use of the room will influence these choices. Rooms receiving constant use, such as kitchens and family rooms, require wall and floor finishes which need minimum care. The background of a room is also determined by the character or idea you wish to express.

GUIDELINES FOR STUDY

GENERAL IDEAS
TO CONSIDER

1. The treatment of main backgrounds—walls, ceilings, and floors—sets the decorating theme, provides a setting for furniture, and also changes the physical characteristics of a room.
2. The choice of a wall finish is determined by personal tastes, condition of the walls, cost, use of the room, and decorating theme.
3. The choice of a floor finish is determined by the home-furnishings budget, family preferences, condition of the floors, and decorating theme.
4. The consumer has a wide choice of floor finishes and floor coverings, making consumer education in these areas necessary.
5. The choice of main backgrounds will vary with family attitudes toward maintenance, family preferences, and costs in relation to the budget.

WORDS, TERMS, AND NAMES
TO KNOW

acoustic tile
Aubusson
Bigelow, Erastus
Brussels carpet
ceramic tile
dado
epoxy paint
flat finish
flocked paper
French toile
grass cloth
hardwood
India print
lacquer
latex paint
linoleum
metallic finishes

monk's cloth
Moors
parquetry
plywood
precut panels
resilient flooring
rigid flooring
satin finish
scenic wallpaper
semigloss finish
shellac
silk-screen printing
softwood
terrazzo
varnish
vinyl

WALL FINISHES

Walls (including windows) are the largest areas in a room, and the treatment of these areas must conform to the character or decorating theme and the structure of the room—size and shape. In addition, the main backgrounds (walls and floors) must complement the furniture and accessories. The wide variety of wall finishes available offers a number of choices for any room in the house and for any expression or idea in decorating. Familiar wall finishes are evaluated.

Paint

Paint is one of the most satisfactory wall finishes available because it is easy to apply and maintain, and the color choices are unlimited. If it is not possible to buy a *ready-mixed* or *formula-mixed* paint to match a fabric or wallpaper, the experienced painter can mix any desired color. This is easily done by adding color pigments to white paint for light values, or by adding a color to medium paints to change the color slightly. If you should need to mix paint, take the following precautions: (1) Avoid using pigments and paint with different bases—for instance, an oil-base pigment will not mix with a latex-base paint. (2) Mix a little paint in a jar, and paint a small area of the wall. Wait until the paint dries, and mask off the old paint with white paper to see the true color. (3) After mixing the desired color in a small amount, mix enough to do the entire job. Keep the sample in case you run out of paint. (See Chapter Twenty-seven for estimating paint needs.) (4) If you run out, stop at a corner, so that the new paint will not contrast too much in case it does not match exactly. (5) Remember that white will lighten a color and that the opposite color on the color wheel will tend to subdue a strong color.

The less-experienced person will find a fairly wide choice of colors in ready-mixed and formula-mixed paints. Ready-mixed paints are available at any place selling paint, but color choices are somewhat limited. Formula-mixed paint may be mixed by any store having a paint-mixing machine. Paint cards give the exact proportions for hundreds of colors. Colors can be thoroughly mixed in about twenty minutes. The introduction of the paint roller and paint that is water-soluble caused a boom in painting by amateurs. About three-fourths of all paint sold is applied by the homeowner.

There are three major types of paints: *oil base, latex* or *acrylic,* and *epoxy.* Oil paint is soluble in turpentine, mineral spirits, or odorless paint thinner. Many professional painters prefer to use oil paint, and many also prefer using a brush instead of a roller, unless the areas are very broad. Good oil paint, properly applied, holds up longer under wall washing. Most do-it-yourself painters prefer to use latex or acrylic paint because it goes on fast, covers old paint nicely, has little odor, and dries fast. It is soluble in water, which makes cleaning clothing and brushes easy if they are washed before the paint has a chance to set.

A flat-finish paint is recommended for all rooms of the house, except the kitchen and bathroom. A semigloss or satin finish is more serviceable in rooms where there is steam or grease because it is easier to maintain. It is also often used to cover wood trim.

Sometimes people paint over wallpaper. If the wallpaper has not begun to separate from the wall, the finish will be satisfactory. However, the wallpaper will be difficult for an amateur to remove. It must be removed without

Painted walls provide a neutral background for an attractive display of art objects and books, and also for the interesting textures used here—in the woven window shade, shag rug, and large plant.

steam by a dry method. This is usually a job for a professional paperhanger.

A newer paint product is epoxy or polyester enamel, which looks like porcelain. This is a durable and glossy-finish paint used in kitchens and bathrooms for refinishing tile walls that have become discolored. Colors are limited to white, black, and pastels. The paint comes in two cans and must be mixed shortly before using because a chemical reaction takes place immediately upon mixing to solidify the paint. The paint in one can acts as a catalyst; and in the other, as a reactor. There is a special thinner to keep the paint at the proper consistency for application.

Aside from paints that produce color in home decoration, there are several clear products: *varnish, shellac,* and *lacquer.* Varnish (soluble in turpentine and paint thinner) comes in dull, semi-gloss, and high-gloss finishes and may be used on natural wood doors, window frames, and wood paneling. Shellac (soluble in alcohol) comes in a clear and an orange color, and is used as a wood sealer or base for paints. Lacquer (soluble in lacquer thinner) is used more on furniture and wall screens than on walls. Lacquer comes in pressurized spray cans, and if directions are followed carefully, a very smooth surface can be obtained. It is more difficult to apply by hand than paint, varnish, or shellac because, like nail polish, it dries rapidly.

For a discussion of how to apply paint turn to Chapter Twenty-seven, page 453.

Wallpaper

Although wallpaper is more difficult to apply than paint and it usually costs more in materials and labor, it has some advantages over paint—for instance: (1) If the walls are rough or uneven, textured or figured wallpaper will de-emphasize the imperfections. (2) Wallpaper comes in a wide range of textures, designs, and colors. (3) It gives warmth to a room; a scenic wallpaper at one end of a room gives greater depth; and a large pattern in wallpaper makes a large room look smaller. (4) It establishes a color scheme. (5) Companion wallpapers and wallpapers that have matching fabrics make color transition from one room to another easy.

Wallpaper may be had to simulate almost any texture—grass cloth, monk's cloth, silk, brocade, metallic effects, French toiles, India prints, wool plaids, wood grains, ceramic tile, brick, stone, and marble. Surface design, which is applied commercially by steel-roller or silk-screen methods, has no limits. However, it is generally advisable to avoid wallpaper that is a blatant imitation of something else.

HISTORY. The Chinese developed the first civilization to use paper resembling wallpaper as we know it. As early as 200 B.C. the Chinese made small twelve- by eighteen-inch rectangles of paper, and decorated them by hand with designs of flowers and birds. Early decorated papers were used for wall hangings or screens. The Chinese also perfected tea-chest papers, or metallic papers with a small pattern, used as a liner for their tea chests exported to foreign lands. By the eighteenth century, the Chinese had developed scenic wallpaper designs to such a high degree that one scene required an entire room for proper display.

Increased trade between England and the Orient during the eighteenth century coincided with the Georgian period in England, when the cabinet-maker Thomas Chippendale was having the greatest influence upon English interiors. The exquisite Chinese scenic wallpaper not only provided a beautiful

A practical background for a laundry and planning area: washable vinyl-coated wallpaper and simulated-wood formica paneling.

background against which to display the fine furniture of the period, but the Chinese influence was reflected in many of Chippendale's furniture designs. Long before the Georgian period in England, Louis XI of France (1423–1483), according to legend, had a court artist design a wallpaper with angels holding scrolls inscribed to the glory of God— perhaps to assure the monarch that the Lord was on his side. Flocked wallpaper, resembling cut velvet, dates from about 1620. In this process the design is printed with an adhesive and a fine fuzz is blown onto the adhesive. These designs are used in elegant restaurants and other formal rooms today.

During the 1700's the French artist Jean Papillon produced wallpaper with design repeats similar to the wallpaper of today. During the reigns of Louis XIV and Louis XV the artists Fragonard and Boucher provided scenic designs for wallpaper, but it was a long time after the invention of the printing press before wallpaper was printed by machinery. The first roller-printed wallpapers came into use in 1839. For the first time commercially produced wallpaper became available to families in the middle class, who could never afford hand-printed wallpaper. Wallpaper with large repeats is often printed by a silk-screen method because large prints require too large a roller to be practical. Screen printing is done by hand, but it is similar to stenciling and is not especially time-consuming.

Brocade fabric applied within wall panels heightens the formality of this traditional living room.

USE OF WALLPAPER. When figured wallpaper with a pronounced pattern is used in a room, it dominates the decorating scheme. Solid-colored wallpaper is sometimes used in place of paint, but it is more difficult to maintain than paint, unless the surface of the wallpaper is coated with a washable finish. Wallpaper manufacturers have designers who coordinate wallpaper designs, so that two or three related papers may be used in adjoining areas. Some wallpaper patterns are also available with matching drapery fabrics.

Many wallpapers are labeled washable, but not all of these are completely resistant to water, grease, and other stains. In truly scrubbable wallpapers, the color itself is a plastic substance. A fabric-backed wallpaper has several advantages. It covers uneven surfaces and cracked plaster, and it is easy to remove. If you find a wallpaper that is not resistant to grease and stains, you can increase its resistance by having the factory give it a vinyl coating at a small additional cost. It is also possible to apply a clear varnish made especially for wallpaper. It is applied after the paper is on the wall. This varnish, which is available under several trade names, changes the color very little and gives extra protection to ordinary wallpaper. Of course it cannot compare with a vinyl finish.

The amateur decorator is often disappointed in wallpaper after it is on the wall. The following suggestions will help the inexperienced person to avoid mistakes:

☐ Bring home a strip of paper several feet long, tape it to a wall in the room where it is to be used, and study the effect. (Use masking tape to avoid damage to the wall.) Designs always look different in wallpaper books than they do on the wall.

☐ Avoid wallpaper designs that appear to be busy, spotty, or restless because this effect will be exaggerated on the wall.

☐ Avoid three-dimensional repeats that seem to be jumping off the wallpaper.

☐ Keep wallpaper designs in scale with the room. Large motifs or repeats will overpower a small room, and small motifs will be lost in a large room.

☐ Avoid using scenic wallpaper or wallpapers with large repeats if the walls are broken up with doors, windows, or a fireplace.

☐ Use scenic wallpapers on unbroken areas if they are needed to give a room a feeling of depth. Keep the colors in harmony with the color scheme and the design in scale with the room. Scenic papers are often used above a *dado*. This is a term used to refer to the lower part of the wall, which may be paneled in wood or painted a solid color, with a chair rail separating it from the upper part of the wall.

☐ For an interesting effect, use figured wallpaper on two or three walls and identical drapery fabric on the other wall or walls. If a solid-colored wall is used, it should repeat the background color of the figured wallpaper.

☐ Use vertical stripes to give an illusion of height and horizontal stripes to give an illusion of breadth.

☐ Avoid using wallpaper that imitates wood, stone, or marble unless you have a special reason for using such finishes.

☐ Avoid flocked designs, rough textures, and metallic finishes unless you are an experienced decorator. They are difficult to use, and you may tire of them.

☐ Try using scenic wallpaper (entire scene) or a wallpaper with an interesting repeat in paneled areas. For example, you can use a small wood molding to frame a panel in a hallway

Walnut paneling used on one wall and repeated on the door lends warmth to a contemporary dining room.

or over a bedstead. The dainty French toile designs are especially interesting in small areas.

Wallpaper is also effective as a lining for drawers and closets and as a covering for closet accessories, such as hat boxes and shoe racks.

Wood Paneling

Until wallpaper was introduced, expensive wood paneling was an accepted wall finish in the palaces of royalty and the homes of the wealthy. Exquisite tapestries and later hand-painted wallpaper were often set in paneled sections of the wall.

Today relatively inexpensive precut and prefinished wood panels are available in plywood or pressed wood. The panels are four feet by eight feet (sometimes larger) and come in a wide variety of surface finishes—grained off-white and grained tinted wood, birch, walnut, mahogany, pine, fruitwood, maple, and oak. A less-expensive grade of paneling may be had if it is to be painted. These panels interlock, so that the joints are concealed. They are not difficult to install. However, if they are to be applied to basement walls where there might be some dampness, sheets of insulation (available where panels are sold) should be placed between the wall and the panel to act as a moisture barrier. This insulation will also help to keep out the cold in areas of the house that receive sharp winds.

Wood paneling not only helps to keep out moisture and cold air, but it also conceals badly damaged walls in any section of a room. This is a popular treatment for the walls in a den, library, family room, laundry room, or recreation area.

Ceramic Tile

Ceramic tile is frequently used for bathroom walls because it is not harmed by heat, steam, or water, and it is easy to maintain. Plastic tile simulates ceramic tile, but it lacks the richness and permanence of ceramic tile.

The use of ceramic tile dates from the time of the Old Kingdom in Egypt. The Moors, who occupied northern Africa and the Iberian Peninsula from the 700's on, used exquisite tiles on exterior and interior walls. If you ever visit Portugal, you will see scenes from Portuguese history depicted on the walls of cathedrals and palaces in blue and white tiles. Tiled walls are popular in the southern and southwestern United States. Plain tile is sometimes used as a dado with scenic wallpaper or a wall painting above it.

This wall-hung desk unit is enhanced by a painted brick background.

Other Wall Finishes

With greater emphasis upon integrating outdoor with indoor living, structural materials are becoming more popular for inside walls. These materials include glazed or unglazed brick in many color tones and glass (clear, patterned, opaque, or in brick form). Linoleum and sheet vinyl are also used for walls, and where quiet is important, carpet and cork are occasionally used.

CEILINGS

In the days of the Renaissance the ceiling was very important in decorating a cathedral or a palace. During the eighteenth century, English and American homes had ceilings that were sometimes dome shaped and often decorated with wood or molded-plaster motifs. Wood beams are still used in English-style country homes and in Spanish-style homes in our Southwest

Most contemporary homes have ceilings no higher than eight feet, and a plain plastered ceiling painted an off-white or a lighter value than the walls is the most common finish. High ceilings in older homes may be painted a darker value than the walls to lower the ceiling by optical illusion. In many instances in older homes the ceiling is lowered to a distance of eight or eight and a half feet from the floor by the use of acoustic-tile panels. This ceiling treatment permits the use of lighted panels in rooms of the house where ceiling light is needed. Acoustic ceilings absorb between 55 and 75 percent of the noise, and they are easy to maintain or replace. They are recommended for rooms where noise is a problem. The noisiest rooms in the home are the kitchen, dining room, family room, and recreation room. Acoustic-ceiling tiles may be had in finishes suitable for any room. They will not peel, crack, or chip.

Acoustic tiles of wood fiber are lower in cost than those of mineral fiber, but they are not as luxurious in appearance or nearly as fire-retardant. Both come in 2-foot by 2-foot and 2-foot by 4-foot panels. Acoustic plaster is also available.

Acoustic-tile ceilings are easy to maintain. They can be dusted occasionally with a soft brush and cleaned with wallpaper cleaner or a sponge and mild soap or detergent. Dirt does not clog the small holes in the tiles because the dead air acts as a barrier against dirt-laden air. If it is necessary to change the color of the acoustic tile, a good grade of flat interior oil-base paint can be used. It must be applied lightly and evenly to avoid clogging the pores and thus interfering with noise absorption.

FLOOR TREATMENT

The floor is important in the building of a home and in the decorating plan. Different areas of the home will require different treatments. The homemaker has a wide choice of rigid, resilient, and soft-textured floor surfaces.

Rigid Floor Surfaces

Rigid floor coverings include hardwoods, softwoods, marble, flagstone, slate, brick, terrazzo, mosaic tile, and ceramic tile.

If nicely laid and well kept, wood flooring is preferred by many people and especially by families who own Oriental rugs. Some people like an unadorned wood floor, but such floors present a maintenance problem and provide no resistance to noise or shock. In many apartment buildings, unless wall-to-wall carpeting is used, the landlord requires that all-wood floors be 80 percent carpeted to reduce sound transmission.

Popular hardwoods are oak, maple, beech, birch, and pecan. Pine is the most familiar softwood. A filler, usually shellac, is used on wood floors to fill in the pores. A low-gloss varnish gives extra durability to the finish, and wax helps to preserve the grain and the finish. Dark wood finishes show dust more than medium to light tones. The floor color should not contrast too much with the rugs used on it.

Wood floors may be made of narrow boards set by a tongue-and-groove method, or else of boards nailed inconspicuously to an underflooring. Boards of random widths may be laid side by side and held in place with wood pegs. True wood pegs were used in the floors of Early Colonial homes. It is more common now to nail the boards in place, countersink the nails, and glue in a short wood peg.

Another type of wood flooring is parquetry, or a system of combining two or more kinds of wood in a geometric pattern to form squares of identical size. A modern application of parquetry makes use of odd lots of wood by producing nine- or twelve-inch squares of narrow boards and laying these squares at right angles. They are precut, prefinished, and grooved, so that the amateur can cover a smoothly finished wood or concrete floor with these squares.

Marble has been used for floors for thousands of years. It comes in many colors and grains; it can be cut to produce simple or intricate patterns. Now it is used mainly in vestibules, entrance halls, and bathrooms.

Flagstone is inexpensive and common to many areas of the country. It is especially popular for vestibules, hallways, patios, terraces, paths, and steps. Brick and slate have similar uses. All look better if waxed.

Concrete and terrazzo are poured flooring substances. Many homes now have poured-concrete floors over which carpeting or resilient floor materials are laid. Plain concrete is satisfactory for the laundry or terrace but not very decorative otherwise. Terrazzo has a cement mortar (matrix) which holds together chips of colored marble (aggregate). After the substance is poured and becomes hard, it is polished by machine to expose the fine particles resembling colored glass. Terrazzo is used for floors in almost any room in warm, moist climates; in temperate regions it is well suited for floors in bathrooms, sun rooms, and entrances.

Resilient Flooring

Linoleum was the first resilient flooring material made, and it came into existence by accident over one hundred years ago—1863. Frederick Walton, an Englishman, was experimenting with a number of substances in the hope of producing artificial leather. One morning he noticed a thick rubbery film on the top of a can of paint left open by mistake. In lifting the film off carefully for study, he discovered that the oxidation of linseed oil produced the pliable substance. As he considered some possible use for the new compound, he began to press it onto a piece of burlap. To his surprise he had produced a firm yet flexible floor covering, which he named *linoleum*. *Linum* is the Latin word for the flax plant from which linseed oil is derived, and in Latin *oleum* means oil.

It was nearly a century after Walton's discovery before other resilient floor materials came into existence—asphalt, rubber, and vinyl products which were

Linoleum can provide an elegant background for a formal entrance hall.

combined with asbestos, cork, and other compounds. Resilient floor coverings in tile form have become popular because the amateur can lay tiles more easily than he can lay roll goods. These flooring materials vary in composition and therefore in cost, durability, ease of maintenance, and resilience and in resistance to grease stains and moisture. The mastic or cement used to fasten them to the floor also varies. The grade level and the recommended floor coverings are shown in the chart below.

A capsule description of the various resilient floor coverings follows:

Linoleum is the oldest and best resilient flooring material for general use. Linoleum tile is a heavy-grade linoleum cut in tiles. Linotile is made of very heavy-gauge inlaid embossed linoleum especially processed for longer wear, greater recovery from dents, and greater resistance to abrasives than regular linoleum. Printed linoleum in room-size rugs and roll goods was popular until resilient tiles were introduced. Designs on printed linoleum wear off with traffic. On inlaid linoleum,

which is a heavy-gauge linoleum, designs go through to the back. All linoleum products should be laid above grade level (ground level) or on a suspended floor—that is, a floor over a basement. Linoleum products have more give under foot, and they are quieter than asphalt tile. They have superior resistance to grease and cigarette burns, and they are easy to maintain.

Asphalt tile became popular for floors below, on, and above grade level in the late 1940's. It is the least expensive resilient floor covering and is still popular for basement and family rooms. However, asphalt tile dents easily, shows poor resistance to grease, and is no more shock resistant than a concrete floor. It is only fairly easy to maintain. The production of more attractive flooring with easier maintenance has cut into the sale of asphalt tile.

Rubber tile may be used anywhere. It has slightly more give underfoot than linoleum and has very good recovery from dents; it is very durable and has excellent resistance to cigarette burns. It has good grease resistance and far

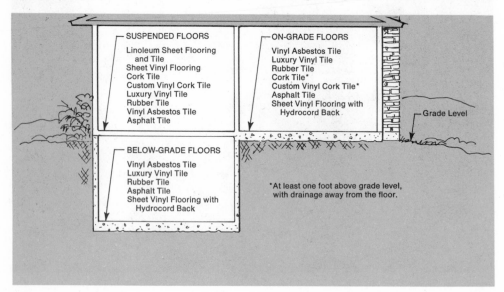

SUSPENDED FLOORS
Linoleum Sheet Flooring
   and Tile
Sheet Vinyl Flooring
Cork Tile
Custom Vinyl Cork Tile
Luxury Vinyl Tile
Rubber Tile
Vinyl Asbestos Tile
Asphalt Tile

ON-GRADE FLOORS
Vinyl Asbestos Tile
Luxury Vinyl Tile
Rubber Tile
Cork Tile*
Custom Vinyl Cork Tile*
Asphalt Tile
Sheet Vinyl Flooring with
   Hydrocord Back

Grade Level

BELOW-GRADE FLOORS
Vinyl Asbestos Tile
Luxury Vinyl Tile
Rubber Tile
Asphalt Tile
Sheet Vinyl Flooring with
   Hydrocord Back

*At least one foot above grade level,
 with drainage away from the floor.

better stain resistance than linoleum. However, it is not quite as easy to maintain as linoleum. It is expensive but not as expensive as linotile.

Cork tile is usually recommended for suspended floors. It has superior resilience and noise resistance but only limited resistance to dents. It has limited resistance to grease, cigarette burns, and alkalies, and poor stain resistance. It is as difficult to maintain as asphalt tile. It is used often in libraries and music rooms where traffic is not heavy and where resistance to noise is desirable.

Pure vinyl flooring is one of the most satisfactory of all resilient floor coverings. Pure vinyl comes in rolls six feet wide and in tile form. Color range and pattern choices are almost endless. Pure vinyl should be used on suspended floors, but if the vinyl flooring has a hydrocord back, it can be used anywhere. It has good to excellent resilience if the backing is cushioned, good recovery from dents, excellent resistance to grease, water-borne stains, and alkalies. It is very durable and easy to maintain, but it is expensive.

Vinyl-asbestos tile is the most popular tile with do-it-yourselfers because it can be cut with scissors to fit around curves and corners, and it comes in a wide choice of colors and designs. It can be laid anywhere, it is durable, and it has excellent resistance to grease, cigarette burns, and alkalies, but stains will leave a mark unless wiped up immediately. Vinyl asbestos requires a minimum of maintenance.

Vinyl-cork tile is twice as expensive as regular-cork tile. The vinyl coating gives the cork excellent stain resistance and greater resistance to grease and alkalies, and makes maintenance especially easy.

Vinyl-cork tile is recommended for installation over suspended floors. It is not quite as quiet as regular cork, but it will take much heavier traffic. It is popular in recreation rooms, family rooms, and living rooms.

Carpets and Rugs

HISTORY. Fabric floor coverings probably had their origin in Turkey, Persia (Iran), and Egypt. During their invasions, the Moors carried the art of rug making to the northern coast of Africa, to southern France, and to Spain. The famous rug factory at Aubusson, France, was established by the Moors during the thirteenth century. In the late sixteenth century Henry IV of France (1553–1610) induced Persian weavers to work in the workrooms at the Louvre Palace.

During the late eighteenth and nineteenth centuries, wealthy families in Europe and America preferred hand-loomed Oriental rugs to domestic rugs, which were either hooked or braided. Imported handmade Orientals became status symbols in the homes of wealthy industrialists and businessmen. It was not until the mid-nineteenth century that the average American family could afford rugs made outside the home. In 1848 Erastus Bigelow invented a power loom for making a patterned carpet in narrow widths requiring seaming. This became known as Brussels carpet. Brussels carpet with beautiful floral patterns and floral wallpaper characterized Victorian homes all over the country.

During the early twentieth century, Oriental designs were imitated by the manufacturers of Wilton or Axminster rugs, and Brussels carpet gave way to factory-produced room-size rugs. Gradually fashion introduced solid-colored rugs of different textures and weaves,

Wall-to-wall carpeting, especially if light in color, can make a room appear larger.

which competed less with figured wall-paper and figured draperies than the popular floral rugs. In more recent years wall-to-wall carpeting has become increasingly popular. Since wall-to-wall carpeting (by using the tackless method) can be laid over concrete slab or ply-wood floors as well as over wood floors, carpeting has been accepted on FHA mortgages as a structural feature of the home.

RUG AND CARPET TYPES. Carpeting is desirable because it absorbs shock and noise and cushions falls. There are fewer falls on steps that are carpeted, and injuries are less severe. With advances in the production of chemical fibers, special weaves, and finishes, the use of carpeting is expanding into kitchens and bathrooms and around swimming pools as well as in offices, hospitals, and classrooms. Special carpeting can be had for outdoor terraces.

Wall-to-wall carpeting gives space and unity to a room, conceals bad floors, and simplifies daily cleaning. However, traffic lanes may appear, and unlike a rectangular rug, carpeting cannot be easily reversed. On-the-floor cleaning does not remove grit and soil thoroughly unless cleaning is frequent. Wall-to-wall carpeting is more expensive than a room-size rug because more yardage is required and the cost of installation must be considered.

The cost of carpet made of synthetic fibers is low in comparison with that of a good wool carpet, so that people no longer think of the floor covering as a lifetime investment. After eight or ten years of use, the average yearly cost of even wall-to-wall carpeting in a living room is not overwhelming if the carpeting is in the medium-price range. Good portions that are left over can be cut for scatter rugs, their edges bound, and the rugs used in bedrooms.

A room-size rug may cover an entire floor, or it may come to within nine or twelve inches of the wall on all sides. A space of more than twelve inches makes the rug seem to float, unless the floor and rug are similar in color; for example, a beige rug that is a little too small may be used on a beige tile floor without calling attention to a wide border. In room arrangements with a large expanse of floor, *area rugs* may be used to define different areas. For instance, an area rug may define a dining area, a conversation area, or a study area. It may be any shape or pattern, but the shape, pattern, and color must bear a relationship to the area, to the furnishings, and to the character of the room.

Scatter rugs are small rugs used in an entrance hall, under a coffee table, in front of a fireplace, or at the side of a bed. It is important to choose a scatter rug with a nonskid back because scatter rugs on slick floors may cause falls.

Accent rugs may be machine- or hand-made, for use on top of wall-to-wall carpeting in front of a sofa or a fireplace to lend interest or to establish a color scheme.

If a rug or wall-to-wall carpet has a pronounced pattern, the use of design will be limited elsewhere in decoration. This means that figured wallpaper or draperies should not be used with rugs that have a pronounced pattern.

MAIN BACKGROUNDS ACCORDING TO USE OF ROOM

The use of the room will determine to a large degree the type of backgrounds chosen and the kind of decoration that is appropriate. As a rule,

An area rug defines the living-room space in this contemporary home. It blends well with the other background materials—cork flooring and wood paneling.

simplicity is the keynote for rooms in which you spend a lot of time and desire a certain degree of relaxation— living rooms, workrooms, or bedrooms. Other rooms may be more stimulating.

Entrances

The entrance, whether large or small, is the introduction to your home, and it sets the tempo for the living area. You can make it more stimulating than the living room by using a gay scatter rug or a wallpaper mural or panel to set the color scheme, or you may use an interesting grouping of pictures or a mirror and wall brackets. A suitable wall choice may be patterned or scenic wallpaper that is coordinated with the paper used in the living room.

Living Room

Plain walls, either wallpapered or painted, are usually preferred to patterned walls in the living room. The trend in recent years has been toward solid-colored carpet also. Pattern may be introduced in paintings or in fabrics for the windows and for upholstered furniture. Since the living room is a meeting place for family and friends, it should be less personal than a room used by only one or two persons.

Dining Room

Backgrounds for dining can be more stimulating than backgrounds for living and sleeping areas because people spend short periods in the dining room and a cheerful atmosphere is conducive to enjoyment of food. If there are small children in the home, it will be necessary to have backgrounds that require easy maintenance. Such a floor covering as tile or a synthetic-fiber rug and such a wall finish as paint or vinyl wallpaper may be suitable. As children mature and as maintenance becomes less of a problem, there is a wider choice of carpeting and wall finishes.

If there is no separate dining room, a dining area can be set apart with an area rug, a mural on the end wall, or a room divider of some kind. All three devices may be used if space permits.

Bedroom

This is a room where individual choice of backgrounds is important. However, the walls should not be too stimulating, unless the occupants like a lot of pattern or color. Nursery walls should not be too active. Large rooms can take greater contrast in color and design than small rooms. Many interesting patterns are available in matching or coordinated wallpaper and drapery fabrics for bedrooms. A rug or wall-to-wall carpeting is safer, softer to walk on, and less noisy than bare floors. Many people prefer bare floors with scatter rugs because they believe they are more sanitary and easier to clean. The height of the beds and the type of vacuum cleaner will have a lot to do with ease of cleaning. If scatter rugs are used, they should have an adhesive on the back, so that they will be well anchored to prevent slipping.

Kitchens and Bathrooms

Wall finishes in kitchens and bathrooms should be thoroughly washable and grease resistant. Suitable wall finishes for the kitchen and bathroom include semigloss paint and rubber- or vinyl-coated fabric or paper. If cost is no problem, a ceramic-tile wall running back of the tub and lavatory in the bathroom will be maintenance free and easy to clean. Ceramic tile is probably the most satisfactory floor covering for the bathroom, followed by vinyl-sheet and vinyl-tile products and linoleum.

Easy-to-maintain carpeting is also available for bathrooms. Kitchen floor coverings include linoleum and vinyl products as well as special carpeting that resists grease and stain.

BACKGROUNDS AND ROOM EXPRESSION

When you choose wall and floor coverings for a room, you should keep in mind the effect you want to achieve. If it is contemporary boldness, you may choose a wallpaper with definite texture or pattern or use a solid-colored paint. The floor may be vinyl or wood with bold scatter rugs, or the floor may be completely covered with a solid-colored, a tweed-effect, or an abstract-patterned carpeting.

If the room is to be traditional in character, backgrounds will have to be more formal. You may paint the walls or use wallpaper with slightly textured background, a formal repeat, or a scenic design. Oriental rugs or a room-size rug or wall-to-wall carpeting with a twist weave, an uncut pile, or a sculptured effect will be appropriate. If a Provincial or Early American effect is desired, the wall may be painted a solid color, repeating the background color in chintz or cretonne draperies, or the wallpaper may have a chintzlike pattern. Wall-to-wall carpeting or a hooked, braided, or tweed-textured rug is suitable.

If an outdoor or rustic effect is your aim, you may choose a flagstone, slate, or terrazzo floor and solid-colored, uncluttered walls. Use lots of plants for emphasis.

You may want to use an eclectic approach, so that you can express your individuality. In this approach to decorating, many of the traditional rules are discarded. However, it takes skill and experience to combine seemingly unrelated ideas and give the room a center of interest and unity.

Before launching into any of these decorating expressions, assemble clippings of well-decorated rooms expressing concepts similar to those you want to express, and study them thoroughly. Also study the illustrations and the captions in the text.

In this Early American room, the braided rug and wallpaper convey a feeling of warmth and coziness.

SUMMARY

Walls in most rooms of a house are usually painted, papered, or covered with wood paneling. Paint is easy to apply and maintain, but paint will not cover wall irregularities. Figured and textured wallpaper will cover some wall imperfections and add warmth and interest to a room. Wood paneling conceals all wall defects. Although expensive, ceramic tile is the best finish for bathroom walls because it is sanitary, long lasting, and easy to maintain. Ceilings should be painted a color lighter than the wall if they are eight feet high or less. A high ceiling will look less high if it is painted a color somewhat darker than the wall. Acoustic-tile ceilings are recommended for rooms that are noisy, such as recreation rooms.

Some people prefer hardwood floors with scatter rugs or larger Oriental rugs, whereas others prefer a room-size rug or wall-to-wall carpeting. The price of carpeting made from man-made fibers is reasonable enough for wall-to-wall carpeting to be within reach of the average budget. Carpet laid wall to wall conceals bad floors. Resilient floor coverings are usually preferred for kitchens, recreation rooms, and bathrooms, but carpeting for these areas is gaining in popularity. Whatever wall or floor finish or covering one chooses, it should be in harmony with all the furnishings or with the total look.

THINGS TO THINK ABOUT AND TO DO

1. Obtain some old wallpaper books from a distributor, and select wallpaper you consider appropriate for the following rooms:
   a. small master bedroom
   b. traditional living room
   c. contemporary living room
   d. large master bedroom
   e. Early American living room
   f. your own bedroom

2. Distinguish between ready-mixed and formula-mixed paints.

3. Name some uses for epoxy paint.

4. Discuss some advantages and disadvantages of oil paint and of latex paint for walls.

5. Display swatches of all types of wallpaper mentioned on page 227, and indicate where you would use each.

6. Make a list of at least six rules to use in the selection of wallpaper.

7. Plan to use wallpaper to cover a closet accessory, such as a hat box, or to line drawers in your bedroom. Several students may go together and buy discarded rolls at low cost.

8. Display on the bulletin board some illustrations showing interesting uses of wood paneling.

9. Contrast ceilings used in English eighteenth-century homes with those used in contemporary homes. You may do this with magazine clippings or with illustrations in books.

10. Display ceiling tile, and discuss the acoustic quality. With the help of a dealer, estimate the cost of installation if you wanted to drop a ceiling about two feet in an older home. You may use a living room that is twelve feet by eighteen feet.

11. Make a list of hardwoods and softwoods available in your part of the country. Collect samples of each if possible.

12. Display on a bulletin board illustrations of interesting floor coverings aside from wall-to-wall carpeting.

13. Assemble large swatches of various kinds of rugs, and discuss where you would use each.

14. Assemble as many kinds of floor tile as possible, and discuss the uses of each.

15. Display some illustrations showing how accent rugs can be used.

16. Write several paragraphs on the history of resilient floor coverings, wallpaper, or carpet and rugs. Expand your information by doing research at the library.

17. Assemble at least three clippings of interesting living rooms. Study the background carefully, and write a caption for each illustration which indicates how the decorator tried to carry out a particular idea.

Assembling a swatch card like this one can help you make decisions about decorating schemes. You can test the effectiveness of different combinations of textures, shapes, and colors for both backgrounds and furnishings.

chapter fourteen

WINDOW DECORATION

Windows may be decorated so that they blend inconspicuously with the walls and serve as a general background for furnishings, or they may become the focal point of the room. In ranch-type homes with average-size rooms and low ceilings, windows are less elaborately decorated than in older homes with large rooms and high ceilings.

We are so accustomed to thinking of windows as an important part of a room that we may be surprised to find rooms with no windows. Although windows provide light and add interest to a room, in some localities where noise has become a problem there are underground, windowless structures. Many large office buildings and department stores also lack windows, but a feeling of space is created because walls are few. A few homes have been built underground with artificially lighted gardens in channels outside window walls. If we had to spend all our time in windowless homes, most of us would have claustrophobia. One study indicated that the error rate of computer programmers increased sharply when they left rooms with windows for those with no windows. In department stores where there is no outside light, employees are not confined to such a limited area as office workers who are shut up within close walls. Most high-rise, centrally air-conditioned apartment buildings have sealed windows, but there is a feeling of space outside. People who spend only evening hours at home do not seem to object to the lack of natural light or the absence of a view, but those who spend a great deal of time at home prefer pleasant surroundings outside.

The term *window* has its origin in the old Norse language and means "wind eyes." The cold and wind in Scandinavian and in other northern European countries necessitated the use of small windows. In southern Europe and in our own South, windows in older homes often reach from floor to ceiling. When low-ceiling ranch houses and the concept of integrating the home with its natural surroundings became popular, picture windows and window walls made their appearance.

Whether you are decorating large windows in an older home, small windows in a Cape Cod cottage, or a picture window in a contemporary

home, you should become familiar with the terms used in window decoration. You should know how to apply the principles of design to make
your windows as attractive as possible and to improve problem windows.
You should know how to choose fabrics that will be in keeping with your
window treatment and decorating scheme.

GUIDELINES FOR STUDY

GENERAL IDEAS TO CONSIDER

1. The original function of windows was to give light and ventilation, and the
climate determined the size. As is still true, beauty was secondary in importance.
2. A lovely outdoor view should not be obscured by heavy or elaborate window
decoration.
3. Window treatments may be chosen to alter the appearance of poorly proportioned or poorly spaced windows or to give unity to a group of windows.
4. Window decoration should be planned in relation to the size and shape
of the room, the placement and size of the windows, and the decorating theme.

WORDS AND TERMS TO KNOW

apron (window)	picture window
Austrian shade	ranch window
baseboard	roller shade
bay window	Roman shade
cafe curtain	sash (window)
cascade	shoji screen
cornice	shutter
drapery liner	sill
draw draperies	swag
lambrequin	valance
louvers	Venetian blind

AUSTRIAN SHADES   ROMAN SHADES

BASIC WINDOW TYPES

If you walk around your own neighborhood or ride by new housing developments, you will find all kinds of windows. You might list the types of windows illustrated in the text on pages 244 and 245 and see how many of them you can identify. Learn the terms for the parts of a window as shown on page 246 because these terms are referred to frequently in window decorating.

STANDARD WINDOW TREATMENTS

Windows should provide light and privacy, and at the same time it should be possible to shut out light when desirable. Window treatments should also meet certain standards of design and complement the furnishings in a room. Window shades, Venetian blinds, shutters, draperies, and curtains are both functional and decorative.

Blinds, Shades, and Shutters

If you are renting a home or an apartment, Venetian blinds, window shades, or shutters are frequently provided. If not, rods are usually provided for draw draperies. Most people like blinds or shades in addition to draw draperies for privacy and light control. If blinds or shades are used, they should be set at the same distance from the windowsill everywhere in the house (especially at the front) to give unity and dignity.

VENETIAN BLINDS. Venetian blinds originated in China, traveled to Europe by way of Venice (therefore the origin of the name), and became popular in both England and America during the Georgian period. Venetian blinds control light and ventilation, but they rattle in the wind and are difficult to maintain. Venetian blinds are available in steel, aluminum, plastic, and wood. They must be dusted fairly frequently and cleaned with a mild detergent at regular intervals. Soiled tapes must be separated from the slats and cleaned periodically. However, new tapes may be adhered to soiled tapes with some degree of satisfaction. Venetian blinds may be used with almost any decorating scheme. It is not necessary to use glass curtains with them, but either side or draw draperies are generally used. Some people use crisscross ruffled curtains over Venetian blinds in bedrooms, especially with patterned wallpaper.

ROLLER SHADES. Roller shades are the most common means of shutting out light and providing privacy. Purely functional shades are made of treated cloth or plastic. Either may be had with a black-out material laminated between two layers, so that very little light enters the room when the shades are pulled to the sill. If dusted and cleaned occasionally with a mild detergent, cloth and plastic shades last a long time. Plain roller shades may be made from any kind of firmly woven cloth to carry out a color scheme.

Matchstick or bamboo roller shades make a good background for rooms showing a Far East influence. Bamboo shades are bulkier and more difficult to handle than matchstick shades. An occasional dusting and sponging with a mild detergent will keep them new looking, but they must be wiped dry.

Translucent-cloth roller shades can be stenciled with textile paint, which is transparent. Colors will show through the light in daytime and appear natural at night. Shades may also be made of fabric to match the wallpaper. Austrian

TYPES OF WINDOWS AND HOW TO TREAT THEM

DOUBLE HUNG   A familiar type that is easy to decorate as a single window or a group of windows. Use
tailored or ruffled curtains, draw or stationary draperies, cafe curtains on both sashes or either upper
or lower cash. Cornices, valances, and swags may
be used.

MULTIPLE DOUBLE HUNG (Group)   Treat as one
window, tying the unit together with crisscross curtains, tailored curtains or draperies with a cornice,
valance or swag across the top.

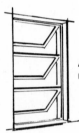

AWNING TYPE   May be treated in the same manner as double-hung windows.

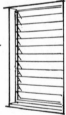

JALOUSSIE   May be treated in the same manner
as double-hung windows.

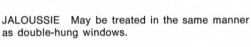

OUT-SWINGING CASEMENT   May be treated like
double-hung windows, whether single or grouped.

IN-SWINGING CASEMENT   Treatment must not
interfere with window opening into the room. Curtains must be fastened to the window and not the
frame. Draperies may be used with swinging rods.
Cornices and valances are not usable.

RANCH WINDOWS   Long narrow group windows
set high in the wall. Use sill-length draw draperies,
or curtains with draperies to the sill. A valance or
cornice may be used. Full-length stationary draperies may be used if a bed or chest is directly under
the windows.

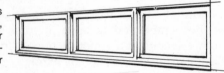

PICTURE WINDOW   May be a glass wall with sliding panes or a long window of ordinary height with
stationary panes. If the view is not interesting, block
it out with semi-sheer glass curtains under draw
draperies. Cafe curtains are also used. A valance or
cornice gives unity.

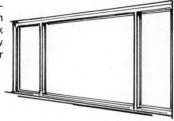

DORMER WINDOW   Simplicity is the keynote. Use
sheer ruffled or tailored curtains or cafe curtains.
For a decorative effect use figured wallpaper on
surrounding walls. A window shade may be covered
with the wallpaper also.

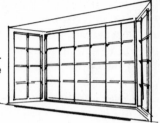

BAY WINDOW   Special rods are available for three-
sided or circular bay windows so that they may be
treated as a group.

CORNER WINDOWS   With special rods these may
be treated as a group, using draw draperies, draw
curtains with end draperies, or cafe curtains with
or without draperies. A cornice or valance may be
used effectively.

OTHER WINDOWS   An ARCHED WINDOW may be
treated like a single window below the arch, and a
special rod will permit a fan-like arrangement over
the arch. A CLERESTORY WINDOW is usually left
plain. A SLANTING WINDOW may be treated with
draw draperies on a special rod.

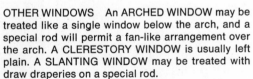

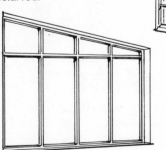

shades (shown on page 242) are rather elaborate and difficult to maintain. Roman shades are simpler. They may be made of cloth to match a chair or a bedspread. Tapes with rings are fastened to the back of the cloth shade. The tapes are looped at the bottom to hold a metal rod. A cord run through the loops pulls the shade up in folds.

SHUTTERS. Shutters are especially popular in areas where heat is intense. In southern European and northern African cities, very heavy wood or metal shutters are used on the outside of windows to keep out the sun during the middle of the day. Many Southern Colonial homes, as well as Victorian homes, have outside louvered shutters. In many homes today, outside shutters are merely decorative and not meant to close.

Decorative shutters are frequently used on the inside of windows—at the upper sash only or at both the upper and lower sash—for a decorative effect, for light control, or for hiding an unpleasant view. (For example, see the photograph on page 253.)

LOUVERS. Louvers are made of metal, wood, or a webbing of cloth or plastic. The slats are usually horizontal and fastened at the sides so that they can be opened or closed like Venetian blinds. Because they are easy to operate, control light and air, and keep out rain, louvers are a popular window treatment in kitchens, nurseries, bathrooms, and bedrooms in warm climates.

Since louvered doors for closets are practical and attractive, the use of louvers for both closets and window treatment can give unity to a room.

Draperies and Curtains

Draperies are important as room decoration and as a means of shutting out light and providing privacy. Curtains diffuse the light, give some degree of privacy in the daytime, and add interest to windows.

Fashions in curtains and draperies have changed along with changes in architecture. Windows in old New England houses and Cape Cod cottages were small and required little decoration except cottage curtains. Georgian homes both in England and in America placed a great deal of emphasis upon woodwork, and frequently draperies or curtains were set inside the window frame to expose the wood trim. The Victorian period in America was an age of opulence, and in the opinion of many decorators, a period of poor taste. The desire for conspicuous display or status led to overemphasis in window decoration to the point of oppressiveness. The bay window became such an important status symbol that people whose homes had no bay knocked out walls to create one. In most contemporary homes, wood window framing

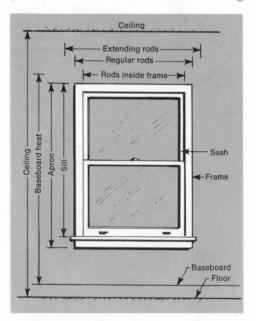

Window Terms Related to Curtain and Drapery Lengths

WINDOW TREATMENTS

TWO-WAY DRAW CURTAINS OR DRAPERIES
Hung on traverse rods. If windows are narrow set ends of rods on wood blocks nailed to the wall beyond the window. Used on double-hung, group, outswinging casement, awning, jalousie, picture, and bay windows.

ONE-WAY DRAW CURTAINS OR DRAPERIES
Hung from traverse rod that operates from one direction. Used on corner windows or on a window wall with a door at one end.

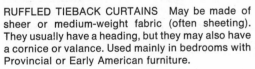

DRAW DRAPERIES ON DECORATIVE ROD
A brass or wood rod may be used in place of regular traverse rods. Rings are usually used on the rod to hold the draperies. Used in same manner as two-way draw-draperies.

SWINGING DRAW DRAPERIES
This treatment must be used on French doors or casement windows that open into the room. Swinging rods are sometimes used at dormer windows.

CAFE CURTAINS
Short curtains hung on a rod by means of rings, clips, or fabric loops. The heading may be plain, pleated, or scalloped. Used on upper or lower half of windows or both upper and lower. They may also be used below the sill. Appropriate for double-hung, group, ranch, dormer, bay, and picture windows.

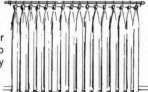

CRISS-CROSS, OR PRISCILLA, CURTAINS
Double-width, sheer ruffled curtains that criss-cross and tie back at sides. They hang to the end of the apron, top of baseboard, or floor. Used on double-hung, group, picture, and bay windows.

RUFFLED TIEBACK CURTAINS
May be made of sheer or medium-weight fabric (often sheeting). They usually have a heading, but they may also have a cornice or valance. Used mainly in bedrooms with Provincial or Early American furniture.

SASH CURTAINS
These are curtains anchored at top and bottom. They cover the glass only to diffuse light and provide privacy. Used on French doors, doors with glass panels, in-swinging casement, ranch, and sometimes clerestory windows.

is practically eliminated, and simple window decoration is more in keeping with our streamlined way of life. Where there is a beautiful view outside a picture window or a window wall, draperies are often kept plain to avoid competing for interest with the view.

When there are no shades, blinds, or shutters, two-way draw draperies on traverse rods are recommended. Draperies need not be lined if the fabric is heavy, firmly woven, or backed with a laminate. However, lining protects the fabric, decreases outside light, and gives the draperies a better hanging quality. To further eliminate light, a specially treated lining fabric or an opaque inner lining may be used. Draperies may start just above the top of the window and stop at the sill, at the bottom of the apron, at a covered radiator, at a low cabinet, at a set of shelves, or just above the floor. They should never dangle in the middle of a wall. Tailored curtains used with draperies may stop at the windowsill, the bottom of the apron, or just above the floor. If curtains and draperies are planned to be the same length, the hems should be as even as possible. Tied-back curtains look better if they stop at the apron or floor. Glass curtains should be twice the width of the window to hang well. The sheerer the fabric, the wider the curtain should be.

Cafe curtains, originally used at the lower sash in street cafes to give a degree of privacy, have become popular in Early American and contemporary homes. They are easy to make and can be quite decorative in kitchens, recreation rooms, small dining rooms, and children's bedrooms.

Valances, Cornices, Swags, and Lambrequins

Valances, swags with cascades, cornices, and lambrequins are used more in period rooms or in older homes with high ceilings than in modern homes. Most newer homes have ceilings eight feet high or less, and any window décor

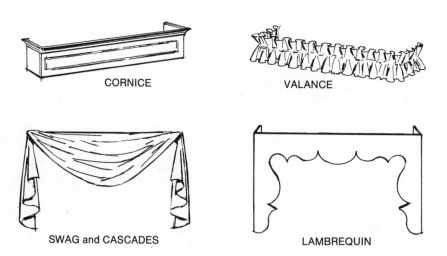

CORNICE   VALANCE

SWAG and CASCADES   LAMBREQUIN

Although the terms "cornice" and "valance" are sometimes confused, the two differ in function as well as structure. Valances harmonize with many styles; cornices, swags, and lambrequins are more formal.

that has a horizontal emphasis tends to make the ceiling seem lower. When any horizontal decoration is used at the top of the window in modern homes, it should come close to the ceiling, and the entire window treatment should not contrast greatly with the main backgrounds.

A valance is a gathered, pleated, or shaped heading, usually hung on the outside rod of a double curtain rod. The depth of the valance should be between one seventh and one eighth of the distance from the top of the window treatment to the floor. Sometimes a valance is suspended on a rod from the ceiling, so that the pleating at the top barely escapes the ceiling. Draw draperies or side draperies may be used with a valance extending all the way across a group of windows.

A cornice may be made of wood, either natural or painted to pick up the background color in the drapery fabric. It may also be made of plastic or mirror glass. Wood cornices are the most popular, and if the cornice is to be covered with fabric, an inexpensive plywood may be used (in which case a layer of outing flannel under the fabric will give a soft effect). Cornices may be made by lumber dealers.

Swags and cascades are used in large formal rooms with tall windows and high ceilings. They may be too oppressive in rooms in an average-size home. Nevertheless, they may be used in traditional-type homes with fairly large rooms and ceilings at least eight feet high, especially if the fabric does not contrast greatly with the walls and if the area between the ceiling and the floor is treated as a window unit to convey height. The depth of the swag at the center should be between one seventh and one eighth of the distance from the ceiling to the floor. The width of the cascade should coincide with the width of the drapery at the window —as a rule about fourteen inches.

Lambrequins are shaped frames made of plywood, masonite, or heavy buckram, all of which may be covered with fabric or a vinyl plastic. Masonite and plywood frames may be painted a solid color or have designs applied.

PROBLEM WINDOWS AND DESIGN PRINCIPLES

If you understand the principles of design, you can make these design principles work for you all over the house. The importance of color and of floor and wall composition in changing apparent room proportions has already been discussed. By applying design principles to awkward-looking or awkwardly placed windows, you can change the entire appearance of a room.

Windows that are too long and narrow, too short and broad, entirely too small, or poorly spaced on a wall can be decorated to give an illusion of good proportions. The illustration on page 250 shows how these improvements can be made.

Many contemporary homes have so-called ranch windows placed high on the wall. This arrangement in small bedrooms facilitates the arrangement of furniture and provide privacy, but the windows do very little for the appearance of the room and it is difficult to see through them. Some effective ways to decorate windows over a bed are shown on page 251. In older homes there are often small windows above high bookcases on each side of a fireplace that present a problem. Bay windows and corner windows may also be difficult to decorate. The illustrations on pages 244 and 245 offer suggestions on how to treat these types of problem windows.

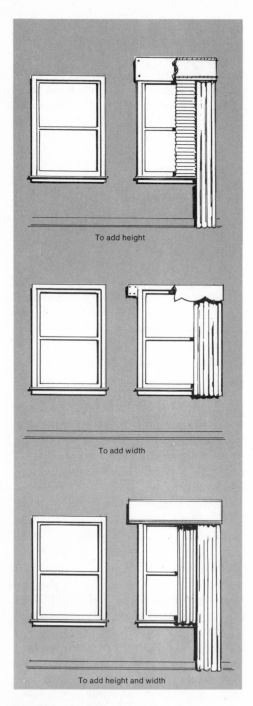

To add height

To add width

To add height and width

To add height: place board above window; use cornice and floor-length draperies. To add width: place wood blocks at sides; hang drapery over wall, and cover with cornice. To add both: nail board above and beyond window for drapery.

USE OF ROOM AND DECORATING IDEAS

Windows, walls, and floors must have unity and must provide a harmonious background for furnishings. The style of architecture and the size, shape, and grouping of windows place some limits upon their decoration. The use of the room and the expression or decorating idea you want to convey further control window treatments.

Use of Room

Windows in a living room may have a more dignified and formal treatment than windows in other rooms. Floor-length draw draperies in a solid color—contrasting with the walls if the room is large, blending into the walls if the room is small, or picking up a prominent color in wallpaper—are always in good taste. If the room is large, the windows are probably important. Figured draperies are good with solid-colored walls especially if the background of the print is repeated in the wall color. Floor-length draw draperies make a very attractive backdrop at night.

Dining room windows should not contrast too greatly with living room windows if the rooms are close together. A dinette separated from the living room may be treated less formally than a regular dining room.

Windows in the master bedroom require a less personal treatment than that in other bedrooms. Some men object to ruffled curtains, delicate prints, and elaborate draping. If wallpaper is used, the window treatment should be simple. If the walls are a solid color, a printed drapery fabric may be desirable. The fabric may be repeated on a chair or in a bedspread.

In bedrooms occupied by boys or by girls, the decoration of windows is an individual matter. Many young people have definite ideas about how they want their windows to look. Even. young children have their own ideas about decorating their rooms.

Room Expression or Character

Architectural features and furniture influence window treatment. If you wish to emphasize an Early American idea, you may choose to use window shades and ruffled curtains in all the rooms of the house. If draperies are used, good choices for drapery fabrics are homespun, crewel embroidery or simulated crewel embroidery, chintz, gingham, or calico.

If you have fine eighteenth-century or traditional furniture, you may choose richer fabrics—cotton or rayon damask or brocade, a mercerized cotton rep, or cretonne or chintz with a formal repeat. Your window treatment may be more elaborate. You may want to use a cornice, valance, or even swags and cascades or lambrequins.

CONTEMPORARY Draperies and cafe curtains on rings.

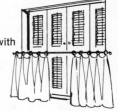

PROVINCIAL Shutters with draw draperies on rings.

SEMI-FORMAL Rings hold swaggered valance in place.

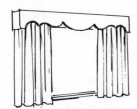

FORMAL Cornice with irregular edge gives unity. Draperies draw.

FORMAL Center panel covers wall area.

TRADITIONAL Swags with cascades.

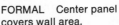

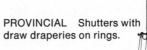

Interesting Treatments for Windows over a Bed.

Contemporary furnishings look best with simple draw draperies in solid colors or bold prints, depending upon the color scheme and use of pattern elsewhere in decorating the room. Textures may be bold also.

A Far East expression calls for simplicity. Often plain-color roller shades (cloth, matchstick, or bamboo) need nothing except shoji screens at either side. The shoji screen was originally made of rice paper with a painted design and a frame of black lacquer. Now interestingly decorated plastic screens are available. If the view outside is unattractive, the screens may be moved to conceal the view without shutting out the light.

OUTSIDE APPEARANCE

In planning window decoration you cannot afford to ignore the outside appearance of the house. You have probably passed homes where there is no uniformity of windows from the street. Pink curtains may blow from one window; blue, from another; blinds may be pulled to the top in some windows and to the sill in others. The effect is very disturbing.

Your own home will present a more attractive appearance from the street if your shades are all set at the same height. The windows will also look better if curtained uniformly. If this is not possible, it is desirable to use the same type of curtains over the downstairs living area and perhaps another style at upstairs windows. In many large apartment buildings, when there are no shades or Venetian blinds, occupants are required to use off-white drapery liners made of a sheer translucent fabric, so that the windows will appear uniform from the street. The liners are usually provided by the landlord. The same idea may be used at home.

SUMMARY

The way you decorate a window will depend upon the style of the house, the size and shape of windows, the size and use of the room, and the decorating idea you wish to project. Large windows in older homes require a more elaborate treatment than average-size windows in newer homes.

There is a wide choice of window accessories available that are both decorative and functional. Although roller shades are the most common means of controlling light, Venetian blinds can control ventilation as well. Shutters and louvers are more limited in usage. Draperies may be stationary or draw, lined or unlined; and curtains can be bought or made in a great variety of styles and fabrics.

For any window decoration to be successful it must provide the occupants of the room with privacy. The treatment should harmonize with the main backgrounds and furnishings of the room and create a feeling of unity. Windows should have some degree of uniformity in appearance from the outside. Often poorly proportioned and poorly spaced windows present problems, but by applying the principles of design, almost any problem window can be given an illusion of good proportions. A narrow window may be made to appear wider by extending the draperies over the wall at each side so that the entire window is exposed. A low window will look higher if one uses a cornice or cascade and swags on the wall above, barely covering the top of the window.

THINGS TO THINK ABOUT AND TO DO

1. Discuss the pros and cons of windowless rooms.

2. Take a walk around a block of homes near you, and identify as many types of windows as possible. Make a list of those you recognize.

3. Distinguish between Roman and Austrian shades, and tell where you might use each.

4. Mount on the bulletin board illustrations of effectively used Venetian blinds, roller shades, shutters, and louvers.

5. Check the windows in your own home from the street. Do they present a uniform effect? If not, consider how you can improve the effect.

6. Assemble swatches of materials used for roller shades, and discuss the cost, maintenance, and usefulness of each.

7. Mount on the bulletin board good window treatments for several decorating schemes—for instance, Early American, contemporary, Far Eastern, and traditional.

8. Borrow from a drapery fixture department a number of fixtures and other items used in window decoration. Display, and discuss their use.

9. Assemble various trimmings used for draperies, and tell how to use them.

10. Collect a number of illustrations of bedrooms and living rooms with interesting window treatments. Indicate your first, second, and third choices, and explain the reasons for your choices.

11. Consider any problem windows in your home and what you might do to improve them.

A modern window treatment in an older apartment house: shutters permit light to enter, provide privacy, and enhance the dignity of this room.

chapter fifteen

DIGEST
OF FURNITURE
STYLES

Basic pieces of furniture had their origin long before recorded history. When man ceased to roam as a hunter and food gatherer and settled down to the role of farmer and herdsman, he began to think in terms of comfort in addition to survival. Hewn logs began to replace rocks as objects to sit upon. A crude bed began to evolve from animal skins or grasses tossed upon the bare ground. Eventually man began to fashion a recognizable chest to replace a hollow log or cave for storage. By this time he had simple pottery dishes and baskets, as well as food to store. These simple comforts and a crude mud or log home with a hearth gave early man his first concept of a home.

The history of furniture, like that of dress, parallels social history, the rise and fall of royal courts, progress in transportation, technological progress, and family living patterns.

Furniture reached its highest degree of opulence and grandeur during the reigns of Louis XIV, XV, and XVI in France. The long reign of Louis XIV (1643-1715) coincided with the latter part of the Jacobean period and all of the William and Mary and Queen Anne periods in England. The reigns of Louis XV and XVI coincided with the Golden Age of Furniture, or the Georgian period, in England when furniture reached its highest degree of refinement.

English furniture styles from the Jacobean period (1603-1688) through the Victorian period (1837-1901) have had a strong influence upon American furniture design. English designs were less elaborate and more practical than those of the French or Italian courts, and therefore they were easier to reproduce and more appropriate for American homes. Furthermore, England was the mother country of the early colonies. The Provincial styles of Italy, France, and Germany enjoy periods of popularity in America, and occasionally Spanish styles, which are strongly Moorish in character, and Oriental styles are introduced. The Scandinavian countries have had the greatest influence of all upon American contemporary furniture designers.

GUIDELINES FOR STUDY

GENERAL IDEAS
TO CONSIDER

1. Many furniture forms we have today had their origin during ancient and medieval times.
2. French Provincial furniture styles are simplified versions of the court style of Louis XV and Louis XVI, and Early American styles are simplified copies of prevailing English styles during the Colonial period—Jacobean, William and Mary, Queen Anne, and early Georgian.
3. England produced some of the most beautiful furniture of all times during the Georgian period, or the eighteenth century.
4. Most furniture produced in America until the mid-twentieth century was inspired by English and French designs.
5. The modern trend in furniture design parallels the modern movement in architecture, painting, sculpture, and dress.
6. Scandinavian designers, especially those of Sweden and Denmark, have been important in the modern movement of furniture styling.
7. Former concepts of furniture design have changed with the introduction of bentwood, metal, glass, and plastics for furniture construction.
8. Structure and texture take precedence over applied decoration in modern furniture.

NAMES AND WORDS
TO KNOW

armoire
baluster leg
Baroque
bentwood
Biedermeier
breakfront
bulbous leg
Byzantine
cabriole leg
commode
cup-turned leg
de' Medici family
Diocletian
Directoire
dower chest
English Regency
Federal period
fretwork
gateleg table
Georgian period

Gothic
highboy
hutch
Jacobean period
lowboy
Low Countries
Middle East
Minoans
Mission furniture
Moors
Neolithic
Pembroke table
Provincial furniture
Rococo furniture
scroll foot
secretary (furniture)
serpentine front
Tudor England
Versailles
X stretcher

FURNITURE ORIGINS
AND EVOLUTION

Furniture in its simplest form resulted from four basic needs of man—a place to lie down, or a *bed;* a place to sit down, or a *chair;* a place in which to store belongings, or a *chest;* and a surface on which to eat or work, or a *table.* The first bed was an animal skin or a pile of grass thrown on the hard earth. The first chair was a rock or a fallen tree, and the first chest was a hole in the gound or perhaps a hollow log. The first table was a flat rock. Man lived as a nomad and hunter for thousands and thousands of years, and until he ceased his wanderings, furniture as such had no meaning.

Excavations of Egyptian tombs give a clue to the furniture and home life of this ancient civilization dating from 2700 B.C. Within the last century, excavations on the island of Crete have given some indication of the furniture, architecture, and dress of this ancient and very sophisticated civilization, which thrived between 2000 and 1200 B.C. The royal courts of these civilizations employed cabinetmakers and stone masons who designed heavy rectangular throne chairs and couches, chests with lids, and small tables decorated with motifs copied from nature. The Egyptians decorated their furniture with motifs of palm leaves, lotus blossoms, and meander borders symbolizing the Nile. The Minoans used motifs of the seacoast—shells and fish.

Furniture of the Greeks and Romans was similar to that of the Egyptians and Minoans, but the motifs used were of local origin or adapted from those of Egypt. The Greeks and Romans conventionalized the honeysuckle, rose, and acanthus, and developed two popular border patterns—the fret and the egg and dart. Roman furniture, like Roman architecture, was Greek in origin but more elaborate than that of Greece. Both civilizations used human and animal forms as supports for tables and beds.

When Roman power shifted to Constantinople in the fourth century, Western and Eastern art and architecture became fused into a style known as Byzantine. Architecture and furniture were mainly church oriented, but closer contact with the Far East introduced luxurious fabrics, rich inlays, and mosaics to Western civilizations.

The first important art period in Europe was the Gothic, originating in France during the late twelfth century. This period brings forth romantic images, such as the castles of princesses and gallant knights. Although these fortified castles with their smoke-filled, drafty, and sparsely furnished rooms were far from romantic, the Gothic period marked a turning point in social history.

The high-poster bed with framework around the top supporting a canopy was brought from the Middle East by the Crusaders during the early Gothic period. This became an important status symbol among feudal lords. It was often placed in the living area and used as a place to sit upon during the day. There was often a trundle bed or two under the master bed. These beds were pulled out at night for children or sometime servants to sleep on. Most servants had to be content to sleep on a blanket in the hall outside the master-bedroom door.

The Crusaders brought back from the Middle East many household refinements entirely foreign to Europeans —table linens, fine china and silver, and exquisite rugs and wall hangings. With the introduction of these items,

IDENTIFICATION OF CHAIRS

UPHOLSTERED STYLES

Until the nineteenth century, furniture styles were named for reigning monarchs (for example, Queen Anne). Victorian furniture took its name from the long reign of Queen Victoria. Biedermeier was named for a fictitious cartoon character; the Windsor chair, for the castle in England; the ladder back, for what it resembles. Other chairs are named for their designers.

IDENTIFICATION OF CHAIRS

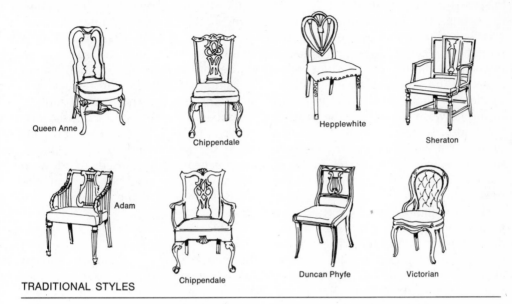

Queen Anne

Chippendale

Hepplewhite

Sheraton

Adam

Chippendale

Duncan Phyfe

Victorian

TRADITIONAL STYLES

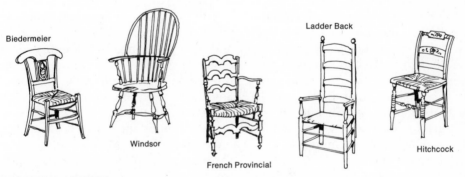

Biedermeier

Windsor

French Provincial

Ladder Back

Hitchcock

PROVINCIAL STYLES

Eames

Wegner

Saarinen

Breuer

CONTEMPORARY STYLES

the concept of eating was lifted to the art of dining. Until this time a set of trestles supported a large, loose board for eating. The expression *room and board* dates from this period in history. As eating became more of a ritual, a permanent dining or banquet table replaced the separate board with its trestles. A chair with arms or a sort of throne was reserved for the head of the house, or master. Thus the origin of the word *chairman*. Other people sat on benches. The master chair, or chair with arms, has survived to the present time.

As the Middle Ages drew to a close there was marked progress in the development of furniture. The Renaissance brought about greater changes as it spread throughout Europe. Italy became the seat of the Renaissance. Italian cabinetmakers were inspired by the massive furniture of ancient Rome and the church furniture of Constantinople. Italian court furniture was heavy, rectangular, and embellished with carving. Although some furniture was upholstered, comfort was of little concern. Glassmaking had developed in Venice to a high degree, and in the 1550's glass mirrors with gilded frames replaced polished metal mirrors.

As Germany and the Low Countries were caught in the spirit of the Renaissance, home and hearth became important. A copy of the Bible was the most cherished possession of every home. The invention of movable type, or the Gutenberg press, about 1450 had made it possible for common people to own this important book, which was carefully guarded in a special box with a hinged lid, lock, and key. Dates of births, marriages, and deaths, and other important family records were kept in the Bible or in the Bible box.

During the 1600's the Dutch, French, and English increased their foreign trade through their East India companies. More and more fine tableware was imported from China, creating a need for more storage space. The ownership of fine cups and plates soon became associated with social and economic status, and these beautiful possessions were conspicuously displayed. Boards with hooks and rails were set up to hold cups and plates. As storage needs increased, boards were set up at the sides to support the shelves. These became known as *cupboards*.

Tables were eventually set against the wall for additional storage and became known as *sideboards*. Shelves were gradually added below the tabletop, and eventually the cupboard and the sideboard were joined to produce a *hutch*.

The Renaissance reached England rather late. Court life in Italy, France, and Spain was highly refined. People dined on damask tablecloths set with fine china and silver, while in Tudor England, especially during the reign of Henry VIII, the refinements of living were unimportant. The de' Medicis under Lorenzo de' Medici had become the most powerful family in Italy during the Renaissance, and under them the arts and social life flourished.

The heavy rectangular furniture that developed under Henry VIII and Elizabeth I was copied from the massive furniture of European courts and was out of place in homes. It was not until the Jacobean period (1603–1688) that furniture became at all practical. Chair designs of the Tudor period were influenced by the farthingale, or the extended skirts of the ladies' dresses, and the bombast breeches of the men. Chairs had to be made wider and arms

Pembroke

Commode

Console

Trestle

Butterfly

Pie Crust

Step

Drum

Step

Nested Tables

Gate Leg

Tilt Top

Coffee

The Pembroke, gate leg, butterfly, and console tables are all extendable. The pie crust, drum, tilt top, step, and console are good lamp tables. The trestle table may be used for eating or for study.

Camel Back

Chesterfield

Tuxedo

Lawson

Duncan Phyfe

Victorian Settee

Contemporary

Charles of London

Sectional

Sofas are identified by their shape, back contour, arms, and cushions. Sofas seat three or more persons; love seats and settees seat two persons. Many sofas can be converted into beds.

had to be eliminated to accommodate these exaggerated fashions. The bombast breeches and trunk hose of the period of Elizabeth no doubt inspired furniture designers to create the bulbous leg, so typical of Renaissance tables.

FRENCH COURT STYLES

The French court had begun to take the lead in the arts during the reign of Henry II (1547–1559), whose wife, Catherine de Médicis, brought many of the refinements of the Italian court to France. Under Louis XIV (1643–1715) and his Finance Minister, Jean Baptiste Colbert, the French court became the most powerful and extravagant in Europe. All other courts attempted to emulate the king's palaces, especially the Palace of Versailles. Since the styles of the three Louis's are mainly museum pieces, we shall discuss them only briefly.

Although French court furniture was too elaborate for the ordinary home, court furniture influenced furniture design in the French provinces and also in England. The period of Louis XIV is known as the Baroque because of its overwhelming grandeur. Royal palaces were furnished with exquisite Gobelin tapestries and rare rugs, massive and elaborately carved furniture upholstered with beautiful brocades, floor-length mirrors with gilded carving, and paintings in the grand style.

During the reign of the next king, Louis XV (1715–1774), the grandiose rectangular forms of Louis XIV were replaced with curvilinear forms carved with rock and shell motifs, referred to as *Rococo*. This was a period when women dominated the French court, especially Madame de Pompadour and Madame du Barry, and therefore furniture expressed feminine curves rather than masculine angles. In keeping with the feminine influence, more feminine furniture forms came into being—toilettes (dressing tables), dainty commodes (end tables with drawers), tea tables, card tables, delicate writing desks, the chaise longue (long-chair-and-high-footstool combination).

After the long reign of Louis XV, Louis XVI (1774–1792) came to the throne. The furniture styles of the period of Louis XVI and Marie Antoinette were influenced by the excavations at Pompeii and Herculaneum. There was a return to classic simplicity, with straight lines predominating except for chair backs. The styles of Louis XV and Louis XVI were copied in more simplified form by craftsmen in the provinces outside Paris. These are the basis for our present French Provincial styles.

Following the French Revolution, France was ruled by a Directory and later a Consulate (1795–1804). During this period of rebellion against wealth and power, the new rulers permitted angry mobs to set fire to Gobelin factories, destroying many art treasures, while other groups destroyed valuable paintings, sculpture, and tapestries in royal palaces. To save some of the valuable pieces of art, the National Convention appointed the well-known artist Jacques David and several other artists to decide what items should be saved, but they found it difficult to reason with the enraged mobs, and many priceless works of art were lost forever.

During the late eighteenth and early nineteenth centuries, there was an avid admiration for Greek and Roman art. New craftsmen introduced classic motifs but changed the furniture forms very little from those of Louis XVI. The furniture of this period, known as

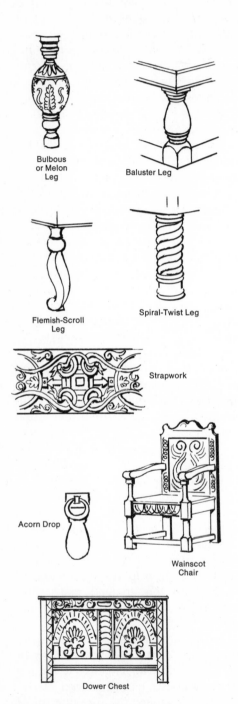

Bulbous
or Melon
Leg

Baluster Leg

Flemish-Scroll
Leg

Spiral-Twist Leg

Strapwork

Acorn Drop

Wainscot
Chair

Dower Chest

Details of Jacobean furniture: Rectangular, massive forms are characteristic of this period. Oak was the favorite wood.

Directoire, is far more attractive than that of the following Empire period.

When Napoleon became emperor (1804–1815), he engaged two craftsmen, Percier and Fontaine, who designed very pompous and ornate furniture from Egyptian, Etruscan, Greek, and Roman sources—chairs, tables, chests, and couches of Empire style. Red mahogany became the most popular wood, and this was carved and decorated with bronze mounts and medallions embossed with Egyptian and classic motifs. Columns and scrolls were a special feature of tables, chests, and beds, and rich upholstery fabrics woven with classic motifs were used.

ENGLISH COURT STYLES

The *Jacobean period* (1603–1688) covered the reigns of James I, Charles I, Cromwell, Charles II, and James II. The period coincided with the reign of Louis XIII and most of the reign of Louis XIV in France.

With the defeat of the Spanish Armada during Elizabeth's reign, England had become a world sea power. England also benefited when Spain's most skilled cabinetmakers fled to English shores during the Spanish Inquisition. Charles II, exiled in France during the period of Cromwell, brought back with him on his return to England many French styles, which also increased interest in furniture making in England.

This was a rigorous period in which change was constant. Power brought wealth, and wealth was reflected in tremendously improved living conditions, which in turn created a desire for better-designed and more luxurious home furnishings. Oak, which became popular in the Tudor period, continued as the most important wood throughout the Jacobean period. Jacobean furniture became far more adaptable to manor houses than Elizabethan furniture. Local craftsmen still depended mainly upon the furniture of the cathedral and parish church for their designs, but they scaled their furniture to fit into country manor houses and simplified the carving. Jacobean designers modified the bulbous leg until it became the baluster leg, conventionalized the folds in church linen for the carved linen-fold borders, and designed drawer pulls from acorns, found in nature. Spanish furniture with its geometric designs also influenced English decoration, after Catherine of Aragon (who came from a province in Spain) became Henry VIII's first wife. The *dower chest,* or what we call the hope chest, became an important piece of furniture. This chest held the bride's contribution to the home, including clothing and household linens as well as firearms. As chests were made larger and deeper, it became inconvenient to find various items; so the concept of drawers came into being. About this time, or during the reign of Charles I, English cavaliers needed a special place to store their large hats. Since chests with drawers proved to be so much more convenient than a chest with a lid, designers began to produce low chests with two or three drawers, or the lowboy.

The long trestle table, better known as the banquet table, was adequate for eating, but as people began to have more leisure, tables for playing games, serving tea, and holding books or sewing supplies came into use. During the Jacobean period an ingenious designer introduced the gateleg table, which became popular immediately. It could be used as a game and tea table, and when not in use, its legs and sides could be folded back, so that it took up little floor space.

Under Cromwell the comforts and pleasures of life were frowned upon, and furniture, like the dress of our own Puritans, became severe. However, Charles II, upon his restoration in 1660, kept craftsmen of all kinds working around the clock. In addition to being influenced by the handsome Baroque furniture of Italy and France and the more homey furniture of the Low Countries, Charles had also inherited a flair for the creative. New furniture forms began to appear. Charles's interest in science inspired him to design the works for an elaborate clock, which we know as a grandfather's clock. With improvements in printing, the possession of fine books became associated with status; thus bookcases became popular. Bible boxes were designed with drawers, pigeonholes, and secret compartments to hide important letters and records. The box was placed on a stand, and the top of the box was slanted as a rest for the open Bible. An increased interest in writing soon turned the Bible box into a slant-top writing desk. By the end of the Jacobean period homes had become much more attractive and more comfortable.

Current reproductions of Jacobean furniture fit nicely into English Cotswold and English Half-Timbered homes, men's clubs and men's apartments, libraries, and large country dining rooms. One or two pieces may be used in any room in a contemporary setting, but Jacobean furniture can be used indiscriminately in very few contemporary homes because it may appear too bulky.

William and Mary (1689–1702) came to the throne when James II was forced to flee from England in 1689. Mary was James II's daughter, and her husband was William of Orange from Holland. Although their rule lasted a

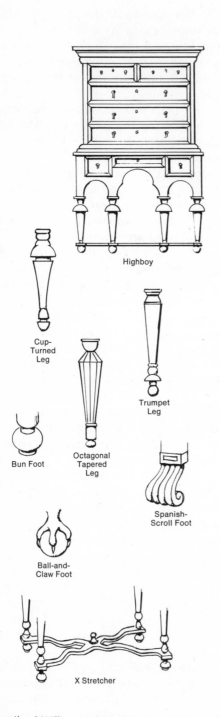

Highboy

Cup-Turned Leg

Trumpet Leg

Bun Foot

Octagonal Tapered Leg

Spanish-Scroll Foot

Ball-and-Claw Foot

X Stretcher

Details of William and Mary furniture: Prevailing forms are less massive and more graceful than Jacobean furniture. Walnut was the favorite wood.

brief thirteen years, their influence upon living concepts was marked. The Dutch were practical business people—not nobility—and they loved their homes, as Dutch painters of this period reveal in their genre paintings. William and Mary brought with them to England many Dutch craftsmen, including Daniel Marot, originally a court favorite of Louis XIV. The young queen was interested in creating an attractive home, and her court cabinetmakers desired to please her. With a woman's influence, furniture became lighter and more practical. Mary's fine collection of china led to the designing of corner cupboards. Writing desks increased in popularity as communication improved. The need for a larger supply of table and bed linens as well as clothing led to the designing of chests with more drawers, or the highboy. This was originally a chest on a table with a drawer, and later a chest-on-chest. As people accumulated more and more books, the flat-top desk and book shelves evolved into the secretary or bookcase.

William and Mary styles were a transition between the almost medieval Jacobean church-inspired furniture and the more feminine styles of Queen Anne. The Low Countries had benefited in cabinetmaking through their early trade with Italy and their proximity to France. For a period during the seventeenth century, Amsterdam was the most active seaport in the world. Although the Netherlands gained its independence from Spain in 1648, Spanish art had left its mark in arts and crafts. As early as 1492 many Jews and Moors, expelled from Spain, settled in the Netherlands. The Moorish arch appears in the apron of highboys and in the double hood of William and Mary secretaries. The scroll foot and X stretcher are also Spanish in origin. The characteristic cup-turned leg was inspired by the vogue for collecting china cups for display.

Except for a few copies of Jacobean furniture, William and Mary styles were among the first to be copied in America after the Dutch settlers arrived in New Amsterdam. William and Mary furniture can be used successfully with Jacobean and Georgian styles. Reproductions are not entirely out of place in contemporary homes.

Queen Anne (1702–1714), Mary's sister, was called to the throne upon the death of William in 1702. As England's wealth increased, comfort and refinements became important. The middle classes began to want more attractive surroundings. Walnut, which became popular with William and Mary, continued to be the favorite wood. It was either carved or veneered, and brass pulls, knobs, and keyholes decorated the drawers of chests. The cabriole leg, adapted from late Louis XIV styles, was used on chairs, cabinets, and tables. Splats in the backs of chairs took many forms. Some resembled fiddles; others, urns; some had shell carving, and others were pierced. Queen Anne styles had such grace and originality that they continued in vogue for more than thirty-five years after Anne's reign and formed the basis for many of Chippendale's early designs.

More leisurely living inspired cabinetmakers to design all kinds of tables for card games, tea, needlework, and dining. Tilt-top tables with piecrust edges replaced gateleg tables. The kneehole desk came into use, with receptacles for pen, ink, and sand. Highboys increased in popularity. Shaving mirrors, to be used on top of high chests, also made their appearance.

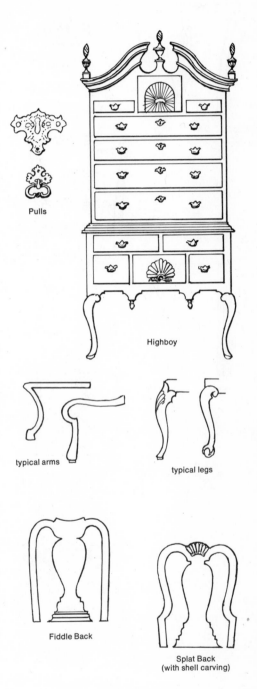

Pulls

Highboy

typical arms

typical legs

Fiddle Back

Splat Back
(with shell carving)

Queen Anne furniture was sturdy and curvilinear, showing strong Rococo influence.

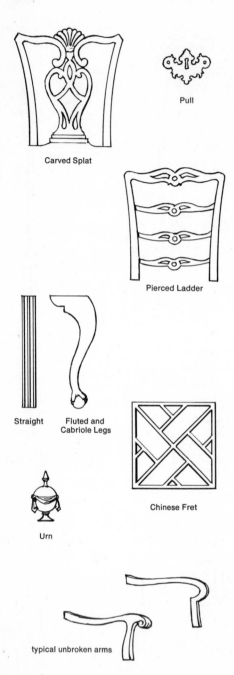

Carved Splat

Pull

Pierced Ladder

Straight   Fluted and Cabriole Legs

Chinese Fret

Urn

typical unbroken arms

Chippendale's designs show ingenuity and varied sources of inspiration. His furniture is widely reproduced today.

The Queen Anne period was one of innovation and refinement in the furniture arts. Queen Anne furniture is at home with Early American, Georgian, and William and Mary styles. Because of its many curves it is a little more difficult to use with extremely severe contemporary furniture.

THE ENGLISH GEORGIAN PERIOD

The Georgian period (1714–1820) covers the reigns of three English kings, George I (1714–1727), George II (1727–1760), and George III (1760–1820). By this time England had become powerful both politically and financially through colonial conquests and world trade. A strong aristocracy had developed, and social competition was keen. Fine china, beautiful silver, and exquisite table linens became the order of the day. Tea drinking became an English institution, inspiring new table and chair designs. Homes became more elegant and furnishings more elaborate as architects and cabinetmakers were inspired by the courts of Italy and France and trade with the Orient. However, Queen Anne furniture forms continued through the early part of the Georgian period. But gradually the names of cabinetmakers rather than those of reigning monarchs became associated with furniture styles. The earliest Georgian architect and cabinetmaker was William Kent (1684–1748), whose designs were rather heavy and were influenced greatly by the Italian Baroque.

As importations of mahogany increased from Cuba early in the Georgian period, mahogany began to replace walnut as a furniture wood. Because it responded to intricate carving better than walnut, it became the favorite wood of the later Georgian cabinetmakers.

Chippendale (1718–1779)

Chippendale was the earliest and most versatile cabinetmaker of the period. His reputation spread so rapidly that he was able to open a shop in London under his own name. In 1754 he published *The Gentleman and Cabinetmaker's Director,* which became the most sought-after book on furniture designs of the period.

He had a knack for selecting the best features of contemporary furniture and creating designs that looked just right in English homes. His early designs, particularly chairs, were influenced by Queen Anne styles. He modified the cabriole leg and pierced the splat back in a rhythmic pattern.

The Rococo styles of Louis XV of France were held in high esteem by the English, and Chippendale's ability to adapt elaborate court style to English country furniture, plus his good timing, increased his popularity. The S and C curves and the serpentine fronts on chairs, sofas, and sideboards reflected the French influence. Furniture and architectural details in Gothic churches also provided an important source of inspiration.

Increased Chinese trade influenced French and English artists and craftsmen, especially Chippendale. Carved pagodas, fretwork, and square legs were characteristic of Chippendale's Oriental period. By combining various details Chippendale gave infinite variety to his designs. The continued emphasis upon the art of table service prompted Chippendale and contemporary designers to introduce new table designs. The Pembroke table, a small drop-leaf table with a drawer, used now as an end table, originated during the mid-eighteenth century. The name is said to have come from the Countess Pembroke, who ordered the table from

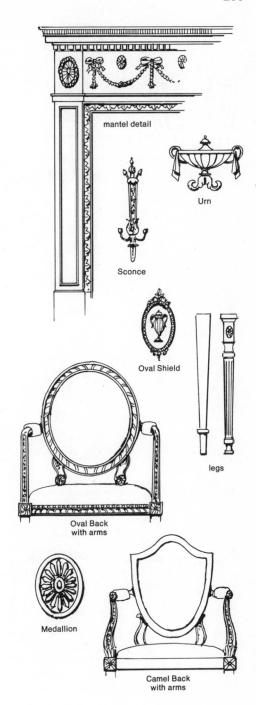

mantel detail

Urn

Sconce

Oval Shield

legs

Oval Back
with arms

Medallion

Camel Back
with arms

The Adam brothers' furniture reflects the classic designs of antiquity. Architectural motifs were repeated in furniture details.

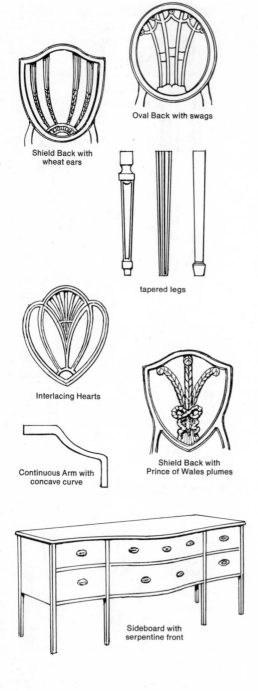

Shield Back with wheat ears

Oval Back with swags

tapered legs

Interlacing Hearts

Continuous Arm with concave curve

Shield Back with Prince of Wales plumes

Sideboard with serpentine front

Hepplewhite's furniture suggests strength and elegance. He preferred to work with mahogany and fruitwood.

Chippendale. Another famous Chippendale table form that has remained popular is the drop-leaf table with console ends. When the leaves of this table are down, the table may be placed against the wall. With the leaves up, it becomes a dining table for eight or more people. When the semicircular console tables are placed at each end, it becomes a banquet table. Another popular Chippendale design was the breakfront or bookcase (sometimes designed as a china cupboard).

Adam Brothers

There were four Adam brothers who were primarily architects catering only to the wealthy. Of the four, Robert (1728-1792) is the best known. In their work the exterior architectural theme was carried inside to the walls, windows, floors, and furniture. The Adam period paralleled that of Louis XVI and Marie Antoinette, when furniture came under the classic influence after excavations at Pompeii and Herculaneum. Robert Adam had studied in Italy, and while there he had recorded measurements from the ruins of the palace of the Roman Emperor Diocletian. When he published his book on the palace of Diocletian, he dedicated it to King George, hoping to be the king's choice as royal architect, but instead the king chose William Chambers.

The Adam firm employed contemporary cabinetmakers, such as Hepplewhite and Sheraton; potters, such as Wedgwood and Spode; craftsmen; artists; and fabric manufacturers to carry out the particular idea for each home they decorated. They considered plaster walls more suitable for their classic-type furnishings than wood paneling, and they used delicately molded classic festoons, fret, honeysuckle, wheatears, acanthus, urn, and medallion motifs in ceiling, wall, and mantel decoration. Similar designs were carved on furniture and woven into fabric and rugs.

Hepplewhite (?-1786)

Few cabinetmakers could equal in their designs the exquisite proportions, refinement, and charm of Hepplewhite furniture. Hepplewhite was influenced by Adam, Chippendale, and Louis XVI designs, but his chairs, tables, chests, dressing tables, desks, and sideboards had a character all their own.

Mahogany continued as the favorite wood, but satinwood was gaining in popularity. Some woods, especially beech, were being painted or lacquered and decorated with Oriental motifs. Hepplewhite used a great deal of carving and inlay. His chairs, like those of Chippendale, had variety. The shield or lyre back is perhaps the most familiar, but the oval, interlacing-heart, and camel backs are also typically Hepplewhite. He used wheatears, honeysuckle, swags, urns, and Prince of Wales plumes on all his pieces. Aside from chairs, Hepplewhite is remembered for his sideboards. Most of these have a curved or serpentine front.

Sheraton (1751-1806)

In the opinion of many people, Thomas Sheraton was the best of the Georgian cabinetmakers, but he did not live long enough to enjoy this distinction. Had he been able to devote his full attention to cabinetmaking, he might have had no equal. However, he was so far outshone by Hepplewhite and the Adams that he could not support his family as a cabinetmaker, and had to supplement his income. His inspiration for designs came from many sources—Louis XVI, Pompeii and Herculaneum, Duncan Phyfe, and French Empire styles. He was inclined to use

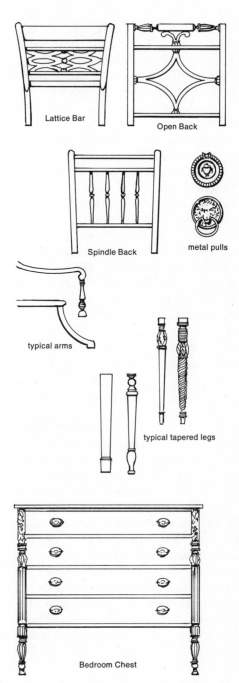

Lattice Bar

Open Back

Spindle Back

metal pulls

typical arms

typical tapered legs

Bedroom Chest

Sheraton's furniture designs were versatile, delicate, and graceful, with more emphasis on straight lines.

straight lines and square tapered legs rather than the curvilinear forms characteristic of Hepplewhite.

Although Sheraton was versatile, he was also lofty, impatient, cynical, and temperamental. His loftiness and temperament often drove potential clients from his little shop. He was forced to supplement his income by preaching in a Baptist church and by teaching furniture drafting. His ability to design and write caused him to turn to writing several books on furniture making. He personally tried to sell his books in England, Ireland, and Scotland, but his income from writing was low. Nevertheless, his designs were copied everywhere. Perhaps Sheraton was a genius, but his versatility and his timing were against him. Sheraton reproductions today harmonize with all but very heavy furniture pieces.

PROVINCIAL AND COLONIAL STYLES

French Provincial (1610–1792)

French Provincial furniture as we know it was copied mainly from the periods of Louis XV and Louis XVI. The cabriole leg is characteristic of most chairs and tables. The styles of Louis XIV were less popular because of their grandiose proportions, but Louis XIV furniture was also copied in the provinces of France. French Provincial furniture was designed locally, and each cabinetmaker interpreted styles a little differently. Local woods, such as fruitwoods, oak, ash, elm, and chestnut, were used in place of expensive imported woods.

In the colder provinces beds were built into walls, and they were equipped with draw curtains. One of the best-known pieces was the armoire, or a large clothes cupboard for the bedroom. Little writing desks and dressing tables were favorite pieces for the bedroom. Another characteristic piece was a sort of hutch for the kitchen or dining room.

Biedermeier (about 1815–1848)

The origin of the name *Biedermeier* is unusual. It is neither the name of a person nor that of a province. In German it means a happy middle-class person who likes solid comfort. A cartoonist, Ludwig Eichrodt, had portrayed this comfortable gentleman in a comic strip with the name "Papa Biedermeier" before the present furniture bore the name. Biedermeier furniture resembles Directoire and Empire styles. However, it was originally made of local wood and had very little carving. Some pieces were enameled or lacquered with black lines to resemble ebony inlay, and classic designs of the French Republic were often painted on individual pieces. Some chairs were enameled yellow and upholstered in black horsehair.

Modern reproductions of Biedermeier combine with French Provincial, Empire, and Directoire styles. Many pieces of Biedermeier furniture fit nicely into contemporary settings.

Early American, or Colonial, Styles (about 1650–1775)

Early American furniture styles usually include those produced between 1650 and 1700 by settlers from England, Holland, Germany, Sweden, and France. These were reproduced from memory to simulate prevailing styles in the old country. Pennsylvania Dutch furniture, painted with hearts, tulips, roosters, and other peasant designs, was among the most charming of the very early pieces.

During the eighteenth century, American Colonial furniture styles prevailed. Sometimes in the eighteenth century furniture was imported, but truly American pieces were made in America. There were adaptations of William and Mary, Queen Anne, Chippendale, Adam, Hepplewhite, and Sheraton designs. The needs of most of the colonists were simple in comparison with the needs of well-to-do families in England for whom the great cabinetmakers of the Georgian period made furniture. However, it was not long before cabinetmakers in New England, Pennsylvania, Virginia, and the Carolinas were turning out beautiful slant-top desks, highboys, small chests of drawers, kneehole desks, secretaries, and all kinds of chairs.

During the Revolution the colonies were cut off from European sources of design. Because of the time lag in communication American Colonial furniture for a long time was patterned after early imports of Queen Anne and Chippendale styles. Not until the late 1700's were Hepplewhite, Adam, and Sheraton pieces copied in America.

NINETEENTH-CENTURY AMERICAN FURNITURE

American Federal (about 1790–1840)

After the Revolution most families in America were impoverished, and there was little creative incentive. As stability returned, designers turned to France instead of England for inspiration. This period coincided with the Directory, Consulate, and Empire periods in France and the revival of Greek and Roman motifs—the eagle, arrows, bowknots, festoons, cornucopia, lyre, acanthus, anthemion, wheat sheaves, and laurel wreaths. In America the new styles symbolized a revolt against the mother country. However, at this time English furniture styles were also being influenced by those in France. This period in England was known as the English Regency, a period when George IV was regent from 1811 until his mentally ill father died in 1820.

It was also during this period that Thomas Jefferson, influenced by the French court, was displaying architectural and artistic talents in designing his home, Monticello, and the University of Virginia, in which the classic influence prevailed. Leading architects all over America were following this trend in their designs for state capitols and public buildings. However, the greatest American exponent of Directoire and Empire designs was the Scotsman Duncan Phyfe.

Phyfe had served as a craftsman-apprentice in Albany, New York, for some time after his arrival in America in 1783. He moved to New York City in 1790 and created furniture after the designs of Hepplewhite and the Adams but soon used the lines of Sheraton, Directoire, and Empire furniture. These were his most successful styles. He preferred to work with mahogany and rosewood, but often used satinwood for decoration. Swags, the pineapple, eagle, and acanthus were his favorite motifs. Damask, brocade, satin, French toiles, and flowered silks were his favorite fabrics. As a designer of furniture Duncan Phyfe enjoyed unprecedented financial success.

Federal furniture designs combine easily with Georgian, English Regency, Directoire, and Empire, and also with Colonial adaptations of these designs. Some Federal furniture may be used with either Victorian or contemporary pieces.

American Victorian

During Queen Victoria's rule wealth increased in England as the British Empire expanded. Large houses and

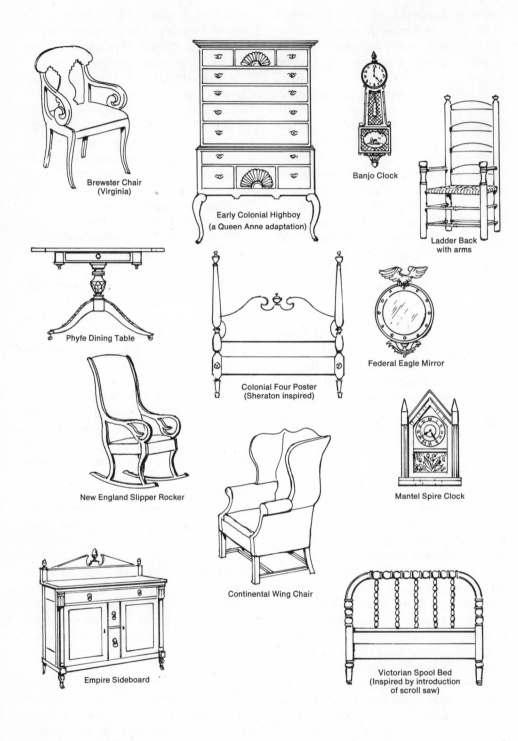

Brewster Chair
(Virginia)

Early Colonial Highboy
(a Queen Anne adaptation)

Banjo Clock

Ladder Back
with arms

Phyfe Dining Table

Colonial Four Poster
(Sheraton inspired)

Federal Eagle Mirror

New England Slipper Rocker

Mantel Spire Clock

Empire Sideboard

Continental Wing Chair

Victorian Spool Bed
(Inspired by introduction
of scroll saw)

pretentious furniture became symbols of status among wealthy industrialists and sea merchants both in England and in America. The cult of the newly rich plus the advent of power machinery tended to cause a period of decadence in home furnishings. During the early and mid-nineteenth century, both in furniture and in home decoration, there were so many competing influences—French Rococo, Egyptian, Greek, Roman, Turkish, Chinese, Moorish, and Gothic—that designers often lost sight of good basic design. Black walnut and many exotic woods became popular; scrollwork, excessive carving, and tufting prevailed. The desire to display imported china inspired designs for all kinds of cupboards and whatnot shelves. An interest in creating beautiful gardens and gazebos led to the designing of intricate "carved" designs in cast-iron outdoor furniture.

In spite of the many poor designs, not all Victorian furniture showed poor taste. Some of the armchairs, sofas, and love seats of the Victorian Rococo period and marble-top bureaus, washstands, and tables of the later and more simplified Eastlake period are among today's most cherished antiques.

Morris and Mission Furniture

William Morris, a craftsman, and Charles Eastlake, an architect, began a rebellion against Victorian opulence and insincerity. Morris was opposed to the Machine Age and endeavored to revive handcrafted furniture. He is remembered for his foursquare or solid-looking rectangular furniture that is associated with early Mission styles. The Morris chair was an item of furniture owned by practically every middle-class American family. The Mission trend in furniture prevailed far into the twentieth century and was typical of the furniture in most

bungalows during the early twentieth century. It was superseded by modernistic and later modern furniture.

TWENTIETH-CENTURY, OR MODERN, FURNITURE

The term *modern* refers to furniture designed since the early 1920's. It resulted from the modern movement in architecture and art—a rebellion against the extremely fussy Victorian styles and awkward-looking Mission styles. The new streamlined homes, schools, and public buildings inspired furniture designers to create simplified furniture styles to go with them. Early modern furniture, referred to as *modernistic,* was heavy, angular, and short-lived. The ugly, massive upholstered pieces are referred to as *Borax.*

The modern movement in furniture dates from the 1920's with the founding of a school of design in Weimar, Germany, called the Bauhaus Institute. The leading exponent of the modern furniture styles and first president of the school was Walter Gropius. With functionalism and simplicity the keynote, a whole new concept in furniture design ensued, using bentwood, metal tubing, polished surfaces, plastics, and geometric forms. The unit method of design (based upon multiples of two), especially in chests, desks, and shelf areas, made it possible to assemble furniture according to personal needs and available space. Many early modern pieces were too clinical and severe in appearance to be generally popular.

The Paris Exposition in 1925 gave impetus to modern furniture designers all over the world. It also stimulated interest in building a museum in New York City in 1929 to house modern art and furnishings. Scandinavian designs, especially those from Sweden, set the standards for modern design in textiles, glass, ceramics, and furniture. Later, Danish, Finnish, Italian, and American designs became popular.

Among the earlier designers to depart from traditional styles were Michael Thonet with his bentwood chairs, Ludwig Mies van der Rohe with his Barcelona lounge chair, Charles Eams and Eero Saarinen with their body-fitting chairs molded from plywood or plastic, and Marcel Breuer with his cantilevered tubular-steel chair and S-shaped supports. (See picture on page 259.)

Among other prominent names associated with good modern furniture are Edward J. Wormley, whose designs have classic simplicity; George Nelson, for his Japanese adaptations to modern American living; Finn Yuhl, for his designs that give the impression that they are floating in space; and Paul McCobb, for his revival of clean-cut Shaker furniture popular with the Quakers who settled in New York and Pennsylvania.

Several manufacturers of modern furniture, such as Knoll Associates, Inc., promote designs under their trade names and also participate in educational programs. Their furniture is designed in a style that is clean-cut, depending upon structure without applied design for its beauty.

SUMMARY

As we trace the social and economic progress of world civilizations, we can understand how the furniture styles we have today came into being. All of our furniture evolved from four basic pieces—a bed, a chair, a table, and a chest. Furniture of antiquity (Egypt, Greece, and Rome) was crude, massive, and limited in design. During the Middle Ages and the Renaissance, church furniture had a strong influence upon the furniture used in castles, palaces, and manor houses.

It was not until the Georgian period in eighteenth-century England that furniture styles became associated with fine homes rather than with royal palaces. Important designers of the period were Chippendale, Hepplewhite, Sheraton, and the Adam brothers. American colonists copied English styles until after the Revolution. In a spirit of independence, designers during the early period of nationalism turned to France for inspiration. It was during this time that French furniture styles were being influenced by excavations at Pompeii and Herculaneum. Furniture of the Federal period in America, the chief designer of which was Duncan Phyfe, was a reflection of the classic influence.

The nineteenth century ushered in the Machine Age, and designers often ignored good design to keep up with constantly changing tastes. Nevertheless, many pieces of Victorian furniture—love seats, chairs, and tables—have become popular as American antiques. Toward the end of the century Victorian furniture with its curves, carving, and tufting began to give way to austere, rectangular Mission furniture as two- and three-story Victorian homes began to be replaced by the popular one-story bungalow.

Contemporary furniture, or modern as it was called originally, was inspired by the modern art movement, the introduction of streamlined ranch-type homes, and Scandinavian furniture designers. Some of our most beautiful furniture today is being designed by contemporary American designers.

THINGS TO THINK ABOUT AND TO DO

1. Select one of the basic furniture pieces and trace its evolution. You may want to locate pictures of these pieces from various historic periods, and show them to the class as you give your report.

2. Discuss the early influence of the Middle East upon the home arts and also later influences when European countries began to organize East India companies.

3. Indicate on the chalkboard the dates of the reigns of Louis XIV, Louis XV, and Louis XVI, and opposite these list the corresponding dates of English rulers. Display illustrations of French and English furniture that is characteristic of these periods.

4. Make a list of as many types of chairs and tables as you can. Display pictures of these types, and label each by its correct name.

5. Make sketches of various kinds of chair legs, and identify each according to its name and the name of the period or designer from which it came.

6. Indicate furniture periods that harmonize with the following:

Jacobean
William and Mary
Queen Anne
Sheraton
Hepplewhite
Duncan Phyfe
Adam brothers
Victorian
Provincial
Early American
Mission
contemporary

7. Discuss the origin of the following terms: *cupboard, chairman, poster bed, slant-top desk, secretary, hutch, grandfather's clock, highboy,* and *Pembroke table.*

8. Indicate furniture periods in which the following woods were popular: walnut, mahogany, oak, satinwood, fruitwoods.

9. Name the most important English furniture designers of the eighteenth century and compare their styles.

10. Indicate four influences upon Chippendale's designs, especially upon his chairs.

11. List the classic motifs Robert Adam used to decorate furniture.

12. Name the motifs used to decorate Pennsylvania Dutch furniture.

13. Give a brief biography of Duncan Phyfe, and display some of his furniture designs.

14. Name four prominent contemporary furniture designers, and display some of their designs.

15. Discuss events that gave impetus to the development of modern furniture.

chapter sixteen

FURNITURE ARRANGEMENT

The arrangement of furniture would be easy if we could start with all new furniture and a new home with nicely proportioned rooms. But only decorators who arrange furniture in model homes have this opportunity. On the other hand, it is more of a challenge when we have to overcome obstacles, such as an awkwardly placed chimney, door, closet, or window, and use furniture that is already on hand.

Most people have to start with what furnishings they have and, each time they move, try to fit present possessions into a new floor plan. A review of the principles of design discussed in Chapter Eleven and space needs discussed in Chapter Five will be very helpful in studying this chapter and in applying its details.

Good furniture arrangement means that little if any traffic should interfere with work areas in the kitchen and conversation areas in the living room. Before arranging furniture in any room, one should understand the activities to be pursued in the room and should provide for artificial light where it is needed—at the sides of lounge chairs, sofas, and beds, and over work centers, such as desks and sewing machines.

The way furniture is arranged can give an impression of order or clutter and can convey an optical illusion of greater space or less space. As a rule large furniture pieces such as beds, chests, dining tables, and desks should not be placed at an angle. Scale is important to good furniture arrangement— large furniture will make small rooms appear smaller, and numerous pieces of small furniture in a large room will appear to float. A very long room can be made to appear shorter by using horizontal arrangements at the long ends of the room. A very large room may require a room divider to identify different areas for such activities as study, television viewing, and conversation. Area rugs also help to serve as room dividers.

In addition to traffic patterns, scale, and the function of the room, one should keep in mind the need for harmonious placement of individual pieces. Furniture of different periods and styles should be combined with care. In arranging a living room it is important to distribute upholstered and wood furniture to achieve good balance and also to relieve monotony.

279

GUIDELINES FOR STUDY

GENERAL IDEAS
TO CONSIDER

1. Good furniture arrangement depends upon the application of the principles of design.
2. Comfort and convenience as well as beauty influence the arrangement of furniture.
3. Planning on paper is an efficient approach to satisfactory furniture arrangement.

WORDS AND PHRASES
TO KNOW

clearance
drop-leaf table
extension table
focal point
king-size bed

queen-size bed
scale drawing
sofa bed
structural features
templates

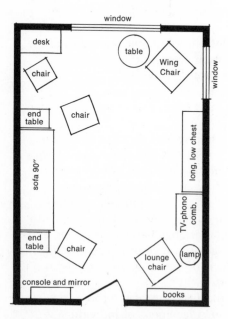

A. OPEN SPACE ARRANGEMENT

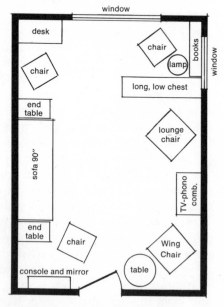

B. CONVERSATION AND STUDY AREA

This 14-foot by 20-foot living room permits a flexible furniture arrangement. In A, the room appears larger. In B, the long chest divides a study area from a conversation and TV-viewing area.

GENERAL GUIDELINES

Whether you are arranging furniture in a living room, dining room, or bedroom, certain general rules apply. The arrangement must be attractive, functional, and expressive of the personal needs and tastes of the occupants of the room. Here are some guidelines to help you with arranging furniture now and in the future:

1. Study the physical structure of the room, and determine a center of interest.
2. Decide where you will place the largest pieces of furniture—usually a bed, sofa, or chest of drawers (buffet in the dining room).
3. Consider where the traffic lanes might be through the room, and arrange furniture to avoid interruption of conversation, work, or dressing (in a bedroom).
4. If the room is large, consider how you can separate it into two or three areas—conversation, television viewing, listening to records, studying, or reading if it is a *living room;* sleeping, studying, reading, or working on a hobby if it is a *bedroom;* eating, studying, or hobbies if it is a *dining room.*
5. Avoid a cluttered arrangement by using built-in cabinets or shelves if storage is a problem, and by rotating accessories if you like to display many interesting possessions.
6. Observe the laws of proportion by keeping furniture scaled to the room.
7. Use optical illusion in changing the proportions of a room. *Shorten* a room that is too long by dividing it into areas or by using a horizontal arrangement at one end or both ends. *Lengthen* a square room by using long horizontal arrangements on two sides and by using an open scenic design on wallpaper at one end or a wall color at one end that is lighter than that of other walls.

8. Avoid placing vertical pieces, such as a secretary or a highboy, between tall windows unless the wall opposite can balance this arrangement.
9. Combine wood and upholstered furniture for pleasing balance.
10. Place wood as well as upholstered furniture away from windows where the sun shines in for long periods.
11. Use even balance on one wall for a feeling of repose, but avoid too much even balance in one room or the effect will be monotonous.

GUIDELINES FOR INDIVIDUAL ROOMS

Your first home may have only a living room, bedroom, bathroom, and kitchenette. You will probably not have an entrance hall or foyer. There are advantages in having some kind of separated entrance. If the living room is large enough, you can make a simulated entrance with a divider—a bookcase with a planter, for instance.

Each area in the home has a different duty to perform, and if the furniture is well chosen and well placed, the people who use the rooms will be able to enjoy better living.

The Foyer, or Entrance Area

A separate entrance area takes much of the traffic out of other rooms of the house and permits family members to pass from the front entrance to the kitchen or bedrooms without going through the living room. The minimum-size entrance should be large enough for a coat closet and have space for a small table or wall shelf and mirror, which provides a last-minute check on one's appearance before leaving the house or answering the doorbell. A little larger entrance may accommodate two additional chairs that can double as dining-room chairs. A still larger foyer may have built-in or movable shelves for books and interesting accessories or a hobby collection, and a small chest of drawers (with a mirror) in place of a small table.

The Living Room

Perhaps your present living room is already furnished, but your family is considering some replacements. If so, a *total plan* should be made before buying anything even if replacements must be staggered over two or three years to spread costs. In this way new purchases—a sofa, chair, tables, slipcovers, or draperies—will fit into the total plan.

When you start to furnish your own home, you will not be able to buy all your living-room furniture at one time. The *first year* you will need some kind of sofa bed or studio couch which can be used in a family room later on. By having something where two persons can sleep, a living room can double as a guest room when necessary. In addition you will need one lounge chair for reading or TV viewing and one or two pull-up or occasional chairs for conversation. Often people buy two dining-room chairs with arms, and use them as occasional chairs in the living room when not in use at the dining table. You will need either two end tables or one end table and a coffee table plus shelves for books, records, magazines, hobbies, and so forth. End tables with drawers or a drawer and shelf will give extra storage space. You can improvise bookshelves if necessary by using ten- or twelve-inch boards about three-fourths of an inch thick with glass brick or regular brick between the boards.

You will need lamps and accessories, but many of these items will be wedding gifts, which, hopefully, will fit into your decorating plans. If you must eat meals in the living room, a card table with folding chairs will serve the purpose temporarily. The table can also be used for playing games, sewing, writing letters, or studying. If you need more space for eating, you can buy a folding round top to fit the card table and to seat six persons comfortably. Inexpensive, round cloth table covers may be bought in all colors should you want to keep the round top on the table as part of the decorating scheme.

The *second year* you may add a drop-leaf or extension table, and one or two small tables and chairs according to needs and space available. When you buy chairs, it is advisable to buy eight dining-room chairs to match (two with arms), and spread these over the house while they are not being used for dining.

The twelve-foot by sixteen-foot living room shown in Floor Plan A on the next page has two windows on one side. It is a nice size room, but in a large home you might want a living room close to fourteen feet by twenty feet, like that shown in Floor Plan B, especially if you have a large family or do a great deal of entertaining. Such a room might serve especially well during the expanding-family period in the family life cycle. The illustrations show the larger room arranged for dining and living, and the smaller room arranged as a living room–guest room.

The center of interest in the living room may be an attractive window treatment or possibly a spectacular view, in which case the window decoration should play a subordinate role. Other possibilities for a focal point in the living room would be a sofa wall and an interesting wall composition above the sofa, *or* on the opposite long wall there might be a low chest for

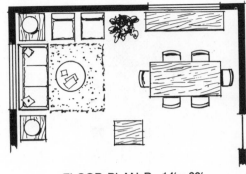

FLOOR PLAN B. 14' x 20'

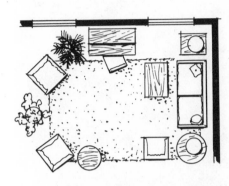

FLOOR PLAN A. 12' x 16'

The Plan A living room becomes a guest room when the sofa is opened into a queen size bed, with lamps providing good light for bed reading. Plan B shows a living-dining area that is both pleasing and functional.

records, radio, television, and storage with a tall table lamp at one end of the chest and a picture collection above the chest. In place of a picture collection, there might be lighted or unlighted shelves to display some other prized collection.

As a rule, a sofa should not be placed in front of a group of windows. But if there is no special view, if the windows can be reached for adjusting without moving furniture, and if the sofa does not compete for interest with the windows, a sofa may be used on a wall where there are windows. Chairs and a sofa should be grouped so that from six to eight persons can be within a conversation range. Two conversation groupings may be better than one large circle especially when traffic may have to pass through a wide circle. The television should be placed where it can be seen by four or five persons at one time without disturbing furniture. Lamps should be placed where people can

read, study, or write letters. Enough table space should be provided for ashtrays, for a decorative object or small flower arrangement, or for people to set down glasses or small refreshment dishes.

Some families have either a spinet, upright, or baby grand piano. A piano should never be placed on an outside wall because of dampness and changing temperatures. A spinet or upright is sometimes placed at a right angle to the wall to serve as a room divider. A mesh fabric may be used to cover the back if this arrangement is desirable. In any case lighting must be provided for playing the piano and some thought given as to where people can sit to listen.

Dining Area or Dining Room

When a living room must serve also as a dining room, the dining table should be near the kitchen. All items to be used in dining should be stored

Top left: A bookcase serves as the center of interest in a room that successfully blends old and new styles. Top right: The black marble fireplace and surrounding wood paneling dominate this evenly balanced, formal room. Bottom left: There are two centers of interest here—the fireplace and the picture window—unified by a curvilinear sectional sofa. Above: Focal point for an Early American room is the sofa and picture collection.

near the dining area to avoid traffic through the living area. If a dining area is used regularly for dining and study, it is advisable to have a good lamp over the table, perhaps one that can be pulled down from the ceiling.

During the expanding stage in the family life cycle, many families prefer a separate dining room if the budget permits, especially if the family places a high social value upon dining, table conversation, and table manners. Preferably a dining room should be large enough to seat eight persons at a table without being crowded, and also hold a buffet and a serving table. A dining table with drop leaves, end extensions, or extra leaves is better than a table that cannot be adjusted. The dining table need not always stand in the middle of the room. A drop-leaf table with one leaf down can be placed against a wall and still seat four persons easily for dining. A dining room can double as a family room, a room for doing homework, or a room for carrying on a hobby. In an emergency it can also serve as a guest room if a folding bed or a daybed is available. It need not stand idle most of the time.

Bedrooms

A comfortable bed takes precedence over everything else in the bedroom. If money must be budgeted, do not skimp on bed springs and mattress. A mattress and a set of springs with four legs can be used until there is enough money to buy a bed frame or a headboard. If a double bed is preferred in the master bedroom, it is advisable to buy a queen size for extra comfort. It may also be wise to purchase twin beds in extra length for the guest room. Bed frames or headboards can be bought later for all beds.

A double bed should have a table at each side. Tables with a drawer and shelf are usually preferred. A table is needed for a lamp, books, and other items. If twin beds are placed together to give the impression of a king-size bed, two tables are necessary, but if the twin beds are parallel to each other with a space between, one table can be used between the beds. If twin beds are placed at right angles in the corner of a room, a square table without a shelf or drawers can be used in the corner. A corner table flanked by beds is inaccessible except for the surface, but the areas underneath can be used for storing articles that are seldom used, such as Christmas decorations or suitcases.

Next to comfort in a bedroom comes convenience, and this means available storage space. Some people like broad twin chests placed adjacent to each other, whereas others prefer a dresser and a tall chest of drawers. It is advisable to have a mirror over a chest or dresser and also a full-length mirror on a door. If space permits, it is nice to have one small lounge chair or a rocker in a bedroom, especially during sickness. One or two other chairs may be dining-room chairs. Often parents like to have a large bed-sitting room during the expanding stage in the family life cycle, so that they can have a quiet place for a retreat. The sitting area may have a small desk, a television, and an extra lounge, an occasional chair, or a chaise longue.

Guest rooms should be more or less impersonal but as inviting and cheerful as possible. Your guests will appreciate little attentions, such as a pencil and pad of paper, magazines, an ashtray, perhaps a small bowl of fresh flowers from the garden, or a little covered dish of small candies.

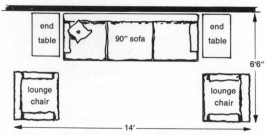

**A. LONG SOFA FLANKED BY
END TABLES AND LOUNGE CHAIRS**

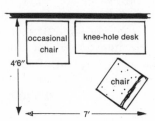

**C. STUDY AREA – DESK, CHAIR
AND OCCASIONAL CHAIR**

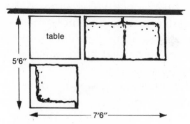

**B. SECTIONAL SOFA AND TABLE
IN CORNER ARRANGEMENT**

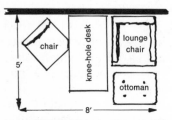

**D. STUDY AREA – DESK, CHAIR,
LOUNGE CHAIR AND OTTOMAN**

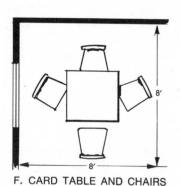

F. CARD TABLE AND CHAIRS

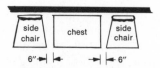

**E. CHEST OR SECRETARY
FLANKED BY TWO CHAIRS**

Popular furniture groupings and space requirements.

The furniture in this bedroom is arranged to give a small child a safe and sizable play area.

Children's rooms should grow with the child. It is easy to purchase furniture in units—chests, desks, dressing tables, shelves, and so on—and add or change units as needs change. Storage space is important, and girls usually like to have a large bulletin board in their rooms.

Often teen-agers like to have a bed-sitting room to which to retreat. As a rule it is advisable to provide a study area composed of a well-lighted table or desk and a suitable chair. Such an area may double for working on a hobby or other leisure activity.

No matter what bedroom you are decorating, begin the furniture arrangement by placing the bed or beds on the longest wall space if the room is small or of average size. Some bedrooms will be large enough so that you will have a choice of two or three locations for the bed or beds. Remember to leave a space of at least eighteen inches

around a bed for making it up; with extra space allowed between twin beds. Place chests or bureaus near closets for convenience. For good day-time lighting on a mirror, place a chest and mirror on a wall adjacent to a wall with a window. A wall lamp on each side of a mirror or very tall, slender lamps on each end of a chest of drawers or dresser will give better artificial light than low lamps.

PLAN ON PAPER

Moving furniture about by trial and error to find a good arrangement is not always necessary. It can be time-consuming, tiring, and exasperating. A little paper planning will save time and strength, and usually produce satisfactory results. Use one-quarter-inch graph paper to make a scale drawing of the room you are decorating. If you are rearranging present furniture, measure each piece and cut out furniture templates to scale. If you want to experiment with templates for new furniture, use templates such as those shown opposite for guidance, and make small copies of the pieces of furniture you need. The suggestions in this chapter may not solve all your furniture arrangement problems, but they should make some solutions easier.

Observe the following measurements for clearances and area groupings:

Living Room

Space between coffee table and sofa or chair	1'6"
Space before chair or sofa for leg room when person is seated	1'6" to 2'6"
Chair or bench space in front of desk or piano	3'
Space for chair, average-size sofa, coffee table, and end table in conversation group	6'6" × 9'
Space for long sofa with end tables, two lounge chairs, and coffee table	6'6" × 14' plus
Bookcase or secretary with flanking chairs (Chairs should be 6 inches away from secretary.)	2' × 7'
Space for card table and four chairs	8' × 8'
Corner group with two chairs, love seat, coffee table, and one end table	7' × 9'
Study area with desk, chair, lounge chair, and ottoman	5' × 8'
Corner grouping with two lounge chairs and corner table	6' × 6'
Fireplace grouping with two lounge chairs, love seat, and two lamp tables	5'3" × 9'

Dining Room

Space between table and wall or buffet	2'8" to 3'
Space for occupied chair beyond table	1'10" to 3'
Space around chairs at table for serving	1'6" to 2'

Bedrooms

Space at each side of bed for making bed	1'6" to 2'
Space between twin beds	1'6" to 3'
Space between chest of drawers and bed	3'

SUMMARY

Good furniture arrangement is more likely to result if you begin your work by studying a room objectively. This means considering the use of the room, the character and the quantity of furniture to be used, the physical characteristics of the room, and the main traffic lanes. With these things in mind the next step is to apply the principles of design so that the room, or the area, or the entire home will be not only functional but attractive. Knowing how to camouflage undesirable features and emphasize desirable features, you can make almost any room look attractive.

THINGS TO THINK ABOUT AND TO DO

1. Collect illustrations of good furniture arrangements for living rooms, living-dining rooms, and family rooms for your scrapbook or portfolio.

2. Bring to class pictures showing good bedroom arrangements for single and double beds. Include master bedrooms, guest rooms, rooms for young children, and rooms for teen-agers. Mount the best on the bulletin board for comment.

3. Draw your own bedroom to scale on graph paper, and see what you can do to improve the arrangement of furniture by using furniture templates.

4. Select a floor plan you think you would like to have in your future home. Plan the furnishings on graph paper.

5. Make a list of your family's activities while occupying the living room. See what you can do to make the furniture arrangement more convenient and attractive.

6. Collect pictures of interesting children's rooms and discuss them from the standpoint of beauty and practicality.

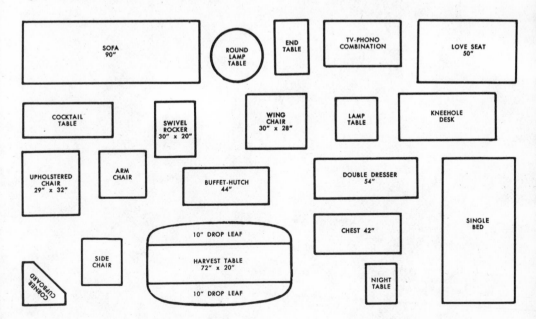

Furniture Templates

chapter seventeen

PICTURES
AND ACCESSORIES

A decorative scheme for any room in the house may start with a picture. It can set the mood and establish the color scheme. However, many people select pictures and other room accessories last instead of first. The poor choice of room accessories can ruin the effect of a nicely furnished room in the same way that the wrong accessories can detract from a beautiful costume. It shows poor taste to clutter the walls with pictures that have nothing in common with each other or the room, and it is also in poor taste to litter tables with all kinds of knickknacks. It is far better to use only a few well-chosen pictures, lamps, and other accessories.

Some people follow the custom of the Japanese and rotate the use of prized pieces of sculpture, wall hangings, and pictures so that each can be enjoyed. Many large cities have art rental galleries, from which people can rent original paintings and other art objects. This arrangement gives the inexperienced decorator an opportunity to experiment and to discriminate between the right and wrong choices. Many people find original art works that they eventually buy, whereas others continue to rent items especially when a family is likely to be transferred frequently.

The human desire to decorate walls dates from the Paleolithic Age, some 40,000 to 30,000 B.C. In the late nineteenth century, drawings of extinct animals dating from this period were discovered on the walls and ceilings of caves in Spain. Archaeologists have since found drawings done by primitive men in caves and on cliffs in many parts of the world, even in isolated parts of the Sahara. For both prehistoric and civilized men, art expressions on walls and in artifacts have been a key to social history. The elaborate Renaissance paintings and sculptures expressed the opulence and grandeur of the palaces and cathedrals. The sentimental art expressions of the eighteenth century were indicative of the bouffant costumes and elegant interiors of the period of Louis XV and Louis XVI. Modern art, stripped of ornamentation and sentiment, is expressive of twentieth-century technology and functionalism.

The guidelines in this chapter will help you in choosing, framing, and hanging pictures and in selecting mirrors, clocks, wall brackets, and other decorative items that enhance the decorating scheme.

GUIDELINES FOR STUDY

GENERAL IDEAS
TO CONSIDER

1. Pictures and accessories can enhance a decorating scheme or detract from it.
2. Paintings, like other expressions of art, are a key to the moods and trends of the times.
3. Pictures used in the same room must have a common denominator in order to give unity—subject matter, feeling, medium, or framing.
4. Wall accessories, such as mirrors, clocks, and wall brackets, add interest to wall composition.

WORDS AND PHRASES
TO KNOW

abstract
aquatint
barometer
block print
candle sconce
ceramic
etching

landscape
lithograph
picture mat
seascape
silk-screen print
still life

The paintings and photographs on this wall are unified by their subject matter—they reflect the occupant's affections and interests. This display is effective in a bedroom, but would be too personal for a living room.

PICTURES AS DECORATION

We use the term *pictures* in a very broad sense to include anything from paintings by great artists to personal photographs. A picture—the subject as well as the medium—should be chosen to fit in with the theme or character of a room. The size and shape should conform to the area in which it is hung. For instance, large pictures require a large wall space, vertical pictures require vertical space, and so on. A picture should give pleasure and perhaps stimulate the imagination. Some people like paintings that look like color photographs or architectural renderings. Others prefer the most abstract forms of art.

A selected group of paintings which represent some of the most important periods in art history can be found on pages 296–299. As you look over these pictures, note those that appeal to you. Do they seem to harmonize with the period you would like to emphasize in furnishings—Early American or Provincial, traditional or eighteenth century, Victorian or contemporary?

Art Mediums

Most of you have had art classes in school. You may be familiar with different mediums and the feelings or textures they convey. For example, oil paintings, block printings, silk-screen printings, and ceramic plaques are strong and bold in texture.

Watercolors; steel, copper, or fine wood engravings; lithographs; etchings; aquatints; and pencil or pen-and-ink drawings are rather delicate in texture. Photographs are in a class by themselves.

As a rule you should not use delicate and bold textures in the same room unless the room is large enough to separate the two mediums. If you choose to group pictures, they should have something in common—the medium or feeling, the subject matter, or the framing. Some people have a natural knack for grouping pictures to give an interesting mass composition, whereas others never manage to achieve harmony.

Subject Matter

Landscapes and outdoor scenes are among the most popular subject-matter choices. There are landscapes by nineteenth-century artists that harmonize with traditional furnishings, contemporary landscapes for modern rooms, and primitive-type landscapes for Early American rooms and Provincial furnishings. Seascapes and winter landscapes with cool colors predominating are a little more difficult to use than regular landscapes, unless a cool effect is desired.

Domestic and folk scenes, typical of the courtyards and interiors used by Flemish and Dutch artists, or the outdoor scenes of Currier and Ives harmonize with Pennsylvania Dutch, Early American, and Provincial furnishings.

Still-life pictures show artistic compositions of bowls of flowers or fruit, groupings of musical instruments, ceramics, or other art forms. Although these may be chosen for almost any room in the house, they often lack the pictorial appeal of scenes from nature and the imaginative appeal of abstract art.

Animal pictures and hunting scenes have limited appeal and should be chosen with discretion.

Flower prints and bird prints have general appeal for almost any room in the house, provided the decorative scheme is not strictly formal or severely contemporary.

Godey and French fashion prints are mainly for Early American, Provincial, or Victorian bedrooms.

Portraits by old masters or family portraits by contemporary painters should be used in large rooms and generally in formal settings. Pastel and watercolor family portraits do not require as formal an atmosphere.

Family photographs are very personal and therefore have limited use in the decorating scheme. A large number of interesting photographs can be grouped on one wall in a family room, study, bedroom, or hall. They may also be mounted on a folding screen. They are not usually mixed in a grouping with other types of pictures. Experienced decorators may, of course, disregard many of these rules.

Framing Pictures

The appeal of a picture can be lost entirely if the wrong frame is used. When you have a picture to be framed, a reliable dealer will be able to make suggestions and let you hold up various picture moldings along the side of the picture. Traditional oil paintings, such as landscapes and portraits, are framed with heavy frames, the width depending upon the size of the picture. The color of the frame should blend in with and not compete with the picture. Large abstract paintings in oil usually have narrow, inconspicuous frames. Glass is seldom used over oil paintings. If it is used, it should be a nonglare type.

Photographs may be framed with or without a mat, and the frame should be narrow. Watercolors, pencil and pen-and-ink sketches, etchings, wood-block prints, and lithographs are usually framed with a mat and a narrow black, gold, or silver frame. Mats may be cardboard or fabric, but in either case the color should harmonize with the picture. It is not always advisable to use a white mat because white may

contrast too much with the background color of the picture or the room. Early fashion prints and flower prints often have a colored edging around the inside of the mat.

Unless you can rely on an experienced craftsman to mat and frame a picture, examine pictures with mats in stores and experiment with cardboard until you have a mat of good proportions. The upper and side margins should be about equal; and the lower margin, a little larger. Mats on horizontal pictures may be slightly wider at the sides than at the top. If you want to buy mat board and frame your own pictures, you can cut smooth edges by using a special knife or a single-edge razor blade held firmly against a metal-edge ruler.

Hanging Pictures

If you plan to hang more than a few important pictures in a room, study current magazines for ideas. If you plan to group a large number of pictures, work out your plan first on quarter-inch graph paper. This approach will eliminate mistakes and possible wall damage. Here are a few simple rules concerning the hanging of pictures:

□ Avoid hanging pictures against figured wallpaper, unless the pictures are matted or the subject is strong enough to hold its own against the wallpaper.

□ Hang a large picture on an important wall at eye level. The average man is 5 feet 9½ inches tall; and the average woman, 5 feet 4½ inches tall. On this basis the center of a large picture should be about 5 feet 7 inches from the floor. (Pictures over mantels may be an exception to this rule.)

□ Place the screws on the back of pictures from a fourth to a third of the way down. Insert the wire for hanging and secure it firmly. When the picture is hung, it will lie flat against the wall.

□ Hang pictures of moderate size so that the lower edge is the same distance from the floor as the lower edge of the largest picture. (Sometimes there may be exceptions to this rule.)

□ Be sure that good proportion exists between the size of a picture, the wall space on which it is hung, and the piece of furniture under it or near it.

□ Make a wall composition of pictures only if you have an interesting collection of related subjects done in a similar medium, such as a group of watercolors, old prints, etchings, and so on.

□ In grouping a large number of pictures keep an imaginary line around the outside, so that the arrangement will hold together and have unity.

□ Use no more than one large grouping of pictures in a room unless you want the room to look like an art gallery.

□ Use cloth-base hangers or small picture hooks for small pictures, and large picture hooks for large pictures. Two picture hooks placed several inches apart will give a large picture greater support and keep it hanging more nearly level. Very large pictures may have to be hung with a special toggle hook.

MIRRORS, CLOCKS, AND WALL BRACKETS

Mirrors

Long before man was able to look into a piece of polished metal and see his reflection, he had to be content with looking into a tranquil stream. In due course silvered glass replaced polished metal. The first true glass mirrors came from Venice. French kings never tired of admiring themselves, and therefore they placed panels of mirrors in walls all over their palaces. Perhaps if we had more full-length mirrors in our homes and school corridors today, there might be a decided improvement in grooming.

Thomas Chippendale, by designing interesting mirror frames, is credited with giving the mirror an important place in home decoration. A beautiful ornamental mirror can be the focal point in the decoration of a living room, dining room, or bedroom, as the illustration on page 290 shows. A bedroom should have a full-length door mirror for function perhaps more than for beauty. An entrance hall benefits by an interesting mirror placed at the proper height, and a good mirror is essential in the bathroom.

Inexpensive mirrors are made of ordinary window glass, which often distorts the image. Better mirrors are made of plate glass free of irregularities. The back of the glass is silvered and given a protective coat of paint. Very expensive mirrors may have a copper coating between the silvering and the paint coating. Some glass is tinted pink or yellow for a warm glow, or blue for a cool glow.

A mirror helps to increase the apparent size of a room. It should be chosen to fit into the decorating scheme. The shape should be in proportion to

"The Swing," Jean-Honoré
Fragonard, National Gallery
of Art, Washington, D.C.,
Samuel H. Kress Collection.
An   eighteenth–century
French painting typical of
ROCOCO art. The exquisite
colors and the graceful, gay
figures reflect the light–
hearted, frivolous life of the
nobility.

"The White Horse," John Constable, National Gallery of Art, Washington, D.C., Widener Collection. Constable, a nineteenth-century ROMANTIC painter, emphasized the glories of nature and
projected emotional appeal.

"A Woman Weighing Gold," Jan Vermeer, National Gallery of Art, Washington, D.C., Widener Collection. A Dutch genre painting of the late *RENAISSANCE.* Domestic interiors like this have wide appeal.

"A Girl with a Watering Can," Auguste Renoir, National Gallery of Art, Washington, D.C., Chester Dale Collection. *IMPRESSIONISM* dominated nineteenth-century French painting. Renoir, like other artists of the period, felt that the total aesthetic impact of a painting was most important.

"Still Life," Paul Cezanne, National Gallery of Art, Washington, D.C., Chester Dale Collection. *POSTIMPRESSIONISTS* felt a renewed interest in problems of form. They emphasized the inner logic of design rather than external appearances, and paved the way for contemporary art.

"Achilles on Skyros," Nicholas Poussin, Courtesy, Museum of Fine Arts, Boston. This seventeenth-century French work is typical of NEOCLASSICAL painting. The mythological theme here is serious, even compelling, but the effect is poetic and dreamlike.

'Self-Portrait," Rembrandt van Rijn, National Gallery of Art, Washington, D.C., Widener Collection. The seventeenth-century Dutch master of the art of portraiture often used himself and his family as subjects. This is a fine example of his high BAROQUE style—sharply lit and intensely introspective.

"Composition," Piet Mondrian, Collection, The Museum of Modern Art, New York, Gift of John L. Senior. Mondrian has been a leading influence in MODERN art. This geometric abstract, painted in 1921, reflects the functionalist emphasis of the twentieth century.

"Christina's World," Andrew Wyeth, Collection, The Museum of Modern Art, New York. This well-known, poignant contemporary work (1948) continues the tradition of REALISM in painting.

Late eighteenth-century mirror and clock, Courtesy, Museum of Fine Arts, Boston. Fine collector's items like these complement almost any furniture style.

the wall space around it. When a mirror is hung over a chest, table, or mantel, the laws of proportion and balance should be observed.

Chippendale, Adam, and Martha Washington mirrors are suitable for traditional rooms. Convex Federal mirrors look well with Early American and Federal furniture. Similar mirrors with less pretentious framing are suitable for Provincial furnishings. As a rule unframed mirrors are best in contemporary homes.

Clocks and Barometers

Long before clocks came into being, man had devised various means of keeping time. The sundial was probably used by ancient civilizations in Mesopotamia and Egypt. It was based upon the observation that the shadow of an object will move from one side to another as the sun moves from east to west. The hourglass, with sand or mercury dripping slowly through a narrow neck between two glass bulbs, came next. It was used until the 1300's. Boys were employed to do nothing except turn the clock as the sand filled the lower bulb. Poets, in denoting the passing of time, often use the expression "sands of time."

The mechanized clock, with its dial and hour hand, had its origin in the 1300's, during a period which is often referred to as the *economic revolution,* or a time when spinning was moved from the home into small factories. The Industrial Revolution, of course, came four hundred years later. Some time before 1700 the pendulum and the minute and second hands were added, giving us our present-day concept of a clock. During the reigns of Louis XIV, XV, and XVI in France, clocks became very elaborate. Until the electric clock came into use, all clocks had to be wound daily or weekly, with one exception. This is the familiar anniversary clock, with its glass dome, which will run for four hundred days with one winding.

Some people make a hobby of collecting clocks, and the collection may be the focal point of a decorating scheme. Clocks and barometers are sometimes matched and hung on opposite or adjoining walls or side by side.

Wall clocks include those that rest on shelves or in brackets, banjo clocks, old American mantel clocks, schoolhouse clocks, cuckoo clocks, and many others—simple or elaborate. Electric clocks are functional, but the cord is objectionable unless the outlet and cord are concealed. For this reason eight-day wind-up clocks and battery-run clocks are preferable to many people.

Hanging Shelves and Other Items

Hanging shelves used to display small collections often make an interesting unit over a chest. Cutout wood wall brackets have been popular since the scroll saw came into use, but long before the introduction of the scroll saw, elaborately carved wall brackets were popular. There is a wide choice of wall brackets today. Other wall accents include candle sconces, plates, tiles, bookshelves, tapestries, and textile prints. The choice of wall items will depend upon their shape, form, and medium in relation to the idea to be expressed in decorating.

OTHER DECORATIVE ACCENTS

Other decorative accents include books, bowls, boxes, vases, bookends, candle holders, figurines, and all kinds of collections. The texture, color, size, and shape of accessories for tables, chests, mantels, and shelves should be in scale and harmony with the room.

In arranging objects on a mantel or chest, an asymmetric or uneven arrangement is often more interesting than a symmetrical arrangement. If there is more bookcase space than is needed for books, such decorative objects as plates, bowls, figurines, or plants may be arranged between groups of books.

Many people like to display special collections, such as spoons, plates, pitchers, tooled-leather books, clocks, and so on. Unless you have a real gift for this type of display or a special niche in a room for displaying a collection, study pictures in books and magazines carefully for a tasteful idea. Otherwise the room may look like a museum.

Art objects skillfully combined with flowers and furniture can add interest and beauty to a room.

Paintings hung on figured wallpaper can be effective if one uses imagination and good taste. In this room, the strong bright colors of the flower print and the still life stand out against the neutral-colored, although busy, paper.

SUMMARY

Instinctively man seems to decorate his body and his home. Cave drawings all over the world reveal that primitive man decorated the walls of his home with scenes from nature, especially hunting scenes. These early art expressions have a great deal in common with folk art and contemporary paintings—boldness and simplicity.

Paintings and other expressions of art have a relationship to the social, economic, and technological progress of the times in which they were created. In our present period of speed and automation, art, dress, furniture, and architecture are speedily created and stripped of superfluous decoration.

Nevertheless, we will have the opportunity to draw upon the past for inspiration if we are not satisfied with contemporary expressions. We also have a wide range of mediums and subject matter from which to choose. Whatever we choose for a picture or other decorative object to hang on a wall, we must make sure that the subject matter and the medium are in harmony with the room.

THINGS TO THINK ABOUT AND TO DO

1. Display on the bulletin board illustrations of paintings showing the following expressions of art: Renaissance, Baroque, Neoclassicism, Romanticism, Impressionism, Post-impressionism, and contemporary. If possible, also show furniture and clothing related to the period.

2. Assemble an exhibit of pictures showing the following mediums: oil painting, watercolor, silk-screen printing, lithograph, block printing, pen-and-ink drawing, and etching.

3. Bring to class illustrations of pictures showing the following subject matter: landscapes, seascapes, hunting scenes, domestic scenes, flowers, birds, folk art, still life, and fashion prints.

4. Demonstrate how to measure for and cut a picture mat.

5. Discuss the use of family photographs in the decorating scheme. Show clippings that demonstrate their use.

6. Collect clippings showing the interesting use of pictures in decorating. Keep these in your decorating file.

7. Discuss and demonstrate the relationship of the frame to the picture. Perhaps you can borrow frame samples from a store that frames pictures. Perhaps you can also borrow prints from a library.

8. Give at least six rules for hanging pictures.

9. Collect illustrations of mirrors, clocks, wall brackets, and so on for your decorating file. Display some of the most interesting ones on the bulletin board.

10. Write a short report on the history of mirrors, clocks, or any other items used for wall decoration.

11. Visit various stores in your community, and make a list of types of pictures and other art objects for sale. Note the quality, art medium used, and price. This may be a group assignment.

12. Plan to improve the arrangement of objects on the wall in one room at home.

chapter eighteen

DECORATIVE LIGHTING AND LAMPS

Lighting as we know it is a fairly modern concept. Until not many years ago man geared his work to the sun, and when the sun set there was not much for the common man to do except go to sleep. Candles, oil lamps, and eventually gas lights gave more meaning to life after the sun went down. The invention of electricity did much to revolutionize living patterns. However, for many years electric lighting was functional but not particularly decorative. Now lighting and lamps are very important to a decorative scheme.

Provision for all kinds of background lighting and outlets for lamps must be included in the blueprint stage. Until recently a ceiling light was the most common form of general lighting, but it is a minor part of home decorating today. Many homes nowadays have one or more different types of decorative lighting with controls to provide any degree of light desired. Lamps are important for their decorative value as well as for local lighting.

In planning lighting it is important to consider the activities to be pursued in the room so that sufficient outlets can be provided in the right places. Light is measured in terms of footcandles, and the number of footcandles needed varies with the activity. For example, card playing requires only ten to twenty footcandles, but prolonged study or reading requires one hundred to two hundred footcandles. The number of footcandles which will register on a light meter will be determined by the lightness or darkness of the ceiling, walls, floor, and furniture, the general background lighting, and the direct lighting on the work. When you have sufficient lighting for your various seeing needs, your eyes will be healthier, you will experience less eye strain and fatigue, and you will be able to pursue an activity for a longer period. If you are buying lamps for any kind of close work, be sure to look for those approved by the Better Light–Better Sight Bureau. If your present lamps do not have a socket for a three-way light, you should have the sockets changed so that you can have extra light when you need it.

GUIDELINES FOR STUDY

GENERAL IDEAS
TO CONSIDER

1. Modern methods of lighting have extended man's hours for work and recreation.
2. Proper lighting for daily activities is important to one's efficiency, enjoyment of work and recreation, and general health.
3. Lighting is both functional and decorative indoors and outdoors.
4. The proper choice of lamps and general lighting is important to the total decorating scheme.

WORDS AND PHRASES
TO KNOW

accent lighting
background lighting
cornice lighting
cove lighting
electroluminescence
fluorescent light

footcandle
harp (lamp)
incandescent light
luminescent ceiling
riser (lamp)
watt

HISTORY OF THE LAMP

One of the First Lamps was a wick dipped in grease. The holder was made of stone.

The Pioneer "Betty" Lamp burned fish oil. The crescent-shaped arm fitted into loops of the linked chain. This made it possible to raise or lower the lamp.

The Discovery of Kerosene and the invention of a glass chimney made possible a greatly improved lamp.

The Candle was a great improvement over fat and oil fuels. Candles were expensive and could only be afforded by the rich.

The "Petticoat" Lamp burned whale oil and was made of tin.

The Gaslight Lamp was the last improvement before electricity became the popular form of lighting.

EVOLUTION
OF ARTIFICIAL LIGHTING

Many of our present-day lamp forms have evolved from early attempts of man to provide some form of artificial light. Torches made from tree branches and resin-soaked pine knots were perhaps the earliest portable lamps. At some remote time in the history of man, someone discovered that animal fat with a twisted yarn in it for a wick would provide a continuous source of light. Later an ingenious inventor made crude candles by wrapping cornhusks or moss around solidified fat. Candles of this type were in common use before the time of Christ. The art of candle-making did not develop until shortly before our Colonial period. The early colonists made candles in molds from any kind of animal fat or cooking grease and added bayberries for fragrance. When candles became plentiful, all kinds of decorative holders from tin plates to crystal chandeliers were designed to hold them. The candle became so important that light is measured today in terms of footcandles. A footcandle is the measured amount of light thrown on a square-foot surface at a distance of one foot from the candle flame. According to this measurement the direct sunlight provides 10,000 footcandles; light under a shade tree on a sunny day, between 500 and 1000 footcandles. If you are sitting at a window on a sunny day, you will be receiving about 200 footcandles of light—about twice the amount of light you need for very close needle-work or detailed drawing.

As the whaling industry increased, oil lamps improved. The pioneer Betty lamp marked a stepping stone in the history of lighting. This lamp could be raised or lowered by a chain; it burned fish oil and produced quite a good light. This quaint lamp is frequently duplicated today.

The discovery of petroleum marked the next step in the history of lighting. For many years the Indians had used oil seeping from the ground for medicinal purposes, but it was not until after the first oil well was drilled at Titusville, Pennsylvania, in 1859 that the kerosene lamp with a braided wick came into use. The gas-lighted lamp was the last fuel source for lighting before Edison produced the first successful carbon lamp in 1879. The invention of electricity coincided with the popularity of Tiffany glass. Colorful Tiffany-glass shades for ceiling lights and lampshades became a status symbol during the late nineteenth and early twentieth centuries.

The incandescent light bulb with a fine filament inside a glass bulb served lighting purposes until fluorescent lighting was introduced toward the mid-twentieth century. A fluorescent light is a long sealed tube with an electrode at each end and a small amount of mercury and argon, a colorless gaseous element, inside the tube. The inner surface of the tube is coated

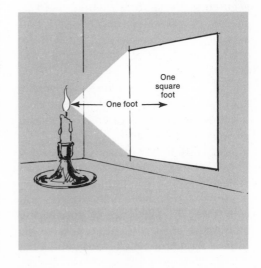

One
square
foot

One foot

with fluorescent powders, which produce light when excited by vapors. Fluorescent lighting is recommended for offices, classrooms, and areas of the home where close work is done.

Lamp styles have not only changed with the times, but they have improved greatly as a source of light. Some lamps provide for a three-way bulb with either 50–100–150 or 100–200–300 watts of electricity. The lamp may provide for the three-way bulb to be supplemented by three smaller bulbs. A lamp of special design for study carries a certified label, which means that it meets the recommendations of the Illuminating Engineering Society and the Better Light–Better Sight Bureau. Homes with lower ceilings than formerly have caused floor lamps to become shorter; emphasis upon functionalism has inspired designers to create taller table lamps, and broader consumer education has forced more manufacturers to improve lamps for close work.

LIGHT REQUIREMENTS

Eyestrain is caused by improper lighting, and continuous eyestrain can cause irritability, eye problems, and accidents. In factories where light is adequate, efficiency is increased and accidents are decreased. Yet we are often negligent about lighting our homes. Function is as important as beauty in choosing lamps, especially if family members spend a great deal of time studying, reading, or doing close work under artificial light.

Many large power companies have home-lighting consultants who can help you with home lighting. However, if you can borrow a light meter, you can check the efficiency of your home lighting against the following footcandle requirements for different jobs:

Visual task	Recommended footcandles
Fine sewing. Hobbies requiring close work	100–200
Prolonged reading. Study. Sewing on medium-colored fabrics. Machine sewing. Piano practice. Shaving.	40–70
Household activities in kitchen and laundry	30–50
Casual reading. Typing. Easy sewing. Personal grooming	20–30
Card playing and other games	10–20
General lighting for halls, stairways, and conversation	5–10

When we indicate five footcandles for conversation, this does not mean the light from five candles will be sufficient for the room, because people will be more than a foot away from the source of light. A light meter held any place in the area should register five footcandles for adequate lighting for halls, stairways, and conversation.

You cannot relate the watts indicated on lights to footcandles because there are too many factors involved. For example, a 100-watt light bulb may provide far more light in a tall lamp with a large white-silk shade than the same bulb in a low lamp with a small opaque shade. Light walls, ceiling, and carpeting will also increase the footcandle reading. The light registration is also influenced by other lighting in the room and by the distance you are away from your main source of light. The load on a particular circuit will also affect the degree of light.

Some evening read or sew in your living room under one lamp with a 100-watt bulb, and measure the light. Turn

 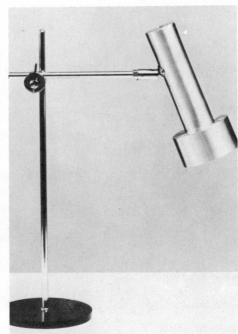

Left: A table lamp for study, recommended by the Better Light–Better Sight Bureau. Right: A bullet-type lamp.

on other lights in the room, and note how much the footcandle reading increases. There are many ways to supplement lamp lighting, such as cove, cornice, or window lighting; accent lighting from recessed ceiling outlets; and luminescent lighting from ceiling or wall panels. Provision must be made in the wiring plans for all kinds of decorative lighting as well as outlets for lamps. (See Chapter Ten.)

DECORATIVE LIGHTING

Luminescent ceiling panels may be suspended from the ceiling in somewhat the same way as large acoustictile panels. An entire ceiling may be lighted, or one or more panels may provide light for special areas—for mirrors in the bathroom, bedroom, and entrance halls and for work centers in the kitchen, laundry, or workshop.

Cove lighting is another type of decorative background lighting. With cove lighting, tubes are set into a cove on one wall or around the perimeter of the ceiling to give soft light to the room. However, if the plaster on the ceiling is not smooth, it is not advisable to install cove lighting because irregularities will be emphasized.

Cornice lighting may be provided in the cornice over a sink or above draperies. Before providing cornice lighting (except over a sink), observe this type of lighting in display rooms or in model homes. It does not appeal to everyone. Similar to cornice lighting is lighting provided in bookcases and shelves displaying glass or china.

Accent lighting is provided by a kind of spotlight recessed in the ceiling. Such lighting may be used over a dining table, a piano, or a desk to increase the light supply. *Pinpoint lighting*

Luminescent ceiling paneling.

Cove lighting.

Luminescent wall paneling (above sink).

is also ceiling light, which comes through small openings to give the effect of starlight.

Electroluminescence is a form of panel lighting in which electricity is directly converted into light by exciting with alternating current a thin film of phosphor sandwiched between tin surfaces. Scenic slides may be used with this form of lighting to look almost like slides projected on a screen. This lighting concept is expensive and not in common use.

CHOOSING LAMPS

In discussing the hanging of pictures, we indicated that there should be some uniformity of height. The same rule applies to the choice of lamps. Years ago tables were higher, and table lamps were smaller. As lower tables have become more popular, table lamps have become taller and more pretentious in design. Certain guidelines may be helpful in choosing lamps:

☐ *Provide enough lamps:* Check each room to find out where you will need light for any activity usually pursued in the room, and be sure to have some source of light to supplement general ceiling lighting. In the living room lamps should provide light for persons sitting on a sofa, on a lounge chair, at a piano, or at a desk. A bedroom should have a lamp for each single bed and two lamps for each double bed. Lamps or ceiling panels also are needed at the grooming area.

☐ *Avoid color contrast:* Lamp shades in any one room should be nearly the same color whether they are cloth or parchment. Although fashion sometimes calls for colored or fancy lamp shades, cream to off-white shades provide better light. If colored or patterned shades are used, they should be grouped as a unit and not used as spots in a room.

☐ *Arrange lamps for function:* The sketches on this page indicate the height lamps should be for various

For casual reading in a chair or in bed, the recommended height of the lamp depends on whether it is behind you or beside you. Prolonged study and sewing require lamps in front of you.

Some basic lamp styles.

activities. If you observe these rules and check the footcandles of light you are receiving for each activity, you can avoid eyestrain and fatigue.

□ *Adjust poorly proportioned lamps:* A lamp base can be made to look taller by using a *riser,* and a larger shade may be used by using a taller *harp.* A riser and a harp are shown in the illustration below.

□ *Avoid a glare:* When you work or read for a long period under only a bullet-type light, the glare as well as the contrast between the light on your reading and the darkness beyond your reading will cause eyestrain. (A bullet-type light is shown in the illustration on page 309.)

□ *Choose good structural and decorative design:* Structure relates to form and texture or a combination of textures, such as brass and alabaster or metal and wood. Decoration is any applied design, such as carving, relief work, or painting. Modern lamps depend largely upon form and texture for beauty.

□ *Choose a style to complement your decorating theme:* With traditional or eighteenth-century themes, you have a choice of the following lamp bases— classic designs, such as an urn or a vase shape and a fluted-round or a square column. The medium may be alabaster, glass, brass, silver, polished wood, china, or perhaps a combination of two materials. Early American and Provincial furnishings do not require so formal a tone, although many of the above types of lamps may be used in more informal designs. Pottery, pewter, hobnail glass, and copper harmonize nicely with a less formal decorating scheme. Contemporary rooms call for lamp bases that are structurally interesting, minus

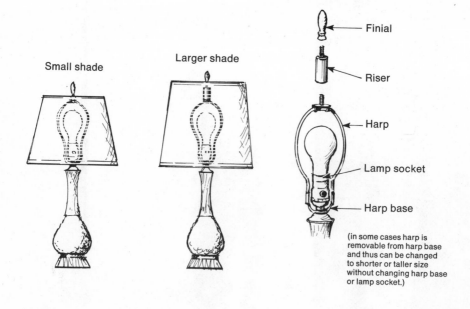

Small shade

Larger shade

Finial

Riser

Harp

Lamp socket

Harp base

(in some cases harp is removable from harp base and thus can be changed to shorter or taller size without changing harp base or lamp socket.)

ornamentation. Wood, wrought iron, brushed brass, spun aluminum, and leather are favorite materials. Figurine and novelty bases are not easy to use, but they can be interesting if properly chosen.

☐ *Choose the right size shade.* Lampshades are usually drum or slightly cone shaped. Floor-lamp shades should be 16 to 18 inches in diameter, and lampshades over lamps where reading is done should be 16 inches at the lower diameter. Other lampshade sizes will vary. When you shop for a lampshade, take the measurements with you—for example, diameter at top and at bottom and depth. Exotic-looking shades seldom fit into any decorating scheme. Sometimes slightly decorative shades are used in a bedroom, but for general use, swags, fringes, and bows are superfluous in less personal rooms.

SUMMARY

Although we have come a long way from candlelight, we still measure light in terms of footcandles, or the amount of light reflected on a flat surface one foot from the flame of a candle. Fuels that have given mankind heat have also provided light, but some have been more adaptable to lighting than others. The oil lamp in the nineteenth century was an improvement over the candle, and gas light gave more light than the oil lamp. Electric lighting, introduced during the latter part of the nineteenth century, has been improved upon greatly since the clear filament bulb dangled from the center of the ceiling as the main source of light. Home lighting is now both decorative and functional.

Decorative lighting is achieved through ceiling panels, cove and cornice lighting, accent ceiling lighting, and pinpoint ceiling lights. Lamps not only provide decorative lighting, but they are important to the entire decorating scheme. They should harmonize with the background in color, shape, size, and texture. As a rule, light-colored shades are preferable to dark-colored shades because they give more light, but sometimes colored shades are important to the decorating idea.

THINGS TO THINK ABOUT AND TO DO

1. List the types of lighting described in the text, and tell how you would use each type. Collect illustrations to show use.

2. Discuss the importance of the candle as a source of light for work and entertaining until the mid-nineteenth century.

3. Collect and display pictures of lighting devices used before electricity came into general use.

4. Show examples of early electric lights and lamps, including some with Tiffany-glass shades.

5. Use a light meter to measure the light you are receiving at home where you do close work, study, prepare meals, do your grooming, and play games. If lighting is inadequate, plan to improve it.

6. Give reasons why lighting-equipment manufacturers cannot give the number of footcandles as well as the number of watts on light bulbs.

7. Go to a lighting-equipment store, and observe examples of cove, cornice, and shelf lighting.

8. Mount on the bulletin board illustrations of types of lamps on the market, and use suitable captions under each.

9. Collect illustrations of lamps you like especially, and keep these in your decorating file.

chapter nineteen

FLOWERS
AND PLANTS
IN DECORATING

In Japan, flower arranging is an art ranking with painting, music, and dancing, and there are many schools for training in this art. In our own country flower arranging, as a hobby, is becoming more popular every year. Library shelves are full of books on growing and arranging flowers. Competition is keen among contestants in local flower shows.

Styles in flower arrangements, like styles in home furnishings and dress, change with the times, but certain basic lines and forms serve as guidelines for good arrangements. These forms may be symmetrical when they take the shape of a cone or fan or asymmetrical when the lines on each side of an imaginary center are not identical. A knowledge of the principles of design, such as balance, proportion, rhythm, and unity, is essential in arranging flowers.

Permanent flower arrangements may be had to complement the colors, period, or theme of a room. People with limited time and little interest in arranging fresh flowers prefer permanent arrangements because they lend interest to a room and require little care except for an occasional washing. People who grow fresh flowers and work with them often object to using artificial arrangements, especially on the table in the dining room. If you like fresh flowers and want to make flower arranging a hobby, you will need proper equipment and a selection of containers.

Plant arrangements either dried or growing are also effective decoration. Potted plants or vines in water provide good year-round decoration. When choosing plants and vines it is necessary to find out from the florist the best exposure and recommended care. One objection to dried arrangements is that they are dust collectors. Nevertheless, a great deal of pleasure and satisfaction can be derived from gathering, drying, and arranging plant materials. The same principles of design apply to arranging dried flowers and plant materials as those used in arranging cut flowers. All flower arrangements should be keyed to the character of the room in which they are used. A contemporary room requires a different arrangement than a traditional room.

GUIDELINES FOR STUDY

GENERAL IDEAS
TO CONSIDER

1. Flower arrangements add an extra touch to room decoration, and flower arranging provides an interesting hobby.
2. Flower arrangements are most effective when they carry out the decorating theme or art period of the room.
3. The successful arrangement of flowers depends upon using the proper equipment, containers, and accessories.
4. Each season of the year produces a choice of flowers and plant materials.
5. The principles of design apply to the arrangement of flowers as well as to other forms of art.

WORDS AND PHRASES
TO KNOW

alabaster
brass
ceramic
china
copper
Dresden china
driftwood
figurine
flower preservative
foliage

forsythia
lotus pods
needlepoint holder
oasis
pewter
pillow vase
pottery
rhododendron
thistle
wood roses

Equipment for arranging flowers: needlepoint holders in various shapes and sizes, adhesive tape, a glass holder for plant arrangements, flexible wire, shears, an oasis, a knife, and modeling clay.

PERIOD FLOWER ARRANGEMENTS

Flower arrangements became an important part of the decorating scheme during the Renaissance. At that time bouquets were colorful, symmetrical, and massive, following the trend of furniture, tapestry, and clothing design. The Baroque period was an outgrowth of the Renaissance and is the period associated with Louis XIV of France. During this sumptuous period, flower arrangements became even more exaggerated but they were less symmetrical. Often branches of trees were used in the arrangement. The term *Baroque,* when applied to flower arrangement as well as period furniture, means irregular curves and exaggerated forms. Renaissance and Baroque arrangements are not suitable for the ordinary home, but you will see them if you ever visit the royal palaces of Europe.

The Rococo period, paralleling the reigns of Louis XV and Louis XVI, was one of delicate curves and pastel colors. Arrangements of this period, like Dresden china figurines, are dainty and popular today.

During the eighteenth century or Georgian period in England (contemporary with the French Rococo), travel increased all over Europe. People brought back mementoes from many places and often used them to complement flower arrangements. Furniture designers, especially the Adam brothers, became more concerned with the total decorating scheme, down to flower arrangements and accompanying accessories. Fine musical instruments, beautiful tooled-leather books, Chinese figurines, and other objects of art began to occupy an important place in flower arrangements. Today also accessories are an important part of flower arrangements.

The Victorian period was a period of potpourri or individual expression and fussiness. Rules of design applied no more to flower arrangements than to furniture. Nevertheless, Victorian flower arrangements today have charm and remind one of an old-fashioned flower garden. Flower arrangements for contemporary furnishings depend a great deal upon structural lines and texture. Driftwood, tree branches, and large waxy leaves form the structure, and large bold-colored flowers provide accent.

All these arrangements are studied and practiced by garden-club members over the country. You may want to attend some of the spring and autumn displays of garden clubs in your community.

You will discover, as you examine flower arrangements or pictures of them, that almost every arrangement assumes one of seven basic shapes, or forms (see the illustration on page 321). Whether flower arranging is pursued as an art form or practiced informally to brighten a home, the basic shape is a vital part of every successful arrangement.

TOOLS AND SUPPLIES

Whether you are cooking, painting, or arranging flowers, an important ingredient in success is proper equipment. Before you attempt to arrange flowers, assemble the following items, and store them in a convenient place:

HEAVY SHEARS OR WIRE CUTTERS. These are necessary for cutting heavy stems and wires.

SHARP KNIFE. A knife is useful in trimming leaves. Leaves should not be left on stems that will be under water because the leaves will decompose in water and cause an odor.

FLOWER HOLDERS. Several sizes of needlepoint holders should be kept on hand to fit into different size containers. Glass flower holders do not permit flexible arrangements, but they are better than metal flower holders when only plants are used because the iron rust from metal holders will cause plants to die.

MESHED CHICKEN WIRE. This can be crumpled and pressed into round bowls or jardinieres, or it can be rolled loosely and placed in tall vases. The wire helps to keep the stems of flowers or plant materials in place.

OASIS. This is a porous mass of material in rectangular form that absorbs and holds water. It permits a more flexible arrangement than flower holders or chicken wire because flowers can be inserted at any angle and receive adequate moisture. The oasis must be soaked thoroughly before using it to arrange flowers.

MODELING CLAY. Flower holders are likely to slide without some kind of anchor. A little modeling clay placed at two or three spots around the flower holder, while the holder and the bowl are dry, will keep the arrangement in place.

ADHESIVE TAPE. This is needed to keep an oasis bar (and sometimes chicken wire) in place. Use two strips at right angles across the top of the container and the oasis. Conceal tape with flowers or leaves.

FLEXIBLE WIRES. Wires come in a number of thicknesses and lengths for various types of flowers. Wires twisted around stems make the stems rigid or flexible. These wires are inserted at the base of the flower or bud and twisted slightly to the end of the stem. A spool of fine covered wire is also useful in holding small bunches of violets and other delicate flowers in an arrangement.

CONTAINERS AND ACCESSORIES

The container and accessories, if accessories are used, should be chosen in relation to the color, size, and shape of the flower arrangement and should also be in keeping with the character of the room. Decorated containers should be displayed without flowers because the surface decoration often competes with the flower arrangement.

Containers

Containers in soft greens, earth colors, and off-whites will not detract from an arrangement. If colored containers are used, some of the flowers should repeat the color of the container. The container should be chosen in relation to the space in which it is to be used and the height and size of the flowers. Low containers are usually best for coffee- and dining-table arrangements. Tall containers should be used against a vertical wall area or on a low chest or table where height is needed to complement a picture or a piece of furniture.

The following containers are popular:
☐ Urns in alabaster, pottery, brass, copper, china, heavy glass, or wrought iron
☐ Vases with open or narrow necks in all sizes and art mediums from glass and metal to pottery and porcelain
☐ Pillow or boxlike containers of various depths
☐ Bowls, either round or oval
☐ Baskets with waterproof containers inside
☐ Buckets made of wood or plastic
☐ Glasses of all kinds

Other containers include teapots, tureens, decorative bottles, and so forth. The illustrations opposite show some of the most popular containers.

THE SEVEN SHAPES

Triangle

Crescent

S-Curve

Spire

Round

Arch

Traditional

Accessories

An accessory keyed to a flower arrangement in color, texture, or idea can add a great deal of interest to the arrangement. Accessories include:

☐ Figurines of china, alabaster, or glazed or natural pottery

☐ Birds and animals in ceramic, wood, or metal

☐ Panels or screens of fabric, bamboo, or pierced metal

☐ Candle holders of brass, silver, copper, wrought iron, wood, glass, china, or pottery

☐ Books with artistic covers

☐ Fruit, either fresh or plastic

☐ Driftwood

SEASONAL FLOWERS AND PLANT MATERIALS

If you can afford to pay the price, almost any kind of flowers can be had throughout the year. They are flown in from halfway around the world. Chrysanthemums, once available only in the fall, can be had at fairly reasonable prices the year round. However, certain flowers and plant materials are more common at some seasons of the year than at others. The flowers and plant material associated with the four seasons over a large part of the country are as follows:

Spring:	Jonquils, tulips, lilacs, iris, forsythia, pussy willow, violets
Summer:	Roses, rhododendron, carnations, peonies, sweet peas, pansies, geraniums, petunias, gladiolus
Autumn:	Chrysanthemums, marigolds, zinnias, asters, berries, pinecones, cattails, wheatears, gourds, fruit, milkweed pods, thistle
Winter:	Poinsettia, dried materials, pinecones, evergreens

Foliage, such as lemon leaves, camellia leaves, croton, and huckleberry leaves, may be used in the winter months alone or with a few flowers. Growing plants of all types may also be used.

GUIDELINES FOR FLOWER ARRANGEMENTS

The arranging of flowers should be an individual expression. The imaginative person with an appreciation for good design can combine many plant materials successfully—flowers, leaves, berries, seeds, pods, cones, grasses, twigs, and fruits. The illustrations in this chapter may suggest ideas, and the application of design principles will prevent an awkward effect. The inexperienced person also will benefit by observing the following guidelines:

1. Select (or grow) flowers that will fit in with the color scheme and character of the room in which you plan to use the arrangement. For example, if green and yellow predominate in the room, an arrangement with green leaves and yellow flowers will harmonize with the background. Flowers used on a dining table should harmonize in color and texture with your table linens and dishes. For example, delicate flowers, such as roses, sweet peas, and carnations, in a china or silver bowl complement fine china. Bold flowers, such as geraniums, zinnias, and sprays of berries, in a wood or copper bowl complement pottery.

2. Cut most flowers in the cool of the morning, and cut stems diagonally for maximum water absorption. Place cut flowers in a deep container of cool water for several hours before arranging them. (Some flower arrangers believe

The triangle shape—in freshly cut flowers and greens, for a formal room—

—or in nuts with a brass container, for an informal room.

Flowers add joy to special events. A charming centerpiece for a baby shower is a bouquet of roses and ivy arranged in a miniature bassinet.

that roses get much of their nourishment from the morning sun, and last longer if cut at noon and placed in a deep container of ice water for an hour before arranging them.)

3. Place a special commercial preservative in the water to keep it clear and fresh and to preserve the flowers.

4. Assemble containers and equipment on a convenient table or counter before beginning an arrangement.

5. Before arranging flowers in a fine silver, crystal, or china container, cut a circle of plastic film to use in the bottom of the vase. This will prevent scratches.

Combining plants and interesting rock forms can add variety and freshness to an interior.

SUMMARY

Flower and plant arrangements add interest to any room in the house. Permanent flower arrangements for coffee tables, mantels, and chests correlated with the decorating idea often complement the decorating scheme. However, many people prefer fresh flower arrangements, especially for the dining table.

In order to enjoy arranging flowers it is necessary to have proper supplies and an assortment of containers, as well as storage space for these items. If one is to be successful in arranging flowers, a knowledge of art principles is essential. When cost is of no importance, one has a wide range of choices. The airplane has made it possible for florists to import flowers from great distances. However, the average person must depend upon seasonal flowers and plant materials. When flowers are scarce and expensive, it takes greater ingenuity to use vines, leaves, driftwood, and dried materials. Many people like to dry their own flowers and plant materials.

THINGS TO THINK ABOUT AND TO DO

1. Display illustrations of Japanese and Baroque flower arrangements. With these illustrations, show pictures of a Japanese living room and a Baroque drawing (living) room. Discuss the differences in the two types, and point out how each flower arrangement complements each room.

2. Display illustrations of Victorian and contemporary flower arrangements, and also show pictures of Victorian and contemporary rooms. Discuss as in item 1.

3. Have someone from a local garden club demonstrate flower arrangements.

4. Assemble and show to the class the supplies listed for arranging flowers. A florist may cooperate on this project. Demonstrate how to use each and how to anchor flower holders or a piece of oasis to a container.

5. Display as many types of flower containers as you can. Assemble fresh or plastic flowers and other plant materials, and practice making flower arrangements. The diagrams on page 321 in the text may be helpful.

6. Bring to class a few accessories you might use with flower arrangements, and discuss how you might use them. If possible, use them with the arrangements made in item 5.

7. Assemble some driftwood and dry materials, and originate some simple arrangements. You may combine fresh or plastic flowers or leaves with them if you wish.

8. Dry some plant and flower materials according to directions. Use references suggested in the bibliography on page 326 or other sources.

REFERENCES FOR UNIT THREE

BOOKS

Better Homes and Gardens Decorating Book. Des Moines: The Meredith Publishing Company, 1961.

Birren, Faber, *Colors for Interiors, Historical and Modern.* New York: Whitney Library of Design, Hill and Wang, Inc., 1963.

Denby, Elaine, *Interior Design.* London: Country Life Ltd., 1963.

Faulkner, Ray and Sarah, *Inside Today's Home.* New York: Holt, Rinehart and Winston, Inc., 1968.

House and Garden's Complete Guide to Interior Decoration. New York: Simon and Schuster, Inc., 1960.

Kornfeld, Albert, *Interior Decoration.* Garden City, N.Y.: Doubleday and Co., 1965.

McDonald, Elvin, *The World Book of House Plants.* Cleveland: The World Publishing Company, 1963.

Nehrling, Arno and Irene, *Gardening, Forcing, Conditioning, and Drying for Flower Arrangements.* New York: Hearthside Press, 1958.

Schmitt, Mimi, *Artificial Flowers, Fruit and Foliage.* New York: Hearthside Press, 1964.

Soutar, Merelle, *Flower Design with Accessories.* London: D. Van Nostrand, 1964.

Stepat, Dorothy L., *Introduction to Home Furnishings.* New York: Macmillan, 1964.

Stevenson, Violet, *Flower Arrangement.* New York: The Viking Press, Inc., 1961.

Sweeney, John A. H., *The Treasure Book of Early American Rooms.* New York: The Viking Press, Inc., 1963.

Van Dommelen, David B., *Designing and Decorating Interiors.* New York: John Wiley and Sons, Inc., 1965.

BOOKLETS AND PAMPHLETS

(Write to the following addresses for current lists of literature.)

General Decorating

Celanese Fibers Company, Consumer Relations, 522 Fifth Ave., New York, N.Y., 10036

E. I. DuPont de Nemours and Company, Education Division, Wilmington, Del. 19898

J. C. Penney Company, Inc., Education Department, 1301 Avenue of the Americas, New York, N.Y. 10019

Sears, Roebuck and Company, Consumer Information Division, 925 S. Homan Ave., Chicago, Ill., 60607

Walls and Floors

American Carpet Institute, Inc., Education Department, 350 Fifth Ave., New York, N.Y. 10001

Armstrong Cork Company, Public Relations Department, Lancaster, Pa. 17604

Columbus Coated Fabrics Company, Public Relations, Columbus, O. 43216

Congoleum Industries, Inc., Box 701, Kearney, N.J. 07032

Hercules Powder Company, Fibers Department, Wilmington, Del., 19899

Kentile Floors, Advertising Department, Brooklyn, N.Y. 11225

Masonite Corporation, Public Relations Department, N. Wacker Dr., Chicago, Ill., 61616

Pacific Lumber Company, 1111 Columbus Ave., San Francisco, Calif., 94133

The Sherwin-Williams Company, Public Relations Department, Cleveland, O., 44101

U.S. Plywood (Weldwood Panels), New York, N.Y., 10017

Wallpaper Council, Inc., Consumer Relations, 969 Third Ave., New York, N.Y. 10022

Window Treatment and Slipcovers

American Viscose Corporation, 1617 John F. Kennedy Blvd., Philadelphia, Pa. 19103

Anderson Corporation, Bayport, Minn., 55003

Celanese Fibers Company (see "General Decorating")

Conso Products Inc., 27 W. 23rd St., New York, N.Y. 10010

Joanna Western Mills Company, 2141 S. Jefferson St., Chicago, Ill. 60616

Kirsch Company, 345 Prospect St., Sturgis, Mich. 49091

National Cotton Council of America, Consumer Education, P.O. Box 9905, Memphis, Tenn. 38109

Rockland Industries, Brooklandville, Md., 21022

Stanley-Judd Division, The Stanley Works, Wallingford, Conn. 06492

Furniture and Furniture Arrangement

Baumritter Corporation (Ethan Allen Furniture), Advertising Division, 145 E. 32nd St., New York, N.Y. 10016

Broyhill Furniture Factories, Advertising Department, 215 Oak St., Lenoir, N.C. 28645

Drexel Furniture, Drexel, N.C. 28619

Henredon Furniture, Morganton, N.C. 28655

Johnson Wax, Consumer Educ. Dept., Racine, Wis. 53403

Kroehler Manufacturing Co., Consumer Education, 666 North Lake Shore Dr., Chicago, Ill. 60680 (*planning kit*)

The Merchandise Mart, Consumer Education, Chicago, Ill. 60654

Mobile Homes Manufacturing Assoc., 20 N. Wacker Dr., Chicago, Ill. 60606 (*planning kits*)

Pennsylvania House, Lewisburg, Pa., 17837

Tell City Chair Company, Tell City, Ind. 47586 (*planning kit*)

Lighting

American Home Lighting Institute, 360 N. Michigan Ave., Chicago, Ill. 60601

Better Light Better Sight Bureau, Consumer Educ. Div., Grand Central Station, New York, N.Y. 10017

General Electric, Large Lamp Department, Nela Park, Cleveland, O. 44112

Lightolier, Inc., Public Relations, Jersey City, N.J. 07305

FILMS, FILMSTRIPS, AND SLIDES

(See page 467 for name and address of source.)

Accent Decor. Shows use of color and pattern in decorating. (10 minutes, color, MTP)

The Armstrong World of Interior Design. Accent on floors. (15 minutes, color, ACC)

Decorate for Living. A film stressing practicality and beauty. (20 minutes, color, ACC)

Decorating Made Easy and Window Treatments. Two filmstrips. (Color, SEARS)

Decorating Unlimited. Shows general interior decorating. (28½ minutes, color, AF)

The Story of Flowers. 2 filmstrips on flower growing and arrangement. (CFGA)

Wall-to-Wall Decorating. On interesting wall composition. (14½ minutes, color, MTP)

unit four

*Consumer
Buying*

chapter twenty

LABORSAVING EQUIPMENT

Advances in the design and function of laborsaving equipment have been taking place at such a rapid pace that it is difficult to make choices without basic consumer information. The push-button age in which we live is a dramatic contrast to the early twentieth century, when women cooked over a coal stove, rubbed clothes over a washboard anchored in a wood tub, bought ice daily from the iceman to place in the top of a small wood icebox, scrubbed floors on their knees, did the ironing with irons heated on the coal stove, and swept the carpet with a broom!

Automated-electrical servants do more for the homemaker today than a couple of maids used to do. Solid-state controls, or semiconductors of energy, have been the most recent stimulant to development in the equipment industry. These tiny, sealed components of germanium and fine gold wires make it possible to program or dial-set automatic washers, dryers, ranges, refrigerators, dishwashers, and all kinds of appliances. The earliest use of solid-state controls, or tiny self-contained batteries, was in transistors for hearing aids and radios. Small replaceable or recharging batteries make it possible to produce cordless appliances. As improvements are made in solid-state controls more and more of our present electrical appliances will be cordless.

The most important factors influencing your choice of laborsaving devices are these: need, storage facilities, and cost. You may use some small appliances so seldom that you will find you can get along without them, especially if storage space is limited. Cost will be a factor not only in the number of appliances you decide to buy, but also in the types of models you will choose. The more completely automatic an item is, the higher will be the cost.

If an appliance is to give satisfaction it must have proper care. All appliances have a warranty and a built-in life expectancy under normal use. With systematic care the life expectancy may be increased considerably. Before using an appliance make sure that you understand the directions that come with it and keep these directions where you can find them. Time taken to learn to operate new equipment correctly is well spent.

GUIDELINES FOR STUDY

GENERAL IDEAS
TO CONSIDER

1. The choice of laborsaving equipment will be determined by need, cost, and storage space.
2. Satisfactory performance of equipment depends upon its construction, the skill with which it is used, and the systematic care it is given.
3. The size and model number of any appliance or major piece of equipment will influence its price.
4. A knowledge of nationally advertised brands and seals of approval is helpful in buying equipment.
5. Special features added to basic models increase the price.

WORDS AND TERMS
TO KNOW

automatic
broiler
canister-type vacuum cleaner
electronic range
free-standing range
heavy-duty upright vacuum cleaner
insulated
nonstick finish

refrigerator-freezer
rotisserie
self-defrosting
semiautomatic
solid-state control
warranty
waste disposer

GENERAL GUIDELINES

Certain general rules regarding choice, use, and care apply to major equipment, such as ranges, refrigerators, freezers, waste disposers, dishwashers, washers, and dryers as well as small appliances. These rules are:

☐ Determine the items you will want to own, and list them in order of need. Plan how you will pay for them.

☐ Study women's and consumers' magazines, so that you will become familiar with brands and models available and with their ratings where possible.

☐ Compare brands, model numbers, guaranties, servicing, installation costs, and methods of financing in different stores before buying.

☐ Buy from a reputable dealer. If you are in doubt about a store or a sales representative, telephone your local Better Business Bureau.

☐ Fill in and return warranty cards, and file receipts in case the merchandise must be returned for failure to meet specifications.

☐ Record the telephone numbers of repair servicemen on all appliances and equipment. When you telephone for service, be explicit and courteous.

☐ Look for the Underwriters' Laboratories (UL) seal which indicates that an item has passed certain safety and performance tests. This is not a guaranty. (Magazines also test and award seals of approval on electrical equipment.)

☐ Read the instructions for use and care that come with each product, and file these booklets with duplicate, dated warranties. A large flat, plastic envelope-type case with a zipper will hold all these items.

☐ Keep the surfaces of all appliances clean. Burned grease, acids, sharp objects, rough scouring substances, and strong detergents cause damage. A mild detergent and a soft cloth wrung out of warm suds will keep most enamel surfaces clean, and it is safe to use soap-filled pads of fine steel wool on some stained metal surfaces.

☐ Note on the kitchen calendar any periodic care required, such as oiling, special cleaning, changing filters, or defrosting a refrigerator or freezer.

RANGES AND WALL OVENS

Some people prefer surface burners set into a counter and a separate wall oven, while other people prefer a free-standing range often supplemented by a wall oven when it is desirable to have two or more ovens. One advantage of a wall oven is that it is at eye level. However, ranges are now available with both an upper and a lower oven, or with two ovens placed side by side. With two ovens it is possible to prepare foods requiring a high and a low temperature at the same time.

Selection

Whether you choose a gas or an electric range is a matter of personal preference and the cost of fuel. Gas and electric ranges are competitive in the features offered.

The most popular sizes of ranges are 30-inch and 40-inch widths. A 21-inch range is adequate for small apartments. Many large families prefer a 30-inch free-standing range with a large oven and an additional large wall oven to a wide range with one large and one small oven. A 23-inch oven (inside measurement) is considered a large oven whether it is built into the wall or into the range. As a rule, ovens are fairly well insulated, but they all give off some heat. Therefore, it is recommended that a range and a refrigerator not be placed adjacent to each other, but sometimes this arrangement cannot be avoided. When a wall oven is used in addition to a free-standing range, it is usually placed beyond the work triangle because it is the least used of any piece of major equipment.

Electronic ranges, which cook food in minutes without heating the utensil, are gradually coming into use. With electronic cooking metal utensils cannot be used because the microwaves cannot penetrate metal. Foods must be cooked in ceramic, glass, or paper containers. Often speed cooking affects the flavor, color, or crispness of foods, so that some foods need to be cooked part of the time in a regular oven. Plug-in electronic ovens with regular controls for finishing the cooking are available.

Here are some additional features the consumer will want to consider:

RANGE SURFACE. The surface controls are usually at the front of a gas range and at the back of an electric range. Most ranges come with an electric-appliance outlet. Both ranges adjust quickly to desired temperatures, and many can be controlled as easily as an electric frying pan. Some ranges have one or more completely automatic burners programmed to begin cooking, cook at a predetermined temperature, and hold the food hot until time to serve it. It is also possible to buy an attachment that will automatically stir sauces, gravy, and soup to prevent sticking.

A number of ranges are equipped with a griddle that can be inserted over two surface burners for making pancakes. This should be dripproof, and it should be easy to control the temperature. It should also be possible to lift out trays or pans under the burners or heating units for easy cleaning.

RANGE OVEN. It is desirable but not essential to have an oven with a glass door and an inside light. If the oven door can be removed, cleaning is made easier. A self-cleaning oven, in which the temperature can be raised to about 750 degrees Fahrenheit for two or two and a half hours to decompose soil, is another desirable feature. The extra insulation in a self-cleaning oven also reduces heat loss, and the kitchen will stay cooler. Ranges with self-cleaning ovens cost more than other ranges; thus it may be advisable to consider a range with a nonstick oven lining, which is not difficult to keep clean, or an oven that can be disassembled and washed in the sink. When a range has an upper oven, there should be a control on it, so that it can be used as a warming oven to keep serving dishes and plates hot. An oven thermostat is more or less taken for granted on a modern oven, but thermostats do get out of order, and they need adjusting once in a while. A difference of 25 degrees can affect the appearance and texture of many baked foods.

Some ovens are equipped so that a special thermometer can be inserted in a roast of meat or poultry and then plugged into an oven wall. If an oven is not equipped with its own meat thermometer, a reliable one can be bought for a very reasonable price at hardware, variety, and department stores.

Solid-state controls make timed cooking, roasting, and baking possible. Solid state means "nothing moves," but explaining these controls is not easy. These tiny, sealed, and extremely sensitive electronic devices have made possible cordless appliances; gas igniters, which have replaced pilots; and speed controls for electrical appliances. They have also revolutionized many other areas in home living. Controls may be set to start the baking or roasting at a predetermined time, complete the cooking, and hold the product at any temperature until needed. In this type of cooking, it is important to read the instruction book, and to avoid leaving certain foods, especially those prepared with dairy products, in the oven too long before serving.

Some gas ovens have fast infrared broilers that improve the flavor of meats. A rotisserie can be had with some ranges to automatically rotate meat under a broiler as it roasts.

Use and Care

It is very important to study the instruction manual and to underscore important points in the use and care of an individual range. Here are a few general suggestions for the use and care of any range:

□ Place small pans on small burners or heating units, and place large pans on large burners or heating units. When a pan extends more than one inch beyond the source of heat, especially at a high setting, the enameled surface around the burner may show small cracks.

□ Avoid cleaning all surfaces until they are cool. Use mild detergent suds and a soft cloth or sponge for most surfaces. Stubborn spots may be rubbed with a fine cleansing powder. When allowed to stand, grease and food may leave permanent marks.

□ Clean metal trays under heating units or burners with soap-filled steel-wool pads.

□ Remove spilled food from electric coils by turning the control to *high* for one minute, and from the holes in gas burners with a wire.

□ Medium-weight aluminum utensils give good cooking results. If heated slowly, cast-iron skillets are satisfactory.

Protect glass by using grids between the glass and burner. Enamelware may chip, and under some conditions, it may melt. Use stainless steel combined with copper, aluminum, or other metals for good distribution of heat.

□ Follow instruction manual directions, if given, about using aluminum foil on trays under burners and inside the oven. Foil should not be placed directly under pies because it will interfere with heat flow. It may be used on the oven floor if it does not touch the heating units.

□ Line the broiler pan and its grid with aluminum foil to reduce cleaning time, but be sure to cut through the openings on the grid and press the edges of the foil firmly around the grid Change often enough to avoid an accumulation of grease under the foil.

□ If the oven is not self-cleaning, use a commercial oven cleaner according to directions.

Range with upper and lower oven.

This laborsaving kitchen includes a portable dishwasher with a chopping block top, a wall oven and a vertically divided refrigerator-freezer.

REFRIGERATORS, REFRIGERATOR-FREEZERS, FREEZERS

Selection

Many people confuse a two-compartment refrigerator with a refrigerator-freezer. The principal differences are: (1) The refrigerator with a freezer compartment is less expensive than a combination refrigerator-freezer. (2) The freezer compartment of the refrigerator is not thermally insulated from the fresh-food storage compartment, whereas the freezer and food-storage compartments in a refrigerator-freezer are separately insulated and have two separate controls. (3) The temperature in the freezer compartment of a refrigerator is about 20 degrees Fahrenheit; and in a refrigerator-freezer, 0 degrees Fahrenheit. This means that food will not freeze as fast or keep nearly as long in a refrigerator freezing unit as it will in the freezer compartment of a refrigerator-freezer.

Refrigerator-freezers are preferable to refrigerators, unless there is also a separate food freezer. *Refrigerators* are available in compact models to fit under a counter in efficiency apartments and in larger size models up to 61 inches high and 30½ inches wide. The compact model has a storage volume, including both the refrigerator and the freezer unit, of about 6.4 cubic feet; and the largest model, of about 24 cubic feet. Some models resemble a breakfront, with a food-storage compartment above and a pull-out freezer bin below. Other models look like wall cabinets. Both of these models are more expensive and less practical than regular upright models. *Refrigerator-freezers* have one or two doors. Some have the storage compartment above and the freezer bin below; some have vertical divisions, and others have the freezer compartment above and the food-storage unit below. Most people prefer a separate door for the freezer compartment. A refrigerator-freezer with a capacity of

13 to 15 cubic feet is the most popular family size.

The term *self-defrosting* is sometimes confusing. A self-defrosting food compartment is highly desirable to keep this area free of moisture. More expensive models are completely automatic so that both the freezer and refrigerator units defrost automatically. However, the freezer unit must be cleaned and the food rearranged periodically, and therefore many people do not object to the semiautomatic defrosting type, wherein the freezer must be defrosted. A convenience but not a necessity is an automatic ice-maker, which dispenses and stores ice cubes. Some models have beverage dispensers also.

Some important points to check when purchasing a refrigerator or a refrigerator-freezer are these.

FLOOR SPACE. The available floor space may limit the width of the unit. Although doors in new models open almost flush with the sides, an inch or more at each side is desirable for moving the unit easily.

CAPACITY. The size of the family, frequency of marketing, amount of entertaining, and proportion of meals eaten at home will determine the capacity needed. It is generally wise to select a refrigerator with a little larger capacity than you think you might need if you have the money and space.

DOOR OPENING AND STORAGE. Doors are hinged to open on the left or on the right, and some are planned to open in either direction. Counter space at the left is needed with a right opening, and vice versa. As a rule, most models provide good door storage for butter, eggs, cheese, bottles, jars, and small cartons.

SHELVES. Shelves should be adjustable, pull out easily and remain stable, and also lift out easily for cleaning. Some models have revolving shelves.

STORAGE BINS. Storage bins should slide easily and fit closely when closed. An airtight meat-storage bin should be located in the coldest part of the refrigerator.

MOBILITY. A wheel base with an automatic stop device will make it easy to move the refrigerator for cleaning.

Separate food freezers come in upright and chest types. In the upright type, all food is easily accessible, but nearby counter space must be provided for loading and unloading. The chest type has the advantage of doubling as counter work space, but it is more difficult to find food in it.

A number of factors will determine whether or not you should buy a home freezer: (1) actual need if the freezer compartment in a refrigerator-freezer is large and if marketing is a pleasure and not a chore; (2) available floor space where the food freezer will be accessible; (3) floor strength, since freezers full of food are very heavy; (4) permanence of location because it is expensive to move a large freezer; (5) dependability of source of power because a power shortage can mean a large financial loss in spoiled food. Some people keep food freezers in unheated areas; it may therefore be important to find out how a freezer will function during long periods of extremely cold weather.

Use and Care

If a refrigerator is to give satisfactory service, various foods must be placed according to instructions in the manual, and overcrowding must be avoided, thus permitting air to circulate. Do not place hot foods in the refrigerator; let them cool first to room temperature.

Avoid using sharp scrapers or rough cleansers. Place foods that have a characteristic odor, such as cantaloupes, in plastic bags. If some foods, such as butter, seem to pick up odors from other foods, place a commercially produced activated-charcoal product in the food unit.

For appearance and sanitation keep the exterior surface clean with a mild detergent. To defrost the freezer section quickly, disconnect the current, remove frozen food and ice trays, wrap in towels, and store in the food-storage area. Place a large pan of boiling water inside the freezer compartment, and close the door. Repeat. Remove the plug at the base of the freezing unit, if there is one, and place a bowl under the opening. Wipe the interior with a solution of two tablespoons of soda in one quart of water. Dry thoroughly, replace the plug, and turn on the current. Set the plug with a little water. Use the same type of soda solution to clean the refrigerator compartment. Remove shelves occasionally for a more thorough cleaning. Every few weeks place a few drops of special fluid in the defrosting drain to keep it from clogging, remove the tray where the defrost water accumulates under the refrigerator, and clean it.

During short vacations (two to four weeks), remove perishable foods, and set the controls at low. During long vacations, remove all food, clean the entire unit inside and out, disconnect the current, and leave the door(s) ajar.

WASTE DISPOSERS

Selection

One research study indicated that the average homemaker accumulates enough waste daily to fill a 25-pound flour sack. A great deal of work may be saved by easy disposal. Two devices are available for disposing of waste—a food disposer and an incinerator. The food disposer is connected with the sink drain, and the incinerator may be installed under a counter near the sink. A food disposer pulverizes food, and a continuous flow of cold water flushes it down the drain. The cold water is necessary to solidify grease. An incinerator decomposes all waste, including paper. It is supposed to be odorless, smokeless, quiet, and to leave little if any residue. Either or both appliances contribute to convenience and sanitation.

Food disposers vary in performance and price. A lightweight unit will not grind up hard bones and rubbery items, and it will not operate as fast as a medium-weight or heavyweight model. Some food disposers must be fed a batch of food at a time, whereas others dispose of waste continuously. Choice will depend upon price and daily needs for disposing of waste. Insulated food disposers are quieter than those that are not, but they cost a little more money. Undercounter incinerators designed for the kitchen are about 15 inches wide. An incinerator may also be installed in a utility room, garage, or basement. No flue is required for the newer models, but a vent must be provided through the wall to the outside. Some have manually operated timers, and others are completely automatic.

Use and Care

Generally a food disposer will do what the directions say it will do and no more. Naturally heavyweight models are more efficient than lightweight models. However, a heavier unit requires a stronger water flow. None will take glass, metal, or plastic. All operate with a steady flow of cold water and electric current.

After grinding stops, the water flow should continue for thirty seconds in order to flush the drain. If the disposer stops or rejects an object, turn off the current and remove the obstacle. Use the tool provided if necessary. Occasionally fill the sink with water and lift the stopper to stimulate flush action, and keep the drain clean.

The incinerator needs little attention, except to keep the vent clear and to remove any accidental waste that will not burn. Combustion is almost complete, but a small amount of ash has to be emptied once or twice a month.

DISHWASHERS

Selection

Dishwashers have taken a great deal of work out of housekeeping, and the demand for them has soared. Models and performance vary. Most people like to have a dishwasher installed under the counter at either the right or left of the sink. A front-loading model with pull-out trays is usually preferable to a top-loading model because the racks are more accessible. The instruction manual will show directions for efficient loading. Spray action differs, either coming from revolving arms at the top or the bottom or coming from a spray at the sides. Look for a model with quiet action; some are very noisy. Some models claim to hold up to eighteen place settings. Some models also have built-in food-waste disposers to eliminate preliminary rinsing. Front panels are available in a variety of color schemes. A top-loading portable model is available with either an enamel or a cutting-board top. Many portable models are convertible; they can be set under a counter later. If you buy a portable model, be sure that you have sufficient floor space and that it will fit along a counter area if you should want to have it permanently installed. Under-the-sink models are available, but the capacity in the top tray is cut in half to accommodate the sink. Extra-large models are also available.

Use and Care

If there are enough dishes to use the dishwasher after each meal, a thorough rinsing may not be necessary unless sticky food, such as macaroni and cheese, clings to the dishes. However, some dishes may be permanently stained if coffee or strong acids remain on them for a long period. Many people sponge or brush off dishes under the faucet before stacking them if the dishwasher is turned on only once a day. Newer models have a rinse-and-hold cycle for the person who objects to prerinsing; other models eliminate prerinsing with the built-in food disposer mentioned previously.

The dishwasher should be loaded so that the spray action reaches the surfaces of all articles. Water must reach a temperature of 150 to 160 degrees Fahrenheit. Recent models also have a superwash for pots and pans and a shorter cycle for fine china. When washing fine china and silver, follow the manufacturer's directions for the kind and amount of detergent to use.

If you have ever had the experience of dumping ordinary detergent into a dishwasher, you will never do it again. The suds will overflow into the kitchen and continue to do so until the wash cycle (and possibly the rinse cycle) is completed. The proper detergent in the right amount must be used. As a rule, the dishwasher manufacturer will specify the amount and indicate that a type made especially for the purpose must be used.

A few items should not be placed in a dishwasher—wood items because they may deteriorate, iron utensils because they may rust, plastics that are not durable enough to hold up under intense heat, and tools or silver knives with handles soldered on that might come loose. Avoid having aluminum and copper come in direct contact with the detergent powder because they will discolor.

WASHERS AND DRYERS

Selection

Washers are semiautomatic and automatic. With a *semiautomatic washer*, the clothes are washed and rinsed, but they must be fed by hand through the wringer. If space is no problem, some people like to have a wringer-washer for items usually labeled "hand wash" as well as an automatic washer. However, new *automatic models* with their solid-state controls can be programmed for any type of washing from that for fine lingerie or permanent press to that for heavy-duty work clothes.

New fibers and finishes force producers of equipment and manufacturers of detergent and other laundry supplies to make constant changes. Recent washers are equipped with automatic dispensers for detergents, bleaches, and fabric conditioners. Dials may be set for a presoak cycle, washing or rinsing at any desired temperature, and a long or a short spin cycle for extracting water. In newer models, the lint is flushed away so that it will not collect on the next load.

A small portable washer that may be stored in a closet is popular with people who send large items to a commercial laundry.

A *dryer* is one of the easiest of all pieces of laborsaving equipment to maintain, and it makes washing possible any day of the year. A dryer must have a vent through the wall to carry off lint, exhaust the vapor, and so on. Permanent-press and wash-and-wear clothing looks better if dried properly in a dryer than if drip-dried. Newer models have a number of heat settings and a tumble-cooling action after drying to reduce wrinkling.

FLOOR-CARE APPLIANCES

The vacuum cleaner is one of the most important of all laborsaving devices and is also one of the oldest. A newer floor-care appliance is the scrubber-polisher, which will scrub and polish floors and shampoo carpets.

An upright vacuum cleaner.

Vacuum Cleaners—Selection

The type of vacuum cleaner and the attachments you choose will depend upon your cleaning needs. Some new homes and apartment houses have built-in plugs for tank-type cleaners, which suck the dust through tubes to a basement receptacle. A *lightweight upright vacuum cleaner* (sometimes called an electric broom) is preferable to a nonelectric hand carpet sweeper for daily brushups of floors and carpets. The hand type of cleaner is not powerful enough to suck up the grit that becomes embedded in the pile. A *canister (tank) type* or regular-size *upright cleaner* is needed for weekly or semi-weekly carpet cleaning. If there is a lot of carpeting in the house, a *heavy-duty upright* or a *canister-type cleaner with a power-driven brush attachment* is the most satisfactory. If the major cleaning jobs are hard-surface floors, draperies, and upholstery, the canister type may be preferred because of the ease-of-use and versatility of the attachments. The American Carpet Institute suggests seven passes over an area of carpet for thorough cleaning with heavy-duty vacuum cleaners and up to eleven passes over a carpet surface with a regular canister-type cleaner or a lightweight upright cleaner. Some cleaners have an adjustment to increase or decrease the vacuum power needed, and most have an adjustment for different pile thicknesses.

Attachments that may be had with vacuum cleaners are: (1) a *floor-and-wall* brush for removing the dust from bare floors, walls, and rug cushions; (2) a *dusting tool* with long soft bristles for removing dust from areas not easily cleaned with a cloth, such as carved furniture and rungs under chairs; (3) an *upholstery nozzle* for removing the dust from upholstered

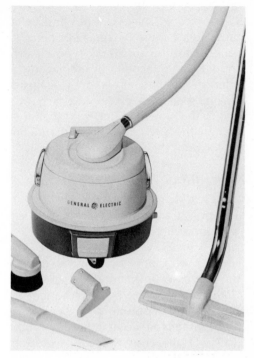

A canister vacuum cleaner.

furniture, draperies, valances, mattresses, furs, and carpeted stairs; (4) a *crevice tool,* or long, slim attachment, to remove dust from the crevices of upholstered furniture, radiators, registers, and carpet edges.

Vacuum Cleaners— Use and Care

Vacuum cleaners will pick up all kinds of small objects, but it is wise to pick up pins and sharp objects before cleaning, since these may damage the motor of the cleaner. When the bag or tank in either a canister or an upright cleaner is too full or when hair and lint accumulate in the brushes, the cleaner will lose efficiency. Disposable bags are easy to insert and remove. However, they reduce the suction and add to maintenance costs. (It is important to use a bag designed especially for the cleaner.) The dust brush should be washed regularly. When cleaners have brushes and belts, these items must be replaced periodically. The filter in a tank-type cleaner should be cleaned or replaced at intervals. If the hose of a canister cleaner becomes clogged, attach one end to the blower outlet, hold the other end to the suction inlet, and run the motor until the hose is free of dust.

Scrubber-Polisher—Selection

A scrubber-polisher will clean, wax, and polish any smooth floor surface—wood, resilient floor covering, concrete, brick, or terrazzo. There are single-, twin-, and triple-brush models, but the twin-brush model is the most popular. There are interchangeable brushes for scrubbing and for waxing. Some models are completely automatic, and will dispense the suds solution, scrub, and suck up the dirty fluid. With others, you have to mop up the

A scrubber-polisher.

soiled liquid. Models are available with an interchangeable brush and detergent hose for shampooing carpets. These models are more expensive.

Scrubber-Polisher— Use and Care

Wood floors should be cleaned with as little water as possible, and the water should be wiped up immediately. Polishing pads must be changed when they become wax coated. After using a scrubber-polisher the wax or liquid detergent should be removed, the container and applicators cleaned, and the cleaner stored upside down, so as not to rest on the brushes.

IRONS

The iron you choose will be determined by your ironing needs. There are three general types—dry, spray, and steam-spray. Some irons are combination dry and steam or dry, steam, and spray. Today the dry iron has limited use because of permanent finishes. However, many people like to own a dry iron for general ironing because it is lighter in weight than the combination irons. If the major part of the ironing is touch-up ironing and pressing, a steam iron is desirable. The steam-spray iron practically eliminates dampening clothes, but it requires frequent filling. All irons should be easy to hold. (See picture, page 345.)

Ironing over rough objects is harmful to all irons and especially harmful to a nonstick coating (fluorocarbon) on irons. The special coating prevents the iron from accumulating starch and sticking to fabrics. Unless distilled water is used, steam and steam-spray irons must be flushed out regularly with a commercial mineral-solvent compound. Be sure to follow directions for use.

MIXERS AND BLENDERS

A mixer is among the most frequently used small appliances. A mixer whips cream and potatoes; mixes icings, batters, and soft doughs; and beats eggs. A blender whips, chops, liquefies, and purees food, but it will not mix cake batters or doughs. The stand-mounted mixer with a detachable head is more versatile than a portable mixer. Most mixers have speed controls suitable for most mixing needs. These should be easy to read. A rubber spatula will push the mixture down from the sides of the bowl, and if it should catch in the beater blades, it will do no harm. A metal spatula should never be used. If you should choose a portable mixer, make sure that it will stand on end or hang up against the wall. Immediately after use the mixer motor casing should be wiped clean and dry, mixer blades and bowls should be washed, and the entire unit should be covered for storage. If the blades in a blender are removable, wash and dry them thoroughly. If not, place warm water with a very small amount of detergent in the blender, and run it a few seconds. Rinse well and wipe dry.

TOASTERS

Toasters are semiautomatic or completely automatic, and models may be had for two or more slices of bread. A completely automatic toaster begins to lower and toast the bread the instant it is dropped into the toaster, and will eject it at any brownness desired. Semiautomatic toasters must be pushed down with a handle. The heating mechanism inside the toaster has changed very little for many years. Solid-state controls, drip pans, and styling have been the reasons for major changes.

People tend to abuse a toaster more than any other appliance. A toaster is not meant to accept buttered bread or fruit-filled goodies. The drippings or raisins and nuts from pastries harm the toaster. Engineers of the Underwriters' Laboratories report that fire hazards result from the misuse of toasters. Metal foil or a metal knife or fork can cause shock if the heating coils are touched with them while the current is on.

A toaster cannot be immersed in water without ruining it. However, the surface should be wiped clean after disconnecting the unit. The toaster should be turned upside down occasionally and gently tapped to release crumbs. The tray underneath should also be kept free of crumbs. When not in use, it is advisable to disconnect the appliance.

WAFFLE IRONS, GRILLS, AND FRYING PANS

Some models of *waffle irons* convert into grills. These are usually square or oblong shaped. The lid of a waffle iron should be hinged to adjust to the rise in the batter, and the drip tray should be wide enough to catch any overflow. The handles should be heat-proof, so that they resist burning, and insulated, so that they stay cool to the touch. A solid-state control with a dial can be set to produce any desired brownness. Follow directions for seasoning the iron before using it. If the waffles stick, let the batter remain until crisp and then brush it off. An *electric grill* is a good buy for the person who likes to grill hamburgers and sandwiches or make griddle cakes. An *electric frying pan* will do all these things, and in addition it will fry and bake. It is available in several sizes with either glass or metal lids.

If a grill or frying pan is coated with a nonstick substance, metal spatulas and cake turners should not be used. However, nylon or plastic utensils will not scratch the coating. Soap-filled pads of fine steel wool can be used on grills and frying pans provided there is no nonstick coating.

COFFEEMAKERS

There are electric percolators that are completely automatic. They will brew the coffee for mild, medium, or strong flavor, and keep it at serving temperature until needed. Measurements will be accurate if the markings on the coffeepot are observed. Vacuum-type coffeepots brew the coffee and regulate the strength according to the amount of coffee used, and will also hold the coffee hot until serving time. The most popular sizes brew from four to ten cups of coffee (5-ounce cups). The secret of good coffee is a clean container.

OTHER APPLIANCES

Another popular appliance is a *can opener,* which should have a magnet to hold the lid and keep it from falling into the can. Some models have an attachment for sharpening knives. *Slicing knives* have gained in popularity. The motor, which is contained in the handle, may be operated by electricity or with a battery.

Electrical cooking appliances take much of the labor out of cooking, but they require storage space and counter space for use. If many small appliances are used at one time, it is advisable to have a separate appliance panel where three or four appliances can be used without blowing out a fuse.

SUMMARY

The increasing array of electrical appliances on the market plus the numerous brands and models available make a study of consumer education almost essential. Perhaps the best initial consumer advice is to buy from reputable dealers, return warranty cards promptly, and read instructions carefully. Equipment that is given proper and systematic care will give better service and last longer.

Major equipment includes ranges, refrigerators, waste disposers, washers, and dryers. Ranges and refrigerators not only come in many sizes and styles, but they also have numerous accessory features. Some ranges have electronic controls, but completely electronic ranges are not in general use. However, many ranges have solid-state controls which may be set at various temperatures and for predetermined times. A surface cooking unit and a wall oven may be chosen, but some people prefer a free-standing range. However, a second wall oven is desirable if a family is large and if a great deal of roasting and baking are done. Refrigerators may have food storage units and a freezing compartment. A refrigerator-freezer has a separate freezer unit where food may be frozen and stored at zero temperatures. Refrigerator-freezers may be completely defrosting or only partially so.

Waste disposers provide for efficient and sanitary disposal of garbage, and the convenience is usually well worth the cost. An under-the-counter dishwasher that loads at the front is easier to load than a top-loading one. Washers and dryers come in several styles. Choice depends upon the type and frequency of laundering, the floor space available, and the family budget. A canister-type vacuum cleaner has easy-to-use, versatile attachments; an upright-type usually cleans rugs more efficiently. Other appliances include scrubber-polishers, toasters, grills, mixers, and so on.

THINGS TO THINK ABOUT AND TO DO

1. What advice would you give someone planning to buy a new electric refrigerator? Consult consumer magazines for brand-name ratings.

2. List some advantages and disadvantages in buying a free-standing range versus a surface burner and a wall oven. Talk with people who use one or the other and get their opinions. Also consult home builders about people's preferences.

3. Why do some people desire two ovens? What are some advantages and disadvantages of an electronic oven? Investigate as in item 2.

4. If you were buying a (1) range, (2) refrigerator, (3) washer, (4) dishwasher, and (5) food disposer, indicate four features you would check for in each. Assemble folders from electrical manufacturers, and study these, as well as observing the actual equipment in stores, before listing these features.

5. Using the equipment in the foods laboratory, demonstrate how to care for each major appliance. One student may be assigned to each appliance.

6. Assemble examples of vacuum cleaners of all types and of scrubber-polishers (real ones or pictures). Discuss each as to how it is used, how satisfactorily it works, and what care is needed.

7. Demonstrate how to use the attachments on a canister-type vacuum cleaner.

8. Demonstrate how to polish floors and how to shampoo a piece of carpet. You may want to call in an appliance agent to demonstrate.

9. Demonstrate the use of a mixer and a blender, showing similarities and differences in what they will do. Indicate the care each requires.

10. Display some new models of irons, and discuss their use and the care they require.

Different types of irons. Note nonstick coating on bottom.

chapter twenty-one

FLOOR
COVERINGS

Soft floor coverings or rugs probably had their origin in the Arab lands of
Persia (now Iran), Turkey, and Egypt. The Moors in the Middle East carried
the art of rug making to the northern coasts of Africa, to southern France,
and to Spain. The famous rug factory at Aubusson, France, was established
by the Moors during the thirteenth century. In the late sixteenth century
Henry IV of France (1553–1610) imported Persian weavers to work in the
workrooms of the Palace of the Louvre.

During the late eighteenth and nineteenth centuries, Oriental rugs became a status symbol among wealthy industrialists and businessmen in
Europe and America. Until the mid-nineteenth century the average American
family made hooked, braided, or woven rag rugs at home. In 1848 Erastus
Bigelow invented a power loom for making a patterned carpet in narrow
widths requiring seaming, which became known as Brussels carpeting.
From this time on factory-made carpets began to replace homemade rugs
in the homes of middle-class people. Brussels carpeting, in beautiful floral
patterns, and floral wallpaper characterized homes of the Victorian period.

During the early twentieth century, Oriental designs were imitated by
the manufacturers of Wilton and Axminster rugs, and Brussels carpeting gave
way to factory-produced room-size rugs. Gradually fashion introduced
solid-colored rugs of different textures and weaves. As our society became
more affluent and carpeting became cheaper, following the introduction
of man-made fibers and simplified production methods, wall-to-wall carpeting became increasingly popular. In fact the Federal Housing Administration will now insure mortgages in homes with wall-to-wall carpeting
laid over either wood or concrete floors.

Resilient floor coverings came into being a little over a hundred years
ago with the introduction of linoleum. In 1863 Frederick Walton, an Englishman, was experimenting with a number of substances in the hope of producing artificial leather. One morning he noticed a thick rubbery film
on the top of a can of paint left open by mistake. He lifted it off carefully

347

for study, and discovered that the oxidation of linseed oil produced the pliable substance. As he considered some possible use for the new compound, he began to press it onto a piece of burlap. To his surprise he had produced a firm yet flexible material which proved to be a successful floor covering. He named the product *linoleum—linum* coming from the Latin word for the flax plant, from which linseed oil is derived, and *oleum* from the Latin term for oil.

It was almost a century after Walton's discovery before other resilient materials came into existence—asphalt, rubber, and vinyl products in combination with asbestos, cork, and other compounds. Resilient floor coverings in tile form have become popular with the amateur craftsman because he can lay them more easily than sheet or rolled goods sold by the foot or the yard.

GUIDELINES FOR STUDY

GENERAL IDEAS TO CONSIDER

1. We are indebted to the ingenuity of past-centuries craftsmen as well as to the know-how of present-day technologists for our modern floor coverings.
2. The satisfaction and enjoyment derived from floor coverings depend upon their beauty, durability, resilience, sound absorption, and light reflection in relation to their cost.
3. A knowledge of rug terminology is helpful in shopping for rugs and carpets.
4. Wear expectancy is dependent upon the rug fiber used, the density of the pile, the type of backing used, and the abuse or care received.
5. Oriental rugs are in a class with works of art, and their selection requires careful study.
6. Resilient floor coverings differ in composition, finish, recommended uses, and care required.

WORDS AND TERMS TO UNDERSTAND

acrylic
Aubusson
Axminster weave
broadloom
carpet pile
filament yarn
linoleum
modacrylic
olefin
outdoor-indoor carpet
pile density

resilient floor covering
rug cushion
savonnerie
soft floor covering
staple yarn
tufting
velvet weave
vinyl asbestos tile
vinyl flooring
Wilton weave

GENERAL CRITERIA FOR JUDGING FLOOR COVERINGS

Not everyone will rate the following criteria in the order given, but these are important factors that influence the choice of floor coverings:

BEAUTY. It costs no more to buy something that is beautiful as well as functional. Manufacturers of all grades of floor coverings are aware of the importance of eye appeal. They try to appeal to many tastes; thus it is up to the individual to assemble the furnishings for a room or a home that will give the occupants of the room or the home the greatest pleasure.

The floor accounts for such a large area that it must be an important part of the color scheme. Often a color scheme begins with the floor, especially if the covering has a pattern in color. The texture and pattern (if any) in the floor covering should harmonize with other furnishings. As a rule, the floor should be the darkest value in the room, and three-dimensional and zigzag effects should be avoided because they make a design seem to move. However, subtle rhythmic effects may be attractive. The floor should not compete with other areas of the room for emphasis, but should serve as a background for furniture. Only in large areas, such as hotel lobbies, may a carpet have a prominent design.

DURABILITY. A floor covering must not only contribute to the decorating scheme, but it must be durable. A floor covering must hold up under a great deal of foot traffic, friction from moving furniture, and spillage of all kinds. Some areas of the house, especially entrances, kitchens, and family rooms, get a great deal more traffic than other rooms. Stair carpeting gets the most abuse—for example, a stair carpeting identical to a living room carpeting will wear out 50 to 60 percent faster. Carpet durability is determined by the fiber content, the closeness and density of the pile, and the backing material. Some resilient floor coverings hold up better than others and require far less care. When you know something about rug fibers, the methods of making carpeting and rugs, and the compounds used in making resilient tile and resilient materials by the yard, you will be better able to judge durability.

RESILIENCE. Resilience in a floor covering reduces human fatigue, noise, injury from falls, and breakage. Some carpet fibers have greater natural resilience than others, and the underlay or padding used increases resilience. Smooth-surface floor coverings, such as linoleum and asphalt and vinyl-asbestos tile, although referred to as resilient floor coverings, are not very resilient. When the backing is "cushioned," resilience is increased.

LIGHT REFLECTION. Ceilings are usually light in color for the maximum light reflection in rooms where light is needed. To create a feeling of solidity, the floor is often the darkest value, but dark flooring materials absorb a great deal of light. Therefore, the darker the floor covering, the more care should be taken that lighting provisions are adequate.

EASE OF MAINTENANCE. Floor coverings with a surface that resists soil, stains, bleaches, abrasion, and moisture require less time and cost for maintenance. Rugs that show footprints and lint and resilient floor coverings that absorb grease and moisture or that require the constant application and removal of wax consume time and energy. As a rule, a carpet with a close, tightly twisted uncut pile will require the least care, especially in tweed effects and in medium-light colors. Shaggy rugs have texture interest, but are more difficult to maintain. Resilient flooring in small patterned effects and in medium to medium-light colors shows abrasion and soil less than do plainer surfaces that are very light or very dark.

SOUND ABSORPTION. Hard surfaces, such as bare floors, walls, and ceilings, reflect noises that can become very disturbing when there is much activity in a room. Carpeting is one of the best sound barriers available, and for this reason it is sometimes used instead of wallpaper on the walls of hotel lobbies and dining rooms. One of the advantages of using carpeting in a kitchen is its sound absorption. The kitchen is a noisy area with so very many motors in use and so very many hard surfaces to intensify noise.

COST. On a limited budget, cost is often a determining factor in the choice of floor coverings. You should avoid being trapped by advertised "carpet bargains" wherein an offer is made to carpet a room of any size for a set price or wherein free installation or similar giveaways are offered, unless you know the full circumstances of the offer. If you are in doubt about a so-called bargain, ask to have the facts and the guarantee in writing. If you are buying a rug or carpeting for a home that you own, buy the best you can afford and deal with reliable merchants. If you are buying something for short-term use, you may be able to "afford" to buy a less expensive carpet.

Broadloom used to connect two rooms, with a two-stair transition, creates a beautiful and very soothing effect. It complements the Mediterranean styling of walls and furniture.

RUG AND CARPET TERMINOLOGY

A knowledge of the terminology currently used to describe carpeting and rugs will be helpful when you have occasion to buy soft floor coverings.

Broadloom refers to carpeting woven on a wide loom. These looms may be six, nine, twelve, fifteen, or eighteen feet wide, and rugs may be cut or sewn from these widths.

Weave refers to any of three common weaves that were more popular in years past than they are now. In the *Wilton weave* the ends of each tuft are buried in the backing to provide a built-in padding, which lengthens the wear of the carpet. Brussels carpet uses a Wilton weave with an uncut pile, whereas traditional Wilton carpet has a cut pile. In the *Axminster weave* the tufts are knotted to a stiff jute back, and there are no yarns buried in the backing. In the *velvet weave* loops of loosely twisted yarn are tied to a jute backing with linen thread to produce a deep rich pile which resembles velvet.

Pile is the so-called "face" of the carpet. It is made of loops of yarn either cut or uncut or in a combination of uncut and cut yarns to give the surface effect. *Density of pile* refers to the closeness with which the yarns are tufted or woven or tied. The denser the pile, the longer the wear.

Filament and *staple yarns* refer to the length of the yarns used in the manufacture of the carpet. Filament yarns are continuous man-made strands of any desired length, and staple yarns are filament yarns cut into short pieces and twisted together to give a textured, less glossy effect. Staple yarns may also be made of natural (cotton or wool) fibers twisted into yarns.

Twist indicates the direction and tautness with which staple yarns—either cotton, wool, or man-made yarns—are twisted. Tightly twisted yarns have longer wearing quality than loosely twisted ones.

Backing refers to the material adhered to the underside of a rug or carpet to give it greater firmness. The backing may be woven from cotton, jute, kraftcord, or other material. It is sprayed with a glue or latex. Latex is usually used on a tufted carpet to hold the tufts in place. A secondary backing is added for extra tuft protection and more dimensional stability.

Tufting refers to a method of rug construction in which the pile is needled into a woven backing in the same way that candlewick bedspreads are made. Multi-needle machines fasten the tufts to a jute or canvas backing. Cotton rugs have been made by this method for a long time, but wool and man-made fibers have been tufted only since 1954. Now about 90 percent of all rugs and carpets made are tufted because this process costs much less than weaving and is just as satisfactory. Sculptured, carved, and striated effects can be produced by varying the height of the pile and by using some cut and some uncut areas.

A *room-size rug* may have a selvage on two sides and either binding or fringe on the other two sides. Wilton and Axminster room-size rugs usually have fringe (to imitate the fringe left on handmade Oriental rugs), but those cut from broadloom are bound. A room-size rug should not be too small for a room for the best effect. The width of the broadloom from which it is made will determine one measurement. For example, either the width or the length must be six, nine, twelve, fifteen, or eighteen feet. The remaining width or length can be any number of feet. The margin around a room-size rug should never exceed twelve inches, unless the room is exceptionally large.

An *area rug* defines one area of a room—an area for dining, writing, watching TV, or conversation. A large room may have a number of area rugs. An area rug may be almost any shape so long as the shape is harmonious with the arrangement of furniture in the area defined.

Scatter rugs are small rugs used in an entrance hall, under a coffee table, in front of a fireplace, or at the side of a bed. Scatter rugs that are used in the same room should harmonize in color, shape, and pattern.

Accent rugs (often Orientals—see page 355) are sometimes used on top of wall-to-wall carpeting in the same way that scatter rugs are used on a bare floor. They may establish the color scheme of the room.

Wall-to-wall carpeting covers the entire floor. Strips of wood with projecting needles are nailed to a wood floor or glued and nailed to a concrete floor. The carpeting is cut to fit the contours of the room; then it is stretched and hooked over the needles. The underpadding, which is laid first, does not go quite to the wall. Wall-to-wall carpeting gives a room unity, conceals bad floors, and under certain conditions simplifies daily cleaning. However, traffic lanes may appear, and unless the room is square or oblong with no projections, the carpeting cannot be lifted and reversed to increase the wear. *On-the-floor cleaning* is not quite as satisfactory as professional factory cleaning, unless cleaning is quite frequent. Wall-to-wall carpeting is more expensive than a room-size rug because extra carpet is needed and installation adds to the cost.

Carpet tile is available in many sizes, fibers, textures, and colors. The wear will depend upon the kind of fiber, the closeness of the pile, the quality of the backing, and the amount of friction the carpet receives. The advantages of carpet tile are that (1) it can be laid by an amateur, (2) worn places can be replaced, (3) patterns can be developed by the way the tiles are arranged, and (4) some tiles can be taken up and moved to any other desired area. Some tiles come with a cushion bonded to the back to give greater resilience; some have an adhesive under a peel-off backing, and others have a waffle-like rubber backing that has enough suction to keep the tiles from being pulled up by a vacuum cleaner.

Outdoor-indoor carpet was limited for a number of years to a green felt-like covering used around swimming pools and on boat docks. It made wet surfaces safer and was not harmed by water or sunlight. Improvements in surface pattern, texture, and color have made this type of carpeting more versatile, and it is now used for patios, kitchens, bathrooms, and recreation rooms. Outdoor-indoor carpet, including the backing, is produced only from man-made fibers. The carpeting resists mildew, rain, sun, and harsh chemicals, and it can be either laid flat on the floor or cemented to the floor. It can be vacuumed, shampooed, or even washed outdoors with a hose.

The surface texture of this all-weather carpet varies according to the method of construction used. A *feltlike surface* is produced by *needlepunching,* a process in which a bat of fibrous material is attached to a fabric base with barbed needles. A traditional *low-pile surface* is produced by tufts on a backing. A *grass effect* is produced by controlling a single filament to give a shaggy surface. The low-pile process, of course, most nearly resembles regular carpeting. It is easier to maintain in kitchens and recreation rooms, for instance, than any other type of carpet.

CARPET FIBERS

Wool was the chief fiber used for carpets and rugs until after the mid-twentieth century. Now wool accounts for only 15 percent of the total carpet production. Nylon accounts for 46 percent; acrylic and modacrylic fibers, for 27 percent; olefin (polypropylene) fibers, for 7 percent; and polyester fibers, for 5 percent. Some fibers, especially nylon, are frequently blended with other fibers in carpet making.

Whereas most carpet fibers are used only in staple form, nylon and olefin are used both in staple and in continuous-filament form. A nylon filament yarn and a nylon staple yarn, for example, produce different effects in the finished rug. Fibers for rug use are commonly dyed before they are made into rugs, but it is now possible to piece-dye or piece-print rugs. In piece-dyeing some portions can be treated with a resist substance, so that a two-tone effect is produced. Piece-printed designs are now available in moderate-priced rugs, though formerly these designs were possible only in Brussels carpet and other carpets with a Wilton or Axminster weave where each color was woven into the design with a dyed yarn.

In studying the following carpet fibers keep in mind that the twist of the yarn, the depth and density of the pile, and the quality of the backing are also important in judging carpet.

Wool wears well, takes dye easily, is resilient, is luxurious, and cleans easily, but wool is the most expensive rug fiber. The increasing demand for carpet wool (most of which was imported) and the diminishing supply were two reasons for the search for a less expensive substitute. Two of wool's weaknesses—shrinkage and its affinity for moths—have been overcome to a surprising degree by special finishes.

Rayon was the first of the man-made fibers used in rug making, but early experiments proved that rayon lacked resistance to abrasion, had little resilience, and soiled easily. However, rayon dyes well and costs little in comparison with most fibers. Rayon scatter rugs are popular for bathrooms and bedrooms because they are machine washable.

Acrylic and *modacrylic* fibers resemble wool in lightweight bulk, resiliency, warmth, and resistance to abrasion. They are also resistant to moths, stains, and mildew, and are as easy to clean as wool. Some trade names for *acrylic* fibers are Acrilan, Creslan, Orlon, and Zefran; and for *modacrylic* fibers, Dynel and Verel.

Nylon has the highest resistance to abrasion of all fibers, and therefore it is popular in medium-priced carpeting for areas where there is heavy traffic. Carpet nylon is made of either staple or continuous-filament fibers. Continuous-filament yarns give a kind of sheen to the pile, whereas staple fibers give a dull effect. Staple fibers tend to pill (cause tiny balls to appear) on the surface. Nylon's weaknesses are its tendencies to collect soil and to generate static electricity. However, nylon is not difficult to clean, except in sculptured weaves. Trade names for nylon carpet fibers are Caprolan, Cumuloft, Nyloft, Enkaloft, and Nylon 501.

Olefin is one of the newest fibers for carpeting as well as for apparel. Outdoor-indoor carpeting with a felt-like surface is perhaps the most familiar

This wool tweed carpet unifies the color scheme in the room. Its deep pile adds textural interest.

carpet made from olefin fibers, but olefin fibers are also used for regular indoor carpeting with sculptured, irregular, or twist surfaces. Olefin fibers are produced from either *polyethylene* or *polypropylene*. A fiber made from the latter is popular as a rug fiber. The fiber compares with nylon in toughness and with the acrylics in lightweight bulk. It is especially resistant to stains, spots, and mildew, and it does not support a flame easily. Its principal drawback, a low affinity for dyes, is being overcome. *Herculon, Marvess, Patlon,* and *Vectra* are familiar trade names for carpet made of olefin.

Polyester fibers have been used in carpeting more for blends than for total fiber content. In a blend they give greater resilience to other fibers needing this property. Recently carpeting made entirely of polyester fibers has become available. Resiliency and cleanability are two important selling points.

Cotton is popular in small rugs for bedrooms and bathrooms. It is sometimes used in larger rugs and in light colors especially for bedrooms. It is not advisable to use cotton in wall-to-wall carpeting. Grease and soil are difficult to remove unless the rug is washed. Cotton wears fairly well, but it lacks resilience.

Other rug fibers, such as sisal, hemp, and similar fibers, have limited use in outdoor and summer rugs in warm climates. At least 20 percent nylon, for instance, is needed in a blend for that fiber's properties to be of influence.

RUG CUSHIONS

Carpets and rugs will wear longer and feel softer if laid over padding, or a rug cushion. Padding also decreases human fatigue. A room-size rug and its cushion should not be so thick that a person risks tripping on them. It may be hazardous to use a rug cushion under a scatter rug unless the cushion is thin and the rug has an adhesive backing. For safety all rugs should have some kind of skidproof backing.

Rug cushions are made of hair (usually cattle hair), a combination of hair and jute, and foam rubber. A 40-ounce hair cushion with a waffle weave is a popular choice for above-grade installation. A heavier grade is recommended for stairs, usually a 50-ounce weight. A combination of hair and jute is cheaper but far less resilient than all hair. However, if the hair-jute combination is rubberized on both sides, it has greater resiliency. For most uses foam-rubber cushions should be ⅜-inch thick.

If rugs have a latex backing or a foam-rubber underlay, dry-cleaning fluids should not be used in cleaning because they will cause the latex or foam rubber to deteriorate. If a floor has radiant heat, foam rubber is not recommended because the heat will cause it to become brittle.

ORIENTAL RUGS

Oriental rugs have been valued western possessions since European traders began to import rugs from the Middle and Far East at the turn of the fourteenth century. During the sixteenth and seventeenth centuries, Persia (Iran) produced the finest rugs ever made. Only the wealthy could afford to own these luxurious floor coverings and the handsome furnishings to go with them.

To be called an Oriental, a rug must be handwoven or knotted, and it must have been made in the Orient, or a country in Asia or the Near East for instance, China, Japan, Iran, India, Pakistan, Afghanistan, Turkey, Hong Kong, or Morocco. The best-known handmade European rugs, in a class with many handmade Orientals, are the French Aubusson and Savonnerie, popular with eighteenth-century French furniture. The Aubusson is characterized by its flat tapestrylike texture; and the Savonnerie, by its deep silklike pile.

Handmade Orientals are never any regular size because each knot is tied by hand and no two weavers tie knots at the same tension. A skilled weaver follows a pattern pinned to the loom, and he or she may tie between 8000 and 12,000 knots a day. The colors and designs show through on the back of Oriental and other handmade rugs, and fringe appears only on the finishing end of the rug.

Some of the most popular Oriental rugs are briefly described:

Persian rugs are very highly prized because of their beautiful designs and fine workmanship. Many patterns have a center medallion, which is said to be inspired by the domes in Persian architecture. Floral, leaf, vine, bird, and animal motifs are used in allover designs. Persia is now Iran, but Persian rugs are still named for the original city in or near which the rugs are made. For example, *Kirman* rugs are characterized by floral forms, especially roses; and *Sarouks,* by foliage motifs in jewel tones. The *Kirmanshah* rug, often confused with the Kirman, is very rare. *Turkoman* rugs are fairly familiar, especially the Bokhara and Turkestan. They have mostly a red background and geometric motifs. These rugs look as though they have been copied from floor tile designs. Tradition implies that the first Oriental rugs ever made were

copied from tile floors used in Moorish palaces from the seventh century on.

India produces a variety of Orientals. Numerous American and British companies have rug factories all over India. Weaving has been an art in India for centuries. Many of the weavers are descendants of the weavers of Kashmir, who made the cashmere shawl popular around the world. Most Indian rugs are woven in Agra, Lahore, and Kashmir. Indian rugs frequently use naturalistic floral, leaf, vine, and animal designs, and the colors are usually brilliant. Indian rugs are not named for the area in which they are made, but are given trade names by the manufacturer.

Caucasian rugs are made in Russia and in sections of central Asia to the northeast of Iran, where weaving has been an established industry since the days of Genghis Khan. These rugs are marketed under such names as *Kazak, Kabistan, Shirvan,* and *Karabagh,* and they are usually scatter rugs or runners.

Chinese rugs are made in large modern factories under skillful supervision. Chinese rugs have always been popular in America, especially with Chinese Chippendale furniture. These rugs are quite different from other Orientals because a large part of the background is a solid color—gold, beige, rose, or blue—and the Chinese use fewer colors than other weavers. There is usually a center medallion and either corner decorations or a border. There is far more symbolism in the motifs used in Chinese rugs than in other Orientals.

Oriental rugs are becoming scarcer as time goes on because of creeping industrialization in Eastern countries and the ever-changing international political situation. For example, not only has Turkey become industrialized, but she has lost many of her skilled Armenian and Greek rug weavers between the two world wars due to persecutions. Since Communists rule in China, beautiful Chinese rugs never reach American shores, except through ports where countries are on better terms with China.

American Orientals are machine-made copies of Orientals and should not be confused with true Orientals. To invest in an Oriental is like investing in a diamond. The reputation of the dealer is of prime importance. With good care Oriental rugs increase in value with age. If you can afford to own Oriental rugs, you will also need to buy furnishings of the same high quality to use with these luxurious carpets.

GENERAL RUG AND CARPET CARE

Research has shown that about 108 pounds of dirt, cinders, and sand are airborne or carried by foot traffic into an average six-room house yearly. There will be less dirt in the suburbs of a nonindustrialized area than in cities near heavy industries and constant traffic. If this dirt is not removed from the heavy traffic areas of a house daily, it settles into the pile of a rug and gnaws away at the fibers until they become loose.

It is difficult to control airborne dirt through windows and doors unless a home is insulated and equipped with either an air-conditioning or air-purification system. However, a great deal of dirt can be kept out if steps and sidewalks are swept regularly, if scatter rugs are kept at entrances, and if family members remove muddy shoes before coming into the house.

Although the care you give carpets and rugs in your home will depend upon where you live, upon daily traffic through the house, and upon the color and texture of the floor covering, you will find the following recommendations useful:

□ Use rug cushions under all room-size rugs, wall-to-wall carpeting, and large area or scatter rugs.

□ Place casters under heavy pieces of furniture.

□ Go over areas *daily* where there is heavy traffic, using a carpet sweeper or preferably a vacuum cleaner to prevent surface dirt from becoming embedded.

□ Use a heavy-suction vacuum cleaner at least *weekly* or *semiweekly* in areas of frequent use.

□ Wipe up all spillage immediately. Carpets made of man-made fibers resist spotting and staining and are nonabsorbent, but the backing is absorbent, and too much moisture may cause the backing to rot or the brown dye from the undercushion to fade through. Lift off any soft food with a knife. Blot moisture with a soft cloth from the outside of the spot toward the center.

□ If spots or stains remain, wipe them with warm water. *Warm water* will remove the following stains: blood, coffee, tea, soft drinks, fruit, fruit juice, milk, ice cream, and most foods. *Water and lemon juice or white vinegar* will counteract urine stains if used before a chemical reaction takes place. A *dry-cleaning solvent* applied lightly will remove chewing gum and grease marks, but avoid having the dry-cleaning fluid penetrate through to a latex backing. The latex may soften and become gummy. A *mild-detergent solution* is more satisfactory if the moisture is not permitted to penetrate to the back of the rug.

□ Reverse rugs occasionally and rearrange furniture on wall-to-wall carpeting (especially heavy furniture, such as pianos, chests, and sofas) to equalize wear. If one person is accustomed to sitting in a particular chair, place a footstool in front of the chair to keep heels from rubbing in one spot. Place a small rug with a soft backing in areas where traffic is heavy. A coarse backing may cause too much surface friction.

☐ To prolong wear on stairs, when laying, turn back a strip of carpet at the top of the stairs. When stair edges appear worn, the fold can be released in order to redistribute worn areas.

☐ To reduce static electricity, keep a certain amount of moisture in the room or use an antistatic spray occasionally.

☐ Keep rug labels for your own information and to present to a professional rug cleaner because a knowledge of the fiber content will be helpful in spot removal and cleaning.

☐ Have carpeting and rugs cleaned professionally about once a year if they receive heavy traffic, or every two years if traffic is moderate. Loose rugs should be sent to a cleaning plant for a thorough cleaning. There will be a slight shrinkage the first time a rug is cleaned, but racks are available for stretching rugs to nearly their original size. On-location cleaning is best for wall-to-wall carpeting. Carpet is woven under tension, and it is difficult as well as expensive to take up wall-to-wall carpet and expect it to fit after cleaning, especially after wet shampooing. (Experienced cleaners can sometimes do it.)

☐ Clean rugs or wall-to-wall carpeting by home methods only if you have the proper equipment, time, and strength. A home vacuum cleaner and a shampoo-scrubber lack the power of professional equipment, but if soil is light, results are often satisfactory.

To foam-clean carpeting: vacuum thoroughly, apply foam cleaner with sponge mop, let dry for two to four hours, vacuum again.

If you do not own a shampoo-scrubber, you may rent one. Make sure that it is a fairly heavy electric one with a liquid-shampoo dispenser and two rotary brushes. (Many rental types are too light to do much good.) You may want to tackle a small, slightly soiled rug before attempting to clean a large one if you clean carpet at home.

SELECTION OF RESILIENT FLOOR COVERINGS

Linoleum, vinyl, asbestos, cork, rubber, and other compounds in sheet or tile form are usually referred to as resilient floor coverings to distinguish them from hard-surface floors, such as wood, marble, slate, terrazzo, and so on. A number of these products, such as linoleum, vinyl, and vinyl asbestos, can be bought by the yard or in tile form. Tiles come in many sizes—9 inches by 9 inches, 12 inches by 12 inches,

15 inches by 15 inches, 18 inches by 18 inches, 24 inches by 24 inches, 36 inches by 36 inches, and 24 inches by 48 inches. Many inserts and feature strips are available in a choice of colors.

The choice of resilient floor covering will depend upon where it is to be laid—below grade, at grade level, or on a suspended floor—the use of the room, and the color scheme. For rooms receiving heavy traffic, it is important to choose a surface or a surface pattern that is resistant to abrasion. A floor covering with a cushioned backing will help to reduce human fatigue in the kitchen and other work areas. A cork surface will reduce noise, but it also has some drawbacks.

Resilient floor coverings in common use are described as follows:

Linoleum is the oldest and best resilient flooring material for general use. *Linoleum tile* is inlaid linoleum cut in tiles. *Linotile* is made of very heavy-gauge inlaid, embossed linoleum especially processed for longer wear, greater recovery from dents, and greater resistance to abrasives than regular linoleum. All linoleum products should be laid *above grade level* or on a suspended floor—that is, a floor over a basement. They have more give underfoot and are quieter than most tiles. They have superior resistance to grease and to cigarette burns, and are easy to maintain.

Asphalt tile became popular for floors below, on, and above grade level in the late 1940's. It is the least expensive resilient floor covering and is still popular for basements and family rooms. However, asphalt tile dents easily, shows poor resistance to grease stains, and is no more shock resistant than a concrete floor. It is only fairly easy to maintain. The production of other more attractive flooring products that are easier to maintain has cut into the sale of asphalt tile.

Rubber tile may be used anywhere. It has slightly more give underfoot than linoleum and very good recovery from dents; it is very durable and has excellent resistance to cigarette burns. It has good grease resistance and far better stain resistance than linoleum. However, it is not quite as easy to maintain as linoleum. It is expensive, but not as expensive as linotile.

Cork tile is usually recommended for suspended floors. It has superior resilience and noise resistance, but only limited resistance to dents. It has limited resistance to grease stains, to cigarette burns, and to alkalies, and resists other stains poorly. It is as difficult to maintain as asphalt tile. It is used fairly often in libraries and music rooms where traffic is not heavy and where noise resistance is important.

Pure vinyl flooring is one of the most satisfactory of all resilient floor coverings. Pure vinyl comes in rolls six feet wide and in tile form. Color range and pattern choices are almost endless. Pure vinyl should be used on suspended floors, but if the flooring has a hydrocord back, it can be used anywhere. It has good to excellent resilience depending upon the backing, good recovery from dents, excellent resistance to grease and other stains and to alkalies. It is very durable and easy to maintain, but it is expensive.

Vinyl-asbestos tile is the most popular tile with do-it-yourselfers because it can be cut with scissors to fit around curves and corners and it comes in a wide choice of colors and designs. It can be laid anywhere; it is durable and has excellent resistance to grease, cigarette burns, and alkalies, but other stains will leave a mark unless wiped up immediately. Vinyl asbestos has the advantage of requiring a minimum of maintenance.

Vinyl cork is twice as expensive as regular cork tile. The vinyl coating gives the cork excellent stain resistance, gives greater resistance to grease and alkalies, and makes maintenance easier. Vinyl cork is recommended for installation over suspended floors. It is not quite as quiet as regular cork, but it will take heavier traffic, so that it can be used in family rooms and recreation rooms.

Poured floors are the latest contribution to resilient flooring. A flooring substance called *polyurethane* comes in cans, and it can be applied with a trowel, spray gun, or roller. It will not blister, and it is not damaged by grease, detergents, or chemicals. It comes in a choice of colors, and it can be used in kitchens, garages, recreation areas, shower stalls, and on counter tops. Coins, sequins, and maps or any other flat object can be inlaid in the substance.

CARE OF RESILIENT FLOORING

Linoleum, rubber, and *vinyl* compounds should be kept free of grit and other particles that with traffic might become embedded in the surface. The frequency with which these floors should be cleaned with a mild detergent will depend upon the use the area receives. Old wax should be removed before applying new wax to prevent the coats of wax from building up. *Asphalt tile* can be kept clean with a mild detergent, but since asphalt has a dull surface, it needs occasional waxing. Never apply wax over soil, and never apply wax with a turpentine base because turpentine will act as a solvent and cause the surface to streak. *Cork* floors should be dusted frequently and waxed only a few times a year with a self-polishing wax. A *vinyl-coated cork* surface responds better to paste wax, or buffing wax.

The application of floor waxes is discussed in greater detail in Chapter Twenty-five.

SUMMARY

All wall-to-wall carpeting and most room-size rugs are woven on wide looms and are called broadlooms. These looms weave carpet in six-, nine-, twelve-, fifteen-, and even eighteen-foot widths. In order to choose carpeting and rugs with satisfaction the consumer must know something about rug fibers, pile length and density, and the material or substance used for backing. The consumer must also consider the size and use of the room, the most suitable color and texture, and the price range she can afford.

Wall-to-wall carpeting has gained in popularity since the introduction of man-made rug fibers and since tufting began to replace weaving, which was an expensive process in the manufacture of carpet. Wall-to-wall carpeting can be laid over old wood floors, concrete, or plywood. Wool sets the standard for fiber comparison. The acrylics and modacrylics most nearly resemble wool, and they are easy to maintain. However, nylon accounts for almost half of all carpet produced. Nylon is durable and fairly easy to clean, but it has a tendency to create static and to attract soil. Oriental rugs are handsome and expensive, and like diamonds, they should be bought with great care. Furthermore, other furnishings to go with them must be equally luxurious. All carpet will wear longer if it is laid over a rug cushion and given methodical care.

Most so-called resilient floor coverings have actually little resilience as far as resistance to human fatigue is concerned. (Cushioned vinyl is by far the most resilient but it is expensive.) However, most resilient floor coverings offer a wide choice of pattern and color and thus add interest to the decorating scheme. Most are easy to maintain. The location of the floor will determine the choice of resilient floor covering.

THINGS TO THINK ABOUT AND TO DO

1. List on the chalkboard all the factors you should consider before selecting rugs or carpeting. Discuss the importance of each.

2. Assemble swatches of carpet in six-inch squares or larger in as many fibers, weaves, and surface effects as you can. Examine these and discuss their characteristics.

3. Work in groups and go to stores to price rugs according to the fiber used, thickness and depth of pile, and construction.

4. Discuss the advantages and disadvantages of wall-to-wall carpeting and room-size rugs.

5. Examine carpet tiles, and discuss how to install them.

6. Indicate some advantages and disadvantages in using carpeting in kitchens and bathrooms. If possible, interview home users. Display swatches of appropriate carpet.

7. List all the selling points and weaknesses of the most popular rug fibers. If possible, show examples of each during the discussion.

8. Indicate the minor rug fibers and their uses. Tell why they are not more widely used.

9. Make a list of the leading rug manufacturers, and assign class members the responsibility of writing for free literature.

10. Distinguish between *woven* and *tufted* carpet and between *Wilton* and *Axminster* weaves.

11. Display several types of rug cushions, and discuss their advantages and disadvantages.

12. Show a film on laying carpet, or observe an actual demonstration.

13. List the areas of the world from which Oriental rugs come. Display illustrations of as many kinds as possible, and discuss them as to colors and motifs used. Go on a field trip to a store, and have a rug salesman talk to your class.

14. Make a list of the kinds of rugs you have in your home. If you are planning to purchase new carpeting or a rug, discuss fibers and construction with your parents.

15. Write a brief report on how to care for rugs and carpeting.

16. Assemble samples of the resilient flooring materials mentioned in the text on pages 358 to 360, and examine each. Discuss the selection and care of resilient floor coverings in regard to appearance, wear, care, and cost.

17. Compare the cost of *poured floors* with the cost of laying a linoleum floor of high quality and a floor of pure vinyl.

18. Give some advantages and disadvantages of floor tile over resilient flooring materials sold by the yard.

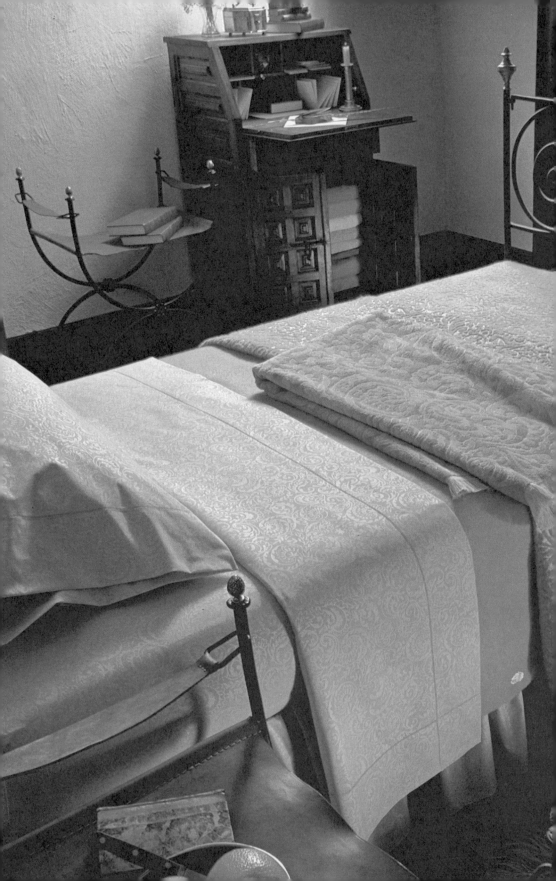

chapter twenty-two

BEDDING AND HOUSEHOLD LINENS

General affluence, easy credit, advanced technology, abundant advertising, and informal living have revolutionized the merchandising of bedding and household linens. Magazines display beautiful colored illustrations emphasizing the importance of the total look in the bedroom, bathroom, kitchen, and dining room. Except for the emphasis upon color, the total look is not exactly a new concept. During the nineteenth and early twentieth centuries, with fewer social and business pressures on them, homemakers spent a large part of their leisure doing fancy needlework. Sheets, pillowcases, spreads, dresser covers, and sometimes curtains had matching crochet, embroidery, or appliqué.

A number of years ago colored sheets with printed borders became popular, but only recently have floral, plaid, arabesque, and geometric patterns decorated sheets, blankets, and spreads in coordinated sets. A substantial argument for spending money on bedding is the fact that the average person spends about a third of every twenty-four hours in bed, and any purchase that can contribute to the enjoyment of rest is a good investment.

The general acceptance of the wider and longer bed has also been a boon to the bedding industry. It will not be long before the queen-size bed outsells the traditional double bed. The standard double bed, fifty-four inches wide, provides each occupant with only twenty-seven inches of width, which is comparable to the width of the average baby crib. The length of traditional single and double beds is no longer adequate because the average height of an adult, due to improved nutrition, is two inches above that of a half century ago. With beds and mattresses wider, manufacturers of sheets, pillowcases, pillows, blankets, and bedspreads have had to provide bedding in larger sizes. New fibers and finishes have all but eliminated the time-consuming task of ironing.

The trend toward informal entertaining has de-emphasized the importance of possessing embroidered and lace-trimmed table linens that require careful laundering. The emphasis today is upon ease-of-care and disposable "table linens." With the ever increasing array of "household linens" in new fibers and finishes, the consumer needs to be better informed in these areas.

363

GUIDELINES FOR STUDY

GENERAL IDEAS
TO CONSIDER

1. Each fiber possesses individual properties, which limit or expand its use.
2. Fiber, yarn construction, and weave affect the appearance and wearing quality of household textiles.
3. Finishes usually alter the natural characteristics of a fiber.
4. The choice of sheets depends upon the size and type of the mattress, laundry facilities, cost, and personal preference.
5. The choice of blankets depends upon climate, wearing qualities, color scheme, size of bed, and cost.
6. Weave, pile density, color scheme, and cost influence the choice of bath towels.
7. The kind of entertaining done, the cost, and the time and facilities available for care determine the choice of table linens.

WORDS AND TERMS
TO IDENTIFY

alkali
appliqué
carded and combed
damask
elastomeric
fiber fill
foam-rubber mattress
generic name
innerspring mattress
metallics

novelty yarns
ply yarns
reprocessed wool
tensile strength
thermal blanket
thermoplastic
thread count
torn size
virgin wool

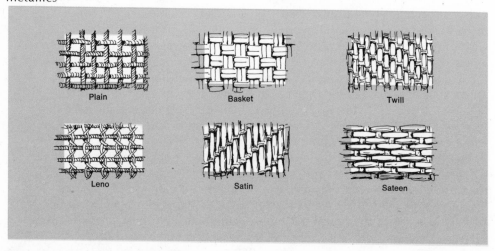

Close-up sketches of common weaves.

FIBERS, YARNS, WEAVES, AND FINISHES

Although many of you may be familiar with fibers, yarns, weaves, and finishes, a quick review may help you to see the reasons why certain fibers, type of yarn construction, kind of weave, and various finishes are suitable for different types of household linens. The term *linen* referring to sheets, pillowcases, towels, and tablecloths dates from a period in history when only flax fibers were used for household textiles. Flax culture originated in Egypt and reached France in the 700's during Charlemagne's reign. Until 1700, flax was the most popular textile fiber in Europe. It was not until later, in the mid-1700's, that cotton production surpassed that of flax.

During the thousand years when flax was important to the economy of Europe, many refinements of living were carried from the Near East to Europe—the heavy poster bed, the refectory table, fine china and silverware, and luxurious fabrics and rugs. All these things became status symbols. Linen was used for sheets, pillowcases, towels, underwear, and damask tablecloths. The ladies and servants of the feudal lords in medieval castles and the women in the manor houses of Renaissance Europe lavished fancy needlework on household linens. Only the wealthy could afford these hand-woven, hand-decorated items. The Industrial Revolution of the nineteenth century and the textile revolution of the twentieth century have brought attractive household linens within the buying power of almost everyone.

Fibers

Each fiber imparts its own individual properties, and no fiber is perfect for every use. To enhance versatility, fibers are blended for extra strength, added luster, increased absorbency, greater crease resistance, or economy. If you are familiar with fibers and their properties, you will be a better judge of the textile products you buy, such as sheets, blankets, tablecloths, curtains, draperies, and upholstery for furniture.

Wool was probably the first recognizable natural fiber. Wool is warm, resilient, wrinkle resistant, and easy to dye. Criticisms of wool have been its tendency to shrink and mat under heat and pressure and its affinity for moths. Wool also pills—that is, the nap or fuzz forms small balls or pills on the surface of sweaters and blankets—but not to the extent of some man-made fibers. Modern finishes, which will be discussed later, have almost eliminated wool's most outstanding problems. *Virgin* wool (new, never used wool) is superior to *reprocessed* wool (wool made from previously woven or felted products but never used). *Reused* wool (wool made from reworked products which have been used and which may have been soiled or damaged) is an inferior quality.

Cotton is extremely absorbent, cool, and hygienic (because it can be laundered at high temperatures). It is inexpensive and is not harmed by ordinary bleaches. Cotton dyes well, and it is so versatile that it can be finished to resemble wool, linen, or silk. However, cotton mildews if it is not cared for properly. Long-staple cotton fibers (Egyptian, Sea Island, and Pima) are *carded* and *combed* in a straightening process prior to spinning, whereas short-staple cotton fibers (upland) are combed only. Long-staple cotton is used for finer fabrics than short staple.

Linen (flax) is even cooler, more

absorbent, and more lustrous than cotton, but linen wrinkles easily, is not quite as easy to dye, and costs far more than cotton. Linen will withstand high water temperatures, but it is a little more sensitive to alkaline bleaches than cotton. Better-quality linen is made from long fibers known as *line,* and ordinary linen is made from short fibers or *tow.*

Silk has always been the luxury fiber because of its appearance, draping qualities, strength, wrinkle resistance, and high cost. The search for a silk substitute led to the introduction of the first man-made fiber, rayon, and opened research into the entire field of modern plastics. Silk for household use is found mainly in satins, damasks, and brocades for draperies and upholstery, but only a minority of people can afford these fabrics.

Rayon is lustrous, absorbent, inexpensive, and takes dye well. But rayon is weak, especially when wet; it is less flame resistant than most fibers, and it will mildew. Many of rayon's shortcomings have been improved by finishes, and in blends it helps to increase absorbency and reduce cost.

Acetate, unlike rayon, is thermoplastic, which means that controlled heat and pressure will set an embossed surface design or make pleats permanent. But acetate fibers will melt under a hot iron. Acetate feels and drapes much like silk. Originally colors, especially blues, changed or faded in the presence of atmospheric gases, but this is no longer a serious problem. *Triacetate* is stronger and less sensitive to higher ironing temperatures than acetate. Acetate is used for bedspreads, draperies, and as a trim on blankets and guest towels. Trade names are *Acele, Avisco, Celanese, Chromspun,* and *Estron.*

Nylon, one of the earliest synthetics, has the highest resistance to abrasion of any fiber. It is also resistant to wrinkling, mildew, alkaline substances, and insect damage. But nylon is low in moisture absorption. It accumulates static electricity, picks up soil easily, and melts under high ironing temperatures. It is important in blends because it increases wear without increasing cost too greatly.

Acrylic fibers can be made to look and feel much like wool. They resist shrinkage, stretching, and wrinkling. They are warm but not bulky, nonallergenic, and resilient. They wash and dry easily, but oil-type soil is difficult to remove. Acrylic fibers are better known by their trade names than by their generic name. Trade names for acrylics include *Orlon, Acrilan, Creslan,* and *Zefran.*

Modacrylic fibers are similar to acrylic fibers in appearance, warmth, wrinkle resistance, and weight. Although modacrylics are very sensitive to heat, they will not support a flame. They wash well and they retain their shape, qualities that make them highly desirable for blankets. *Dynel* and *Verel* are familiar trade names.

Polyesters lead in crease-resistant properties, even excelling wool. Fabrics made of polyester fibers are mothproof, mildew and stain resistant, and dry quickly. These properties make polyester fibers especially popular in blends with other fibers for wash-and-wear and permanent-press items. Familiar trade names are *Dacron, Fortrel,* and *Kodel.*

Olefin is a tough and resilient fiber with lightweight bulk and high resistance to stains and fire. These fibers are nonabsorbent and abrasion resistant. Although Olefin came into household use originally as a fiber for carpeting, now the fiber is also used for bed-spreads, blankets, place mats, and upholstery. Trade names are *Royalene* and *Reevon*.

Metallics are used mainly as decoration on household linens. Metallic yarns, which date from Biblical times, were originally made from precious metals. Now metallics are made mainly of aluminum. A metallic strip is laminated with an acetate, polyester, or other film or yarn to produce a pliable, tarnish-resistant product.

Paper, although not a fiber in the true sense, is an important product for household use. Paper yarns are knitted or woven into place mats and other items. Paper place mats, towels, napkins, cups, and plates are popular disposable items. Informal entertaining has tremendously increased the demand for paper products.

Rubber was the first elasticized fiber. Its main use in household textiles is as a rug backing. *Latex* is probably the most familiar trade name.

Spandex, produced as a substitute for rubber, is popular in elastomeric-stretch clothing, fitted slipcovers, and card-table covers, but as yet has limited use in other household textiles. Usually the spandex fiber is the core around which nylon, cotton, acetate, or rayon yarns are spun. It is cooler and lighter in weight than rubber.

Saran excels in resistance to sunlight, rain, stains, abrasion, and also fire. It is resilient, meaning that it has quick recovery from stretch, making it desirable for outdoor furniture covers. It is also used in outdoor-indoor carpet, in webbing, and in screens. It is more expensive than its closest competitor, olefin. Trade names are *Rovana, Saran,* and *Velon*.

Glass fiber has been popular in hand-washable fabrics for draperies, curtains, or table mats for many years, but only recently have fabrics made of glass fiber been advertised as machine washable. However, they should be washed alone and the washer flushed out afterward because fine glass particles may penetrate other items and cause serious skin irritation. Recent uses of glass fibers are for mattress covers, bedspreads, shower curtains, and window shades. The fiber is strong but nonelastic, fire resistant and waterproof but nonabsorbent. It has very little resistance to abrasion, and therefore is low in durability. Trade names are *Vitron, Fiberglas,* and *Unifab*.

Yarn Construction

All fabrics (except wool felt, which is produced by the interlocking and matting of wool fibers, and certain chemically produced plastics) are constructed from yarn whether the fabric is woven, knitted, or braided. Yarns are made from *staple* fibers of varying lengths, such as cotton and wool staple, or *filament* fibers of continuous length, such as silk and man-made fibers. Often man-made fibers are cut to produce a staple fiber for a different texture effect.

The spinning operation determines the final character of the yarn for weaving. Yarns are classified by the fiber from which they are made, the blend (if used) of fibers in the yarn, the size or thickness of the yarn, and the spinning process used. The raw fiber may be any fiber we have discussed, and any number of fibers may be blended into one yarn or into ply yarns. These yarns may be made any thickness. The method of yarn construction used produces many different surface effects.

The simplest yarn is a *single yarn,* which may be a continuous filament or a single yarn made by twisting fibers together, such as cotton- or wool-staple fibers. *Ply yarns* are produced by twisting together two or more single yarns either loosely or tightly, depending upon the end results desired. For example, a four-ply yarn means that four separate single yarns are twisted together into one yarn. A firmly twisted yarn, such as a worsted, when used in a closely woven fabric, such as a gabardine, gives long wear. A highly twisted long-staple cotton yarn woven closely in percale sheeting will also give long wear.

Novelty yarns are irregular in appearance. One group of novelty yarns is called *core-and-effect yarns,* meaning that different effects are produced by twisting a second yarn around a core yarn. These yarns include *bouclé* and *ratiné,* which have tiny projecting loops; *slub yarns,* which are alternately tightly and loosely twisted to produce a surface such as shantung's; and *nub yarns,* which are twisted to look as though they have been tied in knots at intervals. In addition to core-and-effect yarns, there are *textured yarns.* These yarns may be made from a man-made filament fiber which has been cut into staple length, crimped to produce stretch or resilience, fuzzed to give bulky warmth, or chemically treated to give wrinkle resistance.

When you have occasion to select fabrics for slipcovers or upholstery, be sure to choose those with a smooth surface and firm weave. Novelty fabrics with a looser weave may be used in decorating windows where there is little friction to snag the surface.

Weaves

The kind of weave used affects the appearance, texture, absorbency, and durability of a textile.

The *plain weave* is the simplest weave of all. This is the regular lacing of filling yarns over alternate warp yarns. This is a durable weave, but its durability depends upon how tightly the yarns are spun and how closely they are woven. Percale and muslin for sheets and pillowcases and many fabrics for slipcovers and curtains have this weave.

The *basket weave* is similar to the plain weave, except that two or more filling yarns regularly interlace two or more warp yarns. The most familiar household textile with this weave is monk's cloth. The basket weave is not a durable weave and is not recommended for slipcovers, but it is satisfactory for table mats and draperies.

A *corded weave* is also a variation of the plain weave. In the corded weave heavy warp yarns are interwoven with fine filling yarns, or heavy filling yarns are interwoven with fine warp yarns. Since warp and filling yarns are not evenly balanced, a corded weave is less durable than a plain weave. Rep, poplin, and faille are examples of household textiles with this weave.

A *twill weave* is the interlacing of filling yarn over groups of warp yarns in regular progression to give a diagonal effect. This is an extremely durable weave used in denim, gabardine, and many drapery and slipcover fabrics.

A *herringbone weave* resembles a twill weave, except that the diagonal surface effect is reversed at regular intervals, producing a herringbone effect. It is also a durable weave and is used in fabrics for slipcovers and draperies.

A *leno weave* is produced by lacing filling yarns through warp yarns with a chainlike twist. Curtain marquisette is an example of this weave.

A *satin weave* is identified by

floating warp yarns that pick up light reflection to give a lustrous effect. During the weaving process, a filling yarn goes *over one warp yarn* and *under a number of warp yarns,* with each row of filling yarns interlacing progressively. Silk, rayon, and acetate satins are examples.

The *sateen weave* is identified by floating filling yarns, which seem to reflect less light than floating warp yarns. During the weaving process, a filling yarn *goes under one warp yarn* and *over a number of warp yarns,* with each row of filling yarns interlacing progressively. Cotton sateen is an example. (See illustration page 364.)

Finishes

Chemical and physical finishes are given cloth to improve its appearance. Among the most familiar standard finishes are *dyeing; direct printing* by rollers; *flock printing,* or direct printing with an adhesive capable of attracting and holding minute flocks or filaments; *silk-screen printing* (similar to hand stenciling); *sizing* for a firmer appearance; *napping* to produce a surface fuzz, which holds air cells and produces warmth; *mercerizing,* especially for cotton, to produce luster and strength; *crease resistance* to decrease wrinkling; and finishes for shrinkage control.

In addition to the above finishes, household fabrics may be given certain special finishes. Bedding and draperies for hotels may be given *flame-resistant* finishes. Draperies and bedding may also be given *antiodor* and *antiperspiration* finishes. *Stain-* and *spot-resistant* finishes are given many fabrics for household use. Finishes are also given to *reduce static, affinity for moths,* and *mildew.* A *permanent-press* finish is popular for sheets and drapery fabrics.

Permanent press may be the result of a chemical finish or the result of blending a polyester fiber with cotton or other fibers.

Finishes tend to alter the properties of fibers to some degree. Crease-, stain-, and spot-resistant finishes decrease absorbency in cotton and linen. Some finishes, such as napping, may weaken the fabric if the process is not carefully controlled. Many finishes require special care in dry-cleaning, washing, drying, and ironing.

This brief discussion of fiber properties, yarns, weaves, and finishes should help you to understand what to expect of household fabrics and the need to select them with care.

SHEETS AND PILLOWCASES

The well-dressed bed of some years ago with its snow-white hemstitched sheets and pillowcases and white candlewick spread would seem very conservative in comparison to the colorful array of bed fashions now on the market. Not only are all bed fashions more dramatic, but they are also easier to maintain. Crease-resistant polyester fibers in blends with cotton, rayon, acetate, and other fibers and effective crease-resistant finishes have practically eliminated ironing. Programmed dials on washers and dryers take the guesswork out of timing and temperatures in the washing and drying cycles. When you buy sheets, note the *fabric* or *fabric blend, tensile strength, thread count, style, and size.*

Fabric

Muslin and *percale,* which are usually made of cotton, are the leading fabrics for sheets and pillowcases. Cotton is absorbent, cool, plentiful,

A bedroom and adjoining bath show imaginative use of coordinated accessories. The design motif of the bedding, shower curtain, and towels is repeated with stick-on flowers.

and reasonable in price. It takes bleaching and will withstand high temperatures in washing and ironing. Muslin comes in light and medium weights for home use and in heavy weights for hospital use. Percale is finer than muslin because long-staple cotton is used; the fibers are both carded and combed, and the yarns are finer and more highly twisted. Crib sheets come in *knitted fabrics* either plain or printed, as well as in muslin and percale.

Most *permanent-press* sheets are made of a blend of cotton and polyester fibers or all cotton with a permanent-press finish. A cotton and polyester blend is a little softer than an all-cotton with a crease-resistant finish, and is more wrinkle resistant. Although permanent-press sheets are more expensive than ordinary sheets, tests show that they more than make up the difference in the ease of care, the resistance to shrinkage, and so on. In a cotton-polyester blend, the cotton contributes absorbency and coolness; and the polyester fiber, crease resistance. When a nonabsorbent polyester fiber is blended with cotton, absorbency is slightly reduced but resistance to wrinkling is greatly increased. Finishes are given all-cotton sheets that will retain cotton's outstanding properties of absorbency, coolness, and softness and at the same time impart quick drying and high wrinkle resistance. Nylon is sometimes blended with cotton to give additional strength and quicker drying. A few manufacturers blend rayon and cotton for a silkier appearance. Rayon is absorbent, cool, and dyes easily, but it is weaker when wet than other fibers.

Tensile Strength and Thread Count

Tensile strength refers to the number of pounds of pull, as recorded on a testing machine, necessary to break an inch of fabric. A tensile strength of 50 indicates a weaker sheet than a tensile strength of 70. *Thread count* refers to the number of threads woven vertically and horizontally in one square inch of sheet before shrinking. A heavy muslin sheet may have a thread count of 140, and a fine percale may have a thread count of 180 (90 warp and 90 filling yarns). A very fine percale may have a thread count of 200. The fine percale sheet may outwear the heavy muslin sheet because the long-staple, firmly twisted fine yarns of the percale sheet may be more flexible and resistant to constant friction and folding.

Styles and Sizes of Sheets

A *fitted bottom sheet* has made bedmaking easier because it is contoured to fit over the mattress. However, the fitted sheet must be chosen to fit the mattress properly because a sheet that is too tight will cause the mattress to buckle, and the sheet will wear out quickly because of strain. A sheet that is too loose will wrinkle and become uncomfortable. *Top sheets* come flat or with two fitted corners for the bottom of the bed. An all-flat sheet is frequently preferable because a boxed-in top sheet may cramp the toes.

Sheets should be long enough to stay tucked in at the bottom and to fold back eight to twelve inches over the blanket at the top in order to protect the blanket. Sizes are designated in *torn sizes* and not in finished sizes. Allowing for shrinkage, a bottom hem of one inch, and a three- or four-inch top hem, a sheet with a torn size of 108 inches will actually be somewhere between 96 and 98 inches finished.

Sheets, especially fitted bottom sheets, are bought according to length, width, and thickness of the mattress.

Standard *innerspring mattresses* are about 7 inches thick; and *foam-rubber mattresses, 4½ inches to 6 inches* thick. Not all styles are available for foam-rubber mattresses.

The chart on this page indicates the size sheets to order for different types and sizes of beds. In buying fitted sheets, indicate whether the mattress is innerspring or foam rubber. White sheets are available in all sizes, but colored and printed sheets are available only in popular sizes.

Pillowcase Sizes

Pillows are made in larger sizes to conform to the larger beds. The standard-size pillow used to be 21 inches by 27 inches, requiring a pillowcase 42 inches by 36 inches or 42 inches by 38½ inches. Pillows 22 inches by 28 inches and 23 inches by

29 inches are better sizes for queen- and king-size beds, and these require extra-size pillowcases up to 45 inches by 40 inches. Pillowcases should go over the pillow with ease and they should be at least 6 inches longer than the pillow.

Care of Sheets and Pillowcases

If sheets and pillowcases can be rotated in use, they often last longer. This means allowing six sheets (three top and three lower) for every bed; for example, two in use, two on the shelf, and two in the laundry. If laundry is done frequently at home and if permanent-press sheets are used, it is possible to get along with one or two fewer sheets. The minimum number of pillowcases is three for each pillow. If one can afford the extra cost, it is wise to buy an extra supply of sheets

——————— RECOMMENDED SIZES OF SHEETS, BLANKETS, SPREADS ———————

Type of Bed	Fitted Sheet[1]	Flat Sheet	Blanket	Spread
Crib	27″ × 52″	42″ × 72″	40″ × 60″	
Youth	33″ × 66″	63″ × 108″	54″ × 72″	
Cot	30″ × 72″	63″ × 108″	54″ × 72″	59″ × 100″
Day	33″ × 75″	63″ × 108″	66″ × 90″	
Twin[2]	39″ × 75″	72″ × 108″	72″ × 90″	81″ × 110″
Twin (long)[2]	39″ × 80″	72″ × 120″	72″ × 90″	81″ × 120″
Double[2]	54″ × 75″	81″ × 108″	80″ × 90″	96″ × 110″
Double (long)[2]	54″ × 80″	81″ × 120″	80″ × 90″	96″ × 120″
Queen	60″ × 75″	90″ × 120″	100″ × 90″	105″ × 115″
Queen (long)	60″ × 80″	90″ × 120″	108″ × 90″	105″ × 120″
King	72″ × 84″	100″ × 120″	108″ × 90″	114″ × 120″
King (wide)	78″ × 84″	108″ × 120″	108″ × 90″	
Hollywood[2]	78″ × 75″	108″ × 120″	108″ × 90″	120″ × 120″
Hollywood (long)[2]	78″ × 80″	108″ × 120″	108″ × 90″	

1. Sizes given in this column are for standard innerspring mattresses.
2. Fitted sheets with special boxing are available for foam-rubber mattresses.

and pillowcases during semiannual "white sales" and have enough on hand for emergencies, such as sickness or guests.

White sheets can be laundered in temperatures of 140 degrees to 160 degrees Fahrenheit, but colored sheets require a temperature of 120 degrees Fahrenheit. If the washer should be overcrowded, sheets will not rinse well, and detergent constantly left on the sheets may cause skin irritation. Sheets, especially permanent-press sheets, should not be overdried, because heat-set wrinkles are difficult to remove. (Newer washers have a cool cycle to reduce wrinkling.) Strong solutions of bleach should be avoided on both regular and permanent-press sheets. Folds should not be pressed in because constant pressing over the same fold weakens the fibers. Static electricity can be reduced on permanent-press sheets in cold dry weather by using a fabric softener. Always use a pad between the bottom sheet and the mattress to protect the mattress.

BLANKETS AND BEDSPREADS

Sheets, blankets, and bedspreads are available in coordinated colors and designs. It is fine to have matched sets, but not everyone can afford to buy a complete set of bedding at one time. Moreover, sheets and pillowcases wear out before blankets and bedspreads. Cotton summer blankets with a design and matching sheets are popular, but most people prefer winter blankets in coordinated solid colors.

Blankets
Wool and the acrylics are the chief competitors for use in cold-weather blankets. Wool is expensive, and, unless it is chemically treated, it will shrink and attract moths. Both fibers will pill, but wool pills less and is more resilient than the acrylics. Blankets made of modacrylic fibers are very similar to blankets made of the acrylics, except that they are more flame resistant. Rayon is used for entire blankets or blended with other fibers to reduce cost and add softness. Although rayon blankets are low in warmth and resiliency, their lower cost makes them desirable in moderate climates and in well-heated homes. Cotton-flannel blankets are popular for in-between season use. Thermal blankets, or those loosely woven with a waffle weave to retain air pockets, are good year-round blankets in moderate climates. A cotton bedspread or sheet over them in winter traps the air to generate warmth.

If directions are followed carefully, blankets, even electric blankets, can be machine washed. Presoaking loosens dirt. A very short period of agitation is recommended. Follow the directions on your washer and dryer if you expect satisfactory results. Many people prefer to send acrylic or wool blankets to a professional cleaner once a year, unless they have a washer and dryer with special controls for washing and drying blankets.

Bedspreads
Bedspreads are available in three styles—throw, fitted, and coverlet with a dust ruffle. A bedspread should hang evenly all around and be long enough to tuck over pillows, unless a special covering is used for pillows. Fitted bedspreads must fit well at the corners.

Fabrics for bedspreads run from the traditionally washable tufted heirloom

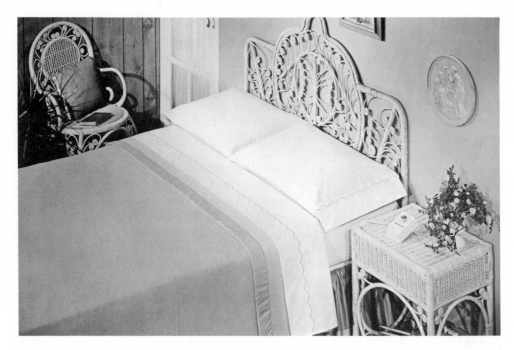

Electric blankets today can be deceptive in appearance, for wires no longer mar the fabric surface.

types or *chenilles* to *sheers* (permanent press) and *quilted* types. The background of the tufted or chenille bedspreads should be firmly woven, and the tufts should be even. Clip—never pull—loose ends. The tufted and chenille types require very little care, except laundering. Thick quilted types made to fit the bed are handsome but heavy to handle, and it is not always easy to find a place to rest them at night. They should be cleaned by a professional cleaner.

If a dust ruffle is used under a coverlet, it should not look skimpy, and it should be keyed to the colors in the coverlet. Coverlets may be patchwork or appliqué quilts or figured quilted types.

BATHROOM TOWELS

First of all, towels should be soft and absorbent, especially bath towels. Bath towels, hand towels, and washcloths should be durable because they receive hard wear. Guest towels and finger towels are made more for beauty than durability. Linen is preferred for decorative guest towels. The trim may be of cotton or metallic yarns or any man-made fiber. All bathroom towels and accessories are usually bought with a color scheme in mind.

Cotton terry-cloth towels are the most popular bath towels. Fairly close, evenly spaced loops absorb moisture and a closely woven gound provides durability. A terry weave has a plain ground weave. A third set of yarns is loosened during weaving to produce the terry loops or pile.

These are the features that make some bath towels look and wear better than others:

□ *Quality and twist of cotton yarns:* Long-staple cotton yarns wear better than short-staple. Evenly twisted smooth yarns wear better than loosely twisted, uneven yarns.

□ *Density of weave:* An even, close

upright pile with a firm feel is superior to a soft pile that is not erect. Elaborate reversible sculptured weaves give color and design interest, but they increase cost and sometimes reduce absorbency.

□ *Printing and dyeing:* Some colors hold up better than others, and printed designs do not always hold up as well as solid colors.

□ *Price:* As a rule, price relates to quality up to a certain point. Cheap towels are loosely woven and less absorbent. On the other hand, an applied design or a special weave, for eye appeal, will run up the cost without giving any better performance.

□ *Laundry methods:* Terry towels should not be washed in extremely hot water. Recommended temperatures are 130 degrees to 140 degrees Fahrenheit. If towels are not dried in a clothes dryer, they should be shaken to loosen the pile.

KITCHEN TOWELS

Cotton and linen are the principal fibers used for kitchen towels because they are absorbent and sanitary. Plain and terry weaves are most common. An all-linen towel is more lint free, more absorbent, and dries more quickly than an all-cotton towel, but it costs a great deal more. A towel containing 25 percent linen does not cost much more than a cotton towel and absorbs much more moisture. Many people prefer terry towels for the kitchen because of their absorbency.

TABLE LINENS

Kinds of Table Linens

The damask, lace, and embroidered linen tablecloth has all but disappeared except for formal dining. Embroidered and damask tablecloths were once a symbol of affluence, but they are difficult to launder at home, and very expensive to have hand laundered elsewhere. If you use any kind of tablecloth, it should extend at least six inches below the edge of the table all around.

Cloth napkins come in several sizes. Dinner napkins are usually 22 inches by 22 inches; breakfast and luncheon napkins, 18 inches by 18 inches or 15 inches by 15 inches; and tea napkins, 12 inches by 12 inches. Paper, straw, plastic, and cork table mats are in general use for family meals. Embroidered linen, lace, and hand-crocheted table mats are formal enough for company dinners. Cloth table mats of linen or cotton wear somewhat better than those made of rayon because linen and cotton withstand somewhat higher laundering and ironing temperatures. Blends and special finishes make most table mats durable enough with proper care. If you entertain a lot at sit-down meals rather than at buffet-type meals, you may want to own one or two sets of embroidered-linen table mats that will look attractive with fine china. These will be so expensive that it is wise to take time in making a choice.

Care of Table Linens

Many brides tuck beautiful linens away for special occasions and then forget about them. It is a pleasure and satisfaction to dine in a charming atmosphere, and the dinner hour can be the highlight of the day. Even if guests are not expected, it is fun to surprise the family occasionally with a nicely set table.

Most table linens are machine washable, but lace, crocheted, and embroidered linens should be hand washed. They should be squeezed to eliminate water because wringing will break the needlework. Good linens should never be sent to an ordinary commercial laundry. It is not difficult to hand wash table mats, napkins, and guest towels. All linens should be laundered soon after use. Spots and stains may be indicated with a running stitch of light-colored thread or even a small safety pin before the item is wet, so that they can be easily located. It is very difficult to remove old spots and stains or those that have been heat set. Most spots can be removed by wetting the spot and lightly rubbing it on the wrong side with a little detergent. Avoid prolonged or vigorous rubbing, which may cause the nap to fuzz or the fabric to wear thin. Scrape food or candle wax off with a dull knife before attempting to remove the stain. A chlorine bleach can be used on white linen and cotton if directions are followed. A grease solvent will remove oily food and chewing gum.

Colored linens should be washed separately so long as there is any sign of fading. Avoid drying linens in an automatic dryer with any item that might run. Remove linens from the dryer while slightly damp—never over-dry. Linens should be pulled into shape and ironed on the wrong side, with special emphasis on hems, and finally on the right side to restore the luster. Embroidered linens may be ironed slightly for a third time to make the embroidered areas stand out; this should be done over a pad or several thicknesses of an old sheet.

When you store linens, keep them in airtight plastic folders or folders of brown wrapping paper to avoid soiled or yellowed edges. Do not store linens in a cedar closet because cedar will cause linen to turn yellow.

RECOMMENDED QUANTITIES OF HOUSEHOLD LINEN

The following lists give the recommended quantities of linen that will be required in an average household. Of course, the needs and preferences of individual homemakers will vary a great deal. If laundry is done at home and done frequently, you can reduce the number of some items slightly. If you have house guests often and entertain frequently, you may want to increase the number of some items.

The Bedroom (per bed)

6 sheets
3 pillowcases for each pillow
1 or 2 mattress covers
1 or 2 mattress pads
1 or 2 wool or acrylic blankets
1 cotton blanket or lightweight quilt
1 or 2 bedspreads

The Bathroom

4-6 bath towels per person
4-6 face towels per person
3-4 washcloths per person
2 bath mats
1 shower curtain (for shower stall or tub with shower)

Dining Area

1-2 tablecloths
3 sets of place mats with napkins
2-3 bridge cloths with napkins
tea napkins, extra dinner napkins, and breakfast cloths according to need

Kitchen

1-2 dozen dish towels (fewer are required if you have a dishwasher)
3-4 pliable and heat-resistant pot holders
2-3 absorbent dishcloths

Kitchen towels come in a variety of sizes, styles, and textures. Notice the convenient towel storage rack.

A handsome setting for lunch or an informal dinner is arranged with woven place mats and linen napkins.

SUMMARY

The term *household linens* dates from a period prior to the mid-1700's when linen was the only fiber used for sheets and tablecloths. Cotton did not become an important commercial fiber in the Western world until later. White linens, hemstitched or embroidered, were an established tradition of elegance until the mid-twentieth century. Although linen is still popular for tablecloths, table mats, and napkins, cotton is mainly used for sheets and pillowcases.

In order to be able to judge textile products for the home, you should have some knowledge of the fibers, weaves, and finishes used for these products. Not long ago, sheets and pillowcases came only in a few limited sizes. With an increasing demand for larger beds and pillows, these items now come in many sizes and also in fitted styles. Man-made fibers compete with wool for use in blankets. Acrylic and modacrylic fibers are nearly as warm as wool, are non-allergenic, and are easy to launder. The trend toward informality has affected the choice of table linens. Fewer tablecloths and embroidered table mats are being sold. Table mats and napkins which require minimum care are more popular. Cotton terry bath towels have been less affected by informal living and the advent of new fibers than any other household textile because cotton is extremely absorbent, relatively inexpensive, and hygienic.

All household textiles require good care if they are to retain their color and shape and render maximum service.

THINGS TO THINK ABOUT AND TO DO

1. Display on the bulletin board magazine illustrations of sheets, pillowcases, and blankets. Include as many different colors and styles as possible.

2. Visit a furniture store and find out from the buyer of bedroom furniture how single beds and double beds in regular, queen, and king sizes rate in popularity.

3. Give brief reports on the development of the cotton and flax industries.

4. List the fibers currently used for *sheets* in addition to cotton; for *blankets,* for *tablecloths,* and for *table mats.*

5. Name the *strongest,* the *weakest,* the *most lustrous,* the *warmest,* and the *coolest* fibers.

6. Display labels with trade names for a number of man-made fibers used for household linens.

7. Name some uses for the following fibers: glass, metallic, olefin, paper, and spandex.

8. List the most common weaves, and display a fabric illustrating each kind.

9. Name the various kinds of finishes that may be used on sheets, blankets, and drapery fabrics.

10. Discuss the acceptance of electric sheets and blankets, of fitted sheets, of colored or printed sheets.

11. Make up a bedding wardrobe for twin beds and for a double bed. Choose either regular, queen, or king size; indicate fabrics and sizes used for all bedding, and give current costs.

12. Display illustrations of as many different types of bedspreads as you can find.

13. Demonstrate points to look for in buying bath towels. Compare the weight and weave of inexpensive and moderate-priced towels.

14. Estimate the cost of the items listed for household linen needs on page 376 at low, middle, and high figures. You may visit stores or use newspaper advertising.

15. Investigate the potential savings one may make at a traditional January or August "white sale."

chapter twenty-three

DINNERWARE— DISHES, GLASSWARE, FLATWARE

In reviewing history we can see that past social standards were determined mainly by the rise and fall of empires or feudal kingdoms or by the development of trade routes over land or sea. When the Roman Empire fell, in 476 A.D., social progress in Europe came to a standstill. The center of civilization shifted to the Eastern Roman or Byzantine Empire (especially Constantinople) until after the Crusades. Benefiting from the rich heritage of Rome, the Byzantines developed a high type of culture and set social standards which were later carried to Europe.

Although the Crusades failed in their goal, Italy benefited tremendously from this religious movement because of her geographic location. Florence and Venice, on the crossroads between East and West, soon became second only to Constantinople in economic and social importance. Among the great merchant families of the period was the de' Medici family. Catherine de Médicis (1519–1589), upon her marriage to Henry II of France, brought many of the refinements of the Italian courts to France, especially the arts of cooking, table service, and fine manners.

During the late Middle Ages, or the French Gothic period, France set the pace for all of Europe in architecture and fashion as well as in many other arts. Her strategic location in central Europe gave her certain trade advantages early in the Renaissance period. Later, under Louis XIV and his finance minister, Jean Baptiste Colbert, all kinds of luxury industries were established, and the palace at Versailles was built. During Louis' long reign, the French court set the standards for court manners and fashion, which all the rising courts of Europe tried to emulate. French became the international language. The term *etiquette* dates from the reign of Louis XIV, when social behavior became so important that the king issued etiquettes, or *tickets*—forms of accepted social behavior—for well-to-do French nobles, so that they would know how to behave at court. The social graces continued to be emphasized until the French Revolution.

GUIDELINES FOR STUDY

GENERAL IDEAS TO CONSIDER

1. We are indebted to Far and Middle Eastern peoples for their contribution toward the development of our present-day dinnerware—china and pottery, glassware, and silverware.
2. Modern technology has provided less expensive, more durable, and easier-to-care-for dinnerware than was previously available, and the mode of casual living has influenced its acceptance.
3. The type of clay and other ingredients, and the firing temperature used, determine whether the final product is porcelain, earthenware, stoneware, or pottery.
4. The type of entertaining done and the kind of table appointments used, such as linens, bowls for flower arrangements, and flatware, will determine the choice of dishes and glassware.
5. The care given dishes, glassware, and flatware will influence the length of service and personal enjoyment derived from using them.

WORDS AND NAMES TO KNOW

alloy
apothecary
artifacts
Beau Brummell
Beau Nash
bone china
ceramics
crystal
earthenware
etiquette
glaze
hollow ware
melamine

open stock
place setting
porcelain
Sandwich glass
sericulture
Sheffield silver
spa
Josiah Spode
sterling
stoneware
translucent
tumbler
Josiah Wedgwood

TABLE APPOINTMENTS
AND SOCIAL HISTORY

Silversmithing, making ceramics, weaving exquisite textiles, and other crafts of the Middle East related to gracious living reached Spain through the Moors, who had traveled to the Iberian Peninsula by way of North Africa. Moorish occupation of Spain lasted from 711 until 1492, when the last Moorish stronghold at Granada fell to the Spanish Christians. The Moors introduced beautiful ceramics, leather tooling, glassmaking, rug and tapestry weaving, and many metal crafts. If it had not been for the Moors, Spain would have remained an isolated peninsula because the formidable Pyrenees between Spain and France prevented Eastern culture from penetrating Spain.

Because of her isolated location, England was slow to experience the Renaissance and the social concepts that accompanied it. Many of the crafts and patterns of etiquette of the Middle East and Italy had penetrated Europe by way of trade routes through Nuremberg, Frankfurt, and Augsburg, Germany. While other countries in Europe were concentrating on armies, Henry VIII of England was busy building a fleet of warships. He was little interested in the social graces, but his first wife and brother's widow, Catherine of Aragon, who was the daughter of Ferdinand and Isabella of Spain, brought to England many court refinements.

Before the English defeat of the Spanish Armada under Queen Elizabeth, Spain had been a world power, and Spanish had become the international language. After the defeat, under the rule of Elizabeth, England began to compete for world supremacy. Social etiquette became far more important under Elizabeth than under Henry. During the Jacobean period (1603–1688), Charles II was exiled in France while Cromwell ruled England. Charles was greatly impressed with French court life under Louis XIV, and upon his return to England brought back new concepts in dress and court etiquette.

During the period of European competition for trade and colonial possessions, the Netherlands had become an important trade center, and for a time during the seventeenth century Amsterdam was the most important port in the world. When William and Mary (reigned 1689–1702) succeeded James II on the throne of England, Mary, in keeping with the Dutch tradition of being a home-loving people, exerted her influence on furniture design and social behavior. Mary's fine collection of china cups inspired the designing of a china cupboard to display them. Queen Anne, the next English monarch (1702–1714), further encouraged social refinements.

The Georgian period marked the real turning point in England's attempt to exceed other countries in the art of gracious living. Wealth from her expanding empire brought about a new leisure class, who spent a great deal of effort in planning fine homes and a great deal of time in visiting spas. The popular spas had masters of ceremonies, among the best known of whom were Beau Nash during the late eighteenth century and Beau Brummell during the early nineteenth century. The emphasis upon dress and etiquette gave rise to finer table appointments and a period of furniture design that has never been equaled. This was a period when manor houses were designed by fine architects and furnished by such well-known craftsmen as Chippendale, Hepplewhite, Sheraton, and the Adams.

While the socially elite of England learned gracious manners and the use of silver knives, forks, and spoons, the common man, eating at a tavern, carried his knife and spoon with him. Utensils for eating were not provided in public eating places. When knives and spoons were not available, people used their fingers to eat any solid foods from a wooden communal bowl after dunking bread into the broth.

POTTERY, PORCELAIN,
AND PLASTICS

Exactly when the first ingenious individual fashioned the first dish, bowl, or jar from clay to carry water is a matter of speculation. Pottery making is one of the oldest of the arts, and pottery itself is one of the most important artifacts in identifying prehistoric periods. Designs on pottery are a clue to how people dressed, what they produced, and what they ate. Pottery is as ancient as the caveman and as modern as tomorrow.

The date when fine porcelain came into being is not certain, but we do know that the technique was already highly developed in China during the Sung dynasty (960–1280), and, like the secret of sericulture, the process was carefully guarded. It was not until 1709 that an apothecary's apprentice in Berlin developed a formula and a method for the production of porcelain. True porcelain, or china, is made from a hard paste, which after being fired and glazed produces a product that is translucent when held up to a light. In 1710 the world-famous Dresden (Meissen) china factory opened.

With the importation of tea, coffee, and cocoa beans, the drinking of tea, coffee, and chocolate became popular. When they were first used, teacups had no handles, but as the drinking of these new beverages became more and more a ritual of the leisure class, handles were added for convenience. In Oriental countries, where people sat on the floor and ate at low tables, handles were not important.

In their efforts to reproduce fine porcelain, English craftsmen accidentally produced a different kind of hard paste made from pulverized bones. This paste, first made in the mid-1700's, is the substance from which English bone china is made today. The earliest English china factories were at Bow and Chelsea in the late eighteenth century. Among the earliest producers of bone china were Josiah Wedgwood and Josiah Spode. As apprentices in the trade, they soon surpassed their masters and invented new tools and methods as well as original designs. The Adam brothers used many of Wedgwood's black, red, white, and jasper medallions in home decoration. *Wedgwood* is recognized by its interesting relief patterns as well as its traditional smooth surfaces. *Spode* designs use motifs of seaweed, flowers, and birds.

To be able to display fine china was a symbol of prestige, especially among the rising leisure class in America during the late nineteenth and early twentieth centuries. Since a glass china cabinet was a mark of social status, no one would have thought of hiding china behind closed closet doors.

Pottery and porcelain products dominated the dinnerware market until plastics were introduced toward the middle of the twentieth century. During World War II, the United States Navy asked that industrial designers make an attempt to produce indestructible dishes for use at sea. Thus there developed a new kind of dinnerware made from melamine, a granular powder produced

English Bone China

Earthenware

Poreclain

Stoneware

from calcium cyanamide. Plastic dinnerware is available in many qualities, and for many years the trade name *Melmac* was synonymous with quality. Now many well-known manufacturers of china and glassware are producing high-quality dishes from melamine.

Meaning of Terms

Such terms as *open stock, starter sets,* and *place settings* can be confusing to the inexperienced consumer. Open stock indicates that you can buy individual pieces without buying a complete set of dishes. This makes it possible to replace broken cups, saucers, or plates. However, open stock does not guarantee that the pattern you choose will be available indefinitely.

A starter set refers to a service for four, which includes dinner plate, dessert or salad plate, and cup and saucer. Bread-and-butter plates can be bought later, or you can always rest a butter spreader on a salad plate. If salad and dessert are served, glass plates may be used for all but very hot desserts.

The old custom of buying a piece of dinnerware by the half dozen or dozen is out of date. It is more popular now to buy place settings in multiples of four, and to buy only the serving dishes you need. When people buy *sets of dishes,* many pieces remain on the shelf collecting dust. Casseroles of silver, chrome, or pottery may substitute for extra serving dishes; wood bowls or glass plates, for salad plates; and a silver or chrome cream pitcher and sugar bowl, for those matching the china dinner service.

Types of Dishes

Clay is the substance from which all dishes, except plastics, are made. The kind of clay and other ingredients,

the kind and number of glazes, the firing temperatures, and the method of decoration determine whether a ceramic is *china, bone china, pottery, earthenware,* or *stoneware.*

China, or more properly *porcelain,* is made from china clay, or kaolin (a fine white clay), and feldspar, a crystalline mineral substance. These make a very hard clay, which produces a vitrified, nonporous, and nonabsorbent substance after being fired in a kiln at temperatures up to 2600 degrees Fahrenheit. This is the "biscuit" stage. A glaze is applied next and fired under the same high temperature. After this second firing, artists apply designs by hand in color or in 24-karat gold. The pieces are again fired, so that the decoration is fused with the china.

Porcelain is easily distinguished from other dinnerware because: (1) it is translucent when held up to the light; (2) it has a clear bell-like tone when tapped; (3) on a broken piece, the color is the same throughout. Bone china is also porcelain in which fine bone ash, instead of feldspar, is mixed with fine clay to produce a white, translucent body with a soft clear glaze. American porcelain, or vitreous (glasslike) china, is noted for its resistance to chipping and breaking, and the glaze is highly resistant to scratching.

Earthenware is a semivitreous dinnerware made from coarse clay. It is opaque when held up to the light and produces only a flat tone when tapped. It is baked at higher temperatures and for a longer period of time than pottery. Some high-grade earthenware may be priced as high as porcelain.

Stoneware is made from coarser clay than porcelain and finer clay than earthenware. It is fired at higher temperatures than earthenware but not as high as the temperatures used to fire

Pewter, pottery, and stainless steel, with a centerpiece of garden flowers, provide a harmonious breakfast setting. Notice how the kitchen color scheme is picked up in details on the table.

porcelain. The product is nonporous and more durable than earthenware. Stoneware comes in darker colors with either a glazed or a mat (dull) finish.

Pottery is not as hard as earthenware and is more porous. It has a crude natural charm. The designs are usually informal, and the colors are gay. *Ovenware* is glazed pottery, which will stand high baking temperatures and from which food may be served at the table.

Plastic dinnerware has been improved so greatly in recent years that many brands are acceptable for all but formal occasions. Melamine is the basic substance from which plasticware is made, but quality may vary greatly. These dishes are practically breakproof, but severe impact will cause cracks and chipping. Designs are imprinted on a melamine base with impregnated paper foil which is then molded into the dish. Cups come in solid colors because it is difficult to build a design into deep curves.

Some objections to plasticware are (1) its low resistance to knife scratches in comparison with ceramicware; (2) its low resistance to heat, making it necessary to keep plastic away from hot areas; (3) its tendency to absorb coffee, tea, and food stains; (4) a quick turnover of stock and difficulty in replacing or adding to service.

On better grades of melamine an extra layer of glaze on the inside of cups gives added resistance to stains, and a tougher glaze in the curing process on all pieces increases resistance to surface scratches. High-quality melamine dishes are expensive in comparison with the type of ceramic dishes a family might buy for general use. If breakage is no serious problem, it is often advisable to buy attractive pottery or earthenware.

Guidelines for Selection

Until well into the twentieth century Americans imported most fine china from Europe, but now many American manufacturers are exporting china to European countries. English names are well known in the manufacture of china—Derby, Bow, Chelsea, Royal Doulton, Spode, Minton, and Wedgwood. Germany is known for Dresden, or Meissen, china, especially figurines; France for Limoges and Sèvres; Ireland for Belleek, an extremely fragile china with a characteristic glaze; and Holland for Delft, which has an unsurpassed underglaze. Among the best-known American manufacturers are Haviland (made originally at Limoges, France, in 1839 by David Haviland for American trade), Castleton, Lenox, and Syracuse.

Perhaps the best bit of advice is to buy familiar brands from well-established stores. If you buy so-called seconds, examine each piece carefully. Furthermore, keep these points in mind:

□ Select dinnerware in four-piece place settings and in multiples of four. Buy serving dishes and other extra dishes as needed. It is also wise to buy one extra place setting and an extra cup or two.

□ Make sure that colors, texture, and design will harmonize with the color scheme and theme of the dining area.

□ Avoid choosing patterns in china, glassware, and flatware that are all fancy. Choose some plain ones, so that all parts of the dinner service will not be competing for interest.

□ Examine surfaces of pottery, earthenware, and especially plasticware for defects, such as rough edges, bulges or indentations, pits, and uneven glaze. As a rule fine china is more carefully inspected before shipment than other kinds of tableware.

□ Examine cup handles for comfort in holding and firmness in joining.

Care of Dishes

Most people take pride in setting an attractive table and want to prevent damage to good china, pottery, or plastic dishes. Here are some guidelines:

☐ Never use any kind of abrasive on dinnerware because it will remove the protective coating and increase the tendency to stain.

☐ Rinse cups and food from dishes as soon after use as possible. Coffee allowed to adhere to the sides of cups and greasy or colored foods allowed to remain on plates may stain the dishes.

☐ Never place dishes in an oven unless they are marked *ovenware*. Vitreous and semivitreous china will yellow and craze or break; plasticware will melt or warp out of shape; glassware will break.

☐ Avoid sudden changes in water temperature.

☐ If you wash decorated china in an automatic dishwasher, use the kind of detergent recommended by the manufacturer. Wash valuable and antique dishes by hand, using rubber mats in washing and stacking. Never hold a cup handle while drying a cup. To avoid chipping, dry plates one at a time.

☐ Place felt or paper circles, especially made for the purpose, between good china plates to avoid scratches.

☐ Hang cups on hooks only if you are careful in reaching for and replacing them. Otherwise stack them carefully no more than two deep.

☐ Buy a set of plastic covers to place over dishes not in frequent use.

SILVERWARE AND STAINLESS STEEL

Although silver as a precious metal dates from 2500 B.C., the exquisite silver place settings today had their origin at a much later time. Silverware as we know it developed from the flint knife and the gourd. The flint knife was man's earliest tool, and without it his survival would have been impossible. It provided a means for killing animals, removing the skins for clothing, and cutting the meat for food. Iron and later steel made stronger and sharper knives possible. The stemmed gourd evolved into the ladle and later into the spoon. By the 1400's spoons were in fairly common use in Italy. During Queen Elizabeth's reign when ruffs were in fashion, spoons were designed with extra long handles. Knives and spoons preceded forks, but as early as the eleventh century (during the 1000's) it is recorded that a doge of Venice married a prominent Greek lady who was severely criticized for her arrogance in eating with a fork. Originally forks had two prongs. A fork dated 1632 is on display in the Victoria and Albert Museum in London, which indicates that forks had found their way to England early in the seventeenth century, but the common people used only wooden spoons for many years. With the introduction of tea into England in 1660, teapots and teaspoons became popular. Silver spoons were expensive and so highly prized that it was a special tribute to newborn babies when godparents presented them with silver spoons. Hence the expression "born with a silver spoon in his mouth."

Silver is harder than gold but softer than copper. It is so pliable that it can be drawn into a thread as fine as silk. For any practical use silver must be combined with an alloy. Sterling silver is 925 parts silver and 75 parts copper. Sterling has been symbolic of quality since the 1200's. At that time merchants of the Hanseatic League in northern

Beginning with the carving fork (bottom center) and moving clockwise are the following: pie or cake serving knife, pierced pastry server, steak knife, pierced tablespoon, place fork, place knife, teaspoon, tablespoon, cocktail fork, sugar spoon, salad fork, butter knife, cream soup spoon, butter spreader, cream or sauce ladle, coffee spoon, tomato or flat server, gravy ladle, iced beverage spoon, pickle fork, place spoon, fruit spoon, cold meat fork, berry spoon, carving knife.

Germany made coins with a higher percentage of silver than the low-silver alloy coins produced in England. These high-silver coins were called *easterlings,* which the English language changed to sterling.

During our colonial period only wealthy plantation owners and sea captains could afford to own sterling silver. Pewter and tinware were more prevalent among the colonists. Robert Sanderson and John Hull produced the first silverware in America in the 1600's but their importance in silversmithing has been overshadowed by the patriot Paul Revere, originally a dentist and a coppersmith. The silver Revere bowl is a popular wedding gift today. By 1800 there were 150 silversmiths in Boston alone. Until well into the nineteenth century brides were given silver coins from which to have their flat silver made by silversmiths.

Because of the high cost of silver, chemists began to experiment with ways to produce silverware for the average person's budget. In 1742 a silversmith in Sheffield, England, was repairing a copper knife for a client, and the hot knife happened to touch a little silver. Noticing that the two metals fused, he began to experiment with fusing large sheets of thin silver to heavy sheets of copper. The fusion produced a silver surface but added to the difficulty of molding hollow ware. All exposed surfaces had to be treated by hand, which proved to be a tedious process. Sheffield silver (mainly trays, silver services, and candelabra) was always stamped with the name *Sheffield.* The Sheffield method was abandoned in 1840, at which time silverplating by electrolysis was invented. However, the factories at Sheffield still make fine cutlery. In using electrolysis, finished tableware and hollow ware (teapots, bowls, and so on) made of copper or nickel silver (a silverlike alloy of nickel, copper, and zinc) are immersed in a solution of silver cyanide and bars of silver. By controlling electric current a plating of any thickness can be deposited on the less expensive and harder metal to give a dull or glossy silver finish.

In recent years stainless-steel flatware, once associated with hospitals and cheap public restaurants, has been raised in status tremendously. Stainless steel is appropriate for all but formal table settings and is almost a "must" as a second flatware service. Stainless steel is made of a special steel alloy of iron, chrome, and nickel, which resists rust, peeling, and tarnish. Stainless-steel knife blades with hollow sterling handles have been available since the 1930's, but the formula for this kind of steel was not satisfactory for the kind of flatware a discerning consumer would accept. In the late 1950's a formula for processing shapes resembling flat silverware was discovered. Decorated stainless steel is still somewhat limited, but the simplicity of the shapes and decoration is what gives stainless-steel flatware special appeal.

Types of Flatware

The term *flatware* includes sterling silver, plated silver, and stainless steel as it is used for knives, forks, and spoons as well as for special implements for serving. Plastic knives, forks, and spoons are not discussed here.

Guidelines for Selection

The following guidelines will be helpful in buying flatware or hollow ware for family use:

☐ Buy from a reliable dealer. Prices will be comparable for established brands.

☐ Buy place settings, including a knife, fork, salad fork, and teaspoon, in multiples of four so that you will eventually have a service for eight or perhaps twelve. An extra teaspoon for each place setting will provide a teaspoon for both beverage and dessert.

☐ Buy extra pieces according to need. A sugar spoon, butter knife, pickle fork, and serving spoons are generally considered necessities. Butter spreaders, cream-soup spoons, and other pieces can be accumulated as gifts on special occasions.

Choose a pattern that will harmonize and yet not compete with your china and crystal. Plain flatware is better with fancy dishes than elaborate flatware, and vice versa. Buying flatware, dinnerware, and glassware in exactly matched patterns often produces monotony. However, colors, shapes, and surface design should be interesting coordinates.

Feel the pieces for weight, balance, and ease of handling.

Buy silver or stainless-steel hollow ware only if you expect to use it, and in the case of silver if you are willing to take the time to keep it polished.

Care of Flatware

Stainless steel needs less care than silver. It is tarnishproof and resists stains and scratches. If washed by hand, it should be rinsed in hot water and thoroughly dried to eliminate watermarks. The following points are helpful in taking care of silver:

☐ Keep sterling silver in use because this will help to retard tarnish. The minute scratches from daily use will gradually blend together and give a soft patina. Rotate your service so that all pieces will wear evenly.

☐ Wash silverware in a dishwasher only if the hollow handles of knives are firmly cemented to the blades. Moisture and heat sometimes loosen the cement. Some people prefer to hand wash and dry silverware to eliminate the possibility of watermarks.

☐ Loosen food that may adhere to a fork with a brush. Wipe off egg and mustard immediately because these substances stain very quickly. Keep salt away from the surface during storage to avoid pit marks that are very difficult to remove.

☐ Keep silver in an accessible box or drawer lined with tarnish-resistant cloth. Wrap pieces that are in less frequent use in special cloths or papers to avoid discoloration.

☐ Use a dependable silver polish when needed, and apply it with a soft sponge or cloth. Silversmiths do not recommend mass cleaning in a chemical bath. The chemicals may be harmful to the silver, and furthermore, a chemical bath removes the oxidation in the crevices that lend interest to the design.

GLASSWARE

One story concerning the discovery of glass is attributed to the Roman historian Pliny. He relates that early Phoenician merchants pulled up their ships along the sandy shores of a river in Syria, and finding no rocks upon which to rest their cooking vessels, they set blocks of niter (sodium nitrate) from their ship's wares in the fire on the sand. When the fire died down, rivulets of a molten mass remained. How much truth there is to this story, we do not know, but we do know that the basic ingredients for making glass were there—*silica* (sand), an *alkali* (sodium), and no doubt a third ingredient, *calcium oxide* (lime).

As early as 2500 B.C. the common people of Mesopotamia and Egypt used

Waterford Crystal

Etched Crystal

Crystal with Platinum Rim

Iridescent Crystal

colored glass beads. Egyptian peasants wore collars, bracelets, and anklets made of glass beads to imitate the jewel-studded flat collars, bracelets, and anklets of royalty. The Egyptians fashioned water tumblers as early as 1500 B.C. by winding hot glass rods around a sand core. They also knew how to make blown glass. In Roman times glass vessels were common, and as early as 500 A.D. stained glass windows were used in Constantinople. The Venetians are credited with the invention of colorless glass called "cristallo," from which the term *crystal* is derived. Crystal is used today to differentiate between ordinary glass and fine glass.

Venice had a monopoly on the making of glass until the end of the 1600's. After that time France, England, Spain, and Germany began to produce fine glassware. Among the names associated with glass made in the United States is that of Henry William Stiegel, a German immigrant who established several

Steuben makes wonderful little animal sculptures of solid crystal.

glassworks in Pennsylvania between 1763 and 1774. Stiegel gave America its first flint or cut glass and fine decorative glass. An earlier glassmaker, Caspar Wistar, made bottles almost exclusively.

It was not until the early 1880's that table glassware was made in America in any quantity. Until this time most table glass was imported from Ireland and England. Credit for the invention of a hand press for molding glass goes to Deming Jarves. In 1827 Jarves turned out the first pressed-glass tumbler at Sandwich on Cape Cod, Massachusetts. Men who made a living blowing glass threatened Jarves' life, but the threat was short-lived because the market proved to be large enough for both blown and pressed glass. The original formula for Sandwich glass has been lost; thus Sandwich glass made between 1827 and 1888 is highly prized by collectors.

Venetian glass has been highly admired for centuries because of its delicacy, interesting coloring, and unusual shapes. Ireland is famous for Waterford glass; England, for Bristol; and France, for Lalique. Colorful Scandinavian glass, especially Orrefors, is popular in modern decoration. Among well-known manufacturers of table glass in America are Libby, Fostoria, Duncan, and Hershey. Many museums have collections of American Stiegel and Steuben glass.

Types of Glassware

Many different types of glassware are produced by blowing, by pressing, and by surface decoration, some of which are described:

☐ *Crystal* is a term applied to fine clear (uncolored) glassware. When tapped, crystal rings like a tiny bell. In Europe the amount of lead in the molten mixture determines whether or not the term *crystal* can be used. *Lead* improves the quality of the glass. *Lime* is used in the manufacture of less expensive glass, and as a rule in pressed glass only.

☐ *Frosted* glass is produced by sandblasting to give a finish resembling frost.

☐ *Bubble* glass is made by forcing air bubbles into molten glass.

☐ *Hobnail* glass is made by pressing small bumps evenly over the surface.

☐ *Cameo* glass is made by fusing two layers of contrasting colored glass together and incising a design through the top layer.

☐ *Cut crystal* is made by cutting a design into glass with a rapidly revolving abrasive wheel. The amateur may not be able to distinguish between cut crystal and pressed glass which has been made to resemble it. Pressed glass is less clear and the "cut edges" are somewhat rounded.

☐ *Etched crystal* is made by the same method artists use for making metal plates for etchings. The background of the glass is covered with a waxy substance, and a design is cut through the wax. When immersed in an acid bath, only the cut portions are eaten away, after which the wax is dissolved and the glass is washed and polished.

☐ *Painted crystal* is produced by applying gold or platinum and then firing the metal until it is fused into the glass. (Glass may also be painted with enamels.)

☐ *Sculptured glass* is produced by masking out all portions of the glass except that for the design and then blowing an abrasive under pressure against the exposed sections.

☐ *Milk glass* is an opaque white glass that is made by adding chemicals to produce a milky effect.

☐ *Iridescent* glass is a rainbow-colored glass made by the application of silver or bismuth.

Guidelines for Selecting Glassware

Many people like to use ordinary glasses and glass plates for every day and keep a good set for special occasions. If you are buying good glass, buy familiar brands from an established merchant. In addition, follow these guidelines:

☐ Buy glassware to harmonize in texture and form with your dishes and flatware. Delicate crystal harmonizes with fine china and sterling silver; and bubble or hobnail glass, with pottery and plated-silver flatware or stainless steel.

☐ Buy glassware in place settings the same as china. A place setting consists of a goblet or tumbler for water, a sherbet glass, a dessert-salad plate, and usually glasses for iced beverages and fruit juices.

☐ To test for quality (either blown or pressed glass), tap the edge and listen for a bell-like sound.

☐ Hold the glass to the light and look for imperfections, such as raised places, bubbles, or shadows. Feel the top and lower edges to detect uneven spots.

☐ If the surface is decorated, look for clear-cut edges around the design.

☐ Decide whether or not you want water glasses and sherbet dishes with stems or with flat bases. Stemware is very pretty, but is more vulnerable to breakage.

Care of Glassware

The following points should be helpful in taking care of glassware:

☐ If you hand wash glass, place a rubber or cloth pad in the sink and on the drainboard. Wash glassware in clean, moderately hot soapy water before washing ordinary dishes. Rinse with hot water, and dry with a lintless towel.

□ Never place ice-cold glasses in hot water. Rinse them first with lukewarm water.

□ If you use an automatic dishwasher, rest the glasses where they will not fall over. Be extra careful in stacking stemware. Heavy-coated dishwasher racks are kinder to glassware than hard uncoated ones.

□ Avoid using an overdose of detergent because excessive detergent may make glassware cloudy. It is safer to wash glasses that have a metallic decoration by hand.

□ Note the hardness of the water if you use an automatic dishwasher. Hard water leaves a film that dishwasher heat may bake on. A weak vinegar or lemon solution will dissolve a film or remove stains if they have not been on too long.

□ Rinse milk or iced coffee served with cream from glasses soon after use to avoid cloudy marks.

□ Wash bowls and vases used for flowers frequently, and keep them free of odor and stains with a diluted chlorine rinse.

□ Avoid prying tumblers apart if they are stuck. Pour cold water into the inner glass to contract it, and rest the outer glass in lukewarm water for a few minutes.

□ Clean cut glass with a soft brush and a very weak ammonia solution.

□ Never stack glasses inside each other. Store them with the rim up. Store low glassware in front of high glassware.

SUMMARY

After the fall of the Roman Empire, Europeans were slow to experience the refinements of living in comparison with people of the Byzantine Empire. China, fine silverware, and crystal found their way into Europe from Constantinople through the ports of Italy and the other crossroads of European trade. England was the last European country to become aware of the fine art of dining.

The art of making fine porcelain began in China. The importation of tea, coffee, and cocoa beans accompanied the rise of a wealthy merchant class in Europe and stimulated the making of china. Not everyone can afford fine china today, and many people who can afford it may prefer more casual dinnerware, such as earthenware, stoneware, or pottery. Plastic dishes often fill the need for an everyday dinner service.

Silverware has always appealed to the bride-to-be, who usually chooses her pattern with a great deal of thought. However, stainless steel is fast becoming popular. Styles are attractive, the finish is appealing, and maintenance is easy.

A knowledge of glassmaking probably goes back as far as the Pyramids, but fine crystal for the table is a later development. Glass tableware was owned only by royalty and the wealthy until an inexpensive means of producing glass was developed in the latter part of the nineteenth century. Today most families can afford attractive glassware in a wide choice of textures.

All dinnerware—dishes, flatware, and glassware—is generally bought in place settings, with a goal of being able to serve eight or twelve people. It is wise to buy good dinnerware under familiar brand names and from reliable dealers. Proper care is as important as wise selection.

THINGS TO THINK ABOUT AND TO DO

1. Give some reasons why it may be important to know something about past social customs in a study of table manners and service.

2. On a European map trace the early trade routes from Constantinople (Istanbul, Turkey) through Venice, Florence, Augsburg, and Nuremberg. Trace the route of the Moors along the coast of Africa to Spain.

3. Review the history of the Crusades, and indicate their importance to the social and economic progress of Europe.

4. Describe the following: (1) life in Italy during the time when Marco Polo returned from Cathay, or China; (2) life in Spain at the height of the Moorish occupation; (3) life in France during the period of Louis XIV; (4) life in Georgian England. Report to the class on these assignments and show slides, if possible, or other illustrations.

5. How did the term *etiquette* originate?

6. How did the term *sterling* originate? Relate Pliny's story of the origin of glass. Why do cups have handles?

7. Distinguish between traditional china (porcelain) and bone china and between semivitreous china (earthenware) and stoneware.

8. Give five important points to consider in (1) choosing dishes and (2) caring for dishes.

9. Show a film on the development of stainless-steel flatware.

10. Display illustrations of a number of patterns of flatware from several manufacturers. The silver department in a local store may be a good source for illustrations. Display as many actual examples of the patterns as possible.

11. Name some famous makes of dishes, flatware, and glassware at different price levels. Prepare an exhibit of these kinds and types if possible.

12. Distinguish between crystal, cut glass, and pressed glass. Show examples of each.

13. List five points to consider in (1) selecting glassware and (2) caring for glassware.

14. Plan a moderate-priced tableware ensemble of four place settings, indicating brands, patterns, and price. Tell why you chose each pattern and why you think each goes well with the other.

Individual candles and embroidered linen place mats make this a distinctive setting for a formal dinner.

chapter twenty-four

FURNITURE AND SLEEP EQUIPMENT

Furniture represents about two thirds of the total home-furnishings budget. The other one third usually goes into carpeting, household textiles, dinnerware, and laborsaving equipment. It is seldom advisable for young people to buy all new furniture at one time, unless they have had more than the average amount of experience or have an income that will permit them to afford to make mistakes. It can be a challenge as well as a satisfaction to furnish a first apartment with discards from older relatives, with refinished furniture from an auction sale, or with restyled furniture from a secondhand shop. Money can also be saved by painting, staining and varnishing, or antiquing unfinished pieces. The demand for rental furniture has increased with increasing physical mobility, especially among unmarried workers and junior executives, who make up the prime upward mobility group.

Whether you buy new or used furniture, you will be able to save time and money if you: (1) become familiar with chair, sofa, and table shapes as well as period styles (discussed in Chapter Fifteen), (2) know woods and methods of decorating furniture, (3) understand construction methods and materials used in wood and upholstered furniture, (4) put into practice certain basic rules in shopping for furniture.

Sleep equipment, from springs and mattresses to studio couches and sofa beds, is an important segment of the home-furnishings industry. The proper sleep equipment is important to one's wellbeing inasmuch as one spends about one third of each day in bed. Studies on bed space requirements have been made in the bedding industry and followed up by advertising to encourage consumers to consider more adequate sleeping space. The newer extra width beds, especially queen size beds, are gradually outselling traditional double beds. Mattresses not only come in a choice of foam rubber or innerspring, but also in varying degrees of firmness. Some people prefer a fairly soft mattress whereas others like a firm one. Sleep equipment—springs, mattresses, mattress covers, and pillows—needs regular care.

GUIDELINES FOR STUDY

GENERAL IDEAS
TO CONSIDER

1. Dual-purpose furniture and furniture with storage space are versatile and functional.
2. Imagination plus ability is an important factor in restyling, refinishing, and improvising furniture.
3. A background of consumer information is necessary in buying furniture if it is to give maximum satisfaction.
4. The choice of furniture woods is influenced by the decorating theme, the character of the room, and personal preferences.
5. The surface treatment given furniture can produce many different effects.
6. The durability of wood furniture will depend upon the kind of wood, the adhesives, the kind of joints, and the surface finish used.
7. The durability of upholstered furniture will depend upon the construction of the framework, the webbing, the springs, the filling materials, and the upholstery used.
8. Systematic care will extend the life of all furniture and add to the enjoyment of it.

WORDS AND TERMS
TO KNOW

atomic wood
bouclé
buffet
camphorated oil
caning
coil springs
console table
corner block
deciduous
dovetailed joint
foam latex
frieze
fruitwood
gumwood
hardwood
inlay
kiln dried

king-size bed
lacquer
laminated
matelassé
mortise-and-tenon joint
polyurethane foam
queen-size bed
rush seat
sectional furniture
softwood
stretcher
studio couch
synthetic wood
veneer
vinyl
zigzag springs

BASIC FURNITURE NEEDS

The following items are considered basic for two persons living in a two-room apartment (not including kitchen or bath):

Living-Dining Area

Sofa or bed sofa or studio bed with back-board

Extendible console table or drop-leaf table for dining and study

Long, low chest for linen storage

Pair of end tables with drawers (or commodes) or a drawer and shelf

Low magazine or coffee table (if space permits)

One lounge or wing-type chair

Two occasional or pull-up chairs with arms[1]

Two straight chairs for writing at a table and for dining[1]

Bookcase or wall-storage unit

Sleeping Area

Springs and mattress (also headboard or full bed if money permits)

Long chest or twin chests or dresser and chest

Two bedside tables, preferably with drawers

Mirror

Two straight chairs[1]

MONEY- AND SPACE-SAVING IDEAS

Whether you marry or secure a job soon after completing your education, you will probably be interested in furnishing an apartment of your own. Some of you may be fortunate enough to acquire a few pieces of furniture from relatives or friends. If you are a do-it-yourselfer with imagination, ability, and

---

1. A group of six dining room chairs—two with arms—will provide two pull-up chairs and two straight chairs for the living area and also two straight chairs for the bedroom.

perseverance, there are many things you can do to stretch your furniture budget and achieve an interesting effect. However, if you dislike working with your hands and your income is limited, you will have to be satisfied with second-hand furniture as it is, or perhaps rent furniture if rental services are available. If you are buying new furniture for an efficiency or a two- or three-room apartment (living-dining area, bedroom, and kitchen), storage space and versatility are important.

Do-It-Yourself Furniture

In the do-it-yourself category, there are four choices: (1) restyling or restoring used furniture, (2) finishing unfinished furniture, (3) assembling precut packaged units, and (4) making improvised furniture from discarded materials.

RESTYLING AND RESTORING. Quite often secondhand furniture shops are full of discarded dining tables, sideboards, china closets, bed frames, dressers, dressing tables, and chiffoniers. If you have work space, a few simple power tools, and time and patience, these seemingly obsolete but not-yet-antique pieces can have a face-lifting that will transform them completely.

FINISHING UNPAINTED FURNITURE. There are many grades of unpainted furniture. When you choose unpainted furniture, compare prices and construction with similar finished furniture to make sure that your time and effort, plus the cost of materials, will produce the results you want. Under experienced hands many pieces of unfinished furniture can be finished to look like high-quality ready-finished pieces. They can be stained, shellacked, and varnished; stained and waxed; painted, lacquered, or antiqued.

ASSEMBLING PRECUT FURNITURE.
This kind of furniture is sometimes advertised as "workshop furniture." A kit contains the units to be put together, the necessary screws, the blocks, and so forth as well as a complete set of directions for assembling the parts and finishing the piece. If this kind of work interests you, look among the advertisements in magazines related to home furnishing or to woodworking for outlets near you. Freight costs from distant points may make the total cost rather high. Experiment with simple projects first.

IMPROVISED FURNITURE. The person with imagination, time, interest, and ability can make a number of pieces of furniture fairly quickly from discarded building materials and odds and ends. For example, a dining, coffee, or study table can be made from a flush door by attaching a set of legs from a mill-supply store. A modern bench can also be made from a flush door by having the width cut down at a lumber mill and attaching a set of legs. With an oblong cushion or with two square ones made of foam latex or polyurethane suitably slipcovered, the bench will fit nicely into a contemporary decorating scheme.

Bookcases can be made from boards and ordinary bricks or glass bricks. If ordinary bricks are used, several should be cemented together and painted with a latex paint to form rests for the boards. Glass bricks can be stacked without cementing. Wood trays can be fastened to campstools to make coffee tables. These are only a few ideas for converting discards into usable furniture for temporary use.

Multipurpose Furniture

When the furniture budget is limited, versatile furniture will help to stretch the home-furnishings dollar. A convertible sofa or a studio-type bed is usually a "must" in an efficiency apartment. It is also useful in a one-bedroom apartment for overnight guests. Styling has made the bed sofa almost identical with the traditional sofa in appearance. A studio couch with a storage unit in a backboard not only serves as a bed or a sofa but provides storage as well. Either a bed sofa or a studio couch is useful in a studio bedroom, a study, or a recreation room, especially during the expanding period in the family life cycle. Before buying either of these items, make sure that they are comfortable to sit on and to sleep on and that you can operate them with ease.

Commodes, or end tables with two or more drawers, provide far more storage space than end tables or nightstands with no drawers or only one drawer.

Dining tables need not take up floor space in a small apartment living room. A drop-leaf or extendible console table is compact when not in use for dining. Either type will fit into a hall or almost any room in the house during the expanding period in the family life cycle when a more permanent dining table may be necessary or desirable.

A nest of tables is also useful. You can distribute them to eat on in the living room when you serve beverages and snacks or buffet suppers.

A chest-on-chest or twin chests placed side by side in a living area or bedroom give maximum storage space within a minimum of floor space.

A number of furniture makers are producing sectional furniture. Sectional cabinets, bookcases, chests, desks, and so on are available in many sizes and finishes. These may be used as separate

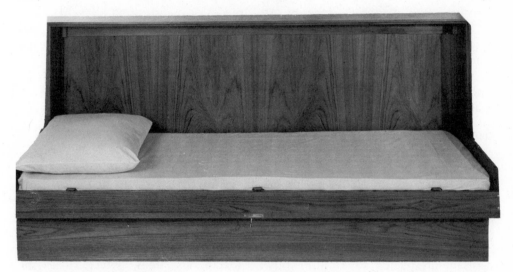

This teak wood convertible bed-chest is of Scandinavian design. Closed, it can serve as a buffet or shelf; opened, it can provide extra seating space or a comfortable guest bed.

pieces or assembled into a continuous unit, according to wall space.

Furniture Rental

Furnishings for home rental are available in a number of large cities. For many years it has been possible to rent pictures and art objects from a museum and special furniture for hospital care from rental outlets for use at home. The rental market for home furnishings is likely to increase with increasing family mobility and rising costs of moving. Already there are enough furniture-rental outlets to justify forming a trade association—The National Furniture Rental Association. A number of furniture manufacturers have entered the field, renting furniture to apartment owners as well as to individuals. Some agencies include decorator services. Surveys indicate that the post-World War II population explosion will bring about the formation of new households at an increasingly rapid rate until 1975. Manufacturers may find it difficult to keep up with the demand for new furniture. Young potential executives may be even more mobile than at present and even less interested in accumulating furniture until they are more permanently settled.

Furniture may be rented on an individual-piece basis or as a packaged unit, which includes furniture, rugs, draperies, appliances, dishes, and accessories. This latter arrangement appeals to young couples or families in temporary locations, those not experienced enough to invest a lot of money in furniture, and those who dislike the details of packing household goods and moving them.

If you are interested in renting home furnishings, consult the yellow pages of your telephone directory for possible services. Find out the monthly costs, and add the rental to your regular rent. Then compare this figure with furnished apartments for rent. As in renting an apartment, you will probably have to rent furniture on a yearly basis and make a deposit for possible damage. For economic reasons, rental furniture appeals far more to apartment renters than to home renters.

SHOPPING SUGGESTIONS

If you are systematic about planning a shopping trip, you will come home less tired and better satisfied. Here are some helpful suggestions for furniture shopping:

□ Study magazine and newspaper advertisements related to furniture buying and become familiar with the merchandise on hand as well as the outlets available.

□ Consider making major purchases at traditional furniture sales, which usually occur in February and in August.

□ Become familiar with nationally advertised brands and reliable dealers.

□ Study labels and guarantees, and learn to ask pertinent questions.

□ Consider carrying charges, which can be a minimum of 18 percent annually, and include these costs in the purchase price.

□ Make a sketch of your room on one-fourth inch graph paper, and indicate where you want to use new furniture. Indicate color scheme and decorating theme. Take this information with you. Measure furniture, and check measurements against available space.

□ Be sure you understand how to judge quality in furniture if you attend "warehouse" or "end-of-season" sales

because sales furniture is not returnable.

□ When you find something you like, you may want to shop around and compare the prices of comparable pieces or brands.

□ Make a long-range decorating plan; project your purchases over several years.

□ Become familiar with various types of sofas, chairs, and tables. This should help you to make suitable purchases.

POPULAR FURNITURE WOODS AND SIMULATED WOODS

Hardwoods and Softwoods

Furniture woods are grouped under two classifications—*nonporous softwoods,* including pine, spruce, fir, and redwoods, and *porous hardwoods* (deciduous trees, which lose their leaves), including walnut, mahogany, oak, gum, maple, birch, beech, and cherry and other fruitwoods.

Pine is frequently used in Early American and Provincial furniture. *Oak* is popular in early English or Jacobean styles; *walnut* and *mahogany,* in eighteenth-century reproductions; and the *fruitwoods,* in Provincial and Early American furniture. *Gumwood* is less expensive than other hardwoods, and it can be stained to resemble walnut, mahogany, or any more expensive wood. You can distinguish gumwood from the more expensive hardwoods because it has finer pores and it dents more readily than walnut or mahogany. When stained and finished, it lacks the richness of the more highly prized hardwoods. Gumwood is frequently used for the sides and backs and the insides of drawers in chests, tables with drawers, and so on (case goods), to reduce cost. Gumwood comes in attractive furniture designs, and many people do not object to nicely stained and well-finished gumwood.

Veneers, Inlays, Lacquers

The fact that a piece of furniture is advertised as *solid* wood does not make it superior to *veneered* wood. Before veneering came into common use among eighteenth-century cabinet-makers, a great deal of carving was used. Veneered surfaces cannot be carved. When the great furniture makers of Georgian England began to design furniture for manor houses rather than for palaces, lighter designs came into being along with new methods of decoration—veneering, inlay, and lacquer. A veneer is made of several fine layers of wood (three, five, or seven) bonded together and then cemented to solid wood. The top layer has a beautiful grain. Veneering is used to improve the appearance as well as the strength of furniture. A veneer may be applied to a wood surface as a continuous piece or in sections to form a stylized pattern. The direction in which a veneer is cut (crosswise, lengthwise, or at the crotch) will determine the character of the surface design. (See the illustration on this page.) A veneer may be poorly cemented on cheap furniture and tend to buckle with changes in temperature and moisture. However, as a rule, a firmly applied veneer will not warp. *Inlays* of contrasting or exotic woods, of metals, or of mother-of-pearl can be set into either veneered or solid surfaces. *Lacquering,* or a type of painting with a smooth, hard surface, became popular with the importation of Chinese lacquered furniture. Red and black are popular lacquer colors.

Bleached Wood

Some woods, such as maple, birch, and light oak, are naturally light. Other more exotic light-colored woods are satinwood, myrtle, and holly. Walnut and mahogany can be artificially bleached to a light blond color. Some people prefer bleached dark woods to naturally blond woods because of the grain. Bleached woods darken slightly with age.

Laminated Plastics

Plastic veneers, ingrained to reproduce any wood grain, are cemented to solid wood for table, desk, and chest tops in much the same way that plastic sheets are cemented to kitchen counters. The resulting surface is resistant to dents, scratches, water spots, and stains. This durable finish is popular with families where there are small children as well as in hotels, motels, hospitals, and offices.

Atomic Wood

An increasing demand for furniture and a decreasing supply of many natural

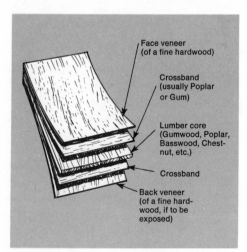

Face veneer
(of a fine hardwood)

Crossband
(usually Poplar
or Gum)

Lumber core
(Gumwood, Poplar,
Basswood, Chest-
nut, etc.)

Crossband

Back veneer
(of a fine hard-
wood, if to be
exposed)

Veneered wood.

furniture woods have stimulated research related to new materials.

Furniture has been produced from plastics for many years, but plastics have not been a substitute for wood. A new kind of wood, currently referred to as *atomic wood,* has been the result of government-sponsored research at the University of West Virginia. In this research process, softwoods are placed in a vacuum to draw out air and moisture, after which they are saturated with a liquid chemical and bombarded with nuclear radiation. The liquid chemical fills in the pores and is hardened by the radiation, thus giving the wood many times its original strength. Atomic wood can be bent easily; it has increased resistance to abrasion, stains, cigarette burns, and warping; and it takes a beautiful finish.

Furniture producers are finding other methods for treating wood surfaces to make them as durable as laminated wood-grain plastics. *Completely synthetic wood* is also available; it may be finished and varnished in the same way as natural wood. Areas can be molded to look like carving. True carving, like cut glass, is done by hand. Synthetic wood can be molded to resemble carving in much the same way that glass is molded or pressed to resemble cut glass. This permits the mass production of "carved" wood furniture.

Furniture Labeling

The furniture industry, in cooperation with the Federal Trade Commission, has formulated trade-practice rules to protect the consumer. The regulations apply to sofas, chairs, and case goods but not to bedding equipment, television sets, radios, or laborsaving equipment. The rules apply to statements which can be made on labels and in advertising as to the kind of wood used in furniture. The following terms are examples of acceptable labeling:

□ *Solid walnut* or *solid mahogany* indicates that all exposed parts are made of the wood named.

□ *Cherry-finished plastic* indicates a plastic, not a wood, piece of furniture.

□ *Mahogany-finished hardboard* does not indicate solid wood but a wood substitute.

□ *Veneered* means that a fine layer of wood is cemented to hardwood or to softwood.

□ *Laminated* indicates that layers of one or two materials are cemented together.

□ *Danish walnut* is not walnut but hackberry, a variety of elm.

□ *Vinyl* indicates that a material is not genuine leather, and all vinyl must be so labeled.

□ *Fiber content* and percentages of each fiber in the upholstery and in the hidden areas must be indicated. A typical label reads: "All new material consisting of all new blended cotton felt 75%, latex rubberized hair (hog) 25%, cushions 100% latex foam."

CONSTRUCTION OF WOOD FURNITURE

For aesthetic reasons most of the construction of furniture is hidden. If all joints, bracing, and screws were visible, furniture would lose its eye appeal. Nevertheless, it is possible to judge construction to a degree without turning a large piece upside down or tearing any piece apart. If a chair seems weak when you sit on it, the legs may not all be even or well braced. If a chest of drawers rocks (does not stand evenly), if the drawers stick when opened and closed, or if the space between the edges of the drawer and the opening is irregular, this item will not be a good buy. When you buy nationally advertised brands, prices over the country or sections of the country will be similar because of fair trade practices. Often standard brands are specially priced during periodic furniture sales. Nationally advertised products usually carry a guarantee related to performance under recommended care, and you have recourse to the manufacturer as well as to the merchant.

If you are considering unfamiliar brands of furniture, avoid bait sales, such as *fire sale, forced to vacate, floor samples, discontinued merchandise,* and so on, which some merchants advertise to stimulate business and attract new customers. If you are disappointed in your purchase, there will not be much you can do about it. Although the Federal Trade Commission does a great deal to protect the consumer, many merchants find ways to evade good practices. The following discussion should help you to be a better judge of furniture.

Construction techniques will differ among different producers, but certain kinds of joints and methods of support in assembling chairs and case goods are commonly used by all manufacturers of good furniture.

Chairs

Dining room and occasional living room chairs have seats about 18 inches from the floor in front, slanting down slightly at the rear. Dining room chairs are 15 or 16 inches deep, and arm chairs with padded seats are 18 to 20 inches deep. A chair back should extend at least 17 inches above the seat to support the shoulder. The chair back should be contoured so as to be comfortable when a person leans back.

Chairs may be all wood or wood with rush, cane, or upholstered seats. Cane and rush seats require more frequent replacement than wood seats. Box frames with all-wood seats or replaceable upholstered seats are more durable and easier to maintain. Upholstered seats usually have a padded plywood base that can be easily removed from the box frame for re-covering.

Backs of chairs take numerous designs, as we observed in our study of furniture design. Among the most popular backs are ladder, spindle, splat, and other conventionalized art forms. Whatever the shape of the chair back, it must be rigid enough to withstand hard use because chairs are usually picked up by the arms or back. Legs may or may not have stretchers for support, but they should be braced with corner blocks or metal bracing.

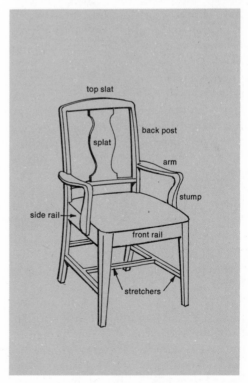

Construction of a box-seat chair.

Case Goods

Case goods is a term used by the trade to mean chests, tables, desks, bookcases, dressers, serving tables, and buffets. Table-leg and table-top construction is similar to chair-leg and seat construction. Table legs may or may not have stretchers.

Chests, buffets, and desks should first of all stand firmly. Areas to examine are these:

EXPOSED SURFACES.   The sides and front should have the same grain and finish. If the back is seen (for instance, the back of a desk), it should also match other exposed surfaces. The label will show the kind of wood used.

UNEXPOSED SURFACES.   Plywood is commonly used for backs and undersides. In better furniture the back will be set into the sides, glued, and then screwed in place. The surface will also be stained and rubbed smooth. In inexpensive furniture the backs may be flush with the sides and nailed in place.

DRAWERS.   In better furniture, drawers will have dovetailed joints (see the illustration on this page) at the front and usually at the back. Sometimes the drawer will have a lap-butt joint at the back. In most medium- and high-priced furniture, there will be a dust panel under the drawer. This gives added strength and helps to keep out excess dust. If a drawer is to slide easily, it must have a center runner or two side runners. Inexpensive furniture has few of these desirable features.

HINGED PARTS.   Doors should be flush with the framing and firm enough to open and close with no pressure; the space around the sides should be even and airtight. Hinges should be firm. Table leaves should have overlapping grooves to make them firm and flush with the table when they are raised into place. Hardware for supporting leaves should be fitted properly and tightly.

PULLS, KNOBS, AND HANDLES. Contemporary designs in case goods may omit pulls, knobs, and handles, and use a grooved lower panel to pull out drawers. If pulls, knobs, or handles are used, they should be spaced evenly for good balance in operation. The size, shape, and texture should be in harmony with the piece of furniture. They should be well attached so as not to pull off easily.

JOININGS AND SUPPORTS. The following joints and supports are characteristic of well-made furniture: mortise and tenon, dowel, dovetail, tongue and groove, and screwed-in corner blocks. (Metal braces are sometimes used.) Some of these features are illustrated on page 410.

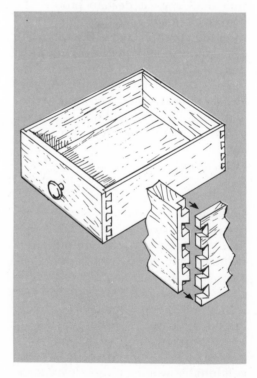

A drawer with dovetailed joints.

CONSTRUCTION OF UPHOLSTERED FURNITURE

Upholstered furniture consists of the wood framework, the interlaced webbing that is stretched over the seat and back frames, the springs, the padding or cushioning product, and the upholstery. The unexposed wood framework is as important in the construction of upholstered furniture as the webbing, springs, padding, and type of material used in the cushions. Some large stores have upholstered chairs with one side cut away to expose the construction.

Framework

The framework of the chair should be made of *kiln-dried* hardwood to prevent warping and to keep screws or tacks from coming loose. Gumwood is the most frequently used hardwood for this purpose. Softwoods, such as pine and poplar, may be used in less expensive furniture. All corners should be braced with screwed-in corner blocks to make the chair rigid. In less expensive furniture glued blocks may be used, which may or may not be nailed, instead of screwed. Corner blocks are attached on the under side of the chair.

Springs

Without some kind of springs, sofas, chairs, and mattresses would be quite rigid. *Coil springs* are used in heavy sofas and chairs with deep seats. Coil count, or the number of spring coils per chair or sofa, is not as important as the quality of springs and the way they are distributed for comfort. However, all coil springs must be firmly tied with twine to the webbing where the webs crisscross, and then securely knotted. This is so that the springs will act in unison and not interlock. A layer of burlap is stretched over the coils. Then a padding layer of felted cotton moss and hair, or foam latex (rubber), or polyurethane foam is placed over the burlap, and a closely woven fabric is stretched over the top. Excelsior is used as padding in cheaper furniture. In more expensive construction the springs are sewed to the burlap as well as to the webbing.

The trend toward lighter furniture forms led to the production of a less bulky spring construction that is popular at all price levels. This is a *convoluted-* or *zigzag-type spring*, which is used in multiple strips. Both coil springs and flat zigzag springs should be made of tempered carbon steel for maximum support, resilience, and comfort.

Cushions

Sofas with loose seat cushions may have one long cushion or two or three shorter ones. Some people prefer a completely upholstered back with little if any tufting because such a back is easier to clean and less expensive to slipcover or reupholster. Other people prefer either loose or semiattached cushions at the back. If back cushions are loose, they will look better and wear longer if they can be reversed in all directions, not only from side to side. Semiattached cushions fastened to the back tend to sag after use.

Coil springs, foam latex, polyurethane foam, down, feathers, and hair are used for cushions. In spring construction, coils are tied in place and covered with cotton felt or a hair mixture (excelsior is used in cheaper makes), or a layer of foam latex or polyurethane foam may be added. An entire pillow made of foam latex or polyurethane foam may have a trimmer and tighter styling than springs. Of the two foam

CONSTRUCTION FEATURES OF FURNITURE

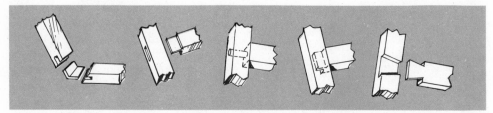

MORTISE AND TENON JOINTS: Loose tenon or feather joint; Common mortise and tenon; Round or peg tenon; Blind housed tenon; Dovetail half-lap joint.

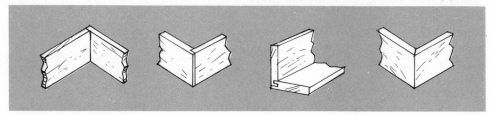

CORNER JOINTS: Plain corner butt; Lap butt; Lock joint; Plain mitre joint.

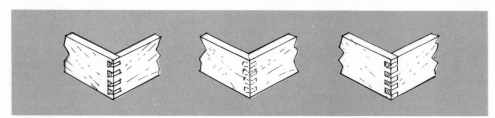

DOVETAIL JOINTS: Open dovetail; Secret or concealed dovetail; Notched.

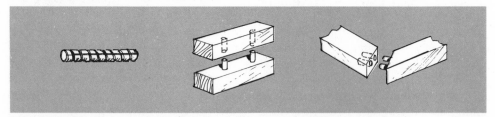

DOWEL JOINTS: Grooved dowel; Glue dowel; Corner or corresponding dowel.

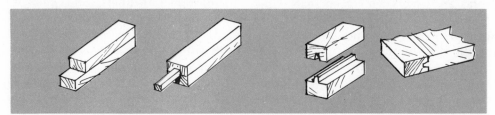

GLUE JOINTS: Plain glue or rub joint; loose-tongue, Double-groove joint, and tongue and groove.

types, latex is heavier and more likely to stay in place than polyurethane. Spring cushions are fabric covered before being upholstered, but foam cushions seldom have a cover under the upholstery. Upholstery on loose cushions is usually held in place with zippers. The cover on foam cushions, especially foam latex, has to be loosened occasionally because heat and pressure cause the cover to crawl and stick somewhat to the foam latex.

The most expensive filling for loose cushions is down. Next is a mixture of down and feathers. Hair (horse, cattle, hog) is sometimes rubber coated and used for filling. Polyester fibers are also used for a fluff pillow. The fill has a foam-rubber core covered with tiny polyester fibers. This gives a fluffed-up appearance without the need for constant fluffing, as with down.

Upholstery

Nylon and wool fabrics with a firm weave are snag and abrasion resistant, and easy to clean. Cotton, or cotton blended with polyester, acrylic, or rayon fibers, if firmly woven and treated to resist spots, stains, and grease, will also wear well. Upholstery fabrics made of these fibers without a soil-resistant finish are difficult to clean because soil, stains, and grease penetrate the fibers. It is possible to apply soil-resistant sprays to these fabrics at home if directions are carefully followed.

Upholstery materials should have a firm, smooth surface or a short pile. Some bouclés, monk's cloth, and similar materials that tend to snag are not recommended. Pile fabrics include velveteen, frieze, velvet, and bouclé. Smooth firmly woven fabrics include damask, brocade, matelassé, tapestry, chintz, needlepoint, cretonne, sailcloth, satin, and twill.

Plastic materials may be had to imitate almost any fabric or leather surface. These coverings appeal to families with growing children, hotel and motel owners, and office managers. Vinyls come in all grades, but a vinyl with a stretch back laminated to it is more attractive and more durable than ordinary vinyl.

Leather is expensive, and it will crack or rot if not well cared for. It is used more frequently in expensively furnished offices and home libraries.

Care of Furniture

Furniture needs protection from heat and sunlight, dirt, water, grease, and stains. The following practices will help keep furniture in good condition:

□ Keep dirt out of the house by keeping steps and entrances swept and a foot rug at the door, and by keeping windows and doors closed on windy days.

□ Avoid letting bright sunlight strike furniture because it will fade upholstered furniture and mar the surface of wood furniture.

□ Avoid using water on wood furniture unless you use a recommended detergent (not soap) solution and a damp cloth for cleaning and rinsing. Wipe dry with a chamois or soft cloth.

□ Clean with a good furniture wax or polish, and follow directions carefully. Avoid using furniture polish or wax over a heavy coat of wax. Remove wax first. Read and follow directions on the remover bottle. Rub in the direction of the grain.

□ When buying upholstered furniture, have the dealer include covers for the backs and arms of chairs and the arms of sofas to protect these areas from dirty and oily hands and hair.

□ Use special vacuum-cleaner attachments for cleaning surfaces and crevices. The amount of dirt in the air will determine frequency of cleaning. A semiweekly light brushing and bi-weekly cleaning with the vacuum attachment will ordinarily keep dirt from accumulating on the surface of the furniture.

☐ Clean evenly soiled fabrics with a foam cleaner used according to directions. Avoid having the fabric absorb too much soil before cleaning.

☐ Have badly soiled upholstered furniture cleaned professionally.

☐ Remove grease spots with a grease solvent. Scrape off excess chewing gum, and then use a grease solvent. Work from the outside in, and keep rubbing the outer edges lightly to avoid a ring.

☐ Remove blood by cold and then lukewarm water, adding a detergent if necessary. Avoid soaking the fabric. Rub lightly with a soft towel until almost dry.

☐ Avoid using regular furniture polishes or waxes on marble, leather, vinyl, or glass, unless certain ones are mentioned in the directions given for the care of these surfaces.

☐ Use treated dustcloths for daily cleaning, and fold back the soiled side as you work. Never shake a dustcloth in the room where you are dusting. If you do not use a treated cloth, use a lintless, soft, porous one, or the dusting attachment on a vacuum cleaner.

☐ Brush carved surfaces with a soft brush to remove dust, or clean by vacuuming.

☐ Eradicate minor scratches by first removing any wax finish with a remover preparation recommended for the purpose. Rub medium-deep scratches with a commercial coloring stick or compound to match the wood. A tiny bit of shoe polish of the right color will often camouflage a scratch. If scratches are minute, a cut nutmeat will act as a stain. Rub off all excess stain, and polish the surface.

☐ Have a professional refinisher restore deep marks made from sharp objects or burns.

☐ Remove white marks made by perfume, alcohol, or a wet glass by rubbing very lightly with camphorated oil. Wipe the surface with a damp cloth and a mild detergent and then with a damp cloth wrung out of clear water. Rub dry immediately, and polish. Some white spots can be removed by rubbing them with cigarette ash or rottenstone combined with either linseed or salad oil.

SPRINGS, MATTRESSES, PILLOWS

If you have to skimp on other home furnishings to buy a good set of springs and a good mattress, do so. A satisfactory night's rest is essential to comfort, health, and a good disposition. Buy a familiar brand of the best quality you can afford. (You can at least report any dissatisfaction to the manufacturer of the brand.) Buy a mattress-and-springs combination that is large enough for comfort. The National Association of Bedding Manufacturers recommends that a bed be 6 to 10 inches longer than the occupant and provide a width of 38 inches for each person. A traditional double bed provides only 27 inches for each occupant. About 85 percent of body weight is distributed between the shoulders and the hips, so that a mattress without adequate support will sag in the center and cause backache. Queen-size double beds and extra-length single beds are rapidly outselling the traditional double and single beds. (See Chapter Twenty-two, page 372, for mattress and bedding sizes.)

Springs

A bed needs bedsprings as well as a mattress, even though the mattress is the box-spring type. There are three types of bedsprings: *covered and padded coil springs, uncovered coil springs,* and *flat springs.* The covered and uncovered coil springs give 4 or 5 inches more height to the bed than flat springs. Flat springs cost much less. They tend to sag under heavy weight, but they are quite satisfactory for children. Uncovered box springs of high quality are comfortable, but they collect dust, and if there are rough edges, sheet corners will catch and tear. Covered box springs are the best investment if you can afford them. In either type, a double-deck coil will give greater support and resilience than a single-deck coil.

Mattress

Under government bedding label regulations, sleep products that have been uncrated or had labels removed cannot be returned. Thus it is important to make sure of your purchases before using them.

Mattress types available are *innerspring* and *foam* in either foam latex or polyurethane foam. Felt and hair mattresses, once very popular, are almost off the market.

Before you buy any mattress, check the following: (1) stretch out on it and make sure it will be comfortable and give adequate support, and (2) make sure a foam mattress is deep enough and heavy enough to keep sheets in place—especially the polyurethane type.

INNERSPRING MATTRESSES. Mattresses with smooth surfaces have replaced the old-fashioned tufted mattresses. A padding of cotton felt, foam latex, or polyurethane foam is placed just under the ticking. The number of coil springs in a mattress may run from 180 to over 1000. However, the type of construction and the quality of the springs are as important as the coil count. Innerspring mattresses may have *cloth-pocketed* or *wire-tied coils.* A standard double-bed mattress with each coil covered with cloth usually has about 800 coils. Since coils that are tied together by wire or steel bands are larger than pocketed coils and use heavier wire, the same size mattress will have 500 coils. The type of coil and assembly methods will cause the number of coils to vary. Strong tempered steel makes the best springs.

FOAM MATTRESSES. Solid-foam mattresses are light in weight and comfortable. They are from 4½ to 6 inches thick, and are intended for use over high-quality box springs. The *compression resistance factor* (density) is important in buying a foam-latex mattress. A compression factor of 25 represents a firm mattress, and one below 17 indicates a low-quality product. A polyurethane-foam mattress is lighter in weight and less expensive than a latex foam. Because of its light weight it tends to shift around on the bed under the pressure of body weight and during bedmaking.

A good mattress, whether innerspring or foam, will have a firm 26-ounce ticking to cover the construction and hold the mattress in shape. Edges and fastenings should be reinforced so that the mattress will not sag if people sit on the edge of the bed.

In addition to considering the above shopping suggestions, look for nylon metal handles at the side of a mattress for turning it and for four or more perforated metal or plastic ventilation panels on the sides of the mattress.

Pillows

Pillows should be made of pre-shrunk, firmly woven ticking or very heavy sateen to withstand constant friction and to prevent the fill from working through. They are filled with (1) acrylic or polyester and acrylic fibers; (2) foam latex, shredded or in one piece; and (3) down, down and feathers, or all feathers. Man-made fibers and foam latex are especially recommended for persons who might be allergic to feathers. Down is the softest and most expensive filling. Goose and duck feathers are superior to turkey or chicken feathers. Goose and duck feathers are sometimes combined with down. A new process applied to feather and down filling will make down and feather pillows dustless, mildew resistant, and machine washable and dryable. A label on pillows must state the fiber content, and it should also indicate that the fabric is preshrunk.

A pillow should be resilient. To test for resiliency, lay the pillow on a flat surface and compress it. Knead fiber and down-and-feather pillows to make sure the filling is uniformly distributed and free of small lumps or hard feather quills. Smell a pillow to detect any unpleasant odor. Buy a size that fits best across the bed and also a size that will be comfortable.

Care of Mattresses and Pillows

Proper care is important if you are to get the maximum satisfaction from any purchase. The following practices will prolong the life of sleep equipment:

□ Clean a mattress and springs regularly with an upholstery attachment for a vacuum cleaner—at least three or four times a year.

□ Turn new innerspring mattresses every two weeks for six months—up and down one time and sideways the next time. After six months turn three or four times a year.

□ Always use a mattress pad, and keep it clean and free of wrinkles. Mattress pads that are treated against shrinkage are highly desirable. If a mattress pad is likely to shrink, you may want to send it to a commercial laundry to be laundered and pressed by a mangle. This will flatten out the quilting and return the cover almost to its original size.

□ Fluff up pillows every day, and air them near an open window once a week. Protect pillows with a zippered white fabric cover.

SUMMARY

Furniture represents a large investment; thus every possible precaution should be taken to prevent mistakes. Regardless of whether you remain single or marry, you will probably be faced with furnishing an apartment or a house. It is best to make a long-range decorating plan, and until you can afford to get what you want, buy essentials only, making sure they are in good taste and are well made. With a little ingenuity, most people can use some makeshift item for a long time. If space is limited, multipurpose furniture is a good solution to the space problem. Tables, chests, and desks with drawers and shelves are recommended for limited quarters.

A knowledge of woods, finishes, fabrics, and construction techniques will be helpful when you shop for furniture. This is especially true for upholstered furniture where the construction is almost entirely concealed.

It is never advisable to skimp when buying springs and mattresses. Proper rest is essential to one's health, efficiency, and disposition. Mattresses should be long enough, wide enough, and firm enough for comfort. Beds larger than traditional single- and double-bed sizes are becoming more popular every year. Bed sofas now resemble regular sofas in appearance; they are fairly comfortable, and they provide extra sleeping space. Upholstery for sofas should be firmly woven and easy to maintain.

THINGS TO THINK ABOUT AND TO DO

1. Mount on the bulletin board pictures or sketches of basic furniture for a living-dining area and for a sleeping area.

2. Assemble pictures of restyled, refinished, and improvised furniture, and discuss some advantages and disadvantages of do-it-yourself furniture.

3. List some distributors of precut and ready-to-assemble furniture. Consult decorating magazines for addresses. If possible, order and assemble at least one item.

4. Mount on the bulletin board or collect for your decorating file illustrations of multipurpose furniture and furniture with good storage space.

5. Collect booklets or other illustrations of good sectional furniture.

6. Look up the addresses of distributors of rental furniture near you. Report to the class information on rental provisions.

7. Collect small finished samples of a number of the kinds of wood mentioned in the text. Study the grain and color of the woods until you can recognize them by sight.

8. Compare similar priced veneered and solid wood furniture—for example, a table or chest. How do they compare in other points of quality? Which, if either, is the more expensive?

9. Display some furniture illustrations showing inlay and lacquer.

10. Collect samples of wood with a laminated plastic finish, atomic wood, and synthetic wood.

11. Assemble a number of furniture labels for display on the bulletin board.

12. Assemble some wood furniture, and point out some construction points described in the text.

13. Invite a representative from a furniture company to discuss the construction of upholstered furniture for the class.

14. Distinguish between coil and flat springs.

15. Write an article suitable for a newspaper or a magazine on the proper care of furniture—wood and upholstered.

16. Show a film on wood furniture construction, and if possible arrange a field trip to a local furniture store.

REFERENCES FOR UNIT FOUR

BOOKS

(See also BOOKS listed for Unit Three.)

Handbook of Household Equipment Terminology. Washington, D.C.: American Home Economics Association, 1965.

BOOKLETS AND PAMPHLETS

(Write to the following addresses for current
lists of literature, with prices.)

Appliances and Kitchen Cabinets

Association of Home Appliance Manufacturers, 20 N. Wacker Dr., Chicago, Ill. 61616

General Electric Company, Appliance Park, Louisville, Ky. 40225

Hoover Home Institute, The Hoover Company, North Canton, O. 44720

Kemper Kitchens, Inc., Richmond, Ind. 47374

Long-Bell Kitchen Cabinets, International Paper Company, Portland, Ore. 97207

NuTone Company, Consumer Relations Division, Cincinnati, O. 45227

Schreirich Kitchens, 250 Ottawa Ave., Louisville, Ky. 40200

Sunbeam Corporation, Home Economics Department, 5400 Roosevelt Rd., Chicago, Ill. 60650

Westinghouse Corporation, Portable Appliance Division, Mansfield, O. 44902

Bedding

Cannon Mills, Inc., Consumer Information, New York, N.Y. 10020

National Association of Bedding Manufacturers, Public Relations Department, 724 Ninth St., Washington, D.C. 20001

Dinnerware—Dishes, Glassware, Flatware

Fostoria Glass Company, Advertising Department, Moundsville, W. Va. 26041

The Gorham Company, Advertising Department, Providence, R.I. 02907

Samuel Kirk and Son., Kirk Sterling, Baltimore, Md. 21218

Lenox, Inc., Education Department, Trenton, N.J. 08605

Libbey Glassware, Owens-Illinois, Toledo, O. 43601

The Melamine Council, Advertising Department, 60 West St., New York, N.Y. 10006

Oneida Silversmiths Guild, Oneida, N.Y. 13421

Royal Worcester Porcelain Company, Inc., Advertising Department, 11 E. 26th St., New York, N.Y. 10010

Sterling Silversmith Guild of America, 551 Fifth Ave., New York, N.Y. 10017

Syracuse China, Household Tableware Advertising, Syracuse, N.Y. 13201

FILMS, FILMSTRIPS, AND SLIDES

(See page 469 for name and address of source.)

The Art of Making Furniture. Traces the manufacture of furniture from the lumber yard to the showroom. (20 minutes, color, AF)

Cindy and Bill's New Carpet. Filmstrip showing a couple planning to decorate a home and shopping for carpet. (FDACC)

Consumers Want to Know. Shows how the Consumers Union functions in evaluating products. (30 minutes, CU)

Convenience in the Modern Way. Shows easier home living with modern appliances. (Filmstrip, SEARS)

Design for Beauty. Shows the manufacture of silver and how silver enhances table settings. (10 minutes, color, MTP)

Fashions in Dining. Filmstrip on table fashions. (Color, SEARS)

The Fine Art of Sterling Design. Shows some of the world's famous silver designers and period table settings. (27 minutes, color, MTP)

Follow It All the Way. Shows how quality controls protect the consumer and how products are tested. (22 minutes, color, AF)

Patterned for Dining. Shows interesting formal and informal table settings. (15 minutes, color, OSG)

The Romance of Early American Furniture. Shows how Early American furniture is designed and produced. (20 minutes, color, AF)

Wedgwood. Shows the manufacture of Wedgwood china and pottery. (15 minutes, color, AF)

Your Money and *You and Your Money's Worth.* Two filmstrips that show money management. (HFC)

unit five

*Maintaining
and Improving
a Home*

chapter twenty-five

REGULAR AND PERIODIC MAINTENANCE

Schools, hospitals, factories, and office buildings operate on regular maintenance schedules. Often efficiency experts are called in to study these schedules, observe workers, and suggest a better organization. If the average homemaker would approach housekeeping from a scientific angle, she would not only be able to reduce the number of hours required for household tasks, but she would be able to develop a better attitude toward necessary housework. Many people who dislike housework seldom take the time to find ways to manage more efficiently, thus making the work more interesting.

There are certain tasks, such as meal preparation, dishwashing, tidying up the house, making beds, and caring for children, which must be done *daily*. The time required for these tasks has been greatly reduced with the introduction of convenience foods, dishwashers, and nonstick cooking utensils. If entrances are swept regularly and a rug is provided at each entrance door, a great deal of dirt can be kept out of the house. If each person can take the responsibility of putting things away after use, the house will seldom look unkempt. Tasks such as marketing, laundering, mending, and general cleaning must be done *weekly* or *biweekly*. Time required for these tasks has been reduced with the availability of self-help supermarkets, automatic washers and dryers, self-cleaning ovens, self-defrosting refrigerators, and versatile floor-cleaning equipment.

Some cleaning is done only *occasionally*—walls, windows, blinds, floors, waxing, and carpet shampooing. Some people call in outside help for some of these jobs if time and energy are more important than money. If you are a homeowner, there are *seasonal* chores in preparation for summer and winter that must also be considered. After an efficient system of housekeeping is mastered and daily and weekly schedules are established, attitudes toward housework will change. Housekeeping tasks may well be shared. When everyone in the family cooperates in taking care of a home, no one person will be overburdened or too tired to enjoy recreation.

GUIDELINES FOR STUDY

GENERAL IDEAS
TO CONSIDER

1. Efficiently planned schedules facilitate performance of daily homemaking responsibilities.
2. Weekly and biweekly cleaning jobs vary according to the number and the ages of people using the home, the number of meals eaten out, and the family's attitudes toward housekeeping chores.
3. Major cleaning jobs, such as floor polishing, rug shampooing, wall washing, and window shade or window blind cleaning, are easier when proper equipment and proper procedures are used.
4. Periodic or seasonal checkups may prevent problems and unnecessary repairs in the future.

WORDS AND TERMS
TO UNDERSTAND

beeswax
carnauba wax
caulking
emulsion wax
flagstone (flooring)
fuller's earth
mortar
mosaic
parquetry
patina
solvent-base wax
terrazzo (flooring)
water-base wax

DAILY HOME RESPONSIBILITIES

If you and your family are willing to make a list of daily housekeeping activities and study the list objectively, it will be surprising how many practices you can initiate to make housekeeping and daily meal preparation easier. Here are a few suggestions:

□ Keep dirt out by keeping entrances clean and by placing a rug outside and inside the doors.

□ Remove muddy, sandy, or wet shoes at the entrance, and place them on newspaper or a sheet of plastic.

□ Use fine screening at open doors and windows.

□ Caulk around loose window frames and sashes.

□ Be systematic about refolding newspapers; replacing books, magazines, and writing materials after they are used; emptying ashtrays; keeping toys picked up; and putting dishes where they belong. Poor practices in these areas soon make a house look very untidy.

□ Make a practice of hanging up or putting away clothing as it is removed. Do not expect someone else to pick up after you.

□ Hang towels neatly over a rack after using them. Do not stuff damp towels in the corner of a rack because they will not only make the bathroom look untidy, but they will soon smell sour.

□ Help to carry dishes to the sink area after meals. A tray or serving cart will save steps.

□ Set the table for breakfast the night before rather than put dishes away at night and get them out in the morning.

□ Turn the bed down to air when you get up and fluff up the pillows. If you work away from home, decide whether it is more efficient to make the bed before or after breakfast.

□ If you do not have time to wash dishes before leaving the house in the morning, rinse and stack them and wipe off the counters.

□ Arrange utensils and food near work centers where they can be used efficiently.

□ Set schedules for children's meals, naps, and play, so that you will have time for daily chores as well as personal recreation.

□ Assign jobs, such as setting and clearing the table, washing dishes, and other tasks, so that everyone will share responsibilities for these daily tasks.

□ Prepare meats and desserts for more than one meal at a time. Freeze or refrigerate them until you are ready to use them.

□ Use convenience foods when time is short, but use a little imagination in serving them.

□ Make the evening meal an experience in eating and in family sociability and not something to be got quickly out of the way.

WEEKLY OR BIWEEKLY JOBS

Marketing, washing, ironing, mending, and general cleaning may be done once or twice a week depending upon the size of the family. The use an area receives, the amount of dirt in the air, and the available time will determine the frequency of cleaning.

Here are a few suggestions for reducing the time spent on weekly or biweekly jobs:

□ Organize laundry supplies conveniently in the laundry area.

□ List all the items you use for floor, furniture, and bathroom care, and store them conveniently. You may want to keep the following items in a cleaning basket ready to carry with you when you clean: dustpan, whisk broom or brush, sponge, dustcloths, furniture polishes, and cleansers.

☐ Separate clothing items before washing so as to avoid time-consuming mistakes. Do not mix white and dark-colored clothes. Avoid washing dark socks with items that shed lint.

☐ Set aside items needing mending, and mend before laundering.

☐ Remove items that require no ironing from the clothesline or dryer, and fold them for storage or place them on hangers. Buy as many items as possible that require little or no ironing.

☐ Dust wood furniture, vacuum-clean or brush upholstered furniture, and dust exposed wood floors before using the vacuum cleaner on rugs.

☐ Keep on hand a well-stocked larder of frozen and canned foods and staple items, so that menus can be easily adjusted to changed weather conditions, unexpected guests, or other fluctuations in number of persons present or in time available for meal preparation.

MAJOR CLEANING JOBS

Years ago it was customary to give the house a thorough spring cleaning and almost as thorough a fall cleaning. Those were the days when housecleaning was a real chore. Rugs were taken up, hung on the clothesline, and beaten with wire or reed rug beaters. Curtains were washed by hand and stretched on curtain stretchers. Floors were scrubbed with a scrub brush and waxed and polished on hands and knees. The coils on bedsprings were tediously hand dusted. Blankets were washed, rinsed, wrung with a hand wringer, and stretched over the clothesline to dry. Basements and attics, bulging with heirlooms and junk, added to the enormity of the annual or semiannual cleaning. When housecleaning was over, every homemaker

and her family were exhausted, but the sense of pride and satisfaction experienced by some homemakers seemed to compensate for the strenuous ordeal.

However, old-fashioned spring and fall housecleaning, along with the carpet beater and the curtain stretcher, has gone out of date. Today most homemakers prefer to rotate cleaning and to do one room at a time rather than have the entire house torn up for several weeks. By concentrating on one room a week, using day help and/or labor-saving equipment, the house can be kept clean with a minimum of confusion. Many families living in large homes and enjoying good incomes contract with professional housecleaning companies for wall and wallpaper cleaning, floor and carpet cleaning, and window washing. These services are becoming more and more popular, especially where husband and wife are both employed.

Even though you may never have to do your own housecleaning, it is a good idea to know the basic principles related to major cleaning jobs, as well as basic equipment.

Types of Waxes

Long before wood floors requiring wax became popular, wax was used by the Egyptians to preserve paintings on walls and inscriptions on stone tablets. The Romans used clear wax to conceal imperfections in marble statues. Both the Egyptians and the Romans used wax on stone and cement floors in temples and in palaces long before wood floors came into use. When the exquisite mosaic floors of Constantinople were imitated in Venice and Florence during the Middle Ages, wax was used to preserve them. France was the first European country to use wood for floors. During the reign of Louis XIV,

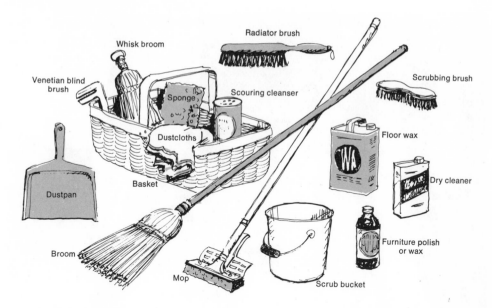

Basic Cleaning Equipment

polished parquetry floors came into use in the palaces in and around Paris.

Beeswax was the only wax known until after the French and American Revolutions. In the early days beeswax was melted into the floors with a hot iron and then polished by servants, who tied rags over their feet and skated over the floors until they had a soft patina. In 1797 palm trees were discovered in eastern Brazil, the leaves of which produced a substance known as *carnauba wax.*

As wood floors became more common, improvements were made in wax. Turpentine was found to be a good solvent, making soft paste wax possible. However, it was not until 1929 that the first water-emulsion, self-polishing wax was marketed. This type of wax originated in the leather industry. Early emulsion wax, like many new products, was not satisfactory, but now there are excellent emulsion waxes for any surface requiring waxing. Waxes are no longer made from natural wax but from synthetic substitutes.

Floor waxes are classified as *solvent base* and *water base.* In using any kind of wax, it is imperative to read the directions on the container label.

Solvent-base polishing wax relies on a chemical, usually petroleum naphtha, to hold the waxy substance in suspension. Solvent-base wax comes in paste and liquid forms, depending upon the amount of solvent in the mixture. Since solvent-base wax has a built-in dry-cleaning fluid, the wax cleans as it polishes. The liquid form is easier to use, and it cleans better than the paste types. Solvent-base waxes smell like dry-cleaning fluid, and they require polishing. *Never use a solvent-base wax on asphalt tile* because the cleaning fluid in it will dissolve the asphalt.

Water-base wax is usually marketed in liquid form, and it is usually self-polishing. Water-base liquid waxes dry either with an abrasion-resistant luster or with a somewhat dull finish requiring buffing. Water-base waxes are not recommended for anything harmed by water, such as leather, worn wood

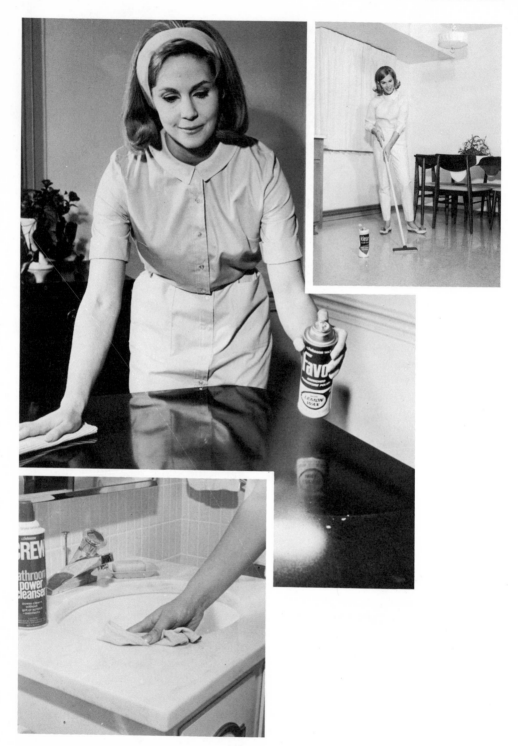

Routine housecleaning chores need not consume too much time and energy if regular schedules are followed and efficient methods used.

floors, or cork floors. The water may penetrate these substances and cause dry rot.

Either solvent- or water-base waxes can be used on (1) wood if it is new or in good condition, that is, finished with shellac or varnish; (2) linoleum, either printed, inlaid, or in tile form; (3) tile, vinyl asbestos, vinyl plastic, and well-sealed cork and rubber; and (4) flagstone, smooth brick, sealed indoor concrete, slate, and sealed terrazzo.

Cleaning
and Waxing Floors

Floors can be cleaned and waxed in one simple operation with a liquid solvent-base wax by following the procedure outlined:

1. Vacuum-clean or dust the floor surface well. Wipe up sticky spots with a damp cloth.
2. Place pads under the polisher brushes on a special polisher attachment *or* use a hand applicator on a handle.
3. Pour or spray a small amount of wax on the floor and spread the wax evenly. Begin in a corner and work toward a door. The dirt will dissolve and adhere to the pads. Replace the pads as they become soiled.
4. After the wax is dry, buff the surface with an electric or hand polisher.

The above method is especially recommended for wood, cork, and inlaid-linoleum floors. If you use a paste wax, apply a very thin coat of paste. It is better to use two thin coats than to use one heavy coat. Polish after each application.

Two operations are necessary if a water-base wax is used. This is the only wax that can be used on asphalt-tile floors. It should never be used on worn-wood or worn-cork floors. The floor must be clean before waxing. Use the following procedure for this type of wax:

1. Vacuum-clean or dust the surface.
2. Use any recommended detergent for scrubbing well-sealed wood floors, linoleum, tile, or stone. Use as little water as possible, and wipe up the water immediately after loosening the soil. Rinse with a mop wrung from clear water and let dry before applying wax. If the old wax is difficult to dissolve, add a little ammonia to the water.
3. Pour or spray puddles of wax on the floor, and spread a thin film evenly with a mop used only for this purpose. Allow at least twenty minutes for the wax to dry.
4. Buff with an electric polisher or soft pads attached to a long-handle brush. Buffing between waxings will help to maintain a lustrous surface.

Shampooing
or Dry-Cleaning Carpet

Rugs and carpet may be kept fresh and clean by home cleaning methods if directions are followed and if the surface is not allowed to accumulate too much soil. There are two types of commercially made rug cleaners—*liquid-detergent shampoos* and *sawdust saturated with a dry-cleaning solvent.* The latter will not clean cotton carpet satisfactorily, and it should not be used on low-pile carpets with a latex back because the cleaning fluid may dissolve the latex.

If a liquid shampoo is used, it is important to avoid soaking the carpet. Acrylic, nylon, and olefin fibers will not readily absorb water, and the excess water will soak into the background and cause the backing to deteriorate. Oversoaked wool carpet will take a long time to dry, and the wool or the backing may shrink in the drying. The surface foam does the cleaning and leaves the soil in suspension on the carpet, ready to be picked up with a vacuum cleaner. The following procedure should be used for home on-the-floor cleaning of rugs and carpets:

1. Move as much furniture as possible out of the room. Push large pieces, such as pianos and sofas, out from the wall.

2. Vacuum-clean the rug or carpet thoroughly (preferably with a heavy-duty, agitator-type vacuum cleaner). Clean the edges of the carpet or rug with the crevice attachment or with a stiff brush before using the vacuum cleaner.

3. Using a small brush or sponge, go around the edges of the rug or wall-to-wall carpeting with the shampoo or dry-cleaning preparation.

4. Apply the shampoo or dry-cleaning substance to an area between two and three feet square as directed on the label. Work the cleaning agent into the fibers of the carpet with a sponge, brush, or electric shampooer. If you are using a liquid detergent in an electric shampooer, switch off the flow of liquid as soon as the detergent begins to foam, and continue to agitate until most of the foam disappears. If you are using a sawdust-saturated cleanser, work the particles into the fibers with a long-handled brush until the surface appears fresh.

5. After completing the above operation, let the carpet dry. Then vacuum-clean the carpet and the edges thoroughly. If you are using a sawdust-type cleaner, make sure the sawdust is dry before using the vacuum cleaner to remove it.

6. Move furniture back into place, and put small pieces of blotter or aluminum-foil pads under all furniture. (This is to avoid the possibility of rust or soil deposit on the rug from the bottom of

the furniture.) When the carpet is thoroughly dry, remove the pads, and brush up the depressed pile with a stiff brush.

Washing Walls and Woodwork

A few precautions will reduce the amount of soil on walls. Before turning on the heat in the fall, clean the registers if you have a hot-air furnace or the radiators if you have a hot-water furnace. Otherwise, the accumulation of dirt that has gathered throughout the summer months will be blown through the house as the heat circulates.

Wall washing is hard work, and it must be done carefully. Some people leave walls so streaked after cleaning that the streaks are difficult or impossible to remove. If walls are allowed to become too soiled, it is not possible to wash them satisfactorily. The following suggestions will facilitate wall washing:

1. Assemble necessary supplies—mild detergent, a bucket for the detergent solution, a bucket for clear water, two large synthetic sponges, drop cloths or old sheets to protect the floor, and a ladder.

2. Read the directions given in the label on the detergent box for mixing and using detergent. Experiment behind a large piece of furniture until you are successful in washing and overlapping an area (see item 3).

3. Begin at the bottom and wash toward the ceiling to avoid streaking the walls. (It is possible to wash from the top down if you do not let the water run down on the soiled wall.) Wash with a rotary motion, covering an area about two feet square at one time. Rinse with a sponge wrung from clean water. Overlap the clean area as you progress. Change the water as it becomes soiled.

Be sure a ceiling is washable, since some ceilings are finished with a water-base whitener. Ceilings are a little difficult to reach, but the procedure for washing them is the same as for walls. Woodwork is less difficult to wash because it usually has a semigloss surface.

Wallpaper Cleaning

There are washable and truly scrubbable wallpapers. Oilcloth and vinyl-coated wallpapers can be washed like painted walls. Other so-called washable papers must be washed with care. Wallpaper cleaners that resemble play dough are satisfactory on most wallpapers. These cleaners will remove only soil and not grease. If a grease spot is fresh, it can be removed by making a paste of fuller's earth or powdered chalk and dry-cleaning fluid. A good commercial chalk preparation in stick form is available where notions are sold. Several applications may be necessary.

The frequency with which walls should be washed or cleaned will depend upon the amount of dirt in the air and the number of people moving about in the house. In areas where there is heavy industry, walls will have to be washed once a year or oftener. In rural areas or in clean cities, a washing every two years will be enough. With complete air conditioning or an air filter system, walls stay clean for a long time.

Cleaning Venetian Blinds and Window Shades

Venetian blinds should be pulled down flat and dusted with a soft absorbent cloth when dust shows on the surface. The tapes should be brushed before the slats are dusted. Once or twice a year (more often in industrial areas) the slats should be washed one at a time with a mild detergent solution and a soft cloth—old bath towels or pieces of knit cotton underwear cut into convenient sizes make good cleaning cloths. Hold one side of the blind with a small cloth while cleaning the opposite side, since wet hands may streak the slats.

It is possible to take Venetian blinds apart for an occasional thorough cleaning if you have a large surface, such as a Ping-Pong table, upon which to work. The tapes and cords can be washed in a washer if you put several large bath towels in the wash with them. Tie the cords to prevent knotting. The slats are easily wiped off by hand with a soft cloth wrung from a mild detergent solution. If you dismantle a Venetian blind, observe the process of dismantling so that you can reassemble it and have it operate properly. Never dismantle more than one blind at a time, unless you have plenty of space to spread out each one and keep the parts separated. You may prefer to have a professional cleaner give Venetian blinds an occasional cleaning.

Vinyl-coated and cloth window shades can be dusted and washed in the same manner as walls. Wash them on a Ping-Pong table or counter surface. Make sure that the surface is clean. If shades are not badly soiled, a wallpaper cleaner can be used. Avoid using too much liquid if you use a detergent solution, and overlap the clean area as you progress. Paper shades cannot be washed, but they can be cleaned fairly well with wallpaper cleaner.

HOMEOWNER'S SEASONAL CHECKUP

The homeowner has more responsibility for general maintenance than one who rents a home, in which case the landlord is responsible for general maintenance. Every spring and fall the homeowner should check lists similar to the following to avoid costly services and repairs.

Spring Checklist

1. Observe condition of paint on brick, clapboard, or shingles, as well as on window frames. Note the condition of caulking or putty around the windows as well as the condition of brick pointing and mortar between the bricks.
2. Note the condition of wood porches and steps.
3. Indicate any need to replace storm windows and doors with screens.
4. Check any need for insulation in roof.
5. Look for signs of termites or mice.
6. Check windows for loose locks.
7. Examine heating system for necessary repairs.
8. Check air conditioners or central air conditioning.
9. Examine walls for signs of leaks.
10. Check for water leakage in faucets and flush tanks.
11. Examine trees and shrubs, and spray, trim, fertilize, or replace if necessary.

If it is not possible to make the necessary repairs yourself, consult the yellow pages of the telephone directory for professional services. If you want quick service, do not wait until late in the season.

Fall Checklist

1. Check the furnace. If it is gas, check the pilot light and clean the burner if necessary. If it is oil, fill the tank. Check water levels in hot water containers.
2. If necessary, replace screens at windows and doors with storm windows and storm doors. Clean and repair screens, hose them, dry them, and store them in a dry place. Cover them to keep them clean.
3. Check for loose caulking or weather stripping at windows. Caulking tubes are available and as easy to use as squeezing toothpaste out of a tube.
4. Cover the outside of air conditioners if they are not to be used until spring.
5. Remove, clean, and store fabric awnings (fiber glass, plastic, and metal awnings may stay in place).
6. Check chimney to furnace or fireplace.
7. Clean leaves from gutters and downspouts, and note the need for any repairs. Consider installing mesh guards for gutters and wire cages for downspouts.
8. Turn off outside water pipes that are likely to freeze.
9. Examine the roof and the flashing around a chimney for possible leaks.
10. Examine walks and drives for hazards that may cause falls.

SUMMARY

Home maintenance can be a burden or a satisfaction, depending upon one's attitude and one's ability. People who approach home maintenance in a haphazard fashion will probably dislike housekeeping, marketing, and meal preparation. Those who approach these necessary responsibilities associated with homemaking from a scientific and analytical point of view will find homemaking a challenge.

When every member of a household forms good personal habits in home management and shares in the work, no one need be overburdened. Clean from the top down; for instance, before attempting to clean and wax floors or shampoo carpeting, clean ceiling, walls, and window shades. It is necessary to know the best products and best procedure to use. Often floors and carpeting are ruined by indifference or ignorance in cleaning.

The homeowner has greater responsibility for seasonal maintenance than the home renter. A spring and fall checklist can be helpful to every homeowner.

THINGS TO THINK ABOUT AND TO DO

1. Make a list of the things you can do every day to facilitate housekeeping.

2. Check the entrances to your home to be sure you have made adequate provision for keeping dirt out of the house.

3. Provide a convenient place for laundry supplies in the laundry area, dishwashing supplies in the sink area, cleaning supplies where they are easily available.

4. Display on the bulletin board illustrations of housekeeping methods used during the early twentieth century.

5. Using a suitable classroom floor, demonstrate how to clean it.

6. Demonstrate how to shampoo a rug with an electric shampooer. Emphasize the importance of cleaning with foam and not with water. You may be able to secure large swatches of discarded rugs at a store. Note the fiber and method of construction. When swatches become soiled, clean them with either a detergent solution or a sawdust and dry-cleaner fluid.

7. Demonstrate how to wash a wall in an inconspicuous part of the classroom. Volunteer to wash or clean the walls in a room at home.

8. If you own your home, use the seasonal checklist with your father to check for needed repairs. Help to make them if possible.

chapter twenty-six

GENERAL
HOME REPAIRS

The person who is handy with tools can make many simple home repairs and save money. The furniture, plumbing, carpenter, and electrical repairs covered in this chapter can be made with simple household tools. Some jobs can be accomplished a little faster with power tools. A workbench is· an added convenience if space permits. If space is limited, basic tools for simple home repairs can be stored on a pegboard wall panel or in a regular toolbox.

Work is always easier if tools are kept in good condition and put in place when not in use. Accidents can be prevented by observing safety rules, especially in using power tools. Mending and painting jobs can be done with greater satisfaction if one follows directions carefully in using adhesives, paint removers, paints, and varnishes. There are many repair jobs that an amateur can do with the minimum of tools, such as mending scratches, dents, and holes in furniture, removing stains from marble, and making sticking drawers operate more smoothly.

Some of you may want to redecorate your room or perhaps give a little face-lifting to a living room or family room. If you own some antiques, perhaps you will want to refinish them. You may want to buy some second-hand furniture and restyle it before restoring the original finish or painting or antiquing it. Many young people are so successful in restoring old furniture that they cherish some restored pieces all their lives. Skill in refinishing furniture is not only satisfying, but also economical.

A number of carpenter and plumbing jobs are not difficult if one has the time, interest, and tools. The amateur carpenter can tighten the legs on a table or chair to make it rest firmly without squeaking, loosen a window that sticks, straighten a door that sags, or reverse a roller shade to double its wear. The amateur plumber can relieve a clogged shower head, repair a dripping faucet, adjust a noisy flush tank, or replace loose caulking around a bathtub.

Of course one should exercise discretion in deciding when a particular task is within one's abilities and when it is best to seek expert help. Knowledge of the basic skills outlined here will help you decide wisely.

GUIDELINES FOR STUDY

GENERAL IDEAS
TO CONSIDER

1. General home repairs made by the amateur are advisable only if one has sufficient interest, time, and ability as well as the proper tools.
2. Strict adherence to safety rules is important in making home repairs.
3. When tools and supplies are conveniently placed for use, home repairs will be less difficult to make.
4. Major furniture surgery and extensive home repairs require special tools and equipment, specific knowledge, and technical skill.

WORDS AND TERMS
TO KNOW

adhesive
antique finish
auger
casein
caulk
chisel
contact-type cement
epoxy
glaze
plastic-resin glue
polyvinyl-acetate glue
pumice
refinish
restyle
resin
resorcinol
shellac

SAFETY RULES

Fewer repair accidents would happen if the home craftsman observed the basic rules of safety set up by industry. If you are working with power tools, it is even more important to be cautious. Here are some suggestions:

☐ *Wear proper clothing.* Avoid long sleeves, exposed shirttails, ties, or any loose clothing that can catch in tools. Wear heavy leather shoes rather than sneakers, which provide no protection from falling objects.

☐ *Keep tools clean and in good repair.* This means keeping handles free of oil or moisture, sharp edges sharp, handles tight, and drill bits properly installed.

☐ *Keep tools in place when not in use, and keep sharp edges turned away from your reach.*

☐ *Provide for proper grounding of power tools.* This is especially important when working in damp areas. A ground receptacle has three prongs instead of two.

☐ *Make sure that surfaces on which you are using power tools are firmly anchored.*

☐ *Turn off power tools before laying them down or replacing any part.*

☐ *Work in a well-ventilated room.*

☐ *Wear safety goggles when grinding stone or metal.*

TOOLS NEEDED

The tools needed for most home repairs are indicated in the diagram on page 436. If tools are to be used conveniently, they must be stored in an accessible place and kept in good condition. In addition to tools, the repair shelf should contain small jars of nails, screws, and picture hooks of assorted sizes; picture wire; fine sandpaper; mending tape; and adhesives.

ADHESIVES

The terms *glue* and *adhesive* are used almost interchangeably. Success in using any glue will depend upon selecting the right glue for the job and following directions carefully. If joints are to be firm, they must be clean, snugly fitted, clamped, and allowed to dry for the recommended period and at the specified temperature. Some of the most common glues are listed according to use.

WHITE POLYVINYL ACETATE. These are popular all-purpose white glues sold in plastic squeeze bottles under several trade names. They are easy to use, and dry clear. Joints must be clean and held together under pressure for twenty to thirty minutes for preliminary contact. Thorough drying requires twenty-four hours. These glues can be used on paper, fabric, cardboard, cork, leather, and wood.

CASEIN GLUE. This is a powder that must be mixed with water. It is used on heavy wood joints. It can be used at low temperatures, and it tends to fill in between the joints if they do not fit snugly. It is not as waterproof as plastic-resin glue.

PLASTIC-RESIN GLUE. This is a powder that must be mixed with water and used at room temperature—seventy to eighty degrees Fahrenheit. Joints must be closely fitted and clamped tightly for five or six hours. The glue is very strong and waterproof.

WATERPROOF RESORCINOL GLUE. This type of glue consists of two parts —a liquid resin and a powdered catalyst, which must be mixed immediately before using. The glue must be used at room temperature, and the joints must be clamped together for eight to ten hours. This type of glue is recommended for outdoor furniture, outdoor

1. BEGINNER'S TOOLS

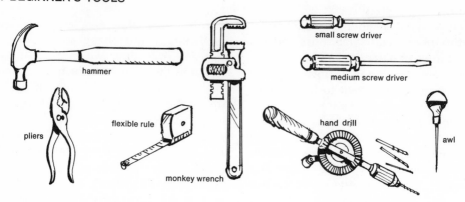

hammer

pliers

flexible rule

monkey wrench

small screw driver

medium screw driver

hand drill

awl

2. ADDITIONAL TOOLS

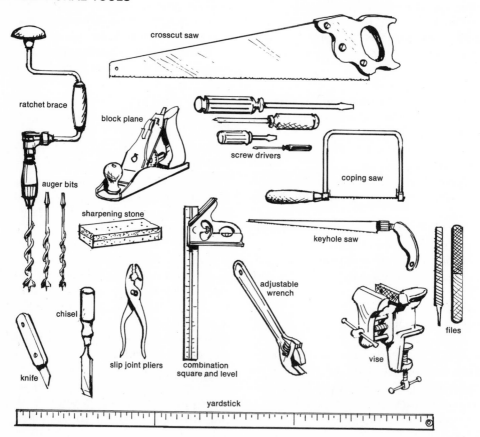

crosscut saw

ratchet brace

block plane

screw drivers

coping saw

auger bits

sharpening stone

keyhole saw

chisel

knife

slip joint pliers

combination square and level

adjustable wrench

files

vise

yardstick

woodwork, and boats. It is also excellent for plastics and pottery.

CONTACT-TYPE CEMENT. This is the adhesive used for cementing plastic sheets, leather, or metal to plywood. This adhesive joins surfaces immediately upon contact. There is no margin for error. An odorless water-thinned cement is safer to use than the highly flammable solvent-thinned type, which has an odor. Contact-type cement must be spread very evenly over each of the two surfaces and allowed to dry according to directions—five to forty minutes. The two surfaces are then pressed together for permanent contact.

EPOXY ADHESIVES. These adhesives come in two parts, including a resin and a catalyst, and in clear, white, or metallic finishes. The adhesive must be used soon after it is mixed, or it will harden. This adhesive has many uses, from repairing drain pipes, masonry, cracked radiators, and rotted wood to fine china, marble, and glass. The surface must be thoroughly clean and dry, and the adhesive should be used at room temperature or higher.

MINOR FURNITURE REPAIRS

If you look around the house, you probably can find many minor repair jobs, such as eradicating scratches, dents, and holes in furniture; tightening joints in chairs and tables; easing drawers that stick; and restoring the surface on marble-top tables and chests.

Scratches

If a scratch is only surface deep, a repair job is simple. A walnut meat can be rubbed over a scratch on most dark woods. Iodine can be "painted" over a scratch in mahogany by using a little cotton on the end of a toothpick. Light shoe polish or crayon can be used on

light woods. The excess stain must be rubbed entirely away. Special furniture shellac wood-stain sticks are available at paint stores for deeper scratches. After staining over a crack, ordinary furniture polish will blend into the scratch.

Dents

Minor depressions in wood can be raised by moisture and heat: (1) Remove furniture polish from the dented area with a dry-cleaning fluid or turpentine. (2) Cover the dent with several thicknesses of a soft thin cloth (a piece of old sheet will do) slightly dampened. (3) Place a flat metal cap from a small can or bottle over the spot, flat side down. (4) Hold an iron over the top for a minute to swell the wood. Repeat if necessary, and then polish the entire surface.

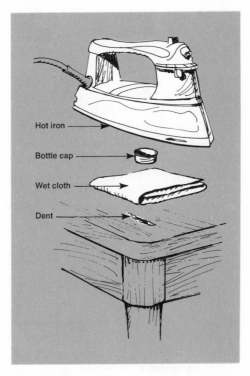

Hot iron

Bottle cap

Wet cloth

Dent

The steam created by this process will often make the wood swell back to its former shape.

Holes

Holes in furniture may be caused by cigarette burns or sharp objects. These are more difficult to mend than scratches or dents. (1) Scrape the hole clean with a sharp knife, and rub it with fine sandpaper or steel wool. (2) Wipe off the residue with a soft cloth dampened with dry-cleaning fluid or turpentine. (3) Fill in the hole with a plastic-wood filler, available at any paint store, that matches the raw wood in color. (4) Touch up the filled hole with clear varnish or shellac, and rub it smooth with pumice and linseed oil. (5) Wipe off excess oil with turpentine, and polish the entire surface. (If the hole is not very deep, thin layers of clear varnish can be built up over several days until the surface is even.)

Sticking Drawers

If drawers stick mainly in damp weather, the solution is simple. Remove the drawer, and wipe the dust or grease off with a dry-cleaning fluid. Rub the sides with paraffin or candle wax. If the wood has absorbed a lot of moisture, it may be shrunk by placing the drawer over a radiator or register long enough to remove the excess moisture. If the drawer sticks badly, place medium-grade sandpaper over a block of wood, and sand the areas that stick. If the front of the drawer must be lifted to close all the way, press a few thumbtacks under the front edge.

Stains on Marble

Marble is porous, and therefore any sticky or colored liquid or even water will mark it. Marble should be kept clean with a soft cloth wrung from a very mild detergent preparation, rinsed, and then dried thoroughly. If the soil is deep, a brushing with a nonabrasive detergent may be necessary. The surface should be thoroughly rinsed with clear water. If tea, coffee, fruit juice, or soft-drink stains remain, a little peroxide may be mixed with a little whiting (sold at paint stores) to form a paste. Spread the thick paste over the area, and add a few drops of ammonia. Cover with a small piece of plastic wrap to hasten the chemical reaction. Remove the dried paste with clear water.

Rust and oil stains are more difficult to remove. Special preparations are available in paint stores for removing these stains.

FURNITURE RESTYLING AND REFINISHING

Often you can find in a secondhand store sturdy furniture with good lines that you can restyle and refinish. Even the amateur can remove a mirror from an old-fashioned dresser, and with a little refinishing have a good-looking chest of drawers. It is often fun to visit shops selling antique and secondhand furniture, and bargain for a piece of furniture that has restyling possibilities.

Preliminary Steps

Before attempting to refinish the surfaces of a piece of furniture that needs restyling, do all the necessary furniture surgery first. No two pieces will require the same restyling and no two people will have the same idea about restyling even the same piece. After a piece is restyled it can be refinished by any of the methods described in the following sections.

These two steps will help prevent accidents and aid efficiency:
1. Work in an area that is well ventilated and where the floor covering will not be harmed—preferably out of doors or in a well-ventilated basement. If you work in the house, protect the floors adequately.

2. Assemble the following items:

  old newspapers and soft rags

  medium and fine sandpaper

  medium and fine steel wool

  a 2-inch brush and an old toothbrush

  paint remover (thick liquid preferred)

  denatured alcohol or turpentine

  putty knife '

  materials required for chosen finish

  rubber gloves

Varnishing a Good Surface

If the surface of a piece of furniture is in good condition, it can be brightened with a new coat of varnish. To do so, take these steps: (1) Repair surface; then glue and screw loose parts as described under Adhesives on page 435. (2) Remove old glossy finish with a commercially prepared product available at a paint store. (You can do this with repeated applications of turpentine and sanding, but it is more work.) (3) Wipe the surface clean with turpentine or denatured alcohol. (4) Apply a satin-finish furniture varnish, which will give a hand-rubbed appearance. You may want to use two thin coats on two successive days for a more durable finish. Avoid using varnish in damp, muggy weather because the wood will be moist and the polish will take a long time to dry.

Removing Old Finish

To remove an old finish, proceed as follows: (1) Use a commercially prepared paint remover—preferably a syrup-like nonflammable liquid. (2) Avoid getting the liquid on any part of the body, especially the eyes. Keep a bucket of clear water nearby and rinse off remover immediately if it touches the skin (change water often). (3) Apply the paint remover with a brush and let it stand the length of time stated in the directions before trying to remove the finish. (4) Scrape off loosened varnish with a putty knife, and wipe the residue onto newspaper. Loosen the varnish in crevices with an old toothbrush or a stiff stencil brush. (5) Clean the surface with turpentine, denatured alcohol, or a fairly strong detergent (avoid using too much water, and wipe the surface dry). Repeat the operation until there is no trace of the original finish. Repair dents or holes as directed earlier.

Bleaching Furniture

Take these steps to bleach furniture: (1) Remove the old finish as described above, and make sure that the surface shows no trace of the old varnish. (2) Use a preparation of oxalic-acid crystals (available at hardware and paint stores) and water if furniture needs only slight bleaching. (3) Use a two-solution commercially prepared bleach on dark woods. Follow the directions on the containers. Repeat the operation until the surface is the desired color. (The bleached wood will darken somewhat with the new finish.) (4) Wash with a soft cloth wrung from detergent solution, rinse with clear water, and rub dry. (5) Sand with fine sandpaper or fine steel wool, and wipe off residue with denatured alcohol or turpentine. (6) Seal the surface with shellac, and finish with pumice and oil or with a satin-finish varnish.

Staining Furniture

If a darker or richer color is desired, prepared stains can be used full strength or diluted with a recommended solvent to give a natural wood or wood-color finish. The old finish must be removed down to the raw wood, and the wood must be clean and dry. Test the stain first on the underside of the furniture to make sure the new stain is the color desired. If it is too strong, dilute it, and remember that the finish will darken with a shellac, oil, or varnish finish.

Furniture Finishes

Every furniture expert has his favorite finish, among which are rubbed oil, satin-type varnish, and antique.

RUBBED OIL AND PUMICE. (1) Prepare the surface by removing the old finish and cleaning the surface as described above. (2) Apply a thin coat of shellac (clear type on blond woods and orange type on dark woods), and allow to dry as directed. (3) Make a thick paste of pumice and linseed oil in a deep saucer. (4) With a soft pad, rub the paste over the surface until the wood feels slightly warm from friction. (5) Wipe off the excess oil with denatured alcohol. (6) Apply a rather thin coat of shellac, and let it dry. Repeat several times, finishing with a final oil-and-pumice rubbing. Finally rub with a soft cloth until an even patina is obtained.

VARNISH. Give the surface one or more applications of the oil finish described above. Wipe off all traces of oil. Using a special satin-finish furniture varnish, apply a thin coat, and let it dry overnight. This varnish will withstand heat. Apply a second coat for a more durable finish, and let it dry twenty-four hours or longer before placing anything on the surface.

ANTIQUE. An antique finish may be applied to furniture without removing the original finish. (1) Repair dents, holes, and loose joints as described on pages 435 to 438. (2) Remove the surface gloss with a commercial preparation or by using turpentine, fine steel wool, and sandpaper. (3) Check the entire surface to make

sure there is no gloss or dirt which might cause the paint to crack. (4) Select a kit that will produce the color you want. The kit will contain a white or a colored base, a glaze, and a satin-finish varnish. (5) Apply the base coat, and allow it to dry thoroughly for forty-eight hours. (6) Spread on the glaze, and with a cloth, sponge, or brush, streak or dab the glaze. (Practice on an old smooth-surface board until you have the effect you want.) (7) Wipe off the glaze to follow the grain of the wood. You can handle edges and joints better if you cut a two-by-three-inch rectangle of cardboard and hold the cloth over it as you pull it over the wood or up and down from the edges or the joints. (8) Apply a clear satin varnish for a resistant finish.

CARPENTER REPAIRS

With a little patience and time you can learn to be your own carpenter, at least for simple jobs. You can tighten table or chair legs. You can ease a window or door that sticks, and reverse window shades for longer use.

Loose Table or Chair Legs

If a chair feels wobbly when you sit in it, the trouble may be in the chair rungs or in one of the three-cornered blocks that support the chair legs at the corners of the seat. If a rung is loose, it must be further loosened and removed. The surfaces must be sanded smooth before the rung is replaced. To reset the rung, it must be glued, clamped, and allowed to dry for twenty-four hours. If a clamp is not available to hold the rung in place while drying, a heavy cord can be tied around the legs and a stick inserted at one part of the cord to act as a tourniquet for tightening the cord.

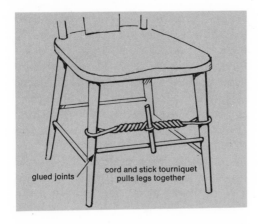

Repairing a chair rung.

If the triangular block is loose under the seat of a dining room chair, or under the top of a small table or desk, the block must be removed and both the contact surface of the block and the chair frame must be sanded smooth. After the glue is applied, screws larger than the original ones should be used to hold the block in place. If these are not available, place a match stem with a little glue on it in the hole first, or insert plastic wood and allow it to harden before inserting the screw.

Windows That Stick

Wood windows stick because they have swelled from dampness or because the edges are sealed with paint. If the window is swollen only slightly, place a cloth-covered wooden block along the edges and tap it with a hammer. Raise the sash, and lubricate the frame with candle wax or soap.

If windows stick after painting, insert a broad, stiff putty knife between the window sash and the frame, and tap it lightly with a hammer. Or hold the blade of a hatchet along the lower edge, and tap it with a hammer. Twist the knife blade or the hatchet slightly after each tap. Raise the window, and scrape off the rough edges with a chisel. Work from the outside of the house. If the window is badly stuck, the molding on the inside may have to be pried off with a chisel, sanded, and then moved out slightly.

A Door That Sticks

A door may stick if the weather is damp or if the hinges work loose. First open the door wide and tighten all the screws that hold the hinges in place. If the holes are loose, remove one hinge at a time and glue in wood plugs, or simply place a wood matchstick in the hole to give the screws a better grip. If the door still sticks, slide a sheet of typing paper faced with carbon paper along the edge of the door to detect the location of the trouble area. Sand the area, and rub wax along the edge of the door. If the door sags at the top or bottom, one hinge may be recessed more than

Fixing a stuck window.

the other (the hinge diagonally opposite from the sag). Unscrew and remove the troublesome hinge from the door-frame side and insert a cardboard wedge, or shim (see the illustration on page 447).

Never take a door off and begin planing it until you have tried the above solutions.

Reversing Roller Shades

The life of a window shade can be doubled by reversing it on the roller: (1) Remove the staples or tacks that hold the shade to the roller, and lift the shade off the roller. Open the hem by running a single-edge razor blade inside the fold to cut the stitches. (2) Dust the shade on both sides, and sponge the surface with a detergent solution; rinse and dry. (3) Using a yardstick, draw a line along the clean, undamaged edge of the shade and trim off the damaged edge with scissors; turn back a hem the width of the original one, and hold the loose edge in place with masking tape. (4) Dust a little cornstarch or powder over the tape to avoid sticking to the presser foot. Machine stitch the hem edge with matching heavy thread, using a long stitch. (5) Remove the tape. (6) Center and tack or staple the opposite edge along the roller. (7) Wind up the shade lightly and evenly on the roller, and replace it in the brackets. Test the ease with which the shade rolls, and release or increase the tension on the roller by inserting the tines of a fork over the ratchet at the end of the roller.

PLUMBING REPAIRS

It is not always possible to secure the immediate services of a certified plumber; so it is wise—even if you are a renter—to know at least where the shutoff valves are in case a washer gives way and water begins to overflow on the floor. As a rule there are valves under a sink, a bathroom lavatory, and a toilet that can be turned to shut off the water until help arrives. Sometimes these valves are in the basement. There are also valves for the bathtub. They may not be visible. If not, they will be enclosed (1) inside a wood panel at the faucet end of the tub or (2) on the wall of an adjoining room or hallway if the tub fits between two walls.

Look for these shutoff valves in your own home because they are important in making some of the plumbing repairs below.

Clogged Shower Head

If your shower head produces a stream instead of a spray, it needs to be cleaned or replaced. Remove the shower-head face and clean the holes with a wire or coarse needle. Soak in a solution of ammonia and water, and scrub the inside with an old toothbrush. Replace. If the flow is not improved, a new shower head is needed.

Dripping Faucet

A dripping faucet can be a nuisance and an expense. The cause may be loose packing beneath the bonnet-shaped cap under the handle, or a worn washer at the base of the stem (see the diagram opposite). Place a cloth around the bonnet-shaped cap to protect the metal, and use a wrench to tighten the cap.

TO REPLACE LOOSE PACKING. If dripping continues, the faucet will have to be dismantled If so: (1) Shut off the water supply to the faucet. (2) Remove the faucet's handle, which

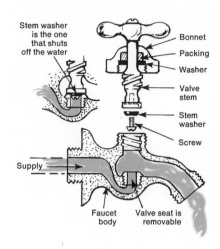

Stem washer is the one that shuts off the water

Bonnet

Packing

Washer

Valve stem

Stem washer

Screw

Supply

Faucet body

Valve seat is removable

Construction of a faucet.

is usually held in place with a screw at the top that may be covered with a decorative cap. (3) Loosen the nut over the bonnet cap with a wrench. (4) Lift up the cap, and pry out the old packing with a screwdriver. Note how the packing is wound in place. (5) Obtain new graphite-impregnated, stringlike material from a hardware store, and wind this around the stem of the valve where the old material was removed. (Newer faucets use a plastic ring in place of wrapping.) (6) Reassemble, and check.

TO REPLACE A WASHER. If dripping continues, a new washer may be needed. (1) Shut off the water supply. (2) Remove handle and bonnet cap. (3) Twist the stem with a wrench or pliers, and remove it. (4) Remove the screw from the washer at the lower end of the stem, and pry off the washer. (5) Purchase a new washer and screw identical with the used ones. (6) Reassemble, and open and close the faucet a few times to set the washer before turning on the water.

Running Flush Tank

The flush tank back of the toilet has three control valves: (1) the *flush valve* at the base of the tank, on which rests a rubber tank ball; (2) an *inlet or float valve,* which lets in water until the tank is full; and (3) the *shutoff valve* below the tank. When the toilet is flushed, the flush valve opens, and the water in the tank runs through the toilet. When the tank is empty, the rubber ball rests in place, acting as a stopper until the tank fills. A metal ball on a rod connected with the inlet valve, or *tank float,* rises as the tank fills again. At a certain water level the float causes the inlet valve to close automatically. (See the illustration on page 444.)

A number of things can happen to cause poor functioning of the toilet. *If the tank fills too slowly,* there may not be enough water pressure, or the rubber ball may not be centered on the flush-valve seat. To relieve this condition, test the shutoff valve to make sure there is a maximum flow of water. If there is a sufficient flow of water, the trouble is not at the shutoff valve; it may be in the tank ball at the base of the flush tank. Therefore: (1) Turn off the water supply at the shutoff valve, or tie the tank float up to prevent the tank from filling, and flush out the water. (2) Examine the position of the rubber ball on the flush-valve seat. If it is not centered, the rod holding it may have to be straightened. (3) Check the condition of the rubber ball, and if it is worn, replace it. (4) Clean the exposed flush-valve seat with an impregnated steel-wool pad, and if the rod holding the rubber ball is in poor condition, replace it. (5) Fill the flush tank, and make sure the rubber ball falls into position.

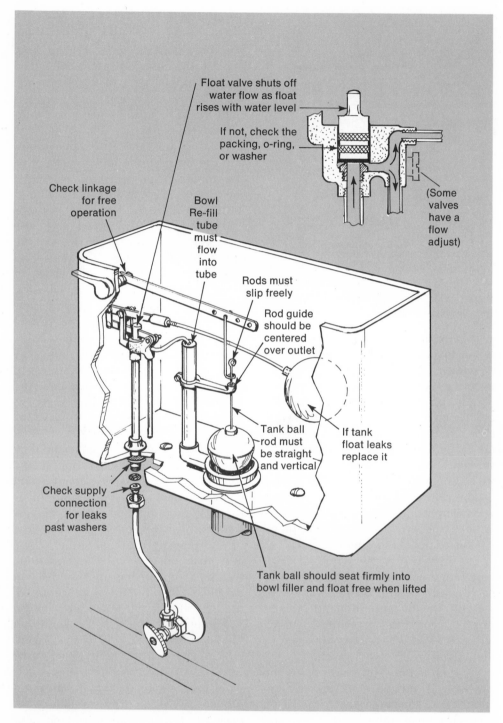

Float valve shuts off water flow as float rises with water level

If not, check the packing, o-ring, or washer

(Some valves have a flow adjust)

Check linkage for free operation

Bowl Re-fill tube must flow into tube

Rods must slip freely

Rod guide should be centered over outlet

Tank ball rod must be straight and vertical

If tank float leaks replace it

Check supply connection for leaks past washers

Tank ball should seat firmly into bowl filler and float free when lifted

Problems involving the shutoff valve or the flush valve and tank ball can often be solved by an amateur.

If water continues to overflow, lift up the float with your forefinger, and if the noise stops, the rod holding the float may have to be bent slightly downward, or the float may have a leak, making replacement necessary. To check for a leak, unscrew the float and shake it.

If the water keeps running, the trouble is in the float, or inlet valve. The overflow constantly runs out through an overflow pipe, and this water loss can run up water bills. Call a plumber at this point, unless someone in the home is adept at mechanics. This operation involves disassembling the valve-inlet section by removing two thumbscrews, or pins, to release the entire float-arm mechanism. The stem and plunger can be lifted so that the washer at the end of the plunger is exposed. It may be necessary to replace the entire unit if it is rusty.

Clogged Drain

If a sluggish drain in a toilet, lavatory, bathtub, or sink is attended to before it clogs up, the job will be simplified. Grease, coffee grounds, and particles of food will clog a kitchen drain; hair, lint, or greasy creams will clog up a lavatory or bathtub drain. Most of the trouble will be in the built-in metal drain stoppers in modern fixtures. These metal stoppers in a bathtub or lavatory can be twisted and lifted out. After pulling off hair and lint, the grease can be cleaned out by soaking the stopper in an ammonia solution.

Most mild stoppage in a sink or toilet can be cleared up by plunging with a force cup (a bell-shaped rubber cup about five or six inches in diameter attached to a wood handle). (1) Fill the sink or toilet with three or four inches of water. (2) Center the cup over the drain, and hold the handle with both hands for the maximum pressure. (3) Force the cup downward, and release it with a jerk to create a suction action. (4) Repeat ten or twelve times to break up foreign matter and to release it down the drain.

If the trouble continues, use a commercially prepared drainpipe cleaner. This is highly poisonous and injurious to the skin and to the porcelain finish; so the following precautions must be taken: (1) Wear rubber gloves. (2) Dip the water out of the toilet or sink. (3) Pour the drainpipe cleaner down the drain below the exposed porcelain. (4) Wait several hours or until waste is dissolved. (5) Flush the toilet several times, or run the water in the sink or bowl for several minutes to prevent the cleaner from damaging the drainpipes.

If the trouble continues in a toilet, a steel auger or snake will have to be used. This is usually the time to call a plumber because few people own an auger or want to be bothered with this messy job.

A sink drain is often clogged at the trap, or U-shaped pipe under the sink. To repair it: (1) Shut off the water supply by turning the shutoff valve. (2) Place a bucket under the drain below the sink. (3) Using a wrench, loosen the trap plug, or nut, very carefully to avoid stripping the threads. Some drains do not have a nut at the base, and if this is the case, the two slip nuts holding a U section in place will have to be loosened. (4) Force a heavy wire or a bent coat hanger through the drain pipe or U-shaped trap in both directions to force out the foreign matter. (5) Reassemble, turn on hot water full force, and if the drain is still clogged, it will be necessary to use an auger or a snake. This is usually a plumber's job.

Loose Caulking around Bathtub

When bathtubs are set in place, the edges along the tile wall and floor are caulked. If the caulking becomes loose, the water from the shower will run between the walls or through the floor, and damage the ceiling in the room below. This is an easy repair job. Purchase a tube of caulking compound at a hardware store. Loosen the cracked caulking, wipe away the residue, and squeeze the compound in the open crevices. Read directions on the container carefully for obtaining the best results.

SUMMARY

Whether or not it is profitable to make minor home repairs will depend upon your attitude, time, and ability. Almost everyone uses glue, hammer, and nails periodically. Many more people would attempt minor repairs if they had the necessary tools in a convenient place. There are some people who like to work with tools not only in making repairs but in creating useful and attractive articles from discards. The experienced person can mend scratches and dents from furniture, refinish damaged surfaces, and often restore family heirlooms at a great saving.

It is hoped that this chapter will not only benefit the experienced home craftsman but will inspire the novice to undertake some simple repairs and furniture restoration. It has become popular for homemakers—both men and women—to take night courses on simplified plumbing and carpenter repairs. The cost of such courses in time and money will be repaid many times over by expenses avoided in years to come.

THINGS TO THINK ABOUT AND TO DO

1. Discuss accidents you or someone you know may have had by being careless about making home repairs.

2. Debate some pros and cons in satisfactions and in savings by making home repairs.

3. Display the adhesives mentioned in the text, and demonstrate how to use each.

4. Demonstrate how to touch up scratches, raise dents, and fill in holes in furniture.

5. Have one member of the class bring in a chair with a loose leg, and show the class how to repair it.

6. Make at least one important repair or restoration job at home, and write or give a report on it in class.

7. Have a class member bring a small piece of furniture to class with the old finish previously removed. Demonstrate how to apply an oil and pumice finish with shellacking in between. Follow the directions on page 440 carefully.

8. Have a plumber demonstrate how to make one or more of the plumbing repairs mentioned in the chapter.

9. Discuss some problems you have had at home, and tell how these might have been corrected or avoided.

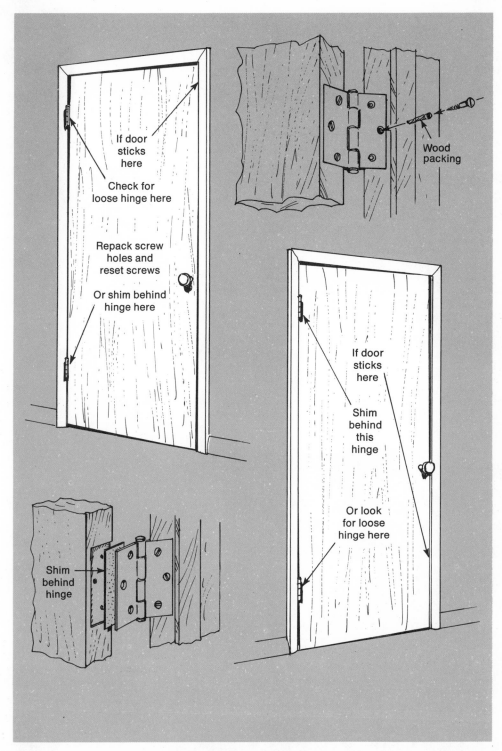

A door that sticks or sags is simple to fix, if these directions are followed.

chapter twenty-seven

HOME IMPROVEMENTS

Fresh walls, floors, and ceilings can completely change the inside appearance of a house. Outside repair jobs, painting, and a neatly kept lawn and shrubs not only improve the appearance of a home but also increase its real estate value. If some or all of these jobs can be done by the homeowner, a tremendous saving is realized. However, unless the homeowner has enough time and the ability and interest to make these home improvements, it is better to pay someone else to do the work.

Of the jobs most commonly undertaken by the amateur, inside wall painting is the most popular. The newer fast-drying, odorless, water-soluble paints and paint rollers have not only simplified wall painting but have eliminated the tedious task of cleaning brushes and clothing after using oil-base paints.

Some of you who have never painted or papered walls, laid resilient carpet or floor tile, refinished floors, or installed ceiling tile may want to undertake some of these projects after reviewing the information and illustrations in this chapter. Results will be more satisfactory if you choose the proper equipment and learn how to use and care for it. Various kinds of paint and recommended uses, suggestions for using wallpaper, and points to consider in choosing ceiling and floor tiles are discussed in Chapter Thirteen.

The beginning painter will find it easier to use water-soluble paint than oil-base paint because it will do less harm if it is spilled on clothing, carpet, or home furnishings, and it is easy to clean equipment and brushes after use. The beginning paperhanger should use prepasted washable wallpaper. Paste is not difficult to mix and use, but it requires a little experience and, if wallpaper is not completely washable, it cannot be wiped off without leaving a mark. Resilient floor tiles are fairly simple to lay if the worker has the tools needed. Most resilient tiles can be cut for fitting with large shears.

Among the home improvements a person with sewing skills can make are draperies and slipcovers. Draperies are not difficult to make, either with pleater tape or with buckram stiffening. Slipcovers are harder, so the beginner should choose a chair with simple rectangular lines and should select a firmly woven fabric without a pattern that requires matching.

GUIDELINES FOR STUDY

GENERAL IDEAS
TO CONSIDER

1. A knowledge of how to buy the proper equipment for painting, wallpapering, and laying floor tile will make the job easier.
2. The proper preparation of walls is necessary if painting or wallpapering is to give satisfaction.
3. A knowledge of the preliminary steps in laying floor tile is as important as knowing how to lay the tile.
4. Since ready-made draperies and slipcovers may be hard to find or unsatisfactory, a knowledge of how to make them is valuable to the home decorator.

WORDS AND PHRASES
TO KNOW

apron (slipcover)
buckram
butted joint
chalk-line
cording
double roll (wallpaper)
French pleats
grain (fabric)
hem gauge
masking tape
masonite
mesh tape

mitering
overlapped joint
patching plaster
pleater tape
plumb line
putty
repeat
selvage
single roll (wallpaper)
sizing
snap-on tape
welting

PAINTING WALLS, CEILING, AND WOODWORK

The choice of brushes, rollers, and paint and the proper preliminary wall treatment are important if a painting job is to be satisfactory.

Equipment and Supplies

There is nothing more frustrating than to be all prepared for painting and to find that you have to stop your work and hurry out to buy a missing item. Use the following checklist before beginning to paint:

BRUSHES. Buy good brushes, and take care of them. Bristles with split ends are more absorbent than those with pointed ends, and hold the maximum amount of paint without dripping. You will need a 4-inch brush for large areas, a 2-inch brush for wood trim, and a 1-inch brush for very narrow places. Even though you paint with a roller, you will need to brush on paint in the corners and near any trim.

ROLLERS. Rollers may be used to paint any interior or exterior surface. Rollers with a short nap are recommended for wood trim; with a medium nap, for walls; and with a long nap, for outside brick, stucco, or cement block. The most popular roller has a ⅜- to ½-inch nap made of lamb's wool or a synthetic fiber resembling lamb's wool.

ROLLER TRAY. Buy a tray to accommodate the roller width. Line the tray with heavy wrapping paper or foil to simplify cleaning.

PAINT AND SOLVENTS OR THINNERS. Water-base paints may be thinned with water, and the brushes used with it may be cleaned with running water. Oil-base paints must be thinned with a paint thinner or turpentine, and the brushes used must be cleaned similarly.

SIZING. A sizing is needed to seal any new plaster or patched plaster before painting. This may be bought at a paint store.

SANDPAPER. This will be needed to smooth rough spots or to take the gloss off wood trim. Buy fine and medium weights.

PUTTY AND PATCHING PLASTER. Putty is used to fill in holes in woodwork or holes made in a wall by picture hooks. A patching compound is available in stick form for hairline cracks. If a crack is wider than a hairline, a groove must be chiseled out, and new plaster set in with a putty knife.

PUTTY KNIFE. This is used to scrape rough spots, to smooth over putty in holes, and to apply plaster in small crevices.

PAINT GUARDS AND MASKING TAPE. These are used to protect the edges of wood trim as you paint or to mark a clean line where one color meets another.

MIXING BUCKETS AND PADDLES. Cardboard mixing buckets are inexpensive and essential for mixing paint and cleaning brushes. Paddles are necessary for stirring paint.

DROP CLOTHS. Plastic drop cloths are fairly inexpensive and protect the floor and furniture. However, old sheets or bedspreads can be used instead.

OLD RAGS AND NEWSPAPERS. Assemble plenty of old rags and newspapers. It will be easier to clean brushes and rollers if the excess paint is wiped, rolled, or brushed off first on paper or cloth.

LADDERS. Two ladders and a long board to stretch between may be needed to paint a ceiling or high wall.

Replaster holes and large cracks before painting.

Use a brush to paint around wood trim.

Rollers are recommended for large wall areas.

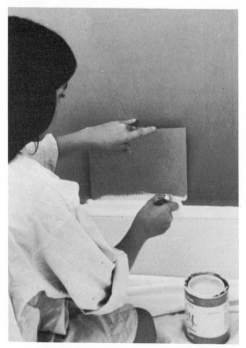

Paint the trim itself last.

Preparation of Room and Walls

Before painting move all tables, chairs, lamps, pictures, and small objects from the room. Assemble large pieces in the middle of the room, and cover them entirely.

If walls and ceilings are very dirty or greasy, the paint will not hold. The walls and ceilings in living, dining, and sleeping areas can be dusted quickly by going over the surface with a dust mop covered with a piece of soft cloth. Walls and ceiling in the kitchen should be sponged clean with a detergent because they are usually greasy.

If there are any fine cracks, they should be filled in with a special plaster stick. All loose plaster must be knocked away, and all deep cracks must be chiseled out and replastered. When the plaster is dry, these areas must be sized. If the walls are to have only one coat of paint, it is necessary first to paint the new plaster as nearly like the old paint as possible to eliminate the possibility of shading when the new coat is applied.

Estimating Quantity of Paint

The label on a paint can will generally indicate the number of square feet the contents will cover. New, rough, or porous surfaces will require more paint. A gallon of paint will cover about 400 square feet of smooth surface in a finish coat, less area in a first coat. It is more economical to buy paint by the gallon unless only a small quantity is needed for woodwork.

Work Sequence

The ceiling should be painted first, walls next, and wood trim last.

It is advisable to use a brush around the edges of the ceiling, at the corners of walls, and around the wood trim. However, it is not advisable to paint all of these areas first because of uneven drying. It is well to remember that wet paint over wet paint dries more evenly than wet paint over dry paint. To avoid streaking: (1) Paint the ceiling across the width of the room, painting a strip three to four feet wide at one time, and overlapping each strip before the paint dries. (2) Paint the wall from the top to the bottom in the same manner. (3) If you must stop, do so at a corner, a window, or a door. (4) Paint the door surface first and the edges last. (5) Protect areas not to be painted by using a paint guard or masking tape. (Avoid using masking tape on fresh paint.) Paint wood trim with a brush, unless you are painting flush doors, in which case a roller works well.

When using a roller, load the cover uniformly with paint, and take the first stroke away from the body whether working on the ceiling or a wall. Use only a moderate amount of pressure, and work fairly slowly.

After painting, roll the excess paint off the roller onto newspapers to simplify cleaning. Remove the roller cover, and clean it in the proper solvent— *water* if paint is water solvent, *turpentine* or *paint thinner* if the paint has an oil base. Clean brushes thoroughly before storing, and as the brush dries comb out the bristles. To store, wrap the brush below the handle with brown paper, and hold the paper in place with a rubber band or masking tape.

PAPERING WALLS

It is advisable to paint the ceiling in a papered room if the ceiling plaster is firm. Ceilings are difficult to paper, and the job requires two persons, unless the work is done by an experienced paperhanger.

Estimating Needs

Wallpaper comes in widths cf 18, 20½, 24, and 28 inches after trimming, but some wallpaper may be even wider. Regardless of width *a single roll covers 30 square feet* of wall space. This is because narrow widths are longer than broader widths, and what is lost in width is gained in length, and vice versa. To estimate the wallpaper needed to cover the walls of a room, *measure the perimeter of the room, and multiply by the height; then deduct 30 square feet for every two doors or two windows or a door and a window.* You generally buy wallpaper by the double or triple roll because when wallpaper has a design, the longer roll cuts to better advantage.

If the panels are to be *overlapped,* which means that the cut edge of one panel overlaps the selvage edge of the other, only one selvage needs to be cut off (be sure it is the same selvage on each panel—either the right or the left). If the panels are to be *butt joined,* both selvages must be cut off, so that the cut sides meet. The latter method gives the smoothest effect, but it is a little more difficult to execute. Always keep leftover wallpaper for patching if an area should become damaged.

Equipment and Supplies

If you do not want to invest in all the items listed, you can make the substitutions that are indicated or rent some items. The following equipment is basic:

BRUSH. A long, slender, flexible brush is required for smoothing out the wallpaper.

PLUMB LINE AND CHALK. A length of firmly twisted string rubbed with colored chalk and with a weight tied to it at the bottom will serve as a plumb line for establishing a line perpendicular to the floor. Hold the ends taut, and snap the cord. The chalk on the cord will mark a perpendicular line on the wall from the ceiling to the baseboard.

SHEARS. Extra-long shears are needed for cutting off the selvage. You can make a sharper and more even edge by cutting along a straight-edge metal strip with a single-edge razor blade or a double-edge razor blade set in a holder.

SEAM ROLLER. This is used to press seams flat when wallpaper is overlapped or butted. A furniture caster or small roller (often inserted in legs of heavy furniture) will suffice if it is clean and smooth.

SPONGE AND BOWL. A soft sponge wrung from clear water will be useful in wiping off smudges.

WHEEL KNIFE. This is a small rotary blade with a handle, and is used for trimming paper at baseboards, doors, and window frames. A razor blade inserted in a handle will do a satisfactory job.

WALLPAPER PASTE. Some wallpaper comes prepasted, making paste unnecessary. Otherwise buy a good paste preparation, and mix it with water to the consistency of mayonnaise.

WALL SIZING. Newly plastered walls require a coat of size, or sizing, in order to make the paper stick.

BUCKET AND PASTE BRUSH. A bucket for paste should have an inside lip that will serve to support the brush out of the paste except when it is in use. A paste brush is a broad, firm brush.

YARDSTICK OR METAL RULE. This is necessary for measuring panel lengths.

TABLE. A large worktable is needed for measuring and cutting panel lengths and for applying paste.

PATCHING PLASTER. This is needed to repair damaged plaster. It is available in small amounts, is easy to mix, and dries fast.

SCRAPER AND SANDPAPER. A scraper is needed to scrape rough plaster before sandpapering it, and the sandpaper is needed to smooth out the surface before applying wallpaper.

STEPLADDER. A sturdy stepladder is needed to stand on and to hold supplies while working.

Preparing Walls

Preparing walls for wallpapering is the same as preparing them for painting. See page 453 for preparing walls for painting, and follow directions accurately.

Special Precautions

The following suggestions may help you to avoid mistakes:

1. Note the kind of wallpaper you are using. So-called *washable* paper will take only a moderate amount of sponging to remove paste marks left on the surface. *Scrubbable* wallpaper will withstand fairly hard cleaning. Some paper, especially plain .paper, will show every spot and require a great deal of care in handling. Other papers have patterns or repeats that require special consideration in hanging.

2. Use the type of paste recommended if the paper is not prepasted. Make sure the paste is free of lumps because lumps will show under the paper.

3. Examine patterned paper for a repeat. Some repeats run straight across,

whereas other repeats drop. If you are a beginner, avoid buying a drop match.

4. Note the top of the pattern, and keep all panels even at the top.

5. Study the room to see where to begin. It is usually best to begin in a corner behind the entrance door where the final joining will be the least noticed. But if the wallpaper has a definite pattern, the pattern should be centered in the most prominent spot in the room—for example, over a fireplace or back of the largest piece of furniture. In applying patterned wallpaper, it is a good idea to mark off the number of panels around the room, and to check your wallpaper repeats before beginning to cut the wallpaper.

6. When cutting strips, match from the top and cut each strip long enough to extend over the baseboard slightly. Trim off the excess along the baseboard.

7. Hang ceiling (if papered) first, walls next, and borders last.

Procedure

The step-by-step illustrations on pages 456–457 show exactly how to proceed for the best results. Directions are given with each illustration.

LAYING FLOOR TILE

Most tiles, such as vinyl asbestos, rubber, cork, and linoleum, can be cut with heavy shears when they are being fitted around pipes or when they are filling in around the edge of a room. Asphalt tile requires heat to soften it before it can be cut. Unless you are experienced with a blowtorch, select another kind of tile suitable for your needs. (See page 359.) It is possible to soften asphalt tile under

To measure height accurately, drop plumb line at several points in room.

Measure and mark at plumb lines. Cut first strip to maximum height of wall, plus 3 or 4 inches.

Cut one strip at a time. Work in paste thoroughly, especially at edges.

Fold wet side to wet side from top and bottom toward center. Do NOT crease. Carry to wall.

Hang first strip to plumb line marking, with overlap onto ceiling and baseboard.

Press firmly to wall with nylon smoothing brush (or broad blunt knife or squeegee). Remove air pockets by brushing to nearest edge.

Hang succeeding strips so that edges butt tightly. Do not overlap seams. Set seams with seam roller so they won't loosen. Wash off excess paste. After 3 strips are hung, trim excess at top and bottom. Then continue around room.

a heat lamp, but never try to heat it in an oven.

Equipment and Supplies

Again, it is important to have good equipment and supplies for laying floor tiles successfully. Perhaps you can rent some of these or improvise substitutes.

CHALK LINE. This is a commercial product. It is a firmly woven cord impregnated with chalk and is used to establish a straight line on the floor before laying tile.

METAL SQUARE. A square is needed to mark right angles and to use as a guide in laying and checking tile.

METAL RULE. A ruler is also useful to measure and check tile lines.

BROAD BRUSH. This is needed to spread the tile cement.

SHARP KNIFE AND HEAVY SHEARS. These are used to cut tiles in fitting them around pipes, wall extensions, and irregular areas around the room perimeter.

ROLLER. Although the tiles may be pressed in place by bearing down hard with a rolling pin, some people like to use a linoleum roller. It may be rented from the outlet selling the tiles.

ADHESIVE OR CEMENT. Use a preparation recommended for the type of tile you are laying and follow directions carefully.

Preparation of the Area

Tiles can be laid on smooth concrete or over a felt or paper base on a wood floor provided the boards are perfectly smooth. Otherwise, plywood or masonite boards must be firmly nailed to the floor, snugly joined, and evenly fitted around the edges. Ask the tile dealer from whom you buy the tile for advice concerning your particular problem.

Procedure

Study each illustration and accompanying directions on pages 458 to 459 before undertaking to measure and lay tile. Save any extra tiles for patching because the color and pattern will be difficult to match later.

HOW TO LAY SQUARE TILES

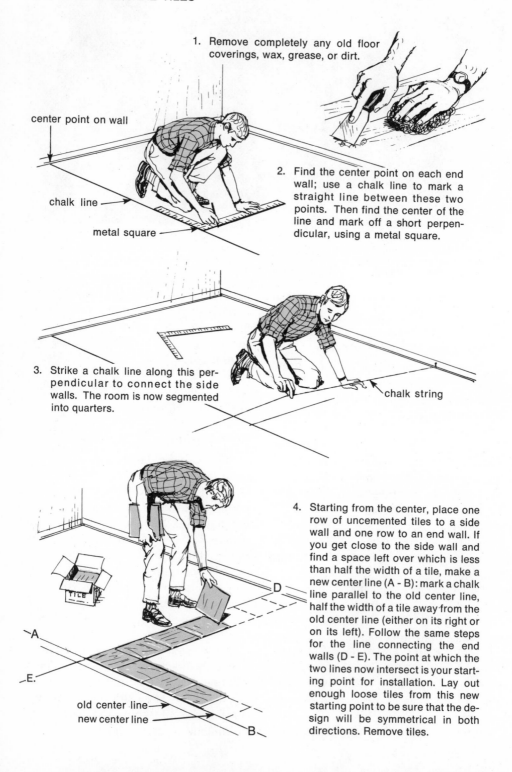

1. Remove completely any old floor coverings, wax, grease, or dirt.

2. Find the center point on each end wall; use a chalk line to mark a straight line between these two points. Then find the center of the line and mark off a short perpendicular, using a metal square.

center point on wall

chalk line

metal square

3. Strike a chalk line along this perpendicular to connect the side walls. The room is now segmented into quarters.

chalk string

4. Starting from the center, place one row of uncemented tiles to a side wall and one row to an end wall. If you get close to the side wall and find a space left over which is less than half the width of a tile, make a new center line (A - B): mark a chalk line parallel to the old center line, half the width of a tile away from the old center line (either on its right or on its left). Follow the same steps for the line connecting the end walls (D - E). The point at which the two lines now intersect is your starting point for installation. Lay out enough loose tiles from this new starting point to be sure that the design will be symmetrical in both directions. Remove tiles.

A

E.

old center line

new center line

D

B

5. Spread cement over one quarter of the floor (bounded by the chalk lines). Let cement set the required time. Working out from the starting point, press each tile squarely into place. Do not slide tiles, but make sure that the first row is flush with the line and that each tile is butted against adjoining tiles. Cover the whole quarter except the border area, where tiles must be cut to fit.

cement

6. Follow the same procedure for the other three quarters. Roll the entire floor. Remove any cement from the surface with steel wool and soap.

7. To lay the border, place a loose tile (A) exactly over one of the full tiles on the edge. (The direction of the graining should match.) Put a third tile (B) on top of this and slide it over against the wall. Using the edge of B as a guide, mark along A with a knife or pencil. Cut A, and repeat for as many border tiles as needed.

wall

B

A

8. To fit tile around irregular objects, make a paper pattern and trace it on the tile. Cut with heavy shears.

MAKING DRAPERIES AND SLIPCOVERS

Most of you will be able to buy suitable curtains. There is a wide selection of curtain fabrics, styles, lengths, and colors. But it may not always be possible to find suitable ready-made draperies, so you may have to make them or have them made. Ready-made slipcovers are not satisfactory, so slipcovers must also be custom-made. If you have the time and interest, you can learn to make draperies and slipcovers and save a great deal of money.

Precautions in Making Draperies

Before deciding upon any window treatment, study the illustrations throughout the text, in magazines, and in publications from manufacturers of drapery fixtures and trimmings. Large department stores have these publications for sale in the *drapery findings* department.

Here are some general guidelines:
□ Determine whether you want to use side draperies or draw draperies—lined or unlined.
□ Determine the length you prefer (see page 248).
□ Study problem windows and determine the best treatment (see page 249).
□ Take measurements and record them before measuring and cutting the fabric. Use a yardstick for measuring.
□ Be sure to match repeats along each length of fabric. This will usually mean wasting some fabric at the end of each length. For example, if draperies are to be 90 inches long and the repeat is 20 inches, you need 5 repeats, or 100 inches, for each panel. Of the 10 inches left over on each panel, you will need to allow about 5 inches for a 4-inch finished hem and a half-inch turn at the top, so the waste on each length will be about 5 inches.
□ Side draperies should be made from 48-inch fabric. If they are made from 36-inch fabric, each panel will require one and a half widths of fabric, or an extra length for each window.

Cutting and Sewing Draperies

These directions are for lined draperies. (If the draperies are not lined, make a one-inch hem at the sides and a top hem the width of the buckram.)
1. Draw a thread across both ends of the fabric and cut along this line to make sure you will be cutting on the grain of the goods. Measure a drapery length (considering the repeat and the amount of waste). Mark with a pin. Mark off all lengths from exactly the same point in the repeat and insert pins. Check these measurements before cutting. *Cut each length on a drawn thread.*
2. Measure, mark, and cut the lining on a drawn thread also. The lining should be 4 inches narrower and 5 inches shorter than the drapery fabric.
3. To prevent hems from puckering, trim off all selvages. (Or, if the drapery fabric is very firmly woven, you may clip the selvage about every 2 inches.)
4. Place the lining over the drapery fabric. Make top edges even, and make sure that the lower edge of the lining is parallel with the lower edge of the drapery fabric. Stitch a 1-inch hem in the lining. Then position lining over drapery with right sides inside.
5. Adjust at the top until the side hems are of equal width; pin sides and top edges together. Stitch a ⅜-inch seam along each side, and then across the top. Turn drapery right side out. Flatten lining to drapery so that 1 inch of drapery extends beyond seam on both sides. Press seams.

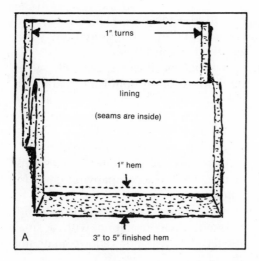

A

1" turns

lining

(seams are inside)

1" hem

3" to 5" finished hem

6-A. *To use pleater tape:* On a 48-inch fabric, pleater tape will make 5 French pleats, with 1 empty slot between each pleat and next to each end pin. This will mean having 28 slots on each pleater tape length for each drapery panel (4 slots for each of the 5 pleats, 2 for the end pins, and 6 for in between). Cut tape and stitch to drapery. Insert 5 four-prong pins and 2 single-prong pins.

6-B. *To use buckram:* Before turning the drapery right side out, measure and cut the buckram. Pin bottom edge of buckram to top of drapery, and stitch parallel to top seam. Turn and press. (No other stitching is necessary, because the buckram will be held in place by the pleat stitching.) Using the pleater tape directions as a guide for spacing, mark off 5 deep pleats. Stitch each pleat the width of the buckram. Pinch in French pleats and sew edges by hand. Insert ordinary drapery pins at lower edge of pleat. *Note:* The use of ordinary pins has an advantage in that the length can be adjusted by moving the pins up a little.

7. Hang one panel overnight, and then mark the bottom hem. Measure the hem evenly across the fabric with a hem gauge and press. Sew by machine or hand. Corners should be mitered by hand. If you need weights, insert one at each corner before mitering.

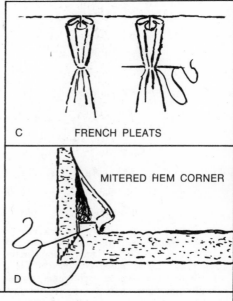

C   FRENCH PLEATS

MITERED HEM CORNER

D

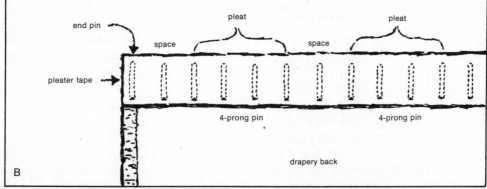

B

end pin

space   pleat   space   pleat

pleater tape

4-prong pin   4-prong pin

drapery back

SLIP COVER YARDAGE*

	Material	Yards
Wing Chair	48" Fabric	8–9
	36" Fabric	10–11
	Cording	18
Lounge Chair	48" Fabric	7–8
	36" Fabric	8–12
	Cording	12–15
Open Arm Chair	48" Fabric	2½
	36" Fabric	3¼
	Cording	7–9
Love Seat	48" Fabric	10
	36" Fabric	13
Sofa (Average)	48" Fabric	12
	36" Fabric	17
	Cording	36
Sofa (Long)	48" Fabric	14
	36" Fabric	24–26
	Cording	40

* Yardage measurements are based on sofas and chairs with a tight back and separate cushions. The yardage given is sufficient for a skirt with a box pleat at each corner, except for the open arm chair where only the seat and back are covered. Fabrics with large repeats require more yardage, in order to center the repeat.

Slipcovers

When you select a chair or sofa to buy, consider the possibilities of slipcovering it when the original cover becomes soiled. Sofas and chairs with cushions semiattached to the back or in tufted styles are difficult to slipcover, and they also require more yardage than simpler styles.

A slipcover, if made carefully, gives the impression of upholstery. Although most slipcovers have a skirt at the base, some stop where the wood frame ends, and the lower edge is held in place with snap-on or mesh tape.

Here are some helpful suggestions:
□ Consult the accompanying chart for yardage.
□ Make your first slipcover from solid-colored fabric or fabric with a small repeat that will not require matching the pattern.
□ Examine several slipcovers custom-made by professionals or by friends who have had experience.
□ Even the fabric at each end by drawing a thread and cutting along the drawn thread line.
□ Cut all pieces on the grain of the fabric. If there is a large repeat, center it on the back and on the cushions.
□ Always fit the slipcover from the right side.
□ Assemble the following items before you start working: a box of straight pins; zippers for the side back of the chair and for the cushion; heavy-duty thread to match the fabric; chalk for any marking necessary, such as center lines on the chair and cushion and a base line for attaching the skirt; tape measure; yardstick; and cording foot.

TO CUT AND FIT SLIPCOVERS. Remove the cushion and mark a center line down the front, back, and sides of the chair and through the center of the cushion. You may use narrow masking tape and remove it later.

1. Fold fabric in half lengthwise along center line, beginning 2 inches beyond back edge of chair. Bring to front edge and pin in a 2-inch fold (to be cut later for a seam with cording). Extend

over chair back to seat. Make a 5-inch tuck (10 inches of fabric) to tuck under the seat. Continue spreading cloth to within 6 inches of the floor. Allow an inch or more at each side all the way down. Open the fabric and smooth over back of chair.

To fit arms: take fabric folded lengthwise; begin 2 inches beyond chair arm and cover arm, allowing for a 5-inch tuck-in at seat. Repeat for other arm. Allow an inch or more for seams at back and at edge of arm.

with pins at corners and center. Pin seams at top of chair.

Cut side panels and side arm pieces and anchor. Pin side panel and side arm piece. Repeat on opposite side of chair.

3. Pin the 5-inch fold at the seat. Fold excess fabric along inside arms. At point where arm joins the seat, slash to within ¾ inch of point so that the fabric can be smoothed down over ends of the chair for joining side seam and mitering corner.

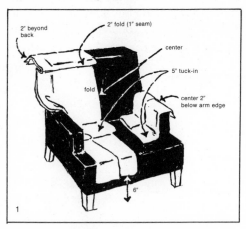

2. Center the fold of the fabric on chair back, allowing a 1-inch projection above top back of chair. Stop 6 inches from floor. Anchor temporarily

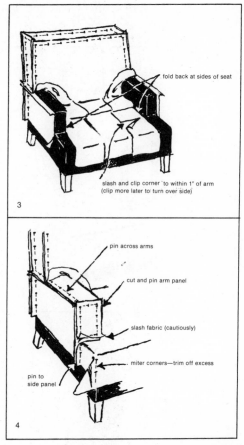

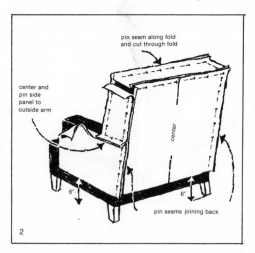

4. Pin along outside arms. Cut front panel and anchor in place by pinning it through the upholstery. Fit and pin around the inside and outside arm pieces.

Slash a little closer at point where

seat covering is to be pinned to front arm panel, and reinforce the cut with a line of close machine stitching. Pin across arm panel at side of chair. Miter corners at front of chair, and trim to make a 1-inch seam. Repeat on opposite side.

5. Smooth inside arms and back covering into crease where arms meet chair back. Mark creases with pins, pencil, or chalk. Trim to about 2 inches around the arm, and make several slashes almost to seam line. Taper tuck-in from about 2 inches at top to 5 inches at bottom.

6. Smooth out fabric at sides and back. Adjust pins if necessary. Unpin at zipper opening and remove cover.

7. Measure depth of band around cushion, and add 1 inch at each side for seams. For the zipper enclosure, cut 2 bands about ¾ the depth, press in turns, and stitch center along center of zipper. Zipper must extend 2 inches around the side of the cushion, and zipper band must be 1 inch longer than the zipper at each end.

Pin one end of zipper band to plain band, and pin the band around the outside of cushion to meet the opposite

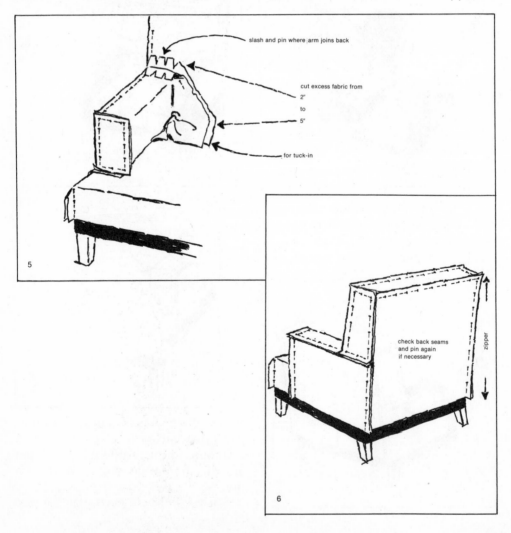

slash and pin where arm joins back

cut excess fabric from
2"
to
5"

for tuck-in

5

check back seams
and pin again
if necessary

zipper

6

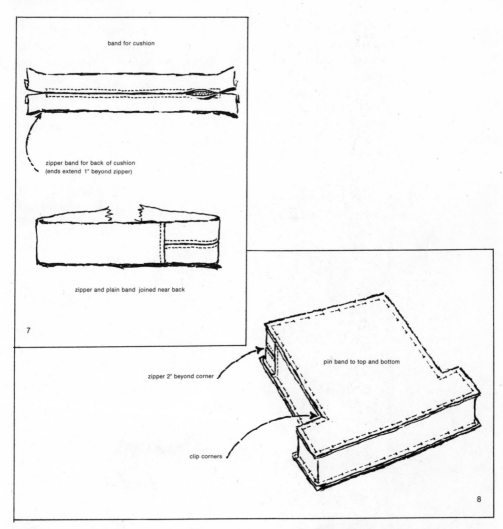

band for cushion

zipper band for back of cushion
(ends extend 1" beyond zipper)

zipper and plain band joined near back

7

zipper 2" beyond corner

pin band to top and bottom

clip corners

8

end of zipper band. Make a seam on the opposite side of the band. Topstitch the seams for firmness.

8. Center the cushion on the top of a center fold of fabric. Press the cushion down so the measurement will not be skimpy. Chalk around the edges, allowing a 1-inch seam all around. Cut fabric for top and bottom of the cushion.

Pin the band around the top and bottom of the cushion. Open zipper to remove.

TO STITCH SLIPCOVERS. Make sure all stitching lines of seams have been marked with a basting thread and notched at intervals. Remove pins, insert cording, and stitch seams in the same order in which you pinned the parts together. *Do not try to stitch the seams together at one time.*

Pin or baste covered cord or welting along stitching line on right side of fabric with raw edges toward the outside. Stitch over stitching on cording. Match notches; pin seams together; and *stitch from the side of the fabric where the stitching shows.* This will keep the cording firm.

Try the cover on the chair and pin along the zipper seam. Make any necessary adjustments. Mark the lower edge evenly 6 inches from floor. Remove cover from chair and stitch cording along this marking.

TO MAKE SKIRT. Measure around chair and add 48 to 64 inches for box pleats (the fold in each side of the pleat should be 3 to 4 inches deep). Cut strip of fabric this length and about 7 inches deep. Optional: cut lining of soft fabric to same dimensions and tack to skirt.

Make a narrow hem. Set box pleats at corners and stitch skirt to cover. Stitch in zipper to within an inch from the edge of the hem.

SUMMARY

Some of you may never have painted or papered walls or laid floor tile, and may never expect to. However, most young married people have a limited income and a limited choice of a place to live. In many instances they will have to do their own decorating or pay to have it done. By knowing how to do some things, the rental dollar will stretch a little further, and besides, it may be fun working together for a more attractive place in which to live.

If is far easier to paint, wallpaper, and lay tile flooring if you are familiar with the best procedures in working. Painting is fairly easy even for the amateur. Wallpapering and laying floor tile require a little more practice. If you can have someone with a little experience help you to get started, of if you can observe someone at work, these jobs will be easier to do.

If you know the fundamentals of simple sewing, you can make draperies. If you can tailor a suit, you can make a slipcover. You can save a great deal of money and carry out your decorating ideas more effectively by sewing for the home if you have the time and interest.

THINGS TO THINK ABOUT AND TO DO

1. Discuss experiences you have had, or someone you know has had, in painting, wallpapering, or laying tile.

2. Ask a paint dealer to help arrange a classroom display of the items used in painting walls and in wallpapering. Examine and discuss these items.

3. Select a room at home to measure for wallpaper or for paint. Determine the wall area to be covered (minus doors and windows except for painting the woodwork in these areas later), and estimate the amount of wall paint or wallpaper needed.

4. Through a wallpaper store, make plans to observe a paperhanger at work, or show a film on hanging wallpaper.

5. If possible, paint or wallpaper a room at home.

6. Show films on painting a room and on laying resilient floor tiles.

7. Price drapery and slipcover materials. Estimate the cost of (1) lined draperies (per pair), (2) chair slipcover, and (3) sofa slipcover if you make them yourself. Contrast these prices with those you would have to pay if you had them made.

8. Display booklets from manufacturers of drapery fixtures showing how to make curtains, draperies, and slipcovers.

REFERENCES FOR UNIT FIVE

BOOKS

(See also BOOKS listed for Unit Three.)

Cassidy, Bruce, *Practical Home Repair for Women.* New York: Taplinger Publishing Company, 1966.

Fitzsimmons, Cleo, and White, Nell, *Management for You.* Philadelphia: J. B. Lippincott Company, 1964.

Gladstone, Bernard, *New York Times Book of Home Repair.* New York: The Macmillan Company, 1966.

Martin, Sara, *The Collier Quick and Easy Guide to Home Maintenance.* New York: P. F. Collier, Inc., 1963.

Nickell, Pauline, and Dorsey, Jean Muir, *Management in Family Living.* New York: John Wiley and Sons, Inc., 1967.

O'Neill, Barbara P. and Richard W., *The Unhandy Man's Guide to Home Repair.* New York: The Macmillan Company, 1966.

Rains, Margaret, *Managing Living Time.* Peoria, Ill.: Chas. A. Bennett Company, Inc., 1964.

Schuler, Stanley, *How to Fix Almost Everything.* Philadelphia: J. B. Lippincott Company, 1963.

Schwartz, Robert, and Cobb, H. H., *The Complete Homeowner,* New York: The Macmillan Company, 1965.

Seymour, Robert G., *Decisions Before the House.* Champaign, Ill.: Guideways, Inc., 1961.

Starr, Mary Catherine, *Management for Better Living.* Boston: D. C. Heath and Company, 1968.

Steidl, Rose E., and Bratton, E. C., *Work in the Home,* New York: John Wiley and Sons, Inc., 1968.

BOOKLETS AND PAMPHLETS

(See also BOOKLETS AND PAMPHLETS listed for Units Three and Four.)

1,001 Decorating Ideas, Conso Publishing Company, 27 W. 23rd St., New York, N.Y. 10010. Booklets on slipcovers and draperies at Singer Sewing Machine Centers.

FILMS, FILMSTRIPS, AND SLIDES

(See list opposite for name and address of source.)

Beauty and the Bride. Housekeeping made easy with modern furniture and proper equipment. (27 minutes, color, MTP)

Is the Modern Homemaker Modern? Shows routine housekeeping jobs with emphasis upon laundering. (14 minutes, color, MTP)

Modern Kitchen Ideas and More Room at Home. Shows dream kitchen planned around seven basic work centers, built-in furniture, and storage units. (9 minutes, color, MTP)

Obligations. Contrasts two households, one poorly managed and one in which family members accept their obligations. (18 minutes, EBF)

Paging Women. Film with tips on clothing, decorating, and foods. (24 minutes, color, MTP)

Planning and Organization. Contrasts good and bad meal planning and organization of kitchen equipment. (10 minutes, MH)

NAMES AND ADDRESSES OF FILM SOURCES

ACC   Armstrong Cork Company, Lancaster, Pa. 17604

AF   Association Films, Broad and Elm, Ridgefield, N.J., 07657 or 799 Stevenson Street, San Francisco, Calif. 94100

BBB   Better Business Bureau, Industry Relations Department, 704 Chrysler Building, New York, N.Y. 10017

CF   Coronet Films, 65 East S. Water Street, Chicago, Ill. 60601

CFGA   Colorado Flower Growers Association, 901 Sherman St., Denver, Colorado 80203

CU   Consumers Union Film Library, 267 W. 25th St., New York, N.Y. 10001

EBF   Encyclopaedia Britannica Films, 1150 Wilmette Ave., Wilmette, Ill. 60091

FDACC   Fibers Division of American Cyanamid Company, 111 W. 40th St. New York, N.Y. 10018

FHM   F. H. McGraw and Company, 780 Windsor Street, Hartford, Conn. 06101

HFC   Household Finance Corporation, Prudential Plaza, Chicago, Ill. 60601

IFB   International Film Bureau, Inc., 332 S. Michigan Ave., Chicago, Ill. 60016

MH   McGraw-Hill Book Company, Text-Film Division, 330 W. 42nd St., New York, N.Y. 10036

MIS   Moody Institute of Science, 11428 Santa Monica Blvd., W., Los Angeles, Calif. 90025

MTP   Modern Talking Pictures, 1212 Ave. of the Americas, New York, N.Y. 10023

NAHB   National Association of Home Builders, 1625 L St., N.W. Washington, D.C. 20036

OSG   Oneida Silversmiths Guild, Oneida, N.Y. 13421

SEARS   Sears, Roebuck and Co., 925 S. Homan Ave., Chicago, Ill. 60607

SEF   Sterling Education Films, Inc., 43 W. 61st St., New York, N.Y. 10023

USDA   U.S. Department of Agriculture, Washington, D.C. 20250

acknowledgments

xvi. Courtesy of The American Museum of Natural History

6. Courtesy of The American Museum of Natural History
7. Hirmer Fotoarchiv, Munich
8. Metropolitan Museum of Art
9. British Travel Association, London
10. French Government Tourist Office
11. German Information Center
14. Oldest House in The United States, in St. Augustine, Florida—Phillip Whitley, Photographer
17. Plimoth Plantation, Plymouth, Mass.
18. (Top) Samuel Chamberlain
18. (Center) New-York Historical Society
18. (Bottom) Fay Foto Service, Inc.
19. (Top) Samuel Chamberlain
19. (Center) Gregory Wilson, Photographer
19. (Bottom) Photo by Charles Phelps Cushing
21. (Top) Samuel Chamberlain
21. (Bottom) Samuel Chamberlain
22. Samuel Chamberlain
23. (Top) Courtesy of Richard Koch, Architect
23. (Bottom) Photo by Sawders, from Cushing
24. Courtesy of the California State Department of Parks and Recreation
26. Samuel Chamberlain
27. Public Relations Consultants for the City of Cape May, N. J.
28. (Top) National Trust for Historic Preservation
28. (Bottom) Boscobel Restoration, Inc.—Joe Barnell, Photographer
29. (Top) Swanlund Photo Lab, Eureka, Calif.
29. (Bottom) *Redlands Daily Facts*, Redlands, Calif.
31. (Top) Courtesy of the Biltmore Estate Office
31. (Center) Edward Teitelman, Photographer
31. (Bottom) Edward Teitleman, Photographer
32. (Top) Gregory Wilson, Photographer
32. (Bottom) Department of Public Information, Travel Division, Frankfort, Ky.
34. Mies van der Rohe, Architect; Hedrich-Blessing Photo
37. Hedrich-Blessing Photo
38. Frank Lloyd Wright, Architect; Hedrich-Blessing Photo
40. Library of Congress
41. Thomas Airviews
42. (Top) Wide World Photos, Inc.
42. (Bottom) Wide World Photos, Inc.
45. (Top) Gregory Wilson, Photographer
47. Gregory Wilson, Photographer
48. Mobile Home Manufacturers Association
51. Hartford Redevelopment Agency
56. Aero Mayflower Transit Co., Inc.
70. Serta Associates, Inc.
79. Gregory Wilson, Photographer
84. Designed by Hans Juergens for Khoury Brothers; Hedrich-Blessing Photo
86. Gregory Wilson, Photographer
100. Helios, Cambridge, Mass.
113. Courtesy of the Boston *Herald Traveler*
114. Courtesy of the U.S. Gypsum Co.; Hedrich-Blessing Photo
123. Drawing Courtesy of Drummey Rosane Anderson, Inc., Architects·
131. Courtesy of the U.S. Gypsum Co.; Hedrich-Blessing Photo
136. Kitchen with island work center, artificial and natural lighting; Hedrich-Blessing Photo
139. Hedrich-Blessing Photo
142. E. T. Barwick Mills, "Renaissance Blue" pattern from Kitchen Classics
144. Uniroyal, Inc.; Hedrich-Blessing Photo
148. John B. Roberts, AIA, Architect; Hedrich-Blessing Photo
150. Designed by Frank and Stein, Architects: A Maytag Promotion; Hedrich-Blessing Photo
155. Ian MacKinley Associates, Architects; Hedrich-Blessing Photo
156. (Left & Right) From *HOUSE & GARDEN*; Copyright © 1968, 1969 by the Condé Nast Publications, Inc.
157. (Left & Right) From *HOUSE & GAR-

DEN; Copyright © 1968, 1969 by the Condé Nast Publications, Inc.

158. Hedrich-Blessing Photo

160. A U.S. Gypsum Project, Designed by Norman Steenhof; Hedrich-Blessing Photo

161. A U.S. Gypsum Research House, Eugene Voita, Architect; Hedrich-Blessing Photo

162. From *HOUSE & GARDEN;* Copyright © 1968, 1969 by the Condé Nast Publications, Inc.

170. Westinghouse

175. General Electric Company

179. A National Home Interior; Hedrich-Blessing Photo

181. Decorator, Marcella Schwarb; Hedrich-Blessing Photo

186. Picasso paintings in the flat of Mr. Berg-Gruen, Courtesy of *REALITIES* magazine

191. (Top) Museum of Fine Arts, Boston

191. (Bottom) Courtesy of Knoll Associates, Inc.

194. Edwin Clark, Architect; Hedrich-Blessing Photo

196. Richard Himmel, AID; Hedrich-Blessing Photo

198. Jerome R. Cerny, Architect; Hedrich-Blessing Photo

200. A monochromatic color scheme—Chicago Historical Society; Hedrich-Blessing Photo

210. Courtesy of the U.S. Gypsum Co., Robert Brockett, Architect; Hedrich-Blessing Photo

211. Designed by Robert McClenahan; Hedrich-Blessing Photo

212. (Top) Courtesy of Fieldcrest, A Division of Fieldcrest Mills, Inc.

212. (Bottom) Designed for Directional Showrooms; Hedrich-Blessing Photo

215. E. Gordon Findley, AID, Designer; Hedrich-Blessing Photo

217. (Top) Designed by Toni Suter; Hedrich-Blessing Photo

217. (Bottom) Designed by Clare Gunderson, NSID; Hedrich-Blessing Photo

220. Hedrich-Blessing Photo

224. Robert Koll, Interior Designer; Hedrich-Blessing Photo

225. Courtesy of the Maytag Corp.; Hedrich-Blessing Photo

226. Designed by Nicholas B. Snavely for S.J. Campbell Co.; Hedrich-Blessing Photo

228. Phillip Meathe, FAIA, Architect; Hedrich-Blessing Photo

229. Hedrich-Blessing Photo

231. Armstrong Cork Co., "Decoresq" pattern

234. Courtesy, Metropolitan Structures; Hedrich-Blessing Photo

235. George Fred Keck—William Keck, Architects; Hedrich-Blessing Photo

237. A Scholz Home; Hedrich-Blessing Photo

240. A St. Charles Kitchen; Hedrich-Blessing Photo

253. Hedrich-Blessing Photo

254. Photographed at Colonial Williamsburg for Pittsburgh Paints Co.; Hedrich-Blessing Photo

278. E. Gordon Findley, AID, Douglas B. Kohler, AID, Interior Designers; Hedrich-Blessing Photo

284. (Top Left) Van Evera Bailey, AIA, Architect; Hedrich-Blessing Photo

284. (Top Right) Interior Design, Rosemary Miley, AID; Hedrich-Blessing Photo

284. (Bottom Left) Courtesy of Royal System, N.Y.C.

284. (Bottom Right) Furniture by Kroehler; Hedrich-Blessing Photo

287. Designed by Mary Jane Graham, NSID, featuring Dexter Hardware; Hedrich-Blessing Photo

290. Hedrich-Blessing Photo

292. A Remodeling Project of U.S. Gypsum Co.; Hedrich-Blessing Photo

294. Gregory Wilson, Photographer

296. (Top) National Gallery of Art, Washington, D.C.

296. (Bottom) National Gallery of Art, Washington, D.C.

297. (Top) National Gallery of Art, Washington, D.C.
297. (Center) National Gallery of Art, Washington, D.C.
297. (Bottom) National Gallery of Art, Washington, D.C.
298. Museum of Fine Arts, Boston
298. (Bottom) National Gallery of Art, Washington, D.C.
299. (Top) The Museum of Modern Art, N.Y.C.
299. (Bottom) The Museum of Modern Art, N.Y.C.
300. (Top) Museum of Fine Arts, Boston
300. (Bottom) Museum of Fine Arts, Boston
301. Designed by Lawrence Peabody; Hedrich-Blessing Photo
302. Interior design, Terry Regner, AID; Hedrich-Blessing Photo
304. Designed by Richard Himmel, AID; Hedrich-Blessing Photo
309. (Left) Keystone Lamp Mfg. Corp., N.Y.C.
309. (Right) George Kovacs, Inc.
310. (Top) James N. Lindenberger, Architect; Hedrich-Blessing Photo
310. (Center) George Fred Keck—William Keck, Architects; Hedrich-Blessing Photo
310. (Bottom) A St. Charles Kitchen; Hedrich-Blessing Photo
312. (Left) Tyndale by Wilmar Co.
312. (Top Right) Tyndale by Wilmar Co.
312. (Bottom Right) Tyndale by Wilmar Co.
313. (Top Left) Georg Jensen
313. (Bottom Left) Tyndale by Wilmar Co.
313. (Bottom Center) Tyndale by MG, Inc. of Pennsylvania
313. (Right) George Kovacs, Inc.
316. Gregory Wilson, Photographer
323. (Top) Courtesy of *FLORIST* published by Florists' Transworld Delivery Assoc.
323. (Bottom) Courtesy of *FLORIST* published by Florists' Transworld Delivery Assoc.
324. Courtesy of the U.S. Gypsum Co.; Hedrich-Blessing Photo
330. The Hoover Company
335. General Electric Company
336. Westinghouse

340. General Electric Company
341. General Electric Company
342. General Electric Company
345. The Hoover Company
346. Designed by Lawrence Peabody, AID; Hedrich-Blessing Photo
350. Courtesy of Lees Carpets, "Simplicity" pattern
354. Laurelcrest's "Danish Delight" Woolmark carpet
358. S.C. Johnson & Son, Inc.
362. Cannon Mills, Inc.
370. Fieldcrest, A Division of Fieldcrest Mills, Inc.
374. Fieldcrest, A Division of Fieldcrest Mills, Inc.
377. Fieldcrest, A Division of Fieldcrest Mills, Inc.
378. Georg Jensen
380. From *HOUSE & GARDEN;* Copyright © 1968, 1969 by the Condé Nast Publications, Inc.
385. (Top Left) Georg Jensen
385. (Top Right) R.F. Brodegaard & Co., Inc.
385. (Bottom Left) Dansk Designs
385. (Bottom Right) Georg Jensen
387. Hedrich-Blessing Photo
390. "WILL 'O' WISP" pattern by Oneida Silversmiths, Ltd.
393. (Top Left) Waterford Glass Inc., "Colleen" pattern
393. (Top Right) Fostoria Glass Company
393. (Bottom Left) Fostoria Glass Company
393. (Bottom Right) Fostoria Glass Company
394. Steuben Glass
397. Hedrich-Blessing Photo
398. Hide-a-Bed sofa by Simmons
403. Scandia Craft Import, Inc., N.Y.C.— Richard DiLiberto, Photographer
420. Helios, Cambridge, Mass.
426. (Top, Center, Bottom) S.C. Johnson & Son, Inc.
432. Gregory Wilson, Photographer
448. Helios, Cambridge, Mass.
452. (all photos) Helios, Cambridge, Mass.
456–457. Columbus Coated Fabrics
466. Hedrich-Blessing Photo

index